Managing Multiculturalism

Managing Multiculturalism

Indigeneity and the Struggle for Rights in Colombia

Jean E. Jackson

Stanford University Press
Stanford, California

Stanford University Press
Stanford, California

Printed in the United States of America on acid-free, archival-quality paper

Library of Congress Cataloging-in-Publication Data

Names: Jackson, Jean E. (Jean Elizabeth), 1943– author.
Title: Managing multiculturalism : indigeneity and the struggle for rights in Colombia / Jean E. Jackson.
Description: Stanford, California : Stanford University Press, 2019. | Includes bibliographical references and index.
Identifiers: LCCN 2018019688 (print) | LCCN 2018021140 (ebook) | ISBN 9781503607705 | ISBN 9781503606227 (cloth : alk. paper) | ISBN 9781503607699 (pbk. : alk. paper)
Subjects: LCSH: Indians of South America—Colombia—Politics and government. | Indians of South America—Colombia—Ethnic identity. | Indians of South America—Colombia—Government relations. | Multiculturalism—Colombia.
Classification: LCC F2270.1.P63 (ebook) | LCC F2270.1.P63 J33 2019 (print) | DDC 3058009861—dc23
LC record available at https://lccn.loc.gov/2018019688

Cover design: Christian Fuenfhausen
Cover photo: Muisca cabildo headquarters in the Bosa section of Bogotá. Jean E. Jackson.

For Louis, again, with love.

Contents

Maps and Figures

Maps

Figures

Acknowledgments

My fifty-year love affair with Colombia began with a letter from Alicia Dussán de Reichel in 1968 inviting me to work in that country after it became clear I could not work in Brazil.[1] From then until their deaths, Gerardo Reichel-Dolmatoff and Alicia helped me in innumerable ways. Many other Colombian anthropologists also graciously invited me into their homes and offices, as well as asked me to give papers and teach in their classrooms. A number of them have become beloved friends with whom I enjoy discussing politics, the indigenous movement, and much more (including, of course, current gossip). These dedicated and generous scholars, whose funding and access to the scholarly literature are often very limited, introduced me to innumerable other helpful people, including potential interviewees and research assistants. Many other Colombians helped the research as well. Some of the people listed below will not remember our interviews or conversations, but I do, and extend my wholehearted thanks to all: Raúl Arango, Jaime Arocha, Diana Bocarejo, Gabriel Cabrera, Margarita Chaves, François Correa, Carlos Eduardo Franky, María Stella González, Abadio Green, Leonor Herrera, Victor Jacanamejoy, Gladys Jimeno, Myriam Jimeno, Dany Mahecha, Germán McAllister, Hernando Muñoz, Victoria Neuta, Guillermo Padilla, Jesús Piñacué, Roberto Pineda, María Clemencia Ramírez, Elizabeth Reichel, Roque Roldán, Enrique Sánchez, Esther Sánchez, Elías Sevilla, the late Nina S. de Friedemann, Adolfo Triana, Carlos Uribe, Simón Valencia, and Martín von Hildebrand. Thanks also to research assistants Marta Lucía Peña, Segisfredo Franco, Ibaná Varón, Sonia Serna, and Juliana Sánchez. Entities that greatly facilitated my research include the Instituto Colombiano de Antropología e Historia (ICANH), the Departments of Anthropology at the Universidad de los Andes and Universidad Nacional de Colombia, various members of the Consejo Regional Indígena del Vaupés (CRIVA), and various officials of the Organización Nacional de Indígena de Colombia (ONIC). Special thanks to Jaime Arocha and María Merecedes Baraya de Arocha, María Clemencia Ramírez, Myriam Jimeno, Esther Sánchez, Marianne Cardale de Schrimpff, and Juana Dávila for hosting me during my stays in Bogotá.

Stateside I have been ably assisted by Juana Dávila, Felipe Gómez, Clare Salerno, and Steven González.

My research in Colombia from October 1968 to November 1970 was supported by the Danforth Foundation and the Stanford Committee for Research in International Studies. Subsequent trips to Colombia were funded in part by the Dean's Office, School of Humanities, Arts, and Social Sciences at the Massachusetts Institute of Technology; and by MIT's Margaret MacVicar Faculty Fellows Program.

In Mitú, Vaupés, Tito Vargas and his wife, Alicia, provided me with generous hospitality and many enjoyable moments at Residencia La Maloka. Thanks also to the León family, proprietors of Hotel La Vorágine, and to the mission staff attached to the Prefectura Apostólica del Vaupés for hospitality, transportation, and many conversations.

I have very fond memories of the original residents of Púmanaka buró on the Inambú River, and especially appreciate the welcome extended to me in Mitú during my later trips by Francisco Escobar (son of Juanico Escobar, headman of Púmanaka buró) and his daughter, María Jesús Escobar. Many Tukanoan residents of the region hosted me and put up with my questions during my river journeys; the same goes for any number of Mitú residents and officials temporally located there. My appreciation and gratitude extend to all.

Thanks also to both Floro Tunubalá, who provided helpful information stateside in October 2004, as did Luis Evelis Andrade in February 2006.

To fellow Vaupés scholars living outside of Colombia, *recuerdos cariñosos* and appreciation for your help and encouragement, above all to Stephen and Christine Hugh-Jones, as well as Patrice Bidou, Elsa Gómez, and Pierre-Yves Jacopin. The late Peter Silverwood-Cope accompanied me on my first flight to Mitú and helped introduce me to the region. I have extremely fond memories of and owe a considerable debt to the late Irving Goldman. Thanks also to

Janet Chernela and Robin Wright, who work in the Brazilian Vaupés, for years of scholarly conversations.

Warmest thanks to the many, many scholars—way too many to enumerate—who, over the years, have commented on my work. Some of you were involved in activism that sought to improve the lives and prospects of Colombians—indigenous, Afro-descendant, and *campesino*—who all too often succumbed to, but often also managed to withstand, grave assaults on their lives, dignity, and future prospects. The late Virginia Bouvier, a former student, represented the very best in advocacy, working tirelessly to end the conflict and achieve a lasting and just peace.

Joanne Rappaport, María Clemencia Ramírez, and my longtime friend and colleague James Howe read this entire manuscript and made extremely helpful comments. I, along with any readers of this book, am indebted to Jim for his hours of editing help. Joanne talked me into doing this project, and María Clemencia helped move things along in many, many ways: thank you, Joanne and Mencha. Thanks also to Lucas Bessire, Margarita Chaves, Carlos Eduardo Franky, Myriam Jimeno, Dany Mahecha, and Peter Wade for reading parts of the manuscript, and to Andy Klatt for help with translations. Thanks also to friends Judy Irvine, Sally Merry, Lynn Stephen, Katherine Verdery, and Kay Warren for their support over the years.

MIT colleagues Manduhai Buyandelger, Michael Fischer, Stefan Helmreich, Erica James, Graham Jones, Amy Moran-Thomas, Heather Paxson, Susan Silbey and Christine Walley have been wonderfully supportive as well; thanks especially to those who commented on the Introduction. Thanks also to my MIT colleague Michel DeGraff, in the Department of Linguistics, for help with Chapter Two. Christopher Donnelley of MIT's Rotch Library provided much-needed help with the figures and maps.

I am enormously grateful for the patience and unconditional and enthusiastic support Louis Kampf has provided throughout this overly long process.

Thanks also to the two anonymous reviewers for Stanford University Press for their careful reading of the manuscript and extremely helpful suggestions. At the Press, heartfelt thanks to Senior Editor Michelle Lipinski and Assistant Editor Nora Spiegel. Copyeditor Elspeth MacHattie saved me hours of work.

Of course, responsibility for the ideas set forth here and any mistakes or omissions is entirely my own.

Some of the ethnographic cases presented in this book have appeared in a different form in the journals *American Ethnologist, Journal of Ethnic Studies,*

Dialectical Anthropology, and *Cultural Anthropology*, and the books *Indigenous Movements, Self-Representation, and the State in Latin America*, edited by Kay B. Warren and Jean E. Jackson, and *The Practice of Human Rights: Tracking Law Between the Global and the Local*, edited by Mark Goodale and Sally Engle Merry. Full citations can be found in the References.

Jean E. Jackson
August 2018

Acronyms and Glossary

Acronyms

ACIN	Asociación de Cabildos Indígenas del Norte del Cauca (Association of Indigenous Cabildos of Northern Cauca)
AICO	Autoridades Indígenas de Colombia (Indigenous Authorities of Colombia)
ANC	Asamblea Nacional Constituyente (National Constituent Assembly)
ANUC	Asociación Nacional de Usuarios Campesinos (National Association of Peasants)
ASI	Alianza Social Indígena (Indigenous Social Alliance)
AUC	Autodefensas Unidas de Colombia (United Self-Defense Forces of Colombia)
CINEP	Centro de Investigación y Educación Popular (Center for Research and Popular Education)
CRIC	Consejo Regional Indígena del Cauca (Regional Indigenous Council of Cauca)
CRIHU	Consejo Regional Indígena de Huila (Regional Indigenous Council of Huila)
DAI	División de Asuntos Indígenas (Division of Indigenous Affairs)
DANE	Departamento Administrativo Nacional de Estadística (National Administrative Department of Statistics)
ELN	Ejército de Liberación Nacional (National Liberation Army)
ETI	Entidad Territorial Indígena (Indigenous Territorial Entity)

FARC	Fuerzas Armadas Revolucionarias de Colombia (Revolutionary Armed Forces of Colombia)
INCORA	Instituto Colombiano de la Reforma Agraria (Colombian Institute for Agrarian Reform)
MAQL	Movimiento Armado Quintín Lame (Quintín Lame Armed Movement)
ILO	International Labor Organization
NT	New Tribes (a missionary group)
ONIC	Organización Nacional Indígena de Colombia (National Indigenous Organization of Colombia)
SIL/WBT	Summer Institute of Linguistics/Wycliffe Bible Translators
WHC	UNESCO World Heritage Center

Glossary of Spanish Words and Phrases

blanqueamiento	whitening
cabildo	council
capitanía	small political unit headed by a capitán (headman)
chuszua (*Muiscubbun*)	temple
Derecho Mayor	"Greater Right"
guaquero	plunderer of archaeological sites
La Violencia	a period (1947–1967) of violent confrontations between Liberal and Conservative parties
llanero	plainsman
maloca	multifamily longhouse
mesa de concertación	consultation roundtable
mestizaje	racial mixture, usually with reference to White and indigenous
Pensamiento Propio	"Our Own Thought"
personería jurídica	legal personhood
rapé	potent tobacco snuff mixed with ashes of the Yarumo tree (Pourouma cecropiaefolia)
resguardo	communally owned indigenous reservation
sede	headquarters
taita	esteemed elder
usos y costumbres	uses and customs
yajé	Banisteriopsis caapi, a hallucinogenic infusion

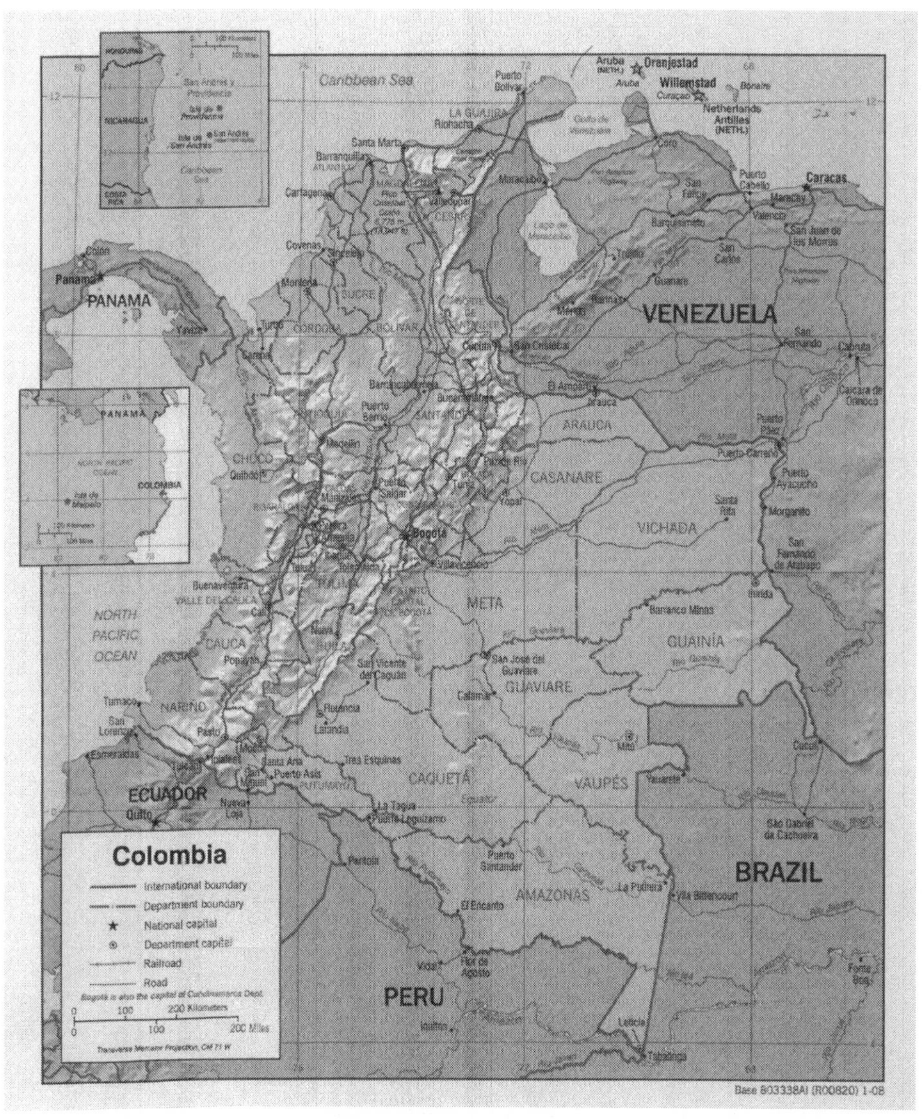

Map 1. Map of Colombia (Courtesy of the Library of Congress).

Managing Multiculturalism

Introduction

In July 1991, upon arriving in the town of Mitú in the southeastern part of Colombia, I heard people talking about a group of nomadic hunter-gatherers who had stayed there until the previous month, when they were flown back to their territory in the neighboring department of Guaviare.[1] The group had emerged from their forest habitat a year earlier, one more case of forcibly displaced victims fleeing the horrendous violence characterizing the region. Surely this group, identifying themselves as Nukak and consisting entirely of women and children, merited a warm welcome from townspeople and humanitarian treatment. But no one had anything good to say about them. In fact, I was treated to a display of appalling bigotry on the part of the locals, both indigenous and White, when they responded to my questions. The Nukak were "not really people." They stole bananas and pineapples from gardens. They ate raw meat, sometimes while their prey was still alive. Worse, they were cannibals. The women were out to seduce other women's husbands. And so on.

It was, as they say, a teachable moment. But I was not there to teach but to do ethnographic research, and so not in a position to tell people what I thought of their absolutely deplorable behavior.

These conversations with Mitú townspeople, some of whom I had known for over twenty years, are described more fully in Chapter Three. I mention them here because the Nukak's sojourn in Mitú illustrates many of the points made in the pages that follow about the state's responsibilities with regard to the country's indigenous citizens; state interventions during crises—particularly in areas beyond state control that were being devastated by violence; the role of nonstate actors, in particular religious missions and nongovernmental organizations (NGOs); indigenous identity; indigenous rights; and indigenous imaginaries—both those held by members of mainstream society and those indigenous people have of themselves.

This book follows the long trajectory of my research in Colombia as a way to explore the evolution of the country's indigenous movement, a subject, I believe, of considerable interest and significance. Given that indigenous people constitute only a small part of the national population, the movement's accomplishments are nothing short of extraordinary. Some leaders became near-celebrities, appearing on television and the front pages of the national press. Amazingly, indigenous communities gained collective ownership of almost 30 percent of the national territory. This struggle occurred during a half century of violent armed conflict among conservative and liberal political parties, state security forces, leftist guerillas, right-wing paramilitary forces, and criminal elements, mostly drug traffickers—an implacable battle for power, control, and territory that profoundly affected the country's indigenous (and Afro-descendant) communities. The truly compelling story of these efforts—how indigenous organizing began, how it found its voice, established alliances, and won battles with the government and the Catholic Church—has important implications for the indigenous cause internationally and for understanding rights organizing of all sorts. I do not offer here a comprehensive history of the movement, one that would encompass all significant organizations, actors, and events throughout Colombia. Rather, I attempt to illuminate what seem to me certain crucial dimensions of the struggle by examining a number of telling ethnographic cases, most of them drawn from my fifty years of research in the country.

Over the five centuries since the Spanish conquest, the indigenous peoples of Colombia—and elsewhere in Latin America—have been forced to confront exploitation, dispossession, and other forms of oppression. In theory this situation ought to have improved in the twentieth century, as the countries in the region championed "universal and undifferentiated citizenship, shared national identity and equality before the law."[2] But while important improvements have occurred, in fact, racial, ethnic, and class inequities continued throughout, revealing a yawning gap between ideals and reality. Late in the century, beginning in the 1970s and taking off in the 1980s,[3] in a period of political liberalization known as the democratic transition,[4] many countries promoted neoliberal reforms,[5] including a turn to civilian rule, reduction of state repression, and the promotion of multiculturalism. Fifteen Latin

American republics instituted constitutional reforms[6] targeting corruption and loss of legitimacy, while at the same time promoting rights discourses[7] that would, it was hoped, go a long way toward solving the "crisis of representation" gripping governments in the region. Responding as well to widespread indigenous and Afro-descendant discontent and mobilization, the move toward democracy and multiculturalism received added impetus from two important international meetings in 1971 and 1977, the first dedicated to the plight of Amazonian peoples, the second to the repression and exploitation of indigenous communities throughout the region.[8] The document that emerged from these meetings, the Declaration of Barbados, drew attention to the plight, until then often hidden, of those communities.

The organizing stimulated by the Barbados meetings departed from previous efforts earlier in the century in several respects. As activists forged links to the international environmental and human rights movements,[9] they began placing greater emphasis on identity and culture, both for the sake of the issues themselves and as a foundation for political and territorial claims. In the crucial matter of land rights, while indigenous organizations demanded territorial control to promote economic subsistence and development, as well as to gain political autonomy and self-determination, they also came to embrace a culturalist notion of territory, one foregrounding the spaces within which indigenous peoples could live their lives in keeping with their traditions, a trend reinforced by emerging notions of intellectual property rights in part resulting from increasing interest on the part of pharmaceutical companies in medicinal plants. In the later 1990s both prospecting for pharmaceuticals and the testing, patenting, and ultimate marketing of human genetic resources occasioned indigenous protests.[10]

During this same period international funders like the World Bank and the Inter-American Development Bank promoted economic and political reforms as part of a comprehensive neoliberal package intended to shrink the corporatist state[11] and strengthen civil society. In the political move from exclusion to plurinationalism, spaces opened up encouraging debate about the definition of democracy, citizenship, and even the state itself. Challenging dominant imaginaries of the ideal national citizen as Spanish- or Portuguese-speaking, Catholic, and "modern," new voices acknowledged the diversity of Latin American countries, now often celebrating their pluriethnic and multicultural citizenry. Many countries redefined the legal status of their indigenous inhabitants, some with constitutions explicitly acknowledging special rights for ethnic and racial groups. Each country's demography, geography, and political history have profoundly shaped its indigenous movement and state policies.[12] For example, Mexico, Guatemala, Ecuador, and Bolivia have very substantial indigenous populations living in both lowland and highland regions. Highland and lowland indigenous communities are also found in Colombia, but the overall percentage of indigenous citizens is quite small, less than 4 percent. Brazil, Venezuela, and Argentina also have small percentages, but these countries lack extensive highland regions with their politically important concentrations of indigenous communities.

Some constitutions incorporated notions drawn from indigenous cosmologies; for example, Article 71 of Ecuador's 2008 constitution refers to "Nature or Pachamama" (Earth Mother). The collective rights gained by indigenous communities through these reforms included formal recognition of the multicultural nature of the nation; self-government at the local level; official status for minority languages in predominantly minority regions; guarantees of bilingual education; and recognition of traditional land tenure systems, medicine, and customary law.[13]

In the early phases of these campaigns, indigenous demands shifted from "rights as minorities" to "rights as peoples." By claiming *inherent* rights deriving from their status as autochthonous peoples, they avoid the assimilationist implications of minority status: minority rights depend by definition on membership in a larger polity, whereas inherent rights imply autonomy and self-determination. These demands were supported by several international covenants and treaties, prominent among them the 1989 International Labor Organization's Indigenous and Tribal Peoples Convention (also known as ILO Convention 169), which was signed by most Latin American governments.[14]

In this rapidly changing environment, the predominant imaginary of indigenous peoples accumulated a number of associations: a spiritual rather than materialistic relationship with the land, decision making by consensus, holistic environmentalism, and restoration of harmony in the social and physical worlds. Implicit in these values was a critique of Western forms of authority and the impulse to control and commodify nature. Also challenged were the nation-state's exclusive claim to sovereignty, its monopoly on legitimate violence, and its pretentions to define and control democracy, citizenship, penal codes, and legal jurisdiction.[15]

Nancy Postero states that the region's democratization in those years, combined with multiculturalism and indigenous activism, brought about an "unprecedented revaluation of indigenous peoples and their culture, customs, and worldviews."[16] This ideological shift, no matter how profound, was often confined, however, in its real-world impact to the formalities of constitution writing and a modest number of protective laws and judicial decisions. Some of these legal and constitutional protections were subsequently eroded, moreover, by neoliberal legislation promoted by international lending agencies. With some exceptions the impoverishment of indigenous peoples—the poorest sector of Latin America and "the most peripheral elements of the periphery of the world system"[17]—continued largely unabated.

Colombia's experience mirrors that of other Latin American countries in the ways spelled out earlier. But it differs in significant respects as well, all of them of interest to us. One is demographic: how, given Colombia's small number of indigenous people—less than 4 percent—did such visible and effective activism and leadership emerge and impact mainstream society in so many remarkable ways? One extraordinary accomplishment has been getting the government to hand over almost 30 percent of national territory to the country's *pueblos.*[18] Newspaper editorials regularly comment on how, despite not having the weight of Bolivian or Ecuadorian indigenous organizations, Colombia's indigenous activists were among the "most organized" sectors in their country, capable, for example, of mustering sixty thousand participants in marches and blockades.[19] The country's indigenous activists and their allies also had an outsize influence, given their numbers, on the international indigenous rights movement.

Second is the fact that no other indigenous rights movement in the Americas had to work in so many regions under threat of serious violence, owing to Colombia's half century of armed internal conflict.[20] At times indigenous communities had to take in considerable numbers of internal refugees, as well as deal with armed combatants—guerrillas, paramilitaries, army soldiers, and police officers—none of whom were interested in respecting pueblo claims to self-determination and autonomy.[21] That conflict is the main reason indigenous organizing in Colombia is not well represented in Anglophone literature, as the insecurity in those times led most foreign anthropologists to opt to carry out their research elsewhere. In contrast, Colombian anthropologists, many of whom are cited here, kept on with their fieldwork, at times under quite difficult conditions. They found themselves analyzing the causes and consequences of the chronic and pervasive insecurity experienced by their study communities that resulted from threats of torture, forced disappearance, and killing, threats that were all too often carried out. While documenting the humanitarian catastrophe produced by an unbelievable amount of repression targeting the country's indigenous, peasant, and Afro-descendant citizens, these researchers faced threats themselves, some of which were brutally carried out. One example is the assassination of Professor Hernán Henao, perpetrated by paramilitaries in 1999 while he was teaching his class at the University of Antioquia. Colombian anthropologists' often impressive publications have, unfortunately, not been widely distributed outside the country, and few have been translated into English.

The pueblos confronted the armed conflict in a variety of ways, some of which are discussed in the chapters that follow. Located for the most part in the countryside, pueblos found the war arriving at their doorsteps and fields with great regularity. Their basic position asserted neutrality, autonomy, and disengagement: they wanted no active role in a war that had parts of the country in paroxysms of terror and would eventually cost 220,000 people their lives. Many pueblos declared their territories off limits to any armed combatants, a policy that led guerrillas to conclude that Indians[22] were working for the military, and led the military to conclude that pueblo members were on the side of the insurgents.

Pueblos also actively sought peace. Their marches and blockades always had peace high on the list of demands, along with denunciations of the kidnappings and murders of hundreds of their leaders. Other attempts at peace making include the 1996 establishment by indigenous organizations of a "territory of coexistence, dialogue and negotiation" in the resguardo of La María, in Piendamó, Cauca, the site of several large blockades of the Pan-American Highway. The aim of this "territory of coexistence" was to bring together civil society organizations interested in finding a space for dialogue that was directly linked neither to the government nor the guerrillas.[23] Another example is the 1998 meeting organized between Abadio Green, president of Colombia's national indigenous organization ONIC;[24] the indigenous senator Francisco Rojas Birry; and Carlos Castaño, head of the umbrella paramilitary organization Autodefensas Unidas de Colombia (AUC, United Self-Defense Forces of Colombia), to negotiate a sixty-day ceasefire in the highly conflictive zones of Córdoba and Urabá.[25]

We will see that a great irony emerges from the fact that war-weary Colombians and others, myself included, have admired the ways certain pueblos resisted the violence that the war brought, despite the at times terrible costs. A profusion of newspaper articles, TV commentaries, and sermons commented on indigenous approaches to achieving consensus and carrying out actions, and by so doing conquering, if only temporarily, the fear-induced paralysis that a long-running armed conflict can produce. These pueblos declared to those who violently challenged their autonomy, "hasta aquí, no más" (you will not advance farther[26]). In the eyes of pueblos caught in the crossfire, a fate "more terrible than death"[27] would have been theirs had they yielded to the guerrillas, paramilitaries, and repressive state security forces, and forsaken their project of securing at least some of their rights. In their vulnerability, but also in their conviction and determination to not give up or give in, we see a complex and diverse set of moral and ethical imperatives in play, in large part due to the shockingly inadequate government response to the violence experienced by the country's indigenous, Afro-descendant, and peasant communities over the past decades.

My own involvement with indigenous Colombia began in 1968, when I went to Colombia for doctoral research among the Tikuna, who live near the Amazon port town of Leticia. As often happens with anthropological fieldwork, I ended up elsewhere, in the Central Northwest Amazon, in a region near the Equator straddling the Colombia-Brazil border, home to indigenous people collectively known as Tukanoans. The region, called the Vaupés on the Colombian side and the Uaupes on the Brazilian side,[28] takes its name from the Vaupés River, a tributary of Brazil's Rio Negro, which in turn empties into the Amazon in Manaus many miles downstream. Also as happens in anthropological research, my initial proposal, which had focused on native Amazonian notions of health, disease, and the body, changed radically in the field. Centered in the approach then fashionable known as ethnoscience, my proposal would have required me to learn *two* languages spoken in my prospective field site; instead I turned my attention to linguistic exogamy, which, as it turned out, was a key component of Tukanoan social structure.

Linguistic exogamy lies at the heart of what is known as the *Tukanoan cultural complex*, an extraordinary regional system in which each person must marry outside his or her settlement and patri-clan, and each clan is linked to a different primary language. This means that marriages must take place between people not only from different communities but with different primary languages. The more I learned about this system, the more fascinated I became, for it gave the lie to all sorts of assumptions about language, culture, kinship, and marriage in so-called tribal societies—assumptions that con-

Figure 1. The author with María Agudero and her daughter in a manioc field at Púmanaka buró, Vaupés, 1969.

tinue to this day. Because we tend to equate language with culture, the system confounded dominant assumptions about the supposed equivalence of the two in small-scale societies. Linguistic exogamy has caused endless confusion among government officials, missionaries, academics, and even members of non-Tukanoan pueblos. For their part Catholic missionaries worked openly to undercut the system.

After receiving my doctorate, I continued to write on the region, now addressing a more diverse set of topics. For reasons quite beyond my control,[29] I was unable to return to the Vaupés until 1987, but during the interim I did travel to Bogotá twice, collecting information on indigenous organizing in the region, learning in particular about the Consejo Regional Indígena del Vaupés (CRIVA, Regional Indigenous Council of the Vaupés), which had been founded in 1973. I found CRIVA puzzling. Colombia's first indigenous rights organization, the Consejo Regional Indígena del Cauca (CRIC, Regional Indigenous Council of Cauca), had been started two years before, in the context of fierce land struggles in the Andean southwest. CRIC's emergence was unsurprising, but CRIVA had begun in an extremely unlikely site for indigenous organizing in those days, with a widely dispersed and small population and rudimentary communications and transportation facilities. When I was finally able to return to Mitú, the capital of the Vaupés, I was eager to interview people about why such undertakings had occurred in such a remote region.

In the 1970s and 1980s, as I discovered, traditional Tukanoan social structure faced new threats, some of them ironically the result of CRIVA's efforts to defend indigenous culture by using models from outside the Vaupés. In this new political space in which activists insisted on rights to difference, a new concept of indigeneity was being developed. My desire to understand these changes led inexorably to expanding my field of view to take in the Colombian indigenous movement as a whole. It also became increasingly clear that the Vaupés was becoming unsafe, due to the expansion of narcotrafficking in the region. I did go back in 1989, 1991, and 1993, but heightened concern about security prevented me from returning after that. As a consequence, while the early chapters of this book deal with the Vaupés, the later ones move to the national level.

A book-length work allows an exposition, via ethnographic case studies, of the ways in which my object of study, methodology, and theoretical approach all evolved over those years. However, one intellectual focus links those decades of investigation: my encounters with, and explorations of, indigeneity. Although early on I was not asking direct questions about its overall nature—but rather about a social structure that confounded received wisdom about Amazonian indigenous culture—my questions about social identity, language, and culture were intimately linked to indigeneity and its representation. Such questions have accompanied my studies up until the present. In addition, my later encounters with, and exploration of, CRIVA led me to delve deeply into the issue of representation of indigeneity, more specifically, self-representation. I have found myself focusing on an ever-increasing role played by indigenous culture in struggles taking place throughout the country aimed at securing rights and the resources that accompany official recognition of those rights.

I also work throughout this book to link Colombian issues with parallel developments in other countries, and to address relevant theoretical issues and debates. For example, I discuss significant shifts in anthropological analytics and, when it occurs, their politicization. I also attend to the relationship between anthropologists and the indigenous communities they study, including my evolving awareness of several highly conflictive issues. In the long history of interactions between indigenous people and anthropologists, misunderstandings, misinterpretations, disagreements, and even out-and-out conflict[30] have occurred.[31] One has only to listen to the denunciations of anthropologists in Floyd Westerman's song "Here Come the Anthros,"[32] or read Vine Deloria's comments in his book *Custer Died for Your Sins: An Indian Manifesto*,[33] to get a sense of the problem. Over time, with the rise of identity politics, awkwardly juxtaposed with postmodernist theory, the nature of such disagreements has changed. The critique of claims to authenticity on the grounds that these claims are socially constructed, as exemplified by James Clifford's well-known essay "Identity in Mashpee,"[34] infuriated many activist Native Americans. Such critics would agree with Jonathan Friedman that while culture might be supremely negotiable for professional culture experts, "for those whose identity depends upon a particular configuration this is not the case. Identity is not negotiable. Otherwise it has no existence."[35] As we shall see is the case for many of the dichotomies explored here, the actual situation is more complex than the opposition of "essentialist perspective" and "social constructionist perspective" suggests. Les Field points out that activists in the United States, both indigenous and nonindigenous, who work to get land titles and tribal status recognized have to deal with legal and political institutions in both tribal societies and mainstream society if they want to be successful.[36] Political projects that base themselves on establishing authentic indigenous identity and culture find they must transcend the rigidity of this opposition, even though their rhetoric might seem to adopt an obdurately unbending essentialist position.

Key Words: Brief Introduction to Theoretical Concepts

Identity

Explicitly spelling out at the beginning how identity is conceived of in this book is necessary if we are to understand the Colombian case, especially given that a main theme is the exploration of indigeneity.

A person's social identity consists of his or her memberships in relevant social groups. Issues of social identity grabbed my attention almost from the beginning of my Vaupés fieldwork. When I found myself with actual people rather than sociological reifications, with kin talking about kin, what had been until then the less than riveting topics of social organization and kinship terminology came to life. So far as I remember, I did not think about identity itself—it was simply something everyone had—probably because other anthropologists were not thinking much about it either.[37] Neither were sociologists, many of whom until recently doubted whether identity was amenable to social study.[38] Too often identity has been taken for granted rather than problematized. Comprehensive definitions have been hard to come by (except perhaps in psychological literature). Steph Lawler in fact doubts whether a single, overarching definition of identity or notion of how it works is even possible.[39] For the same reason Rogers Brubaker and Frederick Cooper recommend throwing the concept out altogether.[40]

Scholarly interest in the topic emerged only during the 1960s, along with the appearance of what came to be called identity politics. The Black power movement, for instance, foregrounded identity in a way that the civil rights movement had not: the two names themselves signal differing foundational premises. Other identity-based movements—women's, Native American, disabled, and gay and lesbian—also appeared in the same years.

One aspect of identity politics in particular has attracted frequent comment and criticism: its alleged reliance on essentialism, that is, as Mary Bucholtz and Kira Hall point out, on claims that socially recognized aggregates "are inevitable and natural, and . . . are separated from one another by sharp boundaries."[41] They add that identity politics have typically, almost inevitably, been essentialist, and anthropology itself has been riddled with essentialist assumptions. By the 1970s, however, with the advent of poststructuralism and postmodernism, social identities of all sorts, including those of indigenous people, increasingly came to be seen as contingent and constructed. Authors today, all too aware of the risks posed by the "dreaded" essentialism that so often attaches to identity,[42] bend over backward to assure their readers that their argument and terminology concerned with identity are not essentialist, rigid, fixed in time, etc. The issue persists precisely because struggles for human rights and self-determination so often entail essentialist claims about culture and identity. In Chapter Five I return to the essentialist debate in a discussion of reindigenization, which occurs when a group of people who see themselves to be descended from indigenous ancestors work to recover their indigenous identity and culture. The topic dramatically illustrates Clifford's point about the "tense interaction" between identity as politics versus identity as inheritance.[43]

In this book identities are seen as social constructions that emerge within, not outside, discourse—there is nothing natural or merely given about them.[44] Identity is about difference as well as sameness: all identities rely on not being something else.[45] Each identity necessarily entails a contrast with that something else, as there can be no identity without an *Other* as foil. Expanding on this idea, Jacques Derrida attributes that same oppositional nature to all "apparently solid pre-given centers or presences," things of all sorts that exist only in relation to something else.[46] Identities are multidimensional, structured by overlapping and intersecting discourses of race, class, gender, and history. Identities reduce the vast complexity of the experienced world to a limited number of social categories, tightly linking those identities to prevailing systems of social classification.[47] Robert Gooding-Williams has proposed the useful concept of *dynamic nominalism*, which holds that "human acts come into being hand in hand with our invention of the categories labeling them."[48] But social identities assigned by systems of identification or categorization are not the same as the identities we experience, and although they are linked, we should not conflate these systems with their presumed result.[49] Identities come into being through behavior, often through performance, the latter attracting much attention in the literature at present. Instances of identity coming into being through performance are found in each chapter. Self-objectifying behavior, succinctly expressed by John Collins as "being ourselves for you,"[50] brings up questions of authenticity and legitimacy.

Although the word *identity* suggests sameness across persons and over time, identities change, and as such are closely tied to process and engagement. Olaf Kaltmeier and Sebastian Thies[51] note that recognition of the flexibility and contingency of biography and belonging leads to understanding identity formations as incomplete and fluid processes. Recent literature on ethnoracial identities, Sara Latorre writes, "focuses on the processes of identity construction and deployment, moving beyond traditional debates on definitions and legitimacy, which are based on reductionist dualisms such as authentic/false, race/ethnicity, or indigenous/nonindigenous."[52] Such dualisms, of course, pervade official treatment of identities, which often cannot move beyond traditional debates because the terminology and definitions are intended to be clear, and broadly and permanently applicable.

While claims based on indigenous identity might initially seem unproblematic, in fact, most other identity categories (e.g., men, women) are not nearly as open to the kinds of challenges that claims based on indigenous identity at times encounter. (Of course, current debates about transgender issues in legislatures, the media, and the courts are complicating what once seemed to be a clear-cut and well-understood contrast.) We shall see instances in which makers of claims confront opponents who impugn the claimants' indigenousness. In some cases the response is to play up the related dichotomy between "currently indigenous" versus only "of indigenous descent." Because the contrast here is not as absolute as indigenous/nonindigenous, making it the crucial binary can open up spaces for action (e.g., performances of indigeneity), and subsequent re-negotiation. Note that *indigeneity* and *indigenousness* are not synonyms. Indigeneity refers to a status, an identity, whereas indigenousness refers to a quality and implies the possibility of a differential amount of that quality. In this sense, the words are opposed, an opposition important to an argument I make about the contradictions that inhere in indigeneity, both as conceptualized officially and in mainstream imaginaries.[53]

Multiculturalism

Indigenous organizing in Latin America and worldwide during the past thirty years emerged in the context of *multiculturalism*, an ideology that celebrates and works to protect ethnic and cultural diversity—the phrase "unity in diversity" captures some of its goals. Partha Chatterjee attributes the emergence of multiculturalism to tensions between the project of universal citizenship and the demands for differential recognition from populations within the citizenry.[54] When defined in political terms as the legal and normative recognition of difference, multiculturalism can be recognized as one form of governmentality. (Note that the phrase "managing multiculturalism" in this book's title refers not just to official multiculturalism but also to multiculturalism as performed and shaped by a wide variety of actors from the indigenous movement and NGOs.[55]) Multiculturalism may not constitute an ideology in the sense of masking a dominant class interest,[56] but one may still ask why elites who previously insisted on cultural homogeneity found it in their interest to embrace diversity.

Modern societies are characterized by multiple kinds of difference, and hegemonic processes maintain some kinds (class stratification, for example) and discourage others, as happened in nineteenth-century Europe when nationalist powers sought to erase ethnic difference. Remedial policies favoring previously excluded and marginalized populations have of course occurred before, with the difference that contemporary multiculturalism now valorizes ethnic difference as a positive good. According to Kriti Kapila, multiculturalist demands for equality are grounded in the notion of equal respect for all cultures.[57] Official multiculturalism reverses prior attitudes and policies by encouraging those considered Others to join the national project—but not at the cost of total embrace of the dominant culture—and by rejecting the multiple forms of discrimination prevalent in Latin America and indeed throughout the world.

When multiculturalism is considered in a wider frame, as it appears in international fora like the United Nations or the international adjudication of human rights, it is apparent that cultural struggle can advance political change at this level as well. As Ronald Niezen puts it, indigenous peoples have "drawn new cultural boundaries, redefined themselves as nations, and, by implication, redefined the foundation of belonging for their individual members not only as kinship or shared culture but also as distinct citizenship, as belonging to a distinct regime of rights, entitlements, and obligations."[58]

The multicultural movement and its ideology are typically identified with democratic, liberal societies, polities with a developed civil society[59] or at least a commitment to promote one. On the one hand, multiculturalist notions of tolerance, coexistence, and equality conform to liberal democratic ideals.[60] On the other, however, the acceptance and sometimes even encouragement of radical differences within a nation clash with the liberal ideal of the unencumbered citizen who has cast off premodern attachments to family, religion, and ethnicity. Citizens who cling to territory or kin or traditional values cannot from this point of view function as the rational, individualistic profit-maximizers modernity often demands,[61] which is why Diana Bocarejo characterizes multiculturalism as "a very widespread political illusion in liberal contemporary democracies."[62]

In the pages that follow, I discuss how official multiculturalism benefits some indigenous people but puts others at a serious disadvantage. I also examine the relationship between neoliberal multiculturalism and indigenous organizing, in particular the kinds of influence nonindigenous stakeholders (e.g., State, Church, NGOs) have had on the emerging indigenous movement in Colombia, and how "indigenous culture" accrued increasing amounts of political capital as recognition politics became the norm. I also look at managed multiculturalism's impact on development project design and implementation, focusing in on the gap between policies developed in Bogotá (and abroad) and their local implementation as fleshed-out programs. I illustrate my points with examples from the Vaupés and elsewhere. Dramatic interactions—often clashes—between Western and Tukanoan assumptions about authority vividly expose these programs' numerous contradictions, despite their well-intentioned multiculturalist framing.

Neoliberalism

Like identity and multiculturalism, neoliberalism is protean, open to multiple definitions and analytic viewpoints. Although the concept has been criticized as analytically unwieldy—insufficiently theorized and "promiscuously pervasive, yet inconsistently defined, empirically imprecise and frequently contested"[63]—it can nonetheless illuminate some key trends that began in the mid-1980s in Latin America and beyond.

The neoliberal project seeks to dismantle the welfare state along with the social, political, and economic structures undergirding it. It encompasses both economic restructuring and market-driven governance models and discourses. Policies are aimed at privatizing, liberalizing, and deregulating national economies in order to promote foreign investment and intensify export production. Neoliberalist reforms are made palatable through appeals to national solidarity and celebration of civil society,[64] which, along with the market, are the mechanisms for reforming a bloated, corrupt, and overall dysfunctional corporatist state. Although such policies are supposed to shrink the state, some authors argue that in fact they reconfigure, rather than weaken it.[65] Note also that the implementation of neoliberalist objectives in fact depends on state policy, which orchestrates the reorganization of legal and political institutions; in turn, the market serves as the basis of state legitimacy.[66]

Neoliberalism reconceptualizes the person: political subjects who govern themselves according to market logics of competition and efficiency and who bear responsibility for their own social welfare are seen to need very little from the state. Educated and entrepreneurial, these self-actualizing subjects are encouraged to see themselves as a project, an enterprise, a consumer.[67]

A striking feature of neoliberal governance is its connection with socially liberal identity politics: economic austerity and pro-market reforms accompany progressive pro-democracy and multicultural reform agendas. Neoliberal multiculturalism plays down social class issues and celebrates what Anders Burman calls a "defanged" notion of ethnicity and cultural diversity.[68] This paradoxical combination of economic, political, and multicultural agendas has produced, according to Mark Goodale, neoliberalism's "dark side." He lists factors such as the consolidation of a late-capitalist mode of production and "the increasing subservience of Latin American states to the imperatives of the World Bank, the IMF, and the United States," which has "made Latin America a site of both enduring exploitation and occasional resistance."[69] For him, the "benign" elements of liberalism,[70] like human rights, are entwined with a particular conception of the individual that, when expressed in practice, has the effect of diminishing liberalism's moral promises.[71]

A number of authors argue that neoliberal reforms, in addition to increasing inequality and decreasing social services and employment, subordinate citizenship rights to security concerns. Violence and the threat of it, they maintain, are integral parts of what sustains the forms democracy takes in Latin America: political leaders overtly and covertly use the notion of an impending breakdown in public order to resist civil society demands for a more inclusive participatory democracy.[72]

It is clear that there is no simple and inherent antagonism between *the indigenous*, *the cultural*, and *the neoliberal*.[73] Neoliberal tenets such as decentralization and political and ethnic pluralism often permitted indigenous communities to strike their own bargains with national and international corporations and NGOs, bypassing paternalistic regional and state agencies. One particularly interesting aspect of indigeneity's emergence as an important way to claim citizenship, rights, and justice was the synergy perceived between certain neoliberally inflected development trends and what Andrew Orta refers to as indigenous communities' "inchoate democracy," which could be tapped for new civic participation: "a civitas at the bottom of the social pyramid."[74] Local communities' accountability and transparency were seen to mesh particularly well with neoliberal governance; Orta mentions celebrations of the neoliberal utility of local knowledge or traits, which were often valorized as local forms of social capital.[75] Sarah Radcliffe demonstrates the penetration of neoliberal thinking in "development with identity" projects. On the one hand, such projects promote participatory methods to foster indigenous and Afro-descendant involvement in project design and decision making. But the policies also promote the adoption of "tightly audited and technically defined terms of reference in order to specify which groups would receive resources."[76]

The degree to which multicultural projects dovetail with neoliberal interests has been hotly debated. Charles Hale finds a close fit between the global logic of neoliberalism and the promotion of indigenous and multicultural rights. For him, the economic reforms guarantee cultural rights in ways that do not "threaten the fundamental tenets of the capitalist economy"; rather, the reforms actually strengthen them.[77] Brooke Larson notes that the state's deployment of managerial devices of co-optation and coercion, which she calls a new version of the colonial divide-and-rule tactic, is aimed at controlling or crushing indigenous movements, "depending on whether they were deemed useful or dangerous to the state and its NGO allies."[78] Orta points out that anti-neoliberal activists "are very often enabled, and in some cases constituted by, the structures of neoliberal governmentality."[79] Although many indigenous leaders do reject the logic of the market and the commercialization of their cultural identity, Thomas Eriksen points out that they "have to do it actively as a form of resistance, surrounded by an encroaching sea of neoliberal thinking."[80]

Hale also discusses the effects of neoliberal governance on subject formation—ways in which regimes open spaces that shape and channel the subjectivities of indigenous actors who come to occupy them. Pushed to become "pragmatic" and compliant, they become "accustomed to the pleasant benefits of working in such spaces, distanced from the communities and community-based processes that produced them as leaders, disinclined toward the radical tactics and demands that helped to produce the spaces in the first place."[81] Although indigenous leaders criticize official discourses of neoliberalism and structural adjustment measures, at the same time they often collaborate with national governments, international institutions, and NGOs that promote neoliberal ideologies.[82] While neoliberally influenced identity work can be effective in strengthening collective pride and boosting self-esteem, states Eriksen, "it can also be controversial, precisely because it moves the project of cultural identity in an individualized, goal-rational, and commercialized direction."[83] In sum, for these scholars, the reforms represent "a parallel mix of opportunity and peril" for indigenous communities.[84]

Indigenous mobilizations did succeed at gaining certain cultural and political reforms from governments and NGOs; however, increased political participation has not significantly lessened socioeconomic inequalities for many of Latin America's indigenous peoples. Rather, as Lucas Bessire points out, participation has resulted in these inequalities being unevenly redistributed, because neoliberalism's cultural project endorses indigenous cultural rights without supporting other necessary changes, so that new political opportunities are accompanied by new economic threats.[85] Indeed, as Carmen Martínez Novo notes, the package of rights to culture has usually been accompanied by an explicit rejection of other demands.[86]

By the end of the 1990s ample evidence revealed neoliberalism's promises to indigenous communities to have been mostly wishful thinking, mainly because the state's social reforms did not "fully confront entrenched structural problems of rural poverty, racism, and marginality."[87] In response to these unmet promises, the first and second decades of the twenty-first century (termed by some the *postneoliberal* era) witnessed a number of challenges to neoliberalism's hegemony, in the form of experiments in democracy. Some Latin American countries are characterized by "a new form of protagonism that both incorporates and challenges the underlying philosophies of neoliberalism" through social mobilizations that "push to make [neoliberal state] institutions more inclusive."[88] Jan Hoffman French documents the way postneoliberalism recognized rights for indigenous and Afro-Brazilians, and linked these rights to tangible resources.[89] The Bolivian constitution's preamble states that "we have left the colonial, republican and neoliberal State in the past." But while the Evo Morales administration ushered in a "hybrid state formation" that mounted specific challenges to the neoliberal paradigm, the country remains subject to the "internal and external constraints of global capitalism."[90] Postero, also writing about Bolivia, asks, "what does multiculturalism mean when 'traditional indigenous' lifestyles are recognized by the constitution but swallowed up by the economic realities of rapid urbanization or resource exploitation?"[91] Eriksen sees this refutation of neoliberalism in Bolivia to in fact indicate its pervasiveness: deregulation, structural adjustment, and marketization negatively impact "peasants, traders, slumdwellers, and civil servants alike."[92]

In sum, while new spaces opened up in the 1990s for celebrating and supporting indigenous political engagement and diversity, a "paradox of simultaneous cultural affirmation and economic marginalization" negatively impacted many pueblos.[93] Some NGOs encouraged the indigenous movement to fashion docile subjects who would focus on strategically claiming resources rather than calling for protests. Neoliberal multiculturalism obscured many of the continuing consequences of historical and political forms of oppression, and avoided addressing certain crucial issues of race, power, and privilege.

My ethnographic cases demonstrate some of the effects of Colombia's efforts to develop an overall neoliberal package intended to shrink the state and enable the development of a much more robust civil society. Multiculturalist ideologies and policies, including new tropes of indigeneity in nationalist rhetoric, were part of that package. Certainly major gains were made, as noted here, but there were significant unintended consequences of those policies, one of them being an increase in income inequality. I also discuss evidence leading to the conclusion that the Colombian version of the neoliberal multicultural state in actuality was *not* fostering social equality but, by seeking to control the process and outcome of indigenous and Afro-Colombian struggles for self-determination and autonomy, was reinscribing racist relations that fostered internal disagreements within, and generated divisions between, communities.

Culture

Culture is perhaps the most protean category of all. So many definitions of culture have been put forward that Alfred Kroeber and Clyde Kluckhohn filled an entire book, *Culture: A Critical Review of Concepts and Definitions*,[94] with nothing else. Since that book's publication in 1952, the definitions and their scholarly applications have increased exponentially. The concept long ago jumped the anthropological corral, turning up frequently in the literature of sociology, history, and (needless to say) cultural studies, as well as in the wider world of popular discourse, so much so that in 2014, Merriam-Webster declared *culture* the most important word of the year.[95] The term's great expansion into the discourses of participatory development perfectly exemplifies neoliberalism's cultural project. Culture has, as Collins puts it, become increasingly fungible.[96] The result is a very ambiguous and flexible concept, one that, as it becomes increasingly "expedient"[97] to mention culture in a wide variety of contexts—constitutions, NGO annual reports, funding proposals, community meetings—runs the risk of becoming almost evacuated of meaning.

A surfeit of definitions makes for a surfeit of debates and issues. Over the years, anthropology has engaged in endless discussions about what culture is and how to study it—how a given culture evolves over time, how cultures differ from and resemble one another, how they are to be classified. Hence the story of my journey also includes comments on the highly dynamic and at times vexed relationship between anthropology and its key concept. One enters the field with a research proposal and a mental folder filled with analytic concepts and their definitions. As the investigation progresses one discovers all the ways such concepts do not fit—well, sometimes they are finally made to fit, but only after a great deal of tinkering. I am not saying this folder should be left at home, as one needs theories and concepts, and not just for the purpose of impressing orals committees and potential funders. My struggles with the culture concept in the pages that follow demonstrate some major features of the *process* of ethnographic fieldwork—how anthropology works.

In this book I limit myself to exploring how the culture concept works in multicultural contexts, what has been called the *politics of culture*. Multiculturalism introduced an array of political applications of the concept, along with actors interested in exploring and using them. The central contradiction at the heart of cultural politics, according to Kapila, is the necessity of recognizing difference in a way that apportions an appropriate degree of redistributive justice.[98]

In popular discourse culture is understood to include tradition, ethnicity, value systems, and language, assumptions also dominant in indigenous self-depictions in terms of autochthony, rootedness, tradition, closeness to nature, rurality, and spirituality. Many authors have pointed out the construction of indigenous culture as the polar opposite of modern life: non-Western, non-Eurocentric, nonmodern, nonurban, and so forth.[99] Politics often requires that indigenous culture, in its essence, be seen as radically different from Western understandings of the world.

Cultural politics necessarily depends on a perceived right to culture. Within a multicultural regime indigenous individuals and communities are no longer wards of the state or the Church; they are citizens, with all the rights and obligations attending that status. In effect, they have gained the right to have rights.[100] Their rights, moreover, include official recognition of their cultures and pledges to protect those cultures. With those rights and privileges comes an implicit demand for authenticity: to secure one's land and natural resources, gain preferential consideration for development projects, and justify exemption from military service, one must demonstrate a worthy, authentic culture. At the same time, official recognition sets in motion machinery to safeguard that culture through special "ethno-" programs in education and health. This circularity—culture as a right but also as the site from which to claim rights—is inescapable in the cultural politics of indigeneity.

Cultural authenticity, moreover, articulates with what Joanne Barker terms legal legitimacy.[101] Latin American pueblos have learned the desirability of establishing and regularly reestablishing their legitimacy—legal and otherwise—through a rhetoric and performance of authentic cultural difference and continuity with a traditional past and place. Such self-authenticating performances ensure their leaders' authority to speak and to be heard, which increases in turn their chances of political success.

In these pages, I describe how my understanding of culture changed as a consequence of my research, first in the Vaupés and later elsewhere in the country. The examples from my early fieldwork show the ways in which what I had absorbed in my coursework at Stanford University regarding the culture concept simply did not allow me to describe and analyze what I was learning about Tukanoan culture, in particular the consequences of the institution of linguistic exogamy. And examples from my early efforts to understand organizing in the Vaupés show how I strained to analyze and write about young Tukanoan activists' efforts to represent their culture in a way that would be understood and approved of by outsiders. To me, their efforts produced inauthentic—in a word, incorrect—representations of Tukanoan culture. What was going on? Is this what they really believed? These young men presumably knew a lot more about Tukanoan culture than I did or ever would. I had to confront a situation in which culture was being politicized, something my graduate school training did not prepare me for at all.

Anyone who seeks to explore the politics of culture, at least when working with indigenous movements, needs a thick skin and a willingness to stand up to the criticism that inevitably follows. I experienced controversies firsthand; for example, in 1984, when I submitted a research proposal to the National Science Foundation to study indigenous organizing in the Vaupés, a reviewer accused me of seeking funding to "do politics." Although studying political organizing in places like the Vaupés became more acceptable, I struggled to write about all this without getting hit on the head, as presentations of my research findings sometimes were met with criticism from both fellow anthropologists and indigenous activists.[102] I found myself encountering several ethical (and epistemological) issues familiar to any researcher investigating indigenous mobilizing around cultural rights. For one thing, new research paradigms were emerging that addressed long-standing ethical issues associated with all kinds of ethnographic research—the researcher's positionality, asymmetrical power relations, and so forth. An example is Lynn Stephen's call for "collaborative activist ethnography," a form of politically positioned and accountable field research that does not subordinate "analytical rigor to conclusions driven by a pre-established political agenda."[103]

In sum, culture is a highly polysemic word. While a discussion of human evolution might profitably and accurately describe culture as adaptive, somewhat in the manner of fur or claws, in circumstances in which culture change is extremely dynamic, it might be helpful to see culture less as like an animal's fur and more as like a jazz musician's repertoire. Yes, the individual pieces come out of a tradition, but improvisation always occurs, and the musician's choices at a particular performance take into consideration the acoustic properties of the venue, characteristics of the instrument(s), knowledge about fellow musicians' intentions, and inferences about what the audience wants. This analogy emphasizes the agentive aspects of culture; we cannot speak of a jazz musician as "having" jazz, and, for the most part, speaking of people as "having" culture obscures the interaction between those people and their traditions. The jazz analogy also highlights the interactive aspects of culture; just as a jazz performer's music depends on engaging an audience and fellow musicians, a culture's existence depends on interaction. I see this perspective to be a more genuinely respectful view of the efforts of present-day indigenous communities to achieve self-esteem, self-determination, and autonomy.

Indigeneity

The word *indigeneity* appeared only recently.[104] However, the history of indianness and attempts to dramatize and appropriate it is long. Philip Deloria's book *Playing Indian* shows White North Americans appropriating indigenous identity as early as the Boston Tea Party.[105] Self-representation by indigenous peoples occurs today virtually everywhere in the world. Latin American pueblos, like indigenous peoples elsewhere, have found since the 1970s that they have to prove to powerful outsiders that they are "naturally" a people. And when such claims are adjudicated, the nature of this "nature"—its essential and distinctive constituents—has to be spelled out, a question that has generated a substantial literature. In the Western Hemisphere such claims may be easier to sustain than elsewhere,[106] given the presence of autochthonous peoples in the Americas long before the European conquest.[107] This historical priority does not mean that in particular cases the criteria for indigenous identity have always been easy to specify, even with respect to official definitions.[108] As indicated previously, in practice, answers to the question, "Are you indigenous now, as opposed to merely of indigenous descent?" may be contested, and not only by opponents. When this happens, the problem usually is not with definitions per se—acceptable ones can certainly be formulated.[109] Sometimes it is a matter of a lack of definitional fit with a particular case. For example, looking only at the countries of South America, we can state that a majority of the Bolivian population is indigenous, but getting all these people to agree on the criteria for such a designation has, at least in the past, been difficult.[110] In other cases, the problem lies in reconciling local identities with those of other pueblos or with the global concept of indigenous. The notion that there is a single overarching indigenous people in the Western Hemisphere, encompassing groups as distant and different from each other as the Ona of Tierra del Fuego and the Cree of Canada's boreal forest, was new and strange for indigenous Colombians in the 1980s and 1990s. Even today, some pueblos remain reluctant to entertain the idea that they are in some way all one people. Several groups, notably the Arhuaco in the north of the country, often seem to be stressing their unique identity far more than celebrating connections.

Complaints that Indians are mystifying, romanticizing, or orientalizing themselves—presenting a non-Western Other that glosses over inconvenient facts or distorts a "native" authenticity—can provoke heated responses. One response is to criticize the ways nonindigenous actors have mystified and exoticized Native Americans.[111] Anthropologists have long been accused of similar practices, of wanting to fix natives in nature, portray them as being without history, discourage them from modernizing. Such attitudes were encouraged on behalf of scientific research goals[112] or because conserving traditional culture and practices was seen as best for the indigenous people themselves. These struggles very often involve the issue of authenticity, and anthropologists often serve as its arbiters. We shall see examples of the unwillingness of state functionaries, some of them anthropologists, to accept certain petitioners' assertions of their right to culture, accompanied by an equal unwillingness on the part of nearby indigenous communities that have a perceived stake in the negative outcome of a given negotiation. In sum, the issue of who qualifies as indigenous and who gets to decide has produced some of the most interesting Latin Americanist work today.[113]

Another recurrent problem arises in the rhetoric of cultural politics phrased in possessive, individualist terms. Richard Handler, in reference to Quebecois nationalism, writes that "the nation and its members 'have' a culture, the existence of which both follows from and proves the existence of the nation itself."[114] Nationalist ideologies of all kinds, he argues, involve accounts "of the unique culture and history that attaches to and emanates from the people who occupy [the nation]."[115] For indigenous populations, what they are usually seen to share and to possess is a history of colonial and neocolonial oppression, genetic relatedness, geographic rootedness, and a primordial culture. Contradictions easily emerge. Joanne Rappaport and Robert Dover critique the anthropologically derived criteria used by the Organización Nacional Indígena de Colombia (ONIC), which are marked by the notion of "culture-as-possessed-object" mentioned by Handler. On the positive side, essentialized trait lists can facilitate production of ethnic "products" capable of acquiring exchange value and political capital, and such capital has increased considerably in present-day multiculturalist regimes.[116] The downside is that when individuals, communities, and ethnicities change, they open themselves to accusations that they are "no longer indigenous."[117] Shannon Speed points out that essentialized ideas of indigenous peoples and their age-old sacred connection to the land can leave some of these people without the ability to conform to those stereotypes "and thus to 'qualify' for land rights."[118]

Indigenous self-conceptions can also change in the face of state action. Such changes may be benign or even useful, as happens with some (not all) government-initiated projects designed to promote tourism or display the state's tolerance and humanity[119] or its environmentally positive role. Virgilio Barco, for instance, when president of Colombia, in 1988 promoted land titling legislation as a weapon against environmental degradation, because "Indians are the best caretakers of the Amazon."[120] We will see that the state's generic construction of indigeneity, *lo indígena*, became reconfigured to portray the pueblos as stewards of the environment, a gaze just as essentializing and homogenizing as what preceded it.[121]

Peace accords signed by states sometimes recognize indigenous groups in new ways and grant them greater autonomy, as illustrated by agreements between the Miskito and the Nicaraguan government,[122] or the Guna (formerly known as Kuna) and the Panamanian state.[123] Coexistence with national and regional governments, nonetheless, demands that even those indigenous groups enjoying the greatest autonomy must be perceived as loyal law-abiding citizens of the states in which they reside, meaning they must renounce armed resistance or even a hint that they might contemplate secession. The unintentionally ironic term *pacification* was used to reference the anything-but-pacific means employed to enforce such cooperation.[124] The newer, gentler approach used today enclaves previously independent groups into reserves, where they can remain culturally distinct, though over time that distinctiveness increasingly follows from a dialogic relationship with national culture. The agendas of NGOs or agencies like the World Bank may also play a role, and a sizeable literature examines "the extent to which not only national but also international legal regimes . . . dictate the contours and content of claims and even of identities."[125]

Outline of Chapters

Chapter One: Indigenous Colombia

This chapter begins with a brief history of indigenous organizing, followed by discussions of the Constitution of 1991 (Constitución Política de Colombia) and in particular its significance for the country's pueblos. A brief introduction to the country's Afro-Colombians concludes the chapter.

Chapter Two: Tukanoan Culture and the Issue of "Culture"

In this chapter I examine the challenges to anthropological theories of culture posed by political organizing around cultural and ethnic rights. The evolution of CRIVA illustrates many of the difficulties activists (and NGOs and state functionaries) encounter when they deploy culture for political ends. I also touch on postmodern questions about authorial reflexivity and ethnographic representation in an account of my search for an analytic approach that would avoid giving the impression that I was judging CRIVA's representations of Tukanoan culture in an entirely negative manner. How do we conduct research on these sensitive topics without inciting opprobrium in our research communities, as well as the larger activist and scholarly communities?

Chapter Three: The State's Presence in the Vaupés Increases

This chapter examines instances of local implementation in the Vaupés of official multiculturalist policies developed at the national level after this previously neglected region became the focus of a remarkable amount of national and international interest owing to its high proportion of indigenous inhabitants. One case deals with interethnic tensions that emerged when ignorant and incompetent officials tried to deal with a very challenging crisis. I discuss shifts in the Nukak's heretofore denigrated status due to their newly valorized identity as authentic, radically indigenous Others, as well as the impact of new discourses of equality and indigenous brotherhood that were entering the region. I also discuss the consequences of differential degrees of indigenousness subsequently being attributed to the Nukak and two other pueblos living in Guaviare department, contradicting the state's overall assumption that all pueblos are equally indigenous. This case demonstrates the analytic utility of the distinction between indigeneity and indigenousness.

In addition, a discussion of two multiculturalist programs carried out in the Vaupés illustrates the unintended consequences that can follow implementation in remote areas of projects designed in the metropole, in particular the numerous contradictions vividly exposed in the dramatic interactions—often clashes—between Western notions of ethno-development and traditional patterns of authority, knowledge production, and collective decision making. These contradictions resonate with Anna Tsing's concept of friction.[126] These two examples also show how development agents can end up fiercely competing for indigenous clients,

Chapter Four: The Indigenous Movement and Rights

I begin this chapter by describing a nationwide crisis in which indigenous activists occupied numerous government offices in Bogotá and elsewhere in the country. The debates that this action sparked vividly reveal the pressures on the indigenous movement to move from a discourse of generic indigenous militancy to one of rights-claiming based on local, culture-specific difference and traditional leadership. The way the crisis unfolded (and was eventually resolved) illustrates many of the issues that have arisen throughout Latin America in standoffs between the state and indigenous activists who attempt to engage the government in a politics of recognition.

I then discuss two examples of clashes between Western criminal law and indigenous communities' traditions with respect to judging, sentencing, and punishing wrongdoers, the result of the Colombian constitution's recognition of special indigenous jurisdiction. They illustrate many of the complexities of legal pluralism and demonstrate the need to examine the vernacularization of human rights discourses,[127] to move beyond transcendent concepts like universal human rights and explore how a community either rejects such discourses or revises and adopts them. An exceptionally interesting aspect of these two cases is the national press's mostly positive coverage, at times arguing that indigenous values and institutions in areas like jurisprudence, spirituality, governance, and communal values are superior to Western values—a quite surprising turn in a country that had, not much earlier, seen its indigenous communities to be greatly in need of rapid assimilation into the dominant society.

The final case in this chapter deals with rights issues connected to manufacturing and marketing products that are branded, so to speak, with indigeneity—what John and Jean Comaroff refer to as "Ethnicity, Inc."[128] An indigenous company's efforts to market coca leaf products exposed contradictory state actions arising from the constitution's guarantees of pueblo autonomy, international antinarcotics treaties signed by Colombia, and powerful international corporate interests.

Chapter Five: Reindigenization and Its Discontents

This chapter discusses several Colombian examples of communities working to recover their indigenous identity.[129] As noted, unlike the many kinds of people claiming rights who are members of fairly clear-cut categories (e.g., women or children), people claiming indigenous rights may be challenged as not indigenous, or not indigenous enough. Given the constitution's failure to provide criteria for determining indigenousness, the government, responding to hundreds of petitions requesting official recognition, periodically issued ever-more stringent requirements. That well-established pueblos may also resist reindigenizing projects becomes apparent in my first example, drawn from anthropologist Margarita Chaves's research in the department of Putumayo. It illustrates the point made by several scholars that in general, the greater the amount of capital (symbolic, cultural, political, economic) that attaches to indigenousness, the more closely those boundaries are policed.

My second example concerns a crisis that arose when a community belonging to a reindigenized pueblo illegally cut a road through part of a UNESCO World Heritage archaeological park. Several significant contradictions inhering within official discourses and practices concerned with indigenous policy, some of them the result of an unstable notion of indigeneity, came into full view. I discuss the increasing links being made between indigeneity and heritage, patrimony, and marketing discourses, and in particular UNESCO's notion of intangible heritage.

I then discuss urban reindigenization projects by looking at recovery efforts in two cabildos that self-identify as Muisca, a pueblo that existed in pre-Columbian and colonial eras. Such communities challenge the assumption in Colombia that indigenous rights are attached to a territory, what Bocarejo terms the spatial exceptionalism of multicultural rights.[130] I discuss my initially ambivalent reactions to these two efforts and then contrast the challenges faced by the Muisca cabildos with those encountered by a community of Tukanoan refugees living in Bogotá who have formed a cabildo and are also searching for ways to perform indigeneity in urban surroundings. Collectively these examples allow further exploration of the issue of authenticity, and in particular the role of anthropologists as authenticators.

By way of conclusion, should any readers question the usefulness of writing about indigeneity and indigenous movements, I would refer them to an essay by Marshall Sahlins, in which he called the veritable explosion of indigenous survival, self-affirmation, organizing, and empowerment one of anthropology's "biggest surprises" of the late twentieth century.[131] A second question might ask whether, given that about 30 percent of Colombia's citizens are of African descent and only a very small minority, under 4 percent, are indigenous, one should write a book about indigeneity in Colombia. The answers, which include major constitutional change, broad national support for indigenous rights, and an exceptional situation when it comes to legal pluralism, are evident in the pages that follow. By examining four notions fundamental to indigenous struggles across the hemisphere—multiculturalism, culture, rights, and indigeneity—as those notions have worked themselves out in one particular country, in one particular era of transformative change, and as seen and understood by one particular ethnographer, I come to terms with this history and with these key concepts in two ways: first, through a series of ethnographic cases, each one the subject of historical and theoretical commentary; and second, through a reflexive look back at my own fieldwork and scholarship, the career trajectory of an anthropologist working to make sense of what she has observed over the course of fifty years in a country she came to care about very deeply. Inevitably, the case histories and how I learned about them are inseparable.

1 Indigenous Colombia

"Informing the members of a community about how they are going to die is not a consultation." Abadio Green, at the time president of ONIC, voiced this sarcastic comment during an interview with me in July 1996. He was referring to recent legislation mandating that "free, prior and informed consent" be obtained before development initiatives, in this case seismic exploration on U'wa territory, could begin.[1] For the most part, the mandate was basically ignored: community members were told about "how they might be affected by the works that are going to happen."[2] This anecdote introduces us to a number of the issues discussed in this chapter: the history of conflict between the pueblos and hegemonic elites like the state and the Church, and the role played by the indigenous movement. Although earlier struggles most often involved threats to indigenous lands that provided subsistence in the form of agriculture or foraging and hunting, increasingly threats are coming from commercial development, at times massive in scale, that harm indigenous communities through the extraction of a given resource (e.g., oil, minerals, hydroelectric power) or through the infrastructural development projects (e.g., new roads, canals, military bases) needed for successful exploitation.

The indigenous peoples scattered across Colombia speak sixty-four distinct languages and form eighty-seven pueblos,[3] as officially recognized by the national government. According to the national census of 2005, almost 1.4 million citizens, constituting 3.4 percent of a national population of about forty-three million, identified themselves to census-takers as indigenous.

Colombia's indigenous peoples, whether living in concentrated Andean villages or the smaller and more dispersed communities of the desert, plains, and tropical forest regions, have always been socially, politically, and economically marginalized. In the colonial era the Spanish Crown, concerned by exploitation of the indigenous population so intense it threatened the very survival of some Andean communities, and with them a crucial source of labor and tribute, created a system of collectively owned *resguardos* (reservations).[4] To centralize and Christianize the region's scattered "savage" populations, the Crown also established *cabildos*, annually elected governing councils, which mediated between communities and their Spanish overlords in such matters as annual tribute and corvée labor.

When Colombia won its independence from Spain, in 1810, the system became, if anything, more repressive: legislation and judicial rulings authorizing the sale of resguardo lands legitimized their expropriation by outsiders, often achieved through violence.[5] A great deal of land was lost in this way. The dominant ideology of the era, enacted into law, facilitated nation-building by fostering a homogeneous, Spanish-speaking, Catholic, and patriotic citizenry. From the early republican period through the 1960s, official indigenous policy worked to incorporate Indians into the general population via biological mixing and cultural assimilation. Communal landholding, in particular, was seen as an obstacle to the nation-building project, and legislation intended to dismantle the resguardos was passed. National elites, however, were divided on these issues: Law 89 of 1890, passed by the Conservatives then in power, slowed the abolition of tribute-paying and the dissolution of collective landholding by recognizing the official status of resguardos and legalizing the cabildos. The latter have since then continued to govern the internal affairs of indigenous communities. Law 89 also strengthened indigenous claims to lands that had been titled in the colonial era, all of them in highland areas. Also during this period a substantial amount of authority over Colombia's indigenous population, especially in parts of the country inhabited by putatively wild Indians, passed into the hands of the Catholic Church. In 1892, Law 72 of that year basically left it up to the missionaries to decide how indigenous societies should be governed;[6] more power was granted by a treaty (*Concordato*) signed in 1887, and by Law 89 of 1890. Ironically, much later, the latter law underlay efforts that began during the 1960s in the departments of Cauca and Tolima to recover illegally alienated territory.

Beginning in the 1970s, many pueblos received land from the government, most of it in the form of resguardos.[7] However, the generosity of this grant was undercut by the presence of nonindigenous Colombians in as much as 80 percent of those lands. In 1988, decree number 2001 recognized the resguardo as a special kind of legal and sociopolitical entity formed either by a single local community or by an entire pueblo. In the tropical forest and plains regions, new resguardos were to be governed by cabildo-like councils called *capitanías*. Unfortunately, these communities, previously without centralized authority, had little experience with democratic self-governance. In one case from 1988, for instance, in which the Colombian president at that time, Virgilio Barco, created new capitanías to manage more than five million hectares in the department of Amazonas, bewildered residents were told to work out arrangements for their capitanías in accordance with tradition, tradition that did not in fact exist as yet.[8]

Twentieth-century changes in indigenous land ownership were accompanied by changes in indigenous education as well. In 1953, another church-state agreement put missionaries in charge of all indigenous education, effectively giving them control over two-thirds of the country's thirteen hundred schools.[9] The church monopoly then started to erode in 1960, with the founding of the government's Divisi6n de Asuntos Indígenas (DAI, Division of Indigenous Affairs).[10] Ostensibly an advocate for indigenous interests, DAI was criticized for its *indigenismo* (indigenism),[11] the adoption of assimilationist policies, mitigated by token gestures of respect for cultural difference.[12]

In 1962, the Catholic Church lost its official monopoly over indigenous education with the signing of a contract between the Ministry of Government and the Summer Institute of Linguistics/Wycliffe Bible Translators (SIL/WBT). SIL was granted permission to insert teams of linguist missionaries into indigenous communities, with the understanding that the organization would facilitate air transportation into isolated regions and promote indigenous education and development, an agreement justified in terms of a scientific and practical investigation to facilitate acculturation.[13] No mention was made in any publically available documents of SIL's evangelical proselytizing goals.[14] Under this agreement, the first concerned with indigenous languages,[15] SIL established bilingual education programs in a considerable number of communities, which in time prompted the Catholic Church to include bilingual education in its curriculum for indigenous students too. Similar agreements were later signed with other Protestant missionary groups, notably the New Tribes Mission, headquartered in Sanford, Florida.

SIL lost power during the 1980s, as the result of protests by the Catholic Church, Colombian anthropologists, and indigenous organizations. The

Minister of the Interior, a supporter of SIL, countered that opposition leaders were "headed by seditious anthropology professors at the National University, Marxists naturally,"[16] indicating just how politicized the issue had become. The numerous organizations that opposed the renewal of the SIL contract in the mid-1970s accused SIL of spying for the CIA, endangering national security, sterilizing indigenous women, and smuggling drugs and emeralds. General José Joaquín Matallana, then head of Colombia's internal security police, argued that SIL should leave because "these foreign missionaries" were subjecting the country's Indians to "cultural suicide"[17]—a highly revealing remark showing just how far the rhetoric of indigenous rights had evolved, since few officials would previously have criticized SIL's integrationist policies.

The Catholic Church's own position regarding anthropology has shown a fascinating ambivalence. Some left-leaning clergy have sympathized with pro-indigenous activism, such as the series of meetings that led to the Declaration of Barbados. In response to its critics, the Church appropriated anthropological language, for example, describing missionary efforts as a means of preserving indigenous culture. The Church formed its own Colombian Missionary Anthropological Center, began a publication called *Etnia*, founded a university program for indigenous students, and in 1973 opened an ethnographic museum in Bogotá, which closed, however, after a few years.[18] In its policies the Church came to accept some anthropological perspectives but remained implacably opposed to others, claiming for instance, that without humanistic bases, anthropological study creates irreligious, indifferent anthropologists and a compromised anthropology.[19]

Another way to approach the history of indigenous Colombia is to compare it to Mexico's history, as the contrasts are instructive. Prior to the current era of multiculturalism, Colombia was among the Latin American countries most oriented to Europe. Although native peoples have always played a role in the country's nationalist narratives, the discourse of collective identity that emerged after independence lacked the foundational reference to indigeneity characteristic of Mexican nationalism. Colombian Indians were included in textbooks, speeches on national holidays, and museum displays; and belated efforts linked the nation to the pre-Columbian Muisca people, but emphasis fell on Indians from the past rather than contemporary cultures.[20] Roberto Pineda writes that unlike Mexico's discourse based in "the glorious Aztec past," Colombia lacks a "fundamental aboriginal ethnicity."[21] As María Teresa Findji remarks, "in the national imagination, the Indians—living evidence of the colonial situation—existed only as those who had disappeared, those who were about to disappear, or those who were ultimately doomed to disappear."[22]

While Colombia's indigenismo resembled Mexico's in that the project failed in both countries, the significant differences begin with the numbers of indigenous people—Mexico's 20 percent as compared to Colombia's 3.5 percent. Second, despite a history of appalling violence, Colombia, unlike Mexico, did not have a revolution. Third, we have seen the important role played by the Catholic Church in Colombia, whereas in Mexico the revolution (1910–1920) severely curtailed the Church's power, and even before then, most Mexican nationalists were very anticlerical. Fourth, Colombia is referred to as a country of regions for a reason; although in both places indigenous communities tend to be found in remote areas, and local elites have played powerful roles in both, the Mexican state nevertheless had a greater impact on rural areas, whereas the Church played a much more dominant rural role in Colombia. Certainly no Colombian president thought it necessary to be a "personal mediator" between the mestizo state and indigenous communities with respect to land reform issues, a role played by Mexican president Lázaro Cárdenas.[23] Fifth, until the 1990s Colombia had no institutionalized urban indigenous intelligentsia inserted into government educational and agrarian reform programs, as happened in Mexico, which also had a much more developed social science sector working on indigenous issues. Sixth, while it is the case that, for political reasons, Mexican agrarian reform was never implemented in many regions,[24] land reform legislation came much earlier in Mexico and played a much more significant role. Finally, Colombian nationalism did not reject European influences nearly as much as did the Mexican version. An explicit goal of Mexican indigenismo was to lessen the damaging effects of three centuries of Spanish rule, a period that was said to have bequeathed to Mexico "an enserfed population dominated by a 'hybrid, defective culture.'"[25]

The official *indigenista* mindset in Colombia had begun to change in the late 1960s, culminating in the 1991 constitution, perhaps the best symbol of the country's shift to official acceptance and even celebration of ethnic pluralism. One of the most progressive charters to emerge in Latin America during what is generally known as the democratic transition, this constitution outstrips all others in its radical stance on indigenous matters.[26]

Two ideologies, indigenismo and *mestizaje* (the production of a new, blended multi-racial population), had underpinned nation-building projects during the nineteenth and twentieth centuries in Colombia and for the most part elsewhere in Latin America[27] until the advent of multiculturalism. They aimed for the radical transformation of indigenous peoples into hispanicized and (with the exception of Mexico) catechized speakers of the national language.[28] The Church, the Language, and the Patria were to be inscribed onto bodies, minds, and souls, thus erasing all traces of indigenousness other than ancestry. Note that the pervasive championing of mestizaje was tacitly undercut by belief in *blanqueamiento*, the gradual "whitening" of that population, leaching out the regrettable indigenous admixture.[29]

Thus, while indigenous people had always figured in Colombia's self-construction as a nation, as ethnic others they were doomed to extinction, since progress was imagined in terms of racial mixture, cultural assimilation, and White superiority. The advent of multiculturalism transformed this imaginary, ushering in a new emphasis on diversity, in which indigenous peoples, Protestantism, and (always something of an afterthought, despite comprising as much as 30 percent of the population) Afro-Colombians received official recognition for their contributions to a uniquely great nation. As Pineda notes, the doctrine of mestizaje had by then been consolidated, helping to create the notion of a national race with triple origins, one in which *lo afroamericano*, and especially Afro-Caribbean culture, finally came to be seen as a fundamental component.[30]

Which is not to say that the old discourse characterizing Indians as savage, superstitious, dirty, and ignorant did not persist. The contentious dialogue between the poles of inclusion and denigration, in Colombia and elsewhere, can be seen in the career of the word *indio*. While *indio* is used at times in academic writing and—rarely and quite self-consciously—by Indians themselves,[31] *indígena* is seen to be more appropriate, precisely because the negative force of indio remains so powerful. Evidence that the people labelled indios have internalized the stigma is overwhelming.

Indigenous Organizing

Andean pueblos began to organize to fight for land rights during the first half of the twentieth century. Beginning in 1914 the most famous leader of that time, Manuel Quintín Lame, a member of the Nasa pueblo, led an insurrection against the hacienda system that turned into a social movement. Activists in the movement, influenced by Marxist values, rejected at least in part the assimilationist positions then held by both the Left and the Right, adopting a discourse of indigeneity and the *indigenous proletariat.* However, Lame, who styled himself as "the great leader of all Indians," did not support outright revolution, and was constantly appealing to the central state as a possible ally in the fight against local and regional elites.[32] He broke with the national Left, as did other indigenous leaders of the time, and ultimately came to espouse indigenous separatism.[33] David Gow notes that Lame felt a dual loyalty, to both his people and his country.[34] He fought elites and centers of power but always trusted that the state could bring about inclusion.[35]

Lame's rejection of universalist values such as egalitarianism and democracy resonates in more recent debates, in Colombia and elsewhere, over whether radically different cultures can coexist within a modern democratic state, even a multiculturalist one. His position presages disputes discussed in Chapter Four that show how some multiculturalist visions encompass far more than just inclusion of minorities with respect to citizens' rights. When implemented as local policy and practice, multiculturalism often overtly goes against liberal notions of fairness, representation, and so forth. For example, recognition of the right to culture, in particular legal recognition of what is called customary law, may require an openness to nondemocratic and exclusionary forms of difference—where, for example, institutions referred to as *Andean democracy* are anything but democratic as understood in the West. Such disputes figure in a considerable amount of Latin Americanist literature concerned with the status of women.[36]

Lame is now widely recognized as the most important ancestral figure by today's activists, who continue to draw on his legacy and example, although by the 1960s his role had greatly diminished, and he died a few years too early, in 1967, to see the fruits of his lifelong struggle.[37] For several years in the 1980s, an indigenous guerrilla group, the Movimiento Armado Quintín Lame (MAQL, Quintín Lame Armed Movement) took his name.

During the 1930s and 1940s the struggle for land by both indigenous pueblos and nonindigenous peasants was taken up by the Agrarian Movement (Movimiento Agrarista) in the department of Tolima in southern Colombia. In the 1950s, guerrillas of Marxist and Liberal persuasions continued this struggle against the Conservative government of the era, forming "independent republics" that evolved into insurgent groups.

In the 1970s the country's newly formed indigenous organizations—beginning with the Consejo Regional Indígena del Cauca (CRIC, Regional Indigenous Council of Cauca), founded in 1971—began to seek, as Lame had, to distinguish themselves from the nonindigenous Left, which saw the ethnically distinct groups mobilizing to regain land and autonomy as threats to proletarian unity, because those groups would not buy into the mestizo-criollo[38] nationalism that constituted the paradigm for most leftist organizing. Although the Left attacked imperialism and capitalism, it did not question the appropriateness of a nation-state model for Colombia's people. Indigenous rights theorizers attacked this position as assimilationist, deeply resenting the way some revolutionaries were dismissing the pueblos as reactionary and racist.[39] A crucial aspect of this split, which has continued to the present, concerns the conceptualization of indigeneity. At the time, the Left saw Indians merely as one more downtrodden sector of Colombian society: they stood to benefit when imperialist domination had been vanquished, but they had no distinctive role to play in the struggle or in the imagined socialist future, which would come about through class warfare. It was obvious to all concerned that Indians were anti-imperialists, capable of organizing and, in some cases, of violent resistance. But pueblo members understood and expressed their resistance in social, cultural, and spiritual terms, even concerning overtly economic struggles about land, which for them is a key symbol of cultural identity as well as a means of production.[40]

The Catholic Church in that era, while quite conservative as an institution, included many young, leftist priests, influenced by Vatican II and liberation theology, and their forcefully delivered arguments at times concerned their work with Indians. In September 1970, at the end of my two-year period of fieldwork, I was invited to speak, along with four other anthropologists,[41] at a gathering of missionary priests in Bogotá organized by the Bishop of the Vaupés, Belarmino Correa. After we made our arguments in favor of respecting indigenous culture, several priests championed similar views. One said, "I went to the Vaupés to teach the Indians about God, but I discovered God in them." Bishop Correa finally stepped in to remind them that their mission centered on teaching the Gospel.

As Christian Gros points out, the Latin American Left spoke three languages: democracy and social justice, progress and modernization, and national independence and the anti-imperialist struggle.[42] Indigenous activists clashed with their leftist counterparts because the two conceptualized democracy and progress differently. Hence, in Colombia, just as elsewhere in Latin America, indigenous resistance movements have sometimes been accused of reactionary separatism, at odds with a leftist stance on ethnicity that at its core is integrationist.[43] In this respect, the Left's dependency theory converged with Liberal modernization theory.[44] The anti-imperialist nationalism of the Colombian Left, despite its pro-peasant rhetoric, is permeated by urban, criollo elitism, which has led it into clashes, some of them violent, with indigenous rights activism.

In 1959 DAI moved to prohibit any more dissolutions of resguardos until further notice, and some DAI employees supported the formation of new cabildos, strengthening existing ones, and protecting collective landholding, all of which, it was argued, helped prevent violence.[45] DAI bolstered the formation of a collectivity based on a regional ethnic identity, and can thus be seen as creating a political and organizational space for indigenous communities to re-create indigenous collective structures.[46] Another aim was to gain allies in a region (Cauca) where the state clearly was not in control. Thus DAI tolerated and even at times encouraged ethnic-based mobilizations in an effort to repress others based on class, and to counter the expansion of guerrilla movements into indigenous areas.[47] These responses helped shape an important state agency's ideas of culture and race.[48]

The history of DAI, established in 1960, illustrates some of the difficulties a state may encounter in its attempts to control ethnic minorities. The agency's creation was supposed to represent a progressive new policy to end forced acculturation, religious domination, and expropriation of indigenous lands. The agency's mandate was to sponsor a gradual integration of the pueblos into the national society, turning marginalized and isolated natives into "useful citizens," largely by integrating them into the cash economy. Traditional authorities were undercut by promoting younger men as managers of cooperatives and training them as primary school teachers and health care promoters.[49] The resguardo system eventually was to be eliminated, with all property transferred to individual families, and nomadic groups were to be sedentarized. Pueblo members in areas of land conflicts were reclassified as peasants, just as had happened in Peru during the Velasco reforms of the late 1960s, and the agency claimed sole authority, in a way that Myriam Jimeno and Adolfo Triana characterize as "obsessive," to determine who was or was not indigenous.[50]

In keeping with the clientelism common in national politics DAI appointees typically arrived in the field with little experience and insufficient or no training. Personnel turned over almost 100 percent with each new administration. As Jimeno and Triana note, both clientelism and *politiquismo* (purely self-interested politics) pervaded DAI politics, particularly at the regional level. Salaries were abysmally low, and funding for programs was paltry, exacerbating the agency's impotence. Taking the Instituto Colombiano de Reforma Agraria (INCORA, Colombian Institute for Agrarian Reform) as a rival, DAI duplicated some of its programs, even though INCORA, with a larger budget and greater technical competence, had a much better track record. DAI's relations with indigenous leaders were chronically difficult, both locally and nationally. A lawyer I interviewed noted that in outlying regions like the Vaupés, DAI agents, chronically short of funds and widely viewed as mired in corrupt politics, lacked all influence and credibility.

During the 1970s a diverse collection of government agencies sponsored a series of uncoordinated programs targeting indigenous communities, which left DAI functionaries with virtually nothing to do. Ironically, new life was breathed into the agency by indigenous mobilizing. By the early 1980s, as the government realized that it could not hold activists' demands at bay purely through repression, it turned to DAI to mediate relations with indigenous organizations, lending DAI a measure of authority.

Despite the many problems that beset DAI during the first three decades of its existence, several of its directors and staff members accomplished important work during their time there. Anthropologist Martín von Hildebrand, for one, was very influential in getting vast amounts of territory designated as resguardos.[51]

In 1967 a semiofficial organization, the Asociación Nacional de Usuarios Campesinos (ANUC, National Association of Peasant Users), was formed by the Colombian government to regulate peasant efforts at ensuring enactment of the land reform laws passed in 1961. But ANUC soon became openly opposed to the government, as it had become clear that INCORA was failing at its task.[52] Peasants everywhere, but especially in Cauca and Huila, invaded haciendas. In response, national policy changed course and met the occupations with repression (which was favored by large landowner associations), and increasingly supported large-scale agriculture. ANUC, further radicalized, became divided by schism, and two lines emerged. The more radical (Sincelejo) line continued to search for solutions to the land tenure problems but also, influenced by leftist mobilizing, embarked on actions directed at upending the social and economic order. Indigenous members of the Sincelejo line, on realizing that ANUC was interested only in *campesinando* its indigenous members, that is, in turning them into mestizo peasants, formed an

Indigenous National Secretariat (Secretaría Indígena Nacional), and subsequently left to form CRIC, a mainly indigenous organization. They vowed to continue the fight for land rights, which included an end to shareholding (*terraje*), and to defend themselves from the severe repression being meted out to indigenous communities, both by guerrilla armies and by the national armed forces. Demanding implementation of agrarian reform laws, which mandated expansion of resguardos as well as reclamation of lapsed resguardos titled by the Crown during the colonial era, CRIC—and later other organizations representing Andean pueblos—fought a number of bloody battles. This confrontational stance responded to a history of more than four hundred years of often-brutal oppression: as one ONIC activist from Tolima told me in 1987, they were united more by harsh memories than by things like a shared language.

When CRIC was founded in 1971, it denounced Law 89 of 1890 (and the resguardo system as a whole) because of its racist and paternalistic language. After six months, however, CRIC leaders changed their mind, as they came to see the law as a tool to fight the powerful landlords who were exploiting indigenous sharecroppers and repressing any form of protest.[53] For their part, state functionaries, when they realized that repossessions of land could not be stopped by imprisoning activists and other forms of repression, reversed official policy and sought a way to place land recovery in a legal framework. INCORA was allowed to create new indigenous territories and resguardos so that indigenous communities could maintain their agricultural practices based on collective traditions. However, INCORA's failure to respond adequately to petitions from Andean pueblos for land titling and resguardo expansion meant that agitation and violence continued.[54] INCORA took as its basic mandate the facilitation of outmigration from the country's heavily populated heartland by assigning plots to peasants who worked them on a small scale, and by creating indigenous reserves in the country's *baldíos*—that is, *terra nullius*, lands legally designated empty. In fact, these territories were inhabited; it was indigenous mobilizing, after all, that had persuaded INCORA to transform most of the reserves into resguardos. Between 1961 and 1986 INCORA created 158 new resguardos, totaling over 12 million hectares; between 1986 and 1989 it created 63 new resguardos, totaling over 13 million hectares.[55] INCORA initially favored dismantling the resguardos, on the grounds that collective tenure did not belong in a modern land tenure regime, which evoked a fierce defense on the part of activists. Protests about the repression widespread in areas where landlessness was most acute often elicited indifference on the part of both DAI and INCORA functionaries.[56] It became clear that agrarian reform, with its goals of lessening conflict over land and making more territory available to modern agriculture, was obviously never intended to bring about the necessary fundamental changes in land tenure that would benefit small-scale farmers.[57] Communities complained about the wide gap between INCORA's announced policies and the autonomy its clients hoped for. INCORA functionaries, according to critics, had taken the part of landlords, and even arranged for funds to be lost when they were for projects that provoked INCORA's hostility or indifference.

Local landowners and some branches of the government were not the only opponents of land repossession; the Catholic Church, which had extensive landholdings in some areas, also fought back. Earlier in the century it had even mounted a campaign to convince pueblos that they had no claim to the lands they were living on. Because pueblos did not engage in Western agricultural practices, so the argument went, the land was therefore available to "whoever would work it and make it worth something."[58]

Although CRIC declared itself an indigenous organization, it never identified itself with a particular pueblo. According to Findji, at CRIC's beginning, it retained ANUC's emphasis on social class rather than ethnicity, and in practice CRIC maintained links with other, nonindigenous sectors of rural society, which helped to amplify its potential for mass mobilization.[59] For example, in its early years CRIC worked to establish government-supported cooperatives.[60] In the fall of 1971, however, CRIC modified its charter to include the defense of "indigenous history, language and customs."[61] CRIC's own version of its history acknowledges that at the very beginning, "we ourselves believed that being indio was not good, and that in order to progress we had to copy what came from the exterior."[62] In 1974 CRIC began the newspaper *Unidad Indígena*, which as of 2018 is still being published. Later on CRIC became nationally known for its efforts to support regional-level negotiations with both state security forces and illegal armed combatants, and to help create organizations committed to promoting peace.

In 1977 another national organization emerged, initially called Gobernadores en Marcha (Governors on the March) and, later, Autoridades Indígenas del Sur Occidente (AISO, Indigenous Authorities of the Southwest). In 1990 this organization, which had strong ties to the Guambiano pueblo, asserted a national presence by changing its name to Autoridades Indígenas de Colombia (AICO, Indigenous Authorities of Colombia), and including other pueblos, such as Pastos living in the southern part of the country and Arhuacos in the Sierra Nevada de Santa Marta in the north. In 2011 it dropped affiliation with the Pastos and changed its name to Autoridades Tradicionales Indígenas de Colombia (Traditional Indigenous Authorities of Colombia).[63]

From the beginning AICO promoted a culturalist line, demanding recognition for the country's indigenous populations as pueblos, with rights to their own traditions and autonomy.[64] Unlike CRIC, AICO maintained a decentralized structure reflecting an insistence on avoiding Western models. The organization's insistence on indigenous autonomy is evident in a document that emerged from a meeting in the resguardo of Guambía in January 1985 and that demanded that all armed actors, including MAQL, quit indigenous territories.[65] CRIC and AICO, for a long time bitter rivals, began in the 1990s to articulate positions more in agreement on basic issues.

CRIC's use of Western forms of organization (its structure followed a labor union model) and its willingness to include nonindigenous advisors (some of them, not even Colombians, were referred to as *misteres*, "Misters") opened up the organization to criticism by AICO that CRIC was betraying indigenous thought and values.[66] Whereas CRIC initially based its position on a Cauca-wide, militant, generic indigenousness that emphasized resistance to colonial and neocolonial oppression and repression, AICO made headway with various sectors, indigenous and not, by engaging in actions and arguments it claimed were based on an authority derived from a traditional and more authentic *Derecho Mayor* (Greater Right) position. But AICO would not have been able to achieve its prominence without CRIC's initial organizing efforts. AICO's prescient critique of CRIC ideology and policy was brilliant, but also ironic, for had CRIC organized along culture-specific lines, rather than generic indigenous ones, it very probably would not have succeeded nearly as well as it did. The phrase "give us a weapon so we can defend ourselves from you" illustrates CRIC's strategy: the discursive and organizational "weapons" it appropriated from the dominant society were effective. The path AICO chose turned out to fit with widespread shifts occurring in Colombian society's understanding of its pueblos and what they needed. All political vanguards sooner or later give way to activists, usually younger, who better understand the situation they are currently encountering. However, they are able to move forward in the new direction because of their predecessors' ability to discern opportunities, evaluate risks, and take appropriate action during the previous era.

During the years 1976 to 1981 the government attempted to pass a repressive Indigenous Law that would effectively have given the state extensive power over the pueblos, including the authority to determine who was or was not indigenous.[67] The bill failed to pass, and the organized resistance continued, buoyed up by press reports highly critical of massacres of Indians, as well as by activists' alliance-building with peasant groups and other leftist organizations. ONIC was founded in 1982, and by 1986 sixteen regional organizations had appeared.[68] In 1983 ONIC received government recognition, and it has since participated in an official capacity in programs concerned with indigenous affairs.

As mentioned, in the 1980s Colombia was handing over land, including some massive tracts, to its indigenous communities, a policy responding, among other things, to the often violent land repossession campaigns, as well as to demands for the effective implementation of the 1961 land reforms. As of 2004 indigenous pueblos had gained collective and inalienable title to nearly thirty-three million fully demarcated hectares, equaling 27.3 percent of the national territory.[69]

An obvious question, one I began asking in the late 1980s, was why Colombia was ceding so much territory to a small segment of its citizenry. Although a comprehensive answer still escapes me, several elements in the national crisis of that moment seem crucial, elements discussed more fully in subsequent chapters. One is the peasant movements of the 1960s and 1970s: the failures and contradictions of class-based politics opened space for alternatives, as envisioned by both the actors resisting state interventions and the state itself. We shall see that nonindigenous allies such as anthropologists, lawyers, some members of the Catholic clergy, and some leftist activists also played important roles.[70] Obviously another element was the disarray in Colombian electoral politics since the end of the National Front in 1974. Another is the armed insurgency that was paralyzing much of the country, producing the "Colombian paradox": a democratic country that lived with endemic and pandemic violence for five decades.[71] Six insurgent groups[72] and counterinsurgency measures wreaked havoc for over half a century. The insurgency would continue until the peace accords of 2016; by then this violence had produced 220,000 deaths.[73] Some five million citizens were forcibly displaced, fleeing kidnappings, massacres, and rapes, an appallingly high number for a country of forty-eight million not formally at war. For a while Colombia had the highest homicide rate in the world. Given this rampant violence, it made some sense to legislate encouragement for indigenous citizens to patrol their lands, and some groups received funding for such surveillance from international NGOs. Note that a great deal of this land was in tropical forest and plains areas, sparsely populated, lacking infrastructure (e.g., roads) that would be attractive to large landowners. Note also that the government had designated some areas as colonization zones, which resulted in at times serious conflicts between indigenous members of the resulting resguardos and settlers (*colonos*) who had migrated there. Finally, the current situation is extremely unstable. Certain units of the Fuerzas Armadas Revolucionarias de Colombia (FARC, Revolutionary Armed Forces of Colombia) have refused to demobilize, and the Ejército de Liberación Nacional (ELN, National Liberation Army) continues its attacks. At least five million displaced citizens, some of them Indians, need to be resettled, and the government must take charge of the areas (some of them in resguardo territory) previously controlled by demobilizing guerrillas, in order to establish state authority and maintain order.

In terms of public relations, the generosity of the land grants improved Colombia's image vis-à-vis international movements for indigenous rights and environmental protection. The grants may also have been intended as a device to keep national resources under wraps until the government was itself ready to tap them. Finally, government functionaries clearly hoped to transform indigenous activists from dangerous antagonists into law-abiding citizens, political actors who might come to see the government as an ally rather than an opponent, a policy that, to some extent, succeeded.

One impediment to indigenous organizing was a lack of a pan-indigenous identity. Notions of a (highly stigmatized) generic indio identity had circulated among nonindigenous Colombians for a long time, but until recently, members of the country's pueblos typically viewed themselves as indigenous only in the limited sense of being non-White. This was the case, for instance, for the Yanacona people, discussed in Chapter Five, who began to forge a pueblo-based identity in the 1980s. Many groups identified with their pueblo but rejected membership in a larger collectivity. Findji discusses a decision by several Guambiano communities to leave CRIC, a choice prompted by disagreements about, among other things, how to conceptualize territory and identity. They wanted, she writes, to be seen neither as campesino (peasant) nor as generically indigenous, but strictly as Guambiano: "We don't want to be 'humiliated' indígenas—we want to defend, for our children's sake, our right to be Guambianos."[74] However, beginning in the 1970s, new incentives and opportunities encouraged the formation of a pan-Colombian indigenous identity, somewhat like Benedict Anderson's notion of "imagined community."[75] During the 1980s state liberalization reduced repressive responses to indigenous demands, thus opening up space for broader efforts at organization and more inclusive claims-making. Resignifications of *indigenous* emerged from the interplay between negotiated otherness and self-conscious efforts to maintain cultural continuity. Paradoxically, a previously stigmatized identity acquired symbolic and political capital, which in turn further encouraged culturalist discourse in indigenous rights-claiming. Meanwhile, the movement, without abandoning efforts to gain access to state political institutions, greatly increased its emphasis on strengthening the pueblos' own institutions. Cultural recovery projects increased in number and visibility, as did their significance, both for the pueblos' self-conceptualization and for their interactions with the nonindigenous world.

These evolving notions about indigeneity and their impact on activist strategizing had far-reaching effects, one of which was to change the meaning of indigenous territory, which in turn produced alterations in the discourse of land claims, in particular in how they were to be justified.[76] Rights to territory were increasingly being asserted in a more comprehensive way: land constituted the underpinnings of self-determination, a "fundamental and multidimensional space for the creation and re-creation of the social, economic, and cultural values and practices of the communities."[77]

The way collective land rights were secured or denied depended more and more on evidence that reflected (or was seen as failing to reflect) evolving imaginaries of indigeneity, imaginaries that were increasingly shared by both indigenous and nonindigenous actors—a theme I discuss more fully in later chapters. Land claims were increasingly based on claims to an intrinsic core identity, which in turn strengthened other kinds of claims—to self-determination, autonomous jurisdiction, and so forth. Such claims increasingly came to be validated by performances of culturally distinct practices and traditions; as we shall see, when the state rejects a petition, it often does so by casting doubt on applicants' indigenousness, a manifestation of what Barker terms the link between "legal legitimacy" and cultural authenticity.[78]

Given that Colombia's indigenous peoples constitute less than 4 percent of the population, the accomplishments of its indigenous movement have been nothing short of extraordinary. During the early 1990s several leaders achieved significant national and international visibility. For example, Lorenzo Muelas, a Guambiano and member of the Asamblea Nacional Constituyente (ANC, National Constituent Assembly), emerged into prominence almost overnight, his charisma winning him abundant exposure on television and in the press. Other movement achievements include pressing for legislation that exempted indigenous Colombians from paying taxes or serving in the military, and that would provide free health care and education up to and through university.[79] Indigenous organizations and their allies claimed a right for pueblo members to be educated in their own languages, to be taught their own history and cosmology in school, and to have indigenous healing systems incorporated into the Ministry of Health's local programs.

These advances, however, have by no means eliminated the poverty, marginalization, and wretched living conditions of most of the country's pueblos. At the same time that Indians cling to their distinct identities, they want less poverty and better health and education services. They have, moreover, suffered constant threats from vested interests, both traditional and recent, in the form of land grabs and misguided development, for instance, hydroelectric mega-projects. Landlords have continued to resort to heinous acts to hold onto land. Armed actors, both official and extralegal, have perpetrated grave humans rights abuses, against the backdrop of a half century of civil conflict that a succession of corrupt and structurally weak governments failed to end until the 2016 peace accords.[80]

The chaos was encouraged by narcotraffickers, who helped to finance and support candidates for national office—support illegal but hard to refuse. Both guerrillas and their paramilitary enemies entered massively into the illegal drug trade, which mushroomed in the early 1980s. In January 2011 the office of Colombia's attorney general reported that 174,618 homicides and 1,614 massacres had been committed by now-demobilized armed groups, with the greatest number belonging to the Autodefensas Unidas de Colombia (AUC, United Self-Defense Forces of Colombia), a coalition of right-wing paramilitaries.[81] Demobilized paramilitary commanders admitted to nearly 50,000 killings.[82] Speeded-up globalization and capitalist expansion only made matters worse. Only in 2014 did peace negotiations begin to gain traction, with the accords signed in 2016.

Indigenous resistance to violence, often at great cost, has elicited favorable commentary from mainstream Colombian society. The ability of some pueblos to arrive at consensus and the resolve needed to act in the face of terrible danger has been noted in the media, church sermons, and everyday conversation, as has the respect of pueblo members for senior indigenous leaders—governors, healers, *taitas* (esteemed elders), and others. For example, in 2000, governors of fourteen indigenous cabildos in northern Cauca were awarded the National Peace Prize for their Proyecto NASA, which involved a coalition working to maintain community neutrality and autonomy in the face of threats by armed combatants.[83] Some pueblos insisted on their neutrality and autonomy in the civil conflict, courageously refusing alliance with any combatant groups. Following the demobilization of MAQL in 1990, the Nasa resolved to oppose the presence of all armed actors in their territory, as AICO had done earlier. Beginning in the late 1990s they embarked on a campaign of pacific civil resistance, enforced by an Indigenous Guard (Guardia Indígena), whose members carry only ceremonial staffs.[84] In 2001, when members of the FARC began firing homemade mortars at a police station in the Nasa community of Toribío, over four thousand unarmed community members flooded its streets, ending the attack.[85] On other occasions dozens of community members traveled to a guerrilla stronghold to obtain release of a kidnapped leader.[86] By 2006 the Nasa Guard had grown to about seven thousand men and women.[87] Several other pueblos have followed their example. The Indigenous Guards have elicited high praise from mainstream Colombia and beyond, as evidenced by media treatment and national and international awards.

Interaction between the indigenous movement and the state has taken many forms, including agitation to get laws already on the books implemented and enforced, as well as complaints that government forces, by their absence from remote areas, have left indigenous and peasant communities at the mercy of armed illegals. Contradictions have proliferated: official programs promoting diversity may sit cheek-by-jowl with others promoting assimilation. When legal protests fail, activists have resorted to conspicuous law-breaking, through highway blockades and other measures, a form of action sometimes called *participatory democracy*.[88] Over time these processes produced a paradoxical dialectic in which the indigenous movement, in protesting and resisting the state, tacitly accepted its structure, ideology, and modus operandi.[89] The governments of Belisario Betancur (1982–1986) and Virgilio Barco (1986–1990), while keeping up repression, opened a dialogue with the indigenous movement, encouraging its consolidation as a counterforce to the guerillas in the countryside.[90] As mentioned, in 1983 ONIC became officially linked to the state—which is not to say that the organization did not continue its adversarial role of critique and resistance. Activists, often reluctantly, accepted collaboration, because the state had the power to fund cultural recovery projects, to accept or deny land claims and other petitions, and to act as final arbiter of disputes over issues of authenticity and legitimacy. The pueblos also engaged perforce with other institutional actors: local and international NGOs, supra-state institutions like the United Nations and the European Community, and North American Protestant missionaries and the Catholic Church.

The much-touted aid program known as Plan Colombia, which ran for six years from its start in July 2000, inspired strong indigenous opposition. Developed by President Andrés Pastrana (1998–2002) with the Clinton administration in the United States, Plan Colombia was supposed to eradicate illegal drugs and at the same time to promote economic and social development and even devise an exit from the country's long-running armed conflict.[91] The pueblos protested the distribution of aid under the program, which assigned three-quarters of each year's budget to military and police campaigns to eradicate illegal drug cultivation.[92] Critics, indigenous and nonindigenous, complained of damage to crops and threats to health caused by aerial spraying of glyphosate, a chemical that has been linked to cancer.[93] They argued that funds should be dedicated to economic and social development, with manual eradication of illegal crops and encouragement for planting legal substitute crops.[94] Indigenous protests also targeted free-trade agreements signed by Colombia, with marches attended by tens of thousands, who argued that the poor had been hit hardest by structural adjustment and by austerity measures to reduce fiscal and political instability and increase foreign investment. No administration has been willing to enter into serious dialogue with the sectors that organized these protests.

In sum, ever since its beginnings in Cauca the indigenous movement has played a key role in changing the Colombian state's relationship with the country's pueblos. By continually incorporating and revising discourses circulating transnationally, the movement fashioned an image of Colombian indigeneity that was both "modern and different."[95] Via a language of collective grievances and rights, ideas about indigenous citizens, autonomy, land, and culture emerged into public discourse and resonated with the dominant culture. Throughout this time the meaning of Colombian indigenous identity was a work in progress. Actors would repeatedly modify their discourses (and demands) in response to the impact of multiculturalism and the openings in the neoliberal environment, drawing most of all on the new valence of indigeneity as a political resource and as a moral reproach to the status quo and hegemonic institutions like the state and the Church.

Constitutional Reform

By the late 1980s there was widespread agreement that Colombia was facing a dire "crisis of legitimacy." A series of presidents had tried to replace the antiquated Constitution of 1886, whose centralist and unitary perspective on politics and the dominant culture was no longer viable, only to be thwarted by the Congress, which had exclusive authority over constitutional reform. The dream of fundamental restructuring had wide appeal to citizens of a country that, however modern-seeming its bureaucratic organization, had proved incapable of curbing violent narcotrafficking, shown most dramatically, perhaps, in the weak response to a series of car bombings in late 1989 that killed or wounded hundreds of people in Medellín and Bogotá. Worse, the long-running armed conflict had produced unprecedented human rights abuses. Unable to protect citizens from abuses by guerrillas and paramilitaries, the state was often compromised by paramilitaries' links to its military and police.[96] The Patriotic Union, a political party born out of the frustrated peace talks between the FARC and the government in 1984, saw more than three thousand of its members killed by paramilitary assassins, in what survivors called political genocide. Successive national governments, failing to enforce the laws, could not control or administer vast swaths of the national territory. With political corruption a staple of newspaper coverage, public discontent with official clientelism and exclusivity grew exponentially, opening a huge gap between the ruling classes and the rest of society, between what commentators called the "political country" and the "real country."[97]

By the end of the 1980s it was clear to many that to reestablish peace, promote national reconciliation, and modernize the state, a new constitution was essential.[98] One key goal of the neoliberal agenda called for moving democracy from representation to participation, thus reordering the political landscape such that power could flow inward from the hinterland rather than always outward from the center. Another goal was to improve Colombia's image abroad, which had been stained by the country's political corruption, drug trafficking, poverty, and horrendous violence.

Demands for a constituent assembly escalated after the assassination in August 1989 of a presidential candidate, Luis Carlos Galán. The following February a petition presented to President Barco stated that the "incompetence of the political class to provide a response to the grave problems of the country" made an assembly imperative.[99] The sense of urgency grew further with the assassination of two more presidential candidates in March and April. After the elections the new president, César Gaviria (1990–1994), deployed his powers under a state of siege to advance the project and put the case for an assembly to elites. Bogotá witnessed a silent protest march, and a petition in favor of an assembly gathered thirty-five thousand signatures. In May an informal referendum organized by students, called the "seventh ballot," was included in a mayoral and congressional election. This pressure from a diverse set of actors led to a referendum in December, with 80.6 percent of the voters in favor of convening the National Constituent Assembly. Seventy-four delegates, with strikingly different, sometimes conflicting positions, were elected, and the ANC was convened on February 5, 1991.

The ANC was favored over other possible reform mechanisms because it was widely recognized that any proposed changes could not succeed without public legitimacy: a diverse set of political actors agreed "that legitimate institutions and norms would result only from a participatory process."[100] Several guerrilla groups had also demanded an assembly as a condition for demobilizing.[101] Of the six insurgent groups, four demobilized and participated in the process,[102] but the two largest, the FARC and the ELN, abstained. As Donna Lee Van Cott points out, the ANC also served to conscientize voters: "In a country where the people rarely have been invited to participate in deliberations on issues of public concern, the generation of an open and participatory process of deliberation fosters a transition from a passive and subservient to an active and participatory political culture."[103]

A great deal more could be said about the ANC—about, for instance, the way delegates were chosen and decisions were reached—but we must move on here from process to results, in terms of the impact of constitutional reform, especially on Indians and Afro-Colombians.

The 1991 Constitution

The 1991 charter is in a number of important ways the opposite of its predecessor of 1886, which was designed to homogenize Colombian society and, as Humberto de la Calle points out, to promote "order rather than liberty."[104] Because the new document emerged from a popular process rather than from elite imposition, it represents "a peaceful, institutional rebellion against exclusion." It facilitates popular consultation and the institutionalization of conflict rather than its suppression. A number of general statements of principle borrow from the constitutions of other countries and from several international covenants, treaties, and pacts that Colombia had signed during the previous fifty years.[105] It contains, finally, a generous Bill of Rights.

Article Seven of the Constitution of 1991 says: "The State recognizes and protects the ethnic and cultural diversity of the Colombian Nation. . . . Culture, in its diverse manifestations, is fundamental to the nation." According to Van Cott, the new charter's espousal of multiculturalism was due more than anything else to political elites' conviction that adopting such reforms "would improve the legitimacy and governability of the state while lifting the psychic burden on state and society of a homogeneous national identity with no basis in reality."[106] In particular the constitution contains unprecedented provisions for indigenous rights, mentioning indigenous Colombians twenty times. Indians are exempt from taxation and military service, and can apply for university scholarships. The government, NGOs, and other actors worked to inform the pueblos about the changes, among other things getting the constitution translated into seven indigenous languages.[107] Although a number of the reforms had been legislated earlier, they were unified in the new constitution.

The constitution confirms that Indians are autonomous citizens with special rights that allow them to participate in civil society as ethnic citizens. While affirming that the basic law of the land must be upheld, the charter promotes indigenous juridical autonomy to an extent unknown in other Latin American nations.[108] In most countries with similar constitutions, when the two legal systems interact, the national system almost inevitably takes precedence, revealing a relationship characterized by hierarchy rather than equality.[109] We will see that such is not always the case for Colombia. Some of the reasons why this occurred in a country with such a minority of indigenous citizens are discussed in the following chapters. In the 1980s indigenous Colombians came to play a symbolic role way out of proportion to their numbers: their plight in some respects was seen to encapsulate much of what was wrong with the system all Colombians were living under. Dissent in 1992 targeting the upcoming celebration of the Columbus Quincentennial was one among many examples. Indigenous protests over the assassinations of hundreds of their leaders increasingly captured mainstream society's sympathy.

Constitutional recognition of customary law in Colombia (and elsewhere in Latin America) has been interpreted by many analysts as a covert critique of the state, an acknowledgment that the state itself needs restructuring. Manuel José Cepeda Espinosa speaks of "weaknesses in the political resolution of conflicts, combined with the traditional ineffectiveness of public administration."[110] The state had been sullied by a 95 percent impunity rate.[111] Utterly ineffective and corrupt national courts failed to act independently, to apply the rule of law to land disputes, theft, interpersonal violence, and other disputes and offenses, particularly in rural areas. Given the perceived efficiency and legitimacy of small-scale, pueblo-based juridical systems, it was even suggested prior to the ANC proceedings that indigenous participatory norms might serve as a model for state democratization. These systems were perceived as more efficient and legitimate than state courts, and the official support these institutions often received arose from a need to ease case backlogs and eliminate extra-institutional conflict resolution and violence.[112]

One institution called for by the constitution was intended to greatly increase pueblo control of jurisprudential and administrative matters; if and when it is implemented, it could provide an opportunity for pueblo governance unparalleled in the rest of Latin America. Article 330 establishes the procedure for turning indigenous territories into "indigenous territorial entities" (*entidades territoriales indígenas*—ETIs), collapsing highland cabildos and lowland capitanías into a new political form: indigenous authorities. ETIs are part of the overall *ordenamiento territorial* process, a countrywide reform of territorial ordinance that restructures local autonomy in a fundamentally new way. ETIs are to be governed by indigenous councils (*consejos indígenas*),[113] which are to be "created and regulated in keeping with the practices and customs of the communities."[114] Council structure and recruitment are to be decided jointly by the pueblos and national government. In bald political fact, however, ETIs so far exist only on paper, since the political will to legislate them into existence has so far been lacking. Territorial units following this model are very unlikely to materialize in the near future.[115]

The 1991 constitution, along with other institutions created by the ANC, has put its mark on almost every aspect of what Cepeda Espinosa terms the "complex Colombian reality."[116] A well-placed government official commented to me in 1993: "Who would have thought we would have such a constitution ten years ago? That an institution like the ETIs would be legislated into existence? That the Church would lose so much power?" Cepeda Espinosa, writing in 2006, speaks of "a wholly new constitutional and, moreover, rights-oriented type of discourse of yet unknown effects."[117] Clearly, many problems remain, including unclear constitutional language on several crucial issues.[118] Concerning legal procedure, for instance, the ambiguous relationship between Western positive law and local customary law, though clarified to some extent by legal challenges, is still fundamentally ambiguous, complicated by the multiplicity of indigenous systems.[119]

The Constitutional Court

To ensure that the country would not revert to the status quo ante, President Gaviria pushed the early implementation of various autonomous democratic institutions created by the ANC.[120] These included a Constitutional Court; the Defensoría del Pueblo (an ombudsman agency); the Fiscalía General, an independent prosecutorial agency linked to the judiciary; and a writ for the immediate protection of constitutional rights, called the tutela (*acción de tutela*). The court, designed to "adjust the judicial review system to the innovative and protective spirit of the 1991 Constitution"[121] began almost immediately to issue decisions righting the uneven distribution of power, "eroding, if only slightly, the prevailing regime of arbitrariness."[122] The court has handed down "increasingly legitimate—albeit in no few cases controversial—responses to the most sensitive and difficult problems facing the country."[123] Cepeda Espinosa notes that requests to the constitutional judge to resolve conflicts have become one of the "prominent forms of participation by ordinary Colombians in the conduct of public and private affairs," giving Colombia what he believes may be the most open system of judicial review in the region.[124] The expansion of issues and topics covered by the constitution "has been accompanied by a corresponding broadening of the scope of judicial review," contributing to the "emergence, merely a decade later, of a striking social, political, and legal process."[125] The court has issued rulings on nearly every aspect of Colombian life.

With respect to the pueblos, constitutional case law has fostered the preservation and development of cultural identity and the promotion of fundamental collective rights.[126] Although the court initially overturned decisions by indigenous authorities, in a breakthrough case from 1996 (T-349) it ruled that indigenous jurisdictions must "comply only with a limited set of rules and not with the whole gamut of national legislation."[127] Since then the court's rulings have tended to favor customary law.

Acción de Tutela

The legal instrument of tutela allows anyone who feels his or her rights are being threatened to make a claim before any judge with jurisdiction in the place where the threat is occurring. The claim must be responded to in ten days.[128] Vendors in the informal economic sector, for instance, might seek legal affirmation of their right to work on the streets. The tutela often allows the weak to win, which is why it has been referred to as "the power of the powerless . . . [t]he social actors who make the most frequent use of constitutional law are those that have the least power within the decision-making processes that affect them."[129] Cepeda Espinosa remarks that the tutela has received praise as an instrument of peace because magistrates' interventions have helped solve conflicts that might otherwise have been "addressed by arbitrary means, often as serious as personal intimidation or murder."[130] The tutela mechanism is widely used by indigenous people seeking protection of their collective fundamental rights. For example, in the Vaupés, CRIVA members worked to win tutelas against New Tribes missionaries and exploratory mining for titanium.[131]

Legal Pluralism

Colombia's formal recognition of customary law and the safeguards established to protect it, like the Constitutional Court and the tutela, offer abundant opportunities to explore the implications and unintended consequences of legal pluralism (also called special jurisdiction). Any number of Colombian court rulings about special jurisdiction have contributions to make to the scholarship on this topic. Scholarly analyses of these decisions and their consequences also have the potential to help indigenous peoples across the globe who are struggling for recognition of their traditional legal systems. I cannot discuss this compelling issue in depth here, but can offer some general comments of a precautionary nature.

My first point is a reminder that the imaginary of indigenous communities as homogeneous and cohesive units that share a consensus on their traditions, daily practices, and so forth, although very appealing, is unfortunately very mistaken. In fact, indigenous communities are like all others in being heterogeneous—along age, gender, economic well-being, and many other dimensions[132]—as well as riddled with conflicts, some of them new and burning hot, others long-standing and more or less quietly simmering below the surface. Faction formation and overall self-interest (i.e., human nature) will ensure, at least some of the time, that certain members are marginalized and excluded from decision making about matters that concern them.

The second point is that in Colombia and across the globe, there is no such thing as a single "indigenous jurisprudence," a notion only moderately useful for drawing a preliminary and very crude distinction between Western positive law and traditional legal systems. In fact, Colombian special jurisdiction comprises numerous systems that have evolved over many years (and continue to evolve) to regulate behavior, provide justification for such regulations, and specify how miscreants who spurn such codes of conduct are to be judged, and punishments determined and carried out.

The third point pertains to the complex ways indigenous customary law interfaces with codified positive law. Among some scholars there is a tendency to assume that Western legal premises and procedures can be "discovered" in systems that are anything but centralized or codified, and that depend on kinship relations, shamanic consultations, and the like. The more one examines cases involving these interfaces, the more one is forced to realize that fundamental differences usually obtain with respect to notions of justice and fairness, as well as assumptions about who is entitled to said justice and fairness.[133] Such differences can wreak havoc with the application of Western notions like due process, evidentiary findings, and legally acceptable ways to resolve conflicts. We shall see that at times pueblos have political reasons to stress the incommensurability between Western positive law and their customary law. The literature on legal pluralism abounds with cases that demonstrate the gulfs separating the Western legal system (which itself is very complex, highly dynamic, and full of contradictions) and so-called traditional ones. This literature informs its readers about the very wide range of values and premises that undergird those systems, by so doing hermeneutically informing us about our own system's often poorly understood and under-examined foundational values and premises. As we shall see in Chapter Four, in two cases involving sentences mandating whipping and stocks, Colombian court verdicts may decide in favor of pueblos that are engaging in what we in the West consider illegal and immoral actions, providing a dramatic opportunity to think carefully about relevant Western values and the contradictions of multiculturalism.[134]

Finally, if it is true that law can be seen both as a form of "social control and of enforcing power relations"[135] *and* as a "space of resistance to the hegemony of nation-state law at the same time as it reinforces the centrality of law as a mode of protest,"[136] it might be very productive to track not only encounters between a given pueblo's customary law and hegemonic state institutions but also that customary law's subsequent evolution, after formal recognition, in order to discover the role it plays as both a site of social control and a space within which pueblo members find ways to resist its power and fashion innovative modes of protest and rights-claiming by activating its role as a guarantor of rights.

Afro-Colombians and the Constitution

While indigenous Colombians continue to suffer from high rates of poverty and racism, the country's multicultural reforms improved their legal status considerably more than that of Afro-Colombians, who are politically much less visible. As Peter Wade notes, "Blacks have not been regarded as legitimate objects of state or intellectual concern" in Colombia.[137] The differential treatment accorded to these two populations during the ANC deliberations, in the constitution, and in subsequent legislation calls for explanation, especially given that the same imbalance crops up elsewhere in Latin America. At stake are more general questions concerning race and ethnicity in the region.

The relative lack of ethnoracial mobilization in Latin America, in contrast with the vigor of indigenous organizing, has attracted commentary. Previously, until the 1970s, discussion of racial inequality was sparse—"censored" is Tianna Paschel's term.[138] The ideology of *mestizaje* promoted the fiction that the region was a "racial democracy," in contrast to the United States or South Africa. The myth of a hybrid nation of mestizos[139] papered over cultural, ethnic, and regional differences,[140] encouraging "submissiveness to a social order in which there is no legal racial domination against which identity formation and mobilization can be targeted."[141] Despite the absence of a legal racial hierarchy, the ideology of mestizaje concealed the belief that improving racial character and promoting progress depended on *blanqueamiento*, making the national population whiter, along with assumptions about how subaltern peoples and their cultures supposedly hindered national development. In this environment, race-based movements could not easily gain traction, as a number of scholars have noted.[142]

In Colombia, Afro-descendants make up a larger portion of the national population than in any other Spanish-speaking South American country (Brazil of course has still more), somewhere between 14 and 30 percent of the whole.[143] Afro-Colombians are predominantly found in urban areas, on the Atlantic coast, and especially on the Pacific Coast, where they make up 80 to

90 percent of the population.[144] Given these numbers, the scant attention paid to Afro-Colombian issues in the constituent assembly calls for explanation, especially given the extraordinary attention paid in that forum to the pueblos. According to Axel Rojas, this neglect exposes disparities in the logics of alterity that have "defined the place of indigeneity and negritude in the country."[145] The very existence of Afro-Colombian communities was acknowledged only in the constitution's Transitory Article 55 and subsequently in Law 70 of 1993, called the Law of Black Communities, which recognizes Black communities and their right to collective ownership of certain territories, as well as sets up mechanisms for protecting cultural identity. These rights, however, are limited to those communities that occupy previously "vacant"[146] lands (*baldíos*) in the riverine Pacific zones.[147]

How to explain this very divergent treatment? First of all, the few Afro-Colombian movements found in rural areas prior to the constituent assembly failed to "project an image at the national level," which doubtlessly limited attention to them during the ANC proceedings.[148] Second, attempts to construct a homogeneous Afro-Colombian identity have stumbled over major variation in that population by region and income level. Third, advancing Afro-Colombian identity as a political category was largely the work of university-educated urban intellectuals influenced by the civil rights movement in the United States.[149] Fourth, many Afro-Colombians dislike the idea of a distinct Black identity, preferring to see themselves simply as Colombians, as potential mestizos, or as natives of a particular region. Some indigenous individuals, especially urban dwellers, feel the same way, but overall, the revitalization of ethnic identity has affected indigenous peoples much more than Afro-Colombians.

Fifth, the two groups have had different histories. During the colonial period the earliest Afro-Colombians came to the Atlantic Coast region as slaves; escaped slaves sometimes formed communities in remote areas, a practice known as *cimarronaje*.[150] After emancipation in 1851, Black community ethnic identity developed in remote areas of the Pacific Coast zone, as well as coastal (and some interior riverine) areas of the Atlantic sector of the country. In settlements established along rivers and near former mining centers, Afro-Colombians maintained and adapted cultural practices and forms of social organization shaped by African, European, and indigenous influences.[151]

During the 1980s and 1990s Afro-descendants in several other Latin American countries also embraced a political strategy based on ethnicity.[152]

Like Brazilian Afro-descendants,[153] Afro-Colombians were encouraged to present themselves as African descendants, "members of an imagined, 'other' continent and 'other culture.'"[154] Rojas points out a paradox: a community's fight to be recognized as an ethnic group supposes that identity to already exist, but in the absence of prior recognition, evidence is often hard to come by.[155] Given that the academic, juridical, and political category of ethnicity is the only route available to a community seeking recognition of their rights, and given that, as Bettina Ng'weno points out, alterity in Colombia was primarily indigenous alterity, Afro-Colombian communities discovered that if they were to succeed with their rights-claiming they needed to be perceived as fitting, "historically and presently, within the structures of indigeneity."[156] However, the situation soon began to change. In 1996, the Constitutional Court recognized a "Black community" in the Caribbean coastal city of Santa Marta.[157] In 2001 the Constitutional Court recognized territorial rights of Afro-Colombian communities in the Pacific sector in a suit challenging the ethnic purification (*saneamiento*) of resguardos in a region with nonindigenous populations.

Given the scholarly tendency throughout Latin America to equate ethnic identity with indigenous identity, scholars who focus on Afro-Colombians have complained bitterly about the "invisibilization" of their research.[158] In Pineda's view, use of ethnic categories to officially recognize Afro-Colombians was a default option ("better analytic models were lacking"[159]), but once enshrined in the language of constitutions and legal texts, Afro-descendants sometimes felt obliged to represent their collective identity using the preestablished logics. In some locations a positive feedback loop was created, establishing "a hegemonic ethnic subject based on the underlying assumption that all ethnic identifications fall within discrete racially homogeneous categories."[160]

Pineda asks, what happens to Afro-Colombians in Bogotá, Barranquilla, and Medellín?[161] To which we can add, what happens to the thousands who were driven out of the lands to which they had gained title? Urbanized Afro-Colombians unable to assert an ethnic identity[162] lack "a solid claim to collective rights even though they suffer from political exclusion and racial discrimination."[163] Unlike urban Indians, who can be seen as "no longer indigenous" mestizos, urban Afro-Colombians retain that identity no matter where or how they live. They find themselves at the racial end of a classificatory continuum that puts ethnicity at one end and race at the other, while rural Blacks in the Pacific sector are placed closer to the continuum's ethnicity end. While indigenousness is also racialized, its phenotypical markers are not coded in the same way, given that only in Latin America did the colonial project produce a majority of racially and ethnically mixed people. With the partial exceptions of Brazil, Chile, and Argentina, most Latin Americans "look" indigenous to one degree or another, and thus such a physiognomy does not signify indigenousness in the same way that looking Black signifies membership in the Afro-descendant category. As anthropologist Nina de Friedemann indicated to me soon after the constitution was promulgated, the fact that Afro-Colombians were in no danger of dying out was in one respect a disadvantage, given that a primary rationale for attention to indigenous pueblos was preventing their disappearance.

To explain why some communities receive official recognition as an indigenous pueblo (as a "people") and some do not, Shane Greene suggests that success depends on the "holy trinity of multicultural peoplehood," a trinity consisting of a distinct culture, a language still spoken, and ancestral territorial claims.[164] Of these, land is crucial according to Ng'weno, because ethnicity "is informed by past racial categories created during colonial times."[165] She argues that land rights legitimate claims to both ethnic identity and culture, which in turn justify differential treatment of land claims—a circular interdependence between culture and territory that "remains a rarely vocalized but ever-present way of thinking about culture in anthropology."[166] This linkage helps explain why urbanized and Atlantic coast Afro-Colombians were not officially recognized by the ANC, whereas those in the Pacific coast sector were. A separate Afro-Colombian population residing in the Caribbean archipelago known as San Andrés and Providencia was also recognized. They are descendants of English Puritan colonists, West African slaves, and Jamaican immigrants, and speak an English-based creole.[167]

Ng'weno notes a double bind, in that Afro-Colombians claiming cultural difference from the rest of Colombia were encouraged to demonstrate historic ties to Africa, but in doing so they open themselves to stigmatization as foreigners, and hence to exclusion from full membership in the nation. A connection with "African culture" territorializes Afro-Colombians not where they are but elsewhere, on another continent.[168] She reports that Indians in Cerro Teta, Cauca, the site of her fieldwork, would say, "go back to Africa!" when they sought to discredit Afro-Colombian claims to land. Anthropologist Jaime Arocha told me[169] that certain indigenous Emberá leaders and their advisors were arguing in 1992 that the solution to the territorial problems emerging between the Emberá and local Afro-Colombians in the Baudó river valley in the Pacific coast's Chocó department was for the latter to return to Africa. Rejecting a publication being distributed about their African origins, local Afro-Colombians stated that they were every bit as Colombian as indigenous peoples.[170]

The differential treatment of the two populations illustrates the ideological confusion between race and ethnicity in Latin America. Wade argues that a false binary is produced: ethnic identity is linked to indigenous populations, and race, historically and socially constructed through a process of phenotypical signification, characterizes Black populations.[171] Indigenousness is thus entirely cultural, blackness entirely culture-free. In fact, as noted, both categories are racialized and ethnicized. Current legal structures associate ethnicity with the premodern, colonized indigenous subject, while race is associated with the modern, national subject.[172] This split can be explained in part, Wade states, by past positions of the two categories in colonial society, with formal institutional placement of Indians but not of Blacks, as well as greater anti-Black prejudice—a structural difference that outlasted independence.[173]

In the wake of the ANC, the "invisibilization" of Blacks has diminished with their inclusion in "state-managed official multiculturalism and corporatism or cooptation."[174] As in other countries, Colombian multiculturalism has made Afro-descendant populations more visible and prompted official acknowledgment of their distinct cultural traditions—in some cases, acknowledgment even of their collective rights to land. Despite the "robust" character of this legislation, however, which brought blackness "into the national frame in an unprecedented, positive way," real equality and inclusion still lie in the future.[175]

Conclusions

Since the Spanish conquest, the indigenous communities of Colombia have both resisted and accommodated to the powerful forces unleashed on them. During the upheavals of the nineteenth century, indigenous communities continued to seek ways to coexist with the nonindigenous actors surrounding them, all the while continuing to struggle against integrationist politics. Pueblo members worked to maintain several colonial institutions, such as tribute-paying, collective land tenure, and cabildos. As the twentieth century brought new pressures, pueblos developed new types of oppositional practices to hold on to lands, cultures, and a measure of autonomy. The last quarter of that century ushered in major changes in the dominant society with respect to indigenous communities and, to a far lesser degree, to Afro-Colombians. New forms of governmentality opened up spaces in which Colombian citizens began to both experience and claim different sets of rights and forms of belonging—dispersed and graduated sovereignties that were to be accessed through authorized cultural difference.[176] The 1991 constitution and subsequent legislation recognized that these "different" populations had rights, including the right to difference, and acknowledged that the variability and diversity found among these sectors needed recognition and protection. Benefits include the right to communal land tenure through the resguardo system, the right to self-govern through locally elected cabildos, including control of development and education, and protections of culture in the form of official recognition of indigenous languages and traditional medical systems.

While indigenous and Afro-descendant mobilizing revealed agency and ability to collectively express political identities and claim rights, it also reflected the power of the neoliberal state to shape the conditions and terms of engagement. The state shapes identity politics with an aim to co-opt activists and transform them into "docile subjects," which Hale, following Silvia Rivera Cusicanqui, characterizes as the notion of the *indio permitido*, the "authorized Indian": someone more interested in finding a space within the system than in fomenting social change.[177] Such co-optation is always a danger if it succeeds in closing off avenues of dialogue and productive negotiation in which both parties come to the table in good faith and are willing to compromise. Pueblo members have at times entered into negotiations and emerged with not much to show for their efforts. Those moments notwithstanding, what is definitely true at present is that indigenous Colombians continue their vehement, and at times very visible, protests against international capital's intense interest in extracting resources like oil, minerals, and water found on indigenous lands;[178] protests against astounding levels of corruption; and protests against a hypocrisy that fails to mask the greed and indifference lying just under elite expressions of concern and caring.

Indigenous sectors voted overwhelmingly in favor of the peace accords in the referendum held in October 2016—which was not surprising, given how they, along with Afro-Colombians and mestizo peasants, were forced to bear the brunt of horrendous violence. Like the rest of society, they experience the distrust and at times pessimism resulting from a half century of armed conflict that by no means solved the country's continuing and deeply serious problems. But pueblo members are firm in their stance that they will not relinquish the advances they have made, from Quintín Lame's time onward, for they paid an immense price to achieve those gains.

2 Tukanoan Culture and the Issue of "Culture"

A very fine anthropologist, writing in a very fine journal, attacked me (or so it felt) for writing about CRIVA (Consejo Regional Indígena del Vaupés) members' distortions of Tukanoan culture. Interested in exploring "what sorts of discursive authority accrue to . . . scholarly critics of invention,"[1] the author, Charles Briggs, a fellow lowland South Americanist, questioned whether we critics overlook the extent to which our analyses of oppressed communities are "dependent upon a privileged position from which to observe, to compare, and most generally, to obtain and disseminate knowledge." In particular, he feels that such studies "are likely to discredit and undermine activist leaders of oppressed social groupings."[2]

Overall I do not have a problem with Briggs's critique; the issues are, as journal editor Daniel Segal puts it, "vexed."[3] Indeed, the title of my first essay on the topic, "Is There a Way to Talk About Making Culture Without Making Enemies?" reveals anxieties about the appropriateness of my venture into these matters.[4] I had sent a draft of this essay to Briggs, asking for comments. He wrote back that he was also working on the topic, and subsequently sent me a preliminary draft of his essay. As a fellow lowland South Americanist and scholar, Briggs's interactions with me were above reproach. But my feelings were hurt.

I responded to his critique[5] in a 1999 essay titled "The Politics of Ethnographic Practice in the Colombian Vaupés." One issue I raised, mentioned in Chapter One, is the assumption that a community has a consensus about its traditions, and that it accepts whatever activists assert those traditions to be. In the Tukanoan case, and many others, such an assumption is mistaken. That a community might present a united front in the face of a perceived threat from outside—for instance an anthropologist criticizing their organization's publications—might very well happen, but such an outcome cannot be predicted ahead of time. Having by no means been resolved, the issues surrounding the politics of culture are examined anew in this chapter.

In the social science of the 1980s, many scholars responded to a set of questions and concerns about culture stemming from what Peter Wade characterizes as social theory's "linguistic turn,"[6] which may also be characterized in terms of postmodern and poststructuralist work on issues of representation, textuality, authorial reflexivity, and the Foucauldian concept of discourse. In my own case, I engaged with this literature, most of all with theoretical debates about the nature of culture, to make sense of what I was seeing in the Vaupés, and in particular to understand CRIVA's misrepresentations of Tukanoan society and culture. These efforts led me, in turn, to confront a number of fundamental issues—methodological, epistemological, and ethical—inherent to the study of cultural politics. That the 1980s were the key decade of change in many countries for indigenous activism obviously played a significant role in determining the issues anthropologists and other scholars working on these topics addressed during that time, issues that became forerunners of subsequent developments.

Introduction to the Vaupés

Tukanoans inhabit a tropical forest region right above the Equator, straddling the border between Colombia and Brazil. They number about twenty thousand, with a very low population density of at most .3 per square kilometer.[7] They speak Eastern Tukanoan and Arawak languages and participate in a regionally integrated social system characterized by extensive multilingualism and language exogamy. The system is unique in the world; it is most accurately referred to as the "Tukanoan cultural complex," but this happens only in the anthropological literature and some official publications (usually authored by anthropologists). During my first fieldwork, apart from a few individuals who worked for wages at mission settlements and people living in the regional capital of Mitú, Tukanoan men hunted, fished, and cleared swidden (slash-and-burn) fields for women to grow bitter manioc and other crops. Settlement size ranged from fifteen to three hundred, though the high figure, which came from a mission town, was far from typical. Traditional Tukanoan settlements consisted of a single, patrilocal *maloca* (longhouse) housing four to eight nuclear families. Today, these malocas have been replaced by nucleated villages with multiple dwellings, although maloca structures persist in some villages as community centers.

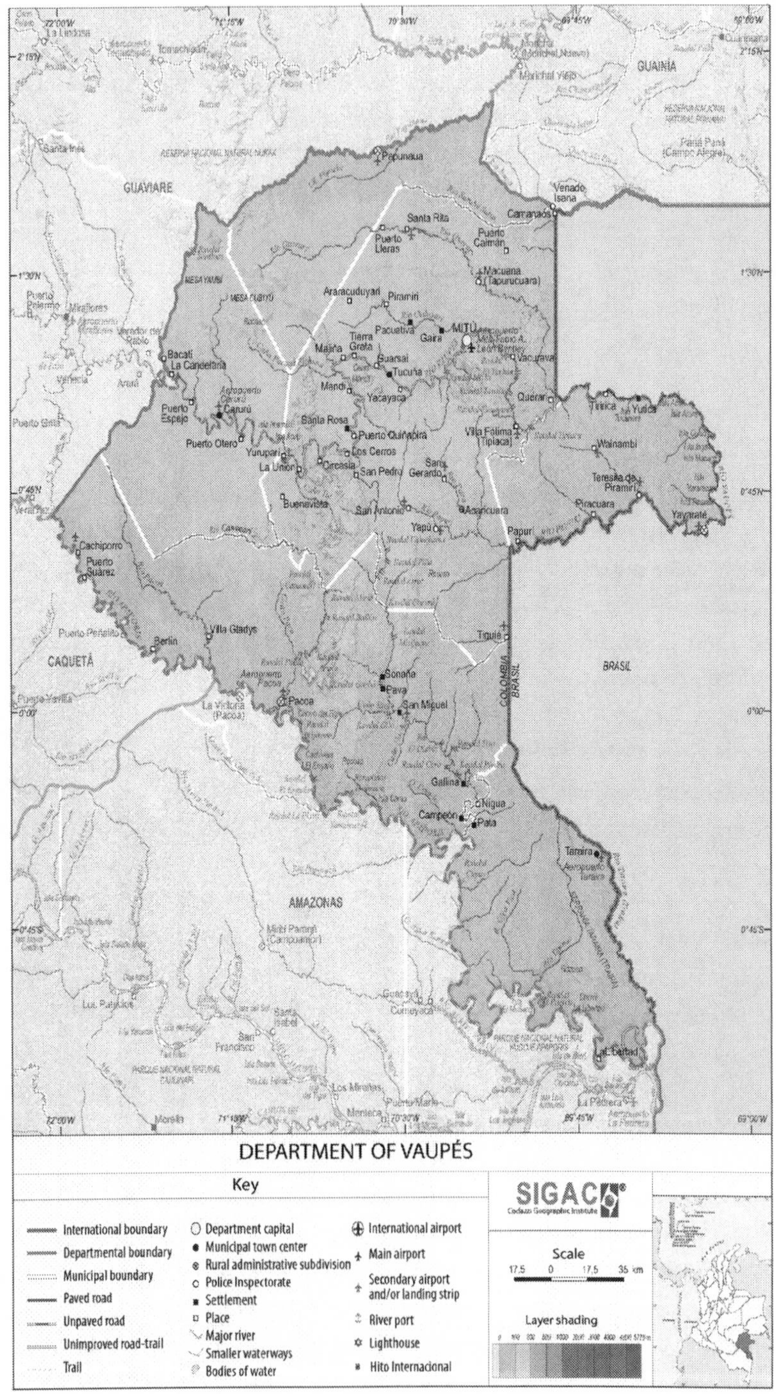

Map 2. Map of the Vaupés (Courtesy of the Instituto Geográfico Augustín Codazzi, Bogotá).

Each Tukanoan settlement traditionally belongs to one of sixteen[8] patrilineal groups, which I call language groups because, at least in the Papurí-Paca drainage area with which I am most familiar, these units each take a distinct language as the primary emblem of unit identity.[9] Individuals must marry exogamously, taking as a spouse someone from a different language group as well as a different settlement. In the hierarchy of kin-based social units in the region, these language groups are one step up the ladder from the smaller, local patrilineal clan (also known in the ethnographic literature as the sib[10]), and one step below the shadowy, more inclusive phratry discussed in the ethnographic literature. The exogamous language groups (which have been mislabeled as *tribes*, and today—equally mistakenly—as *ethnic groups*) encompass anywhere from six to more than thirty clans. Each language group is distinguished by a recurrent set of features: first, its own language and name; second, its own founding ancestors and distinct role in the Tukanoan origin myth cycle; third, the right to ancestral power through the use of certain items of linguistic property such as sacred chants; fourth, the right to manufacture and use certain kinds of ritual goods; fifth, a traditional association with certain ceremonial objects; and sixth, a symbolic association with a territory (though with very imprecise boundaries). In recent years many Tukanoans no longer observe rules of settlement exogamy, but they still marry outside the language group. The actual linguistic difference between languages in the Vaupés, it should be noted, varies widely: some pairs of languages lie far apart, while others (notably for some groups related by marriage) are linguistically trivial. Some clusters of two or three languages, linguists agree, are so closely related that they do not qualify as mutually unintelligible languages, in which case their separation is in fact social rather than linguistic, a matter of ideal types and indigenous fictions. Thus my use of language as the key marker for these groups reflects the prescriptive marriage model of the Tukanoans themselves rather than any technical linguistic reality.

In every significant respect, all these Tukanoan language groups belong to a single cultural universe, with some variation within that universe in custom, manufactures, and level of acculturation. This homogeneity is a function of a fairly uniform natural environment and, even more, of widely shared models for structuring and interpreting the world. Within this regional system, language groups do not occupy discrete territories nor act as corporate groups, and the vast majority of interactions involve participants from more than one language group. Tukanoans see themselves as parts of an interacting whole, in which what might appear to outsiders as cultural diversity unifies more than it differentiates. Within this whole, the various languages facilitate interaction as emblems of the participating groups, somewhat like the uniforms of teams in a football league. Better yet, language groups can be understood as different sections of a symphony orchestra, whose players jointly produce a coherent, harmonious performance using different instruments and different versions of a single score.

Tukanoan Responses to Change in the 1970s and 1980s

As described in Chapter One, in the 1970s and 1980s the Colombian government enacted wide-ranging laws directed at the country's pueblos, and in the 1980s it began handing over land in the form of reserves (*reservas*) and resguardos, reserves being state property whose inhabitants are limited to usufruct rights, whereas resguardos are collectively owned by their indigenous inhabitants.

At the time of my arrival in 1968, the more remote Tukanoan settlements, well upstream on the Vaupés, the Papurí, the Tiquié, and their tributaries and cut off from the outside world by a long series of time-consuming and dangerous rapids, approximated the stereotypical ideal of the barely touched pristine cultural isolate made for anthropological fieldwork.[11] Tukanoans in these areas still lived in multifamily malocas. Older men still wore loincloths. Everyone spoke an indigenous language, and no one, apart from a few residents of mission towns and a few men who had spent time in rubber camps, spoke Spanish. In the 1970s, however, downstream Tukanoans began regularly interacting with representatives of the national society, in particular with NGOs, and in those same years multiculturalist ideas began to enter the region.

Despite the remoteness and low population density of the Vaupés, it is home to the second oldest indigenous rights organization of Colombia, CRIVA, which originated in the regional capital of Mitú in 1973. In that era, early in the movement for indigenous rights, Catholic priests of the Javerian order encouraged indigenous schoolteachers and students at the order's boarding school located upriver from Mitú to organize themselves, with the professed aims of combatting the widely abused system of debt peonage characteristic of rubber gathering,[12] and helping Tukanoans recover their traditions. The local Catholic Prefecture's publications, however, reveal an additional underlying motivation, which was opposing the inroads made by Protestant missionaries from the New Tribes Mission and the Summer Institute of Linguistics/ Wycliffe Bible Translators (SIL). Since New Tribes (NT) and SIL had by then converted a considerable number of Tukanoans to their nondenominational brand of evangelical Protestantism,[13] the Prefecture devised projects, including CRIVA and a program to train missionary-appointed catechists, to keep Tukanoans within the fold and retrieve backsliders. Thus CRIVA, unlike the Consejo Regional Indígena del Cauca (CRIC), its predecessor on the national scene, was in effect birthed by Catholic missionary midwives.

In the mid-1970s international development funds destined specifically for indigenous communities began to arrive in Colombia, with the lion's share going to regions like the Vaupés with substantial indigenous populations.[14] This pro-indigenous financial tide, widely recognized by all parties, encouraged Tukanoans to acknowledge and even highlight their indigenous identity. With multiculturalist rhetoric voiced nearly everywhere, proposals for projects targeting indigenous pueblos promised to preserve and revitalize culture, extending the reach of international indigenous identity politics into the periphery and increasingly influencing how Tukanoans thought and talked about themselves and their culture. CRIVA leaders in particular, most of them from settlements near Mitú, recognized the dangers of assimilation and acculturation, and realized that if Tukanoans were to have a say in deciding their future they had to retain their culture. Self-determination increasingly depended on the ability to act and speak with an authority based on an (Amazonian) "indigenous way" recognizable to outsiders. The ways in which CRIVA members wrote about Tukanoan culture, and the ways they discussed it with me, were clearly influenced by outside notions of indigenous authenticity.

Tukanoan activists, lacking previous experience, learned about political organizing from non-Tukanoan indigenous activists visiting the region (most of them from Andean regions), and from a number of nonindigenous political actors: this latter group included a few young, left-leaning priests influenced by Vatican II and liberation theology; NGO personnel working in the region; and government agents, most of them with anthropological training. CRIVA's intermittent publication, *La Voz de la Tribu* (The Voice of the Tribe), published articles about Tukanoan culture and the mobilizations occurring elsewhere in the country. The Prefecture's newspaper, *Selva y Río* (Jungle and River), also carried articles about Tukanoan culture. Up to this time, with the exception of a few anthropologists (whose influence was negligible), no outsider—missionary, government agent, or rubber gatherer—had celebrated or favored indigenous culture. The Catholic Church had promoted assimilation, while other Whites in the region were dismissive or even contemptuous of Tukanoans and their lifeways. Mitú was the home base for most members of the small collection of Whites in the region, and these individuals also helped to shape CRIVA, for the most part in negative ways.

From the beginning CRIVA experienced severe problems. On the one hand Tukanoans living at a distance from Mitú seldom visited the town and knew very little either about CRIVA or about organizing elsewhere in Colombia, and the organization's own parochial perspective sometimes led it to neglect the interests of distant parts of the region (a theme developed later in this chapter). Tukanoans living near Mitú, on the other hand, some with knowledge of struggles on the national level, came to lose respect for many CRIVA leaders and some of the positions taken by the organization. As CRIVA grew, it evolved into a federation of subregional organizations, which competed and clashed. Paradoxically, CRIVA also suffered from the lack of urgent threats to land or natural resources, which might have motivated greater unity, and from a real threat, namely the coca boom, which was at its height in the early 1980s and drew in quite a few Tukanoans, including some CRIVA activists. Internal divisions, recrimination, and accusations of corruption, all apparent from the beginning, continued to surface.

CRIVA gradually gained some independence from the Catholic Prefecture, acquiring a modicum of authority through the system the Organización Nacional Indígena de Colombia (ONIC, National Indigenous Organization of Colombia) developed of admitting clusters of indigenous communities along with the regional and subregional indigenous organizations representing them.[15] Also, as was noted in Chapter One, CRIVA was put in charge of the Vaupés resguardo, bestowing power on the organization without the legitimacy that would have derived from grassroots mobilizing and struggle. As CRIVA developed, it faced what I later recognized as a perfect storm of obstacles and crises guaranteeing its marginalization and notoriety. In dealing with their peers in the national indigenous movement, CRIVA's leaders were outranked, marginalized, and disrespected. Seen, paradoxically, as more authentically indigenous than members of pueblos that had long since lost their language and many of their distinctive customs, they lacked the political savvy of their counterparts in CRIC and ONIC, and as a result they mostly listened while activists from other parts of the country talked.[16] In later years

CRIVA did improve its understanding of the White world, but its leaders never developed any appreciable clout in the national indigenous movement. They remained, in fact, extremely marginalized, at times to the point of ostracism. CRIVA activists, caught between traditional political forms and expectations and radically different ones arriving from outside, experienced in acute form the conflict and confusion that fence-straddling and culture-brokering almost always entail. Coming out of relatively fluid, dispersed local communities, they had little experience with centralized polities or bureaucracies, and none whatsoever with political mobilizations of any kind. Collective negotiations with non-Tukanoan actors were simply not part of the traditional political repertoire.

In 1998, for example, the national organization ONIC lambasted CRIVA for impeding leadership turnover by restricting candidates for elected positions to members of the highest Cubeo clan. CRIVA's "lack of credibility," ONIC stated, was also the fault of a series of corrupt indigenous mayors of Mitú who "unethically transferred and mismanaged funds."[17] One mayor, Maximiliano Veloz, was accused of blocking the transfer of 152 million pesos (approximately $183,900 in U.S. dollars) from the Ministry of Housing to Tukanoans in the Vaupés resguardo. After his mayoral offices were occupied for several days by more than a hundred protesters, in September 1994 Veloz resigned.[18]

Tukanoan interactions with interested outsiders and change agents were rapidly transforming in this era. In earlier times they had dealt with missionaries and the occasional rubber gatherer, state official, or merchant; now they frequently encountered government teachers, health workers, and NGO employees. Indigenous leaders from elsewhere in the country also turned up from time to time, sometimes accompanied by consultants, known as *asesores.*[19] Most of these change agents sincerely wanted what was best for Tukanoans, but given the wide divergence in their opinions and positions, there was no consensus on what that "best" consisted of, and in some instances would-be outside patrons competed directly for Tukanoan clients.

One of my interviewees in Bogotá commented that indigenous activists from elsewhere visiting the Vaupés would arrive saying such things as, "'we're going to work with the *gente de base* [people at the grass roots].' But [these outside activists are] . . . bureaucrats, they speak Spanish, they manage the White world. Now, it's true the local people may have to learn to manage the White world, but they must do so in pursuit of *their own* interests." A local priest commented that "the Church has to leave CRIVA alone, so that it can mature and not be dependent. When a child falls down, you have to give him a hand up, but sometimes they need to pick themselves up." Another priest advocated severing CRIVA's link to the Prefecture so that the organization could "grow up." A lawyer in Bogotá involved in indigenous land claims, complaining about CRIVA's immaturity, characterized its leaders as "waiting for those in power to do something—now they're waiting for a response from the government, tomorrow they're waiting for an investigator to give them money. It's not an *indigenous* organization at all. Like most indigenous organizations, it is conceived and made rational with White rationality."

One source of trouble was the maze of bureaucratic rules and regulations CRIVA encountered, which violated traditional Tukanoan expectations about hospitality and reciprocity.[20] Internal divisions, as noted earlier, grew from traditional rivalries between settlements, clans, and language groups; this factionalism was exacerbated by the youth and inexperience of CRIVA leaders, which contrasted sharply with the age and gradual accretion of power typical of traditional settlement headmen. CRIVA's leaders, recruited through new and untested procedures like election and appointment, were defensive about their lack of traditional credentials, their youth, their political naïveté, and their ignorance of the rest of Colombia. Worst of all, they had no idea how to manage funds. All of these problems were exacerbated by unscrupulous outsiders and various local people—including, unfortunately a few priests—who offered deplorable advice on how to game the system or even steal funds. CRIVA activists found themselves in a double bind: the more efficient and effective they became at garnering the benefits offered by the system, the more suspect and illegitimate they became in the eyes of their constituents.[21]

Another source of temptation and trouble in the late 1970s and early 1980s was the coca trade. Quite a few Tukanoans began selling coca, quickly acquiring fancy foods and beverages, watches, and outboard motors, and in the process neglecting their traditional lifeways.[22] In some respects the Vaupés was at a particular disadvantage, as one of a very few regions of lowland South America with a tradition of coca cultivation and consumption long antedating the drug trade. Much to the chagrin of SIL missionaries, narcotraffickers began using the airstrips SIL had cleared at their mission stations, and Tukanoan involvement grew apace. Several of my interviewees insisted that indigenous organizing in that era responded as much as anything else to coca trafficking: they characterized one subregional organization as little more than a coca-growers' guild, concerned with regulating prices, the allocation of land for coca cultivation, and the level of payoffs to local officials.

In this context development agencies active in the region typically felt impelled to make a show of promoting traditional culture. A number of my correspondents criticized CRIVA's stance on these issues for being caught up in the White world and lacking an allegiance to tradition. Twenty years earlier, of course, non-Tukanoans in the region had pushed in the opposite direction, arguing for the necessity of teaching Indians the dignity of work and the benefits of civilization. The new pro-tradition rhetoric was undoubtedly motivated in part by fears about the influence of the coca trade and the failures of the Catholic Prefecture and the government: change agents voiced concern about Tukanoan exposure to the worst of the modern world and the dangers of rapid acculturation. Modernist development discourses advocating material change were tempered by caveats about preserving the "good" in tradition. It was by no means clear, however, what that good consisted of, or how to preserve it. The finger was often pointed at certain projects (usually another NGO's) as examples of what not to do, but the route to success was unclear.

In this somewhat chaotic and rapidly changing situation, ideas about the nature and value of local traditions were heavily influenced by received notions from outside—by input from national and foreign indigenous activists and ideas absorbed by CRIVA personnel in their travels around the country and even abroad—ideas that sometimes contradicted local realities. A small book titled *Fundamental Principles of CRIVA*, by Jesús Santacruz,[23] a prominent leader in the early 1980s, was published with the help of the Prefecture and the *comisaría* (the state-appointed local government). Santacruz's account is riddled with errors, some of them undoubtedly deliberate, as is also true of descriptions of Tukanoan life in ONIC's newspaper, *Unidad Indígena* (Indigenous Unity). By no means random, these mistakes offer a stereotyped and highly romanticized portrait of tropical forest indigenousness. One article in *Unidad Indígena* misrepresents the language groups as territorially circumscribed tribes: "To each tribe corresponds a territory whose limits are clearly recognized and respected; in keeping with tradition and mythology, this territory is communal property of the entire tribe."[24] In actuality, associations between territory and language group tend to exist at the ideal level, and claims to exclusive ownership or control occur mainly in mythico-historical accounts. Far from maintaining exclusivity, the norm is nonexclusive usufruct rights to hunt, fish, gather, and raise crops. Local settlements are definitely associated with a traditional territory, but boundaries are vague, and traditionally malocas were typically moved to a new site every generation or so. Some neighboring settlements, moreover, belong to different language groups. In the same vein, another article in *Unidad Indígena* asserts that land is worked communally, when in fact individual labor is the norm: men from one family might help another family clear land for a garden, but not as a regular practice.[25]

Clearly, would-be auto-ethnographers like Santacruz had accepted notions foreign to Tukanoan tradition: to represent themselves in a positive light to external audiences, they had to shape their accounts to fit the preconceptions of those audiences, to conform to the imaginaries of authentic tropical forest Indians circulating in the national culture. As first-generation activists, CRIVA activists lacked the sophistication and skills needed to articulate representations of Tukanoan identity and culture that would resonate with both local and external audiences.

Research Dilemmas

In making social science sense of Tukanoan self-images and self-representation, the dilemma facing me was how best to describe and analyze CRIVA's representations of Tukanoan culture in a way that penetrated beyond the fictions of auto-ethnography without disrespecting its subjects and authors. How is one to avoid sounding judgmental or condescending when observing and analyzing processes in which Tukanoans are being asked to struggle with newly received notions about what it means to be indigenous? How can one deal analytically with distorted versions of what a legitimate native of the tropical forest looked and acted like, accounts obviously written by activists living radically changed lives, heavily influenced in obvious ways by outside input and influence?

My search for some kind of neutral analytic stance led me to see the local issues I was encountering as variants of much larger questions pervasive in anthropology. Why was anthropology's notion of "culture"—highly polysemic, elusive, even protean, but also fundamental to our discipline—so little help here? [26] In the late 1980s I had not encountered colleagues working on these questions, certainly not in lowland South America. Culture as an analytic term was especially problematic in the Vaupés—despite its extensive use in indigenous self-presentation—because several of its fundamental assumptions simply did not fit. Invoking traditional ethnographic notions of lifeways, traditions, and the like concerning the Tukanoan political project seemed to miss the point.

In struggling with these issues I was drawn to the social science literature on ethnicity, to authors who in the 1970s and 1980s were coming to terms with the problematics of ethnic politics, particularly those inherent in nationalist movements.[27] Some authors argued that assertions about fixed ethnic boundaries, whether offered by anthropologists or by the groups themselves, were informed by vested interests and old thinking, missing the fact that such boundaries are typically indistinct, permeable, shifting, or even nonexistent.[28] But the applicability of these new models in the Vaupés was limited, because the social units there did not look like ethnic groups.

It became increasingly clear that none of the various meanings of culture with which I was familiar was apolitical or value-free. Anthropologists have generally valorized traditional culture, treating it as something deserving protection (with the exception perhaps of some of its more violent or disturbing customs). But "good" culture was understood to be collective and long-standing, not some recent innovation, and certainly not the invention of identifiable individuals with an axe to grind. To be sure, anthropologists have always recognized that in some more general sense all culture is invented, but in the case of "authentic tribal" cultures that invention is placed firmly in the past. When tribal culture has been modified in the present or recent past by identifiable individuals and groups (as occurred with the Ghost Dance religion among Plains Indians in the United States), then the process is labelled history rather than culture. Tukanoans before the 1970s constituted—indeed, were a poster child for—what Claude Lévi-Strauss termed a "cold" culture.[29] Despite critiques of Levi-Strauss's hot/cold distinction and Eric Wolf's scorn for the fiction that some societies are "without history,"[30] that fiction remains remarkably persistent, not least in the contested field of identity politics. The task of representing and generalizing about what an anthropologist sees and hears in the field, always daunting, proves especially challenging when contested ethnic identities are in play.

And of course there was also the sticky problem of how to contradict errors in Tukanoan auto-ethnography without seeming accusatory and negative, and without presuming to know more than "the natives." I could not make distinctions between different aspects of their cultural production without assuming the role of cultural critic, able to sort out the good from the bad. How was I to document these processes and products without suggesting that something authentic was being lost, was being replaced by something inauthentic? I did not want to suggest that Tukanoans were "losing" their culture—which suggested an end point of no culture—with only an impoverished version of the previous one. I did not want to follow the example of Theodora Kroeber's book *Ishi in Two Worlds: A Biography of the Last Wild Indian in North America*, whose title made the claim that there are no more "real" Indians left on the subcontinent.[31] Nor could I fall back on an acculturation model of change, since the process I was witnessing was not replacing Tukanoan traditional culture with "modern," "mainstream" Colombian culture.[32]

The vast majority of anthropologists working with indigenous people undoubtedly want to describe them in a respectful fashion, one that grants them "agency, process and social practice,"[33] but even when authors avoid conscious value judgments, their characterizations of ethnic identity often sound negative. Leo Desprès, for example, defines *ethnicity* as "an ascriptive element denoting the fact that certain people are defined, or define themselves, as belonging together by virtue of their *presumed* origin." The hint of dubious or spurious claims resurfaces in Fredrik Barth's remarks on a person's basic identity "*presumptively* determined by his origin and background."[34] Ronald Cohen uses the even harsher term *putative* in reference to permanent, ascriptive identity features.[35] Joan Vincent similarly writes of "the *assumed* givens of a society" whose "*actual* realized organization" has to be demonstrated.[36] Joel Kahn goes still further, characterizing ethnicity as a mere *ideology* needing to be explained rather than taken as a given, a claim echoed by Philippe Bourgois, who calls it "a form of *ideological* expression."[37]

These authors were all reacting against a position previously widespread, both in academic social science and in popular media discourse, that treated ethnicity as a survival, a traditional aberration left over in a modern world, a kind of nonrational attachment—at best a negligible triviality, at worst a form of deep-seated irrationality and an impediment to nation-building and progress, a type of "tribalism" associated with a colonial past.[38] From this point of view, ethnic confrontations were to be seen as cultural or political lag and false consciousness. Needless to say, events following the end of the Cold War proved otherwise.

Here is Cohen again: "Once the ethnic identities and categories are triggered into being salient, cultural *rationalizations* for the legitimacy of the mobilized grouping are actively sought for and created by those involved."[39] Ethnicity, he argues, can "be narrowed or broadened in boundary terms, in relation to the specific needs of political mobilization."[40] Vincent writes of a *manipulation* of a classificatory system according to the needs of the moment: "political actors . . . when articulating ethnic status, are able to define and redefine the rules of interaction according to their changing interests."[41] Elsewhere she denies that ethnicity is "a mystic force in itself"; it is, rather, "a tool in the hands of men."[42]

Indigenous groups deploying their collective identity to buttress their claims and assertions often resent what to them may look like hostile treatment from authors like Cohen and Vincent; Clifford's essay "Identity in Mashpee," mentioned in the Introduction, is a well-known example. In his account of a trial determining whether a treaty from 1798 between the Mashpee tribe and the United States was still in effect, Clifford concedes that the Mashpee might object to his analysis of their arguments.[43] (The decision turned on whether the community had continued as a tribe in the intervening years; the court said no.) In the sheltered world of academic publishing, Wolf's definition of a culture as "a series of processes that construct, reconstruct, and dismantle cultural materials, in response to identifiable determinants" would ruffle few feathers, but in the hurly-burly of ethnic politics it very well might cause offense.[44] Social analysis and political advocacy may differ significantly (even when engaged in by the same individual), but in some arenas the distinction has little force, as I discovered myself.

Today, explorations of ethnicity in this vein, often called constructionist, are commonplace.[45] Colombian anthropologist Myriam Jimeno, for example, writes without hesitation about social actors continually reinventing their individual identities based on their interests and perspectives, and about groups and individuals interacting "to project a continually reinvented 'politics of their own.'"[46] In the 1980s, however, no one was making statements like this.

My concern at that time was not with culture contact in general and the changes it provokes, which had in fact been occurring in the Vaupés for well over a century. Tukanoans in the 1970s and 1980s were responding not only to messages circulating about becoming a proper citizen of Colombia or a Christian of one kind or another but also to exhortations about remaining proper Tukanoans. They were to hold to Tukanoan identity while increasingly hearing from non-Tukanoan stakeholders about what that identity consisted of. If Tukanoan traditions appeared in the pages of *La Voz de la Tribu* in distorted form, if young Tukanoans were giving up a largely unconsidered, even unconscious self-awareness for a highly self-conscious one based on received wisdom from the exterior, how to analyze this process?

We can find numerous historical examples of such self-consciousness. The Plains Indians who signed on to Buffalo Bill's Wild West Show very likely experienced a hermeneutic experience of a sort during their travels abroad, the result of seeing themselves through European eyes.[47] But the advent of multiculturalism in the Americas complicated this process. In the case of the Vaupés, a powerful cultural system that had been intruding into Tukanoan lifeways all of a sudden began sending new messages about the need to remain Tukanoan, messages carried in many cases by some of the same actors who had previously been demanding extensive changes. For an anthropologist, finding a way to talk about this process in nondeprecatory terms was (and remains) a challenge. Simply to speak of "becoming Indian," as I did, suggests something inauthentic.[48] What is intended to be an analytic endeavor may come across as a normative one.

During my first fieldwork in the late 1960s, no Spanish-speaking Tukanoan spoke of *nuestra cultura* (our culture) in this self-conscious sense, although of course many complained bitterly about Whites' efforts to change them. During the 1970s and 1980s, however, they did begin to speak of *lo nuestro* (that which is ours), as Indians in other parts of Colombia were doing. Of course, any indigenous community coming into contact with a radically different culture must become aware of itself in ways previously impossible, and this contact necessarily creates some degree of cultural self-consciousness. What I am talking about here, however—what we might call self-awareness to the nth degree, along with a highly self-conscious version of culture—begins when a group of people start appropriating notions of who they are from outside sources, usually the dominant culture. James Carrier refers to this process as Occidentalism, the inverse of Edward Said's notion of Orientalism.[49]

Ritual is self-conscious in this way when its meaning derives in part from the fact that the audience (both those physically present and those in people's minds) includes people from other cultures.[50] If, for example, a ritual that Tukanoans traditionally performed entirely for themselves is now being shown to outsiders and has an element of "being ourselves for you,"[51] then the ritual is no longer entirely "traditional" in key respects, even if its form is largely unchanged, because the meaning has changed. Two meanings, past and present, stand in a kind of dialogic relationship. How can this complex process be characterized using conventional notions of culture? One suggestion has been to speak of a ritual as having been *folkloricized*, something that happens when participants' involvement in the larger society shapes its performance, determining in part which particular aspects of the ritual are retained or dropped. But seeing this process as a case of folkloricization does not work: the term is a put-down, and it is concerned primarily with state-imposed maintenance of cultural forms.[52]

To resolve this dilemma I began searching for a heuristic that, with a little creative invention of my own, would permit me to describe the situation I was observing in the least negative manner possible. Pidgin and creole studies provided one that I used in an essay published in 1989. At that time pidgin and creole studies offered a useful metaphor precisely because languages of this sort were seen as belonging to a special category of language, due to the fact that they arose in situations of pronounced change and extreme power differentials, usually in state-controlled areas. *Pidgins* are new languages that arise in response to situations, for example, plantations, in which communication is essential yet severely restricted. Would-be speakers, with no language in common, devise a restricted code that everyone can understand. The idea at the time held that if, over time, a pidgin became the first language of the next generation, it would qualify as a creole.[53] This assumption was later discarded. *Creoles* have been stigmatized as inferior, "broken," ungrammatical versions of well-established (usually European) languages. Although linguists for the most part no longer believe this, many nonlinguists continue to see them in these negative terms.[54] In Jamaica, for instance, educators would not recognize the island's creole as a language, seeing it, rather, as a slovenly version of English.

Most useful to me was the way linguists specializing in pidgins and creoles saw them as challenges to conventional assumptions about languages and language change. Just as speakers create creoles when confronting particular communication problems, I wrote, so did Tukanoans, especially CRIVA activists, adjust their representations of their culture to solve their "particular communication problems." Many people liked the article, which was translated into Spanish.

Unfortunately, as pidgin and creole studies developed, the statements I made about these codes turned out not to be true. Today, creoles are not seen as pidgins that have acquired native speakers, and although a substantial amount of controversy continues to characterize this subfield, linguists for the most part agree that creoles are not a special category of language. The reason they were thought to be exceptional, according to my MIT linguist colleague Michel DeGraff, was that European observers could not fathom that

Africans and other non-Europeans could speak anything that would be classified as a language "descended" from their own. The assumption was that, since languages could be used for ranking degrees of humanity, creole languages were to be classified as "lesser" in a world order where Africans were considered to have an inferior nature and thus could be enslaved.[55] The challenge for these Europeans was to explain *away* the similarities between creoles (such as Haitian Kreyol) and European languages (such as French), and so their response was to classify creoles as a special kind of language.

The linguists working on creoles during the 1980s certainly did not see themselves as racists; many of them believed they were countering racist assumptions that informed policymaking, some of it quite consequential. One scholar, Loreto Todd, saw inventors of pidgins and creoles as victims in the five-centuries-long process of domination and exploitation that characterized Europe's contact with the rest of the world.[56] Linguists also struggled to find nonpejorative words to replace terminology like "broken," "bastardized," or "grammarless." And they insisted that creoles be called "languages," rather than "dialects" or "patois." But they did consider them singular languages.

Such is the nature of academic work. Advances in linguistics made my clever appropriation of pidgin and creole scholarship obsolete. But several of the points I made continue to hold. For example, I noted that anthropologists' frustrated and contentious attempts to classify and compare cultures would sometimes involve messy issues being swept under the rug: as Cohen notes, the "fieldwork greats . . . knew they were often as not creating arbitrary and artificial boundaries" when describing indeterminate and shifting groups as separate cultures.[57]

Another point I made in that 1989 article stresses the need to keep in mind that it is *speakers* who construct and change language. Just as linguists need to avoid privileging languages as static entities, and turn their attention instead to those who devise and use them, those anthropologists accustomed to putting culture at the center should give their due to social actors and their adaptations to social transformations. Mikhail Bakhtin's discussion of dialogical interaction, the iterative process through which speakers receive and reconceptualize a word, is apposite: "[a word] enters a dialogically agitated and tension-filled environment of alien words, value judgments, and accents, weaves in and out of complex interrelationships, merges with some, recoils from others, intersects with yet a third group."[58] Bakhtin's remarks apply to the whole field of multicultural discourse pervasive in Colombia since the 1970s and 1980s, not least to the word "culture."

Working on the article led me to see a danger in the enduring notion of culture as a thing—something to be possessed that comes in finite quantities, and that can be retained or lost.[59] It became abundantly clear that the genetic model employed in historical linguistics and (at times) anthropology was not adequate for talking about culture in places like the Vaupés—certainly not the changes in the way activist Tukanoans came to see and speak of their culture from the 1970s on. Surely the lesson to be learned, I wrote, was that the model of culture as a static, unconscious, and slowly changing legacy from earlier generations is a folk model. Although, early on, anthropologists found they needed to acknowledge cultural change—with notions like culture contact, diffusion, syncretization, and acculturation—the organic model of culture was showing remarkable resilience. According to this model, cultures initially resist outside influence, and subsequently they either hang tough or weaken and die, their members in this latter case assimilated into an intrusive dominant culture. Such an organic model offered no help in understanding some of the changes taking place in the Vaupés. At the time I was writing, anthropologists tended to speak of meaning in overly static terms. For example, Clifford Geertz speaks of cultural man as "an animal suspended in webs of significance he himself has spun."[60] I argued that Bakhtin's notion of dialogics could help us see culture and identity as always in flux, always being negotiated, rather than a "thing" inherited or otherwise acquired.

Another lesson to be learned was that outsiders (including anthropologists) who visited for short periods might see only the simplified versions of new Tukanoan cultural forms—versions that, after all, were targeted at outsiders and meant "for public consumption." (And sometimes the public being targeted will include members of the community itself, if the simplified versions have a political role to play.) CRIVA activists were responding to ambiguous and at times contradictory messages coming from mainstream society and non-Tukanoan Indians. Because change agents had their own notions about which cultural forms should be valorized and which needed to be discarded, and because interactions between Tukanoans and outsiders occurred in conditions of seriously asymmetrical power relations, outsiders played a very important role in the creation of these novel representations of Tukanoan identity and culture. Outsiders were not necessarily privy to these meaning construction processes, and we can understand some of these new representations—for example, the booklet by Jesús Santacruz—as a version of Tukanoan culture created "for public consumption."

Another point had to do with linguistic hyper-forms, which, as a general rule, can be considered incorrect so long as some but not all speakers believe an incorrect form to be the correct one.[61] In English, for instance, the use of *premises* to mean real estate, now widely accepted, was once a hyper-form, as seems to be happening with pronouncing the *t* in the word *often*. Using the concept of hyper-form as a heuristic, I argued, might illuminate emerging notions about tropical forest indigeneity: if later generations of Tukanoans should come to believe notions about their traditional culture derived from claims by CRIVA and *Unidad Indígena*, the hyper-form will have become the correct usage. The authors who knowingly misrepresented their customs, were, I believe, responding to disparaging depictions of Tukanoan life, imposed until very recently by government agents, health workers, schoolteacher nuns and their textbooks, and, perhaps, indigenous activists from other parts of the country. The hyper-indigenous auto-ethnography penned by CRIVA writers may have helped heal the hurts suffered from these slights. Most importantly, the authors of the pieces in *La Voz de la Tribu* knew that virtually no one, neither priest, nor nun, nor government official, nor non-Tukanoan indigenous activist really understood linguistic exogamy. Not only did it violate received notions of tropical forest lifeways, it had long inspired scorn and confusion.

I concluded by stating that if, at some future moment, Tukanoans came to believe that their patri-clan ancestors owned land collectively, worked it communally, and married within "the tribe" or the "ethnic group," then the hyper-form would have become the correct form. At the end of the day, it is the actors who create linguistic or ethnographic reality. Ethnicity and culture are not some mystical force existing apart from these actors, even though we (and they) often speak as if their creations were independent realities. Ethnogenesis is a process of constant cultural reinvention,[62] one that demands attention to agency and process as well as to questions of historical and cultural veracity.

The Bigger Picture

During the 1970s and 1980s Colombia's pueblos became much more visible nationally, due to scandals like the Planas affair (discussed in Chapter Three), indigenous mobilizing around land claims, and the rise of identity politics. In many quarters, multiculturalist and human rights discourses reversed the conventional wisdom about Indians (of course, in other quarters they continued to be seen as childlike, ignorant, lazy, and dirty). Positive images of the country's pueblos appeared, originating for the most part in Bogotá and the exterior. In addition to symbolizing a pluralism that would unify the nation, pueblos came to represent a voting bloc to be courted.[63] Also, so the argument went, if welcomed into civil society Indians would be less likely to ally with insurgents. And their exotic alterity would help promote tourism and facilitate indigenous artisanal production and sales, discussed in Chapter Four.

My concern with indigenous self-representation in the Vaupés pointed me toward similar processes going on elsewhere in the country, particularly within national-level indigenous organizations, which opened up more difficult questions about analytic terminology, ethnographic authority, and divergent visions of culture and history. In addition to interviewing indigenous activists in national organizations, I began to investigate the links between what was going on in the Vaupés and in Bogotá by interviewing NGO personnel and state agents in both places, and my conversations with priests in Mitú became much more focused on the Prefecture's multiculturalist-inspired projects and their opinions of CRIVA and other change agents in the region. In Bogotá I set up meetings with Colombian anthropologists who worked elsewhere in the country. For the title of an essay I published in 1995, following the lead of Richard Handler and Jocelyn Linnekin,[64] I borrowed Edward Sapir's phrase "culture, genuine and spurious"—which taught me never to use irony in an article title, because some readers thought I was denigrating Tukanoan cultural forms,[65] and others thought I was denying the existence of culture altogether. Far from repudiating the concept, I was simply pointing to the need to renew anthropology's toolkit in order to make sense of the representations of Tukanoan culture I was hearing and reading about. Although in some respects Tukanoan activists were indeed misrepresenting Tukanoan culture, representations of culture are *never* identical to the culture being represented. Culture consists of what its participants know, feel, practice, and the like, rather than what some members of a given society assert it is, or what we outsider experts (think we) know. Moreover, members of a given society do not share an identical habitus, body of knowledge, or repertoire of emotions.

The 1995 article circulated widely,[66] in part, I believe, because it was one of the first attempts to analyze the effects of identity politics on Amazonian indigenous activists who were under pressure to conform to outsiders' notions of what lowland tropical forest culture and society look like. That those outsiders included indigenous activists from elsewhere in Colombia—who in turn were also under pressure from transnational organizations—made it even more interesting.

I had several axes to grind in that essay. To me, the system of linguistic exogamy was magnificent, and I was taken aback when young Tukanoan activists misrepresented it—after all, the Catholic missionaries bent on destroying the system did not need any help. Over the past fifty years I have encountered very few people willing to confront the system intellectually, since linguistic exogamy deeply challenges accepted wisdom about important topics like tribal societies, marriage, unilineal kinship systems, and the relationship between language and culture. I also regularly experience feminist irritation at the consequences of the disjuncture between patri-centric social structure and values and the actual makeup of Tukanoan communities. No matter what the topic, in-married women are given short shrift in most descriptions of Tukanoan families and lifeways. When I ask activists (always men) about these women's language group membership and natal settlements, they have been forgotten or are explicitly dismissed. The received wisdom considers all members of a given community to belong to a single "ethnic group." End of story. This attitude is in part due to the fact that men, Tukanoan or not, are doing the talking, in part due to the uniqueness of linguistic exogamy, and in part due to the fact that very few non-Tukanoans understand how patrilineal kinship systems work. That in-married women's membership in other language groups might result in their having different perspectives on many issues is seemingly of no consequence—despite the fact that women as a category are symbolically linked with affines (in-laws—to whom we lose our sisters and daughters, and from whom we must get our women), and more broadly with the category "not-us," which would seem to make in-married women's nonmembership rather consequential.[67]

But I was also sympathetic toward CRIVA members who were trying to advance their cause and were learning how to do so from people, indigenous and White, with higher social status. As noted, lowland pueblos were considered more authentic than many highland ones because the lowland ones had retained more of their language and culture, which gave them a kind of cultural purity that carried symbolic clout. But the hierarchy within the indigenous movement was clear: Andean pueblos were on top. One does not have to look far to find examples in the 1970s and 1980s of highland Indians treating their lowland counterparts negatively (we shall see a contemporary example in Chapter Five), and dominant society attitudes toward the country's "savage" inhabitants of the tropical forests and plains doubtlessly contributed. One rather trivial, but telling, example is the visuals in the early years of ONIC's publication *Unidad Indígena*. Members of highland pueblos are invariably depicted in a very respectful manner, usually with a photograph or a sketched portrait. In contrast, every issue is ornamented with several cartoons of an always-smiling, large-eyed, pudgy small boy complete with loincloth, hairband, and feather.

Multiculturalism's Increasing Presence in the Vaupés

By the 1980s multicultural and preservationist rhetoric was penetrating the region in all sorts of ways, accompanied by a contradiction that, at the time, was barely perceptible. Official multiculturalism requires indigenous claims to entitlements to be based on authentic cultural difference, with the obvious implication that development programs should not threaten traditional culture. But change agents, religious or secular, by definition promote change, regardless of their claims that *their* kinds of change did not jeopardize tradition.[68] As early as 1969 I heard an SIL missionary insist that, unlike the priests, SIL wanted to change only Tukanoans' faith, not their culture.

The contradictions inherent in this stance become evident when change agents' agendas are juxtaposed with their disclaimers. A DAI proposal to aid the community of San Miguel on the Pirá-Paraná River to the south, for instance, paid lip service to respect for indigenous tradition, specifically to support for shamanism and mythic conceptions of health and illness. Elsewhere, however, the proposal alludes to studying "stable indigenous societies" as a basis for implementing beneficial cultural, social, and economic changes.[69] Similarly, another proposal, from a Netherlands-sponsored program of health care, urged the importance of spelling out the component of "community participation," because health care agents would be encountering radically different communities whose members possessed "another form of interpreting reality."[70] A proposal from the state agency Family Well-being (Instituto Colombiano de Bienestar Familiar) opens with boilerplate about "ethnic strengthening" and respect for indigenous cultural systems, but then discusses implementation of changes decided on by experts in Bogotá.[71] Which is not to say that Tukanoans might not embrace some of those changes, especially to counter recent declines in self-sufficiency. But the multiculturalism in such proposals was highly formulaic—stereotyped rhetoric trotted out before getting down to the business at hand.

Change Agents

Throughout this period Tukanoans were increasingly being exposed to the worst of the larger society. A gold rush that began in the late 1980s attracted a horde of prospectors, many of them as unsavory as any depicted in Wild West movies. The population of Mitú, which as late as 1969 had been only seven hundred or so, by 1991 had grown to fourteen thousand. The ongoing armed conflict also produced tremendous problems, most dramatically in 1988, when a FARC raid on Mitú led to major change, most of it with terrible effect on nearby Tukanoans.[72] Previously regional security had been left in police hands, as the Vaupés lacked a military presence. Now a military base was built on the edge of town, bringing much tighter control of people's movements, new diseases, and women giving birth to babies with no social fathers—previously, men, whether Tukanoan or White, lived with the mothers of their children in a stable relationship. A second, all-out assault by FARC in 1998 killed sixteen policemen and thirteen auxiliaries (all of the latter Tukanoan), destroyed public buildings, and left three thousand people homeless. Insurgents mined the airport and blew up the communications tower.[73] And the coca boom continued to produce its own massive problems.

In the same period, multiculturalist rhetoric was becoming increasingly evident in Mitú and mission towns, as well as in conversations among Tukanoans. My 1991 and 1993 visits revealed that numerous change agents from NGOs and government agencies were competing in the region, including Family Well-Being, the National Apprenticeship Service, the Agricultural Cooperative, the Ministry of Education, Communal Action, Indigenous Affairs, Public Health, the National Plan of Rehabilitation, and the Office of the Mayor. Competition among missions—called the "War of the Gods" in a film by Brian Moser[74]—was now a War of the Change Agents, what one Cubeo schoolteacher called "the bombardment of our communities."

Inevitably, the poorly designed and executed projects implemented by these agencies would fail, leading to finger-pointing and excuse-making. The endemic backbiting was evident in a letter written by a local DAI agent in 1987 complaining of a health worker scheming to "set the Indians against us, an attitude that we have seen repeatedly, always with hostile intent."[75] The letter also accused Catholic clergy of keeping Tukanoans under their influence by keeping a "monopoly on merchandise." In another letter the writer complained that the president of CRIVA refused to return two outboard motors to the local DAI office.[76]

In this tense atmosphere, the competition between Protestant and Catholic missionaries was intense, underneath a thin veneer of civility.[77] The Prefecture's publications sniped at their rivals: a 1991 interview with the Guambiano leader Lorenzo Muelas in *Selva y Río* quotes him as saying: "I only defend the unity that ought to reign in the entire human community. If there is a religion that defends this unity, it is good, but if the religion brings divisions among Indians, then it is better to reject it."[78] The article suggests that Muelas is referring to the divisions created by SIL. A note from a 1992 issue of *Selva y Río* alleges that "a certain community changed its religious sentiments in exchange for an outboard motor"—venting Catholic anger both at Protestant wealth and Tukanoan fickleness.[79]

The Prefecture's relationship with anthropological ideas was ambivalent and given to rapid changes. When helping to found CRIVA, the Prefecture invoked anthropological, nationalist, and Leftist discourse, and the publications of both CRIVA and the Prefecture were permeated with culturalist rhetoric. But just what the Church meant by culture was often unclear, and the articles and editorials in *Selva y Río* struggled to bridge the gap between Catholic dogma and cultural preservation. The cover of one issue reads: "The God of Life dies anew in the struggles of indigenous peoples, and in the solidarity of all, to achieve recognition of their ethnic rights and to defend their traditional territory."[80] Changed attitudes and ambivalence were also evident in an article on coca, described as

> a sacred plant that has saved and continues to save the life of many of our brothers and sisters who suffer oppression and hunger because of unjust exploitation. The coca leaf is an ancestral good of our people that needs to be defended today, and its cultivation ought to be supported in the way that generates life and not death, which is not the case after coca is transformed into cocaine. Long before the arrival of the Spaniards, even before the Inca Empire, Indians used it above all for medicine and nutrition, as well as to fight against the cold.[81]

Needless to say, such sentiments would have been unimaginable just a few years before.

Another striking reversal concerned the maloca. In 1970 an older priest informed me that it had been his duty ("a mi me tocó") to burn down malocas, as temples of demon-worship and encouragements to promiscuity. In striking contrast, a 1991 *Selva y Río* article featured a photograph of a maloca characterized as "also the temple of God."[82] But ambivalence was obvious: the magazine urged victory over "indigenism . . . just as we must overcome false Christianity . . . we fight to conserve all that is valid and change all that does not conform with Culture and the Gospel." Although positioning itself on the side of indigenous rights, the magazine had a mixed message about culture:

> Today when in Latin America *autonomy, land, culture, and unity* [referring to *Unidad Indígena*'s slogan] of indigenous peoples are insisted upon, it is good to ask ourselves where we have come from and where we are going. Whoever makes an argument based only on culture as the way to demonstrate how great it is to be indigenous . . . is wasting their time.[83]

The Prefecture's rivalry with other change agents and ambivalence about traditional Tukanoan culture colored its relations with any institution or individual that dealt with Tukanoans. At times, anthropologists and the government were almost as suspect as SIL and NT. A 1991 editorial in *Selva y Río* states:

> We have economic problems, but we can overcome them. Have we thought of the possibilities for tourism in our jungle? Gold appears everywhere, it is a benediction of God. . . . We will be an example for Colombia. We will not allow others to set a program for us. Some anthropologists want to see us in the greatest misery, it seems that they are happy to picture us in the worst state of indigence. But we will not permit these intrusions.[84]

The battle over whose model of development would prevail was taken up again in the same issue in a letter to the president of the country from its archbishop, Gustavo Ángel Romero:

> The Division of Indigenous Affairs works to hinder all progress in the Vaupés. Several anthropologists have gone into the communities trying to convince the people that they do not need anything, that they lived well 100 years ago and ought to return to their ancient customs. The Indians are very troubled, because these anthropologists have become ecologists with the pretense of not touching any tree in the Amazon because other countries want it this way. . . . I believe this campaign has something to do with the suspension of the Highway Project.[85]

The fact that DAI's staff was mostly made up of anthropologists doubtlessly heightened the Church's critical stance toward the discipline.

The Prefecture's conflicting messages resulted from its need to work toward a diverse and not always compatible set of goals. First, promote religious teaching. Second, promote development, both to meet Tukanoan demands for some material improvements, and to answer critics who accused the Church of cultural imperialism and indifference to needs other than salvation. And third, promote (or at least appear to promote) indigenous culture and autonomy. Unlike SIL and NT, which had from the start promoted Tukanoan catechists, the Prefecture, responding to changes in Church policy nationally, had difficulty reconciling its long-established paternalism with recognition of the need for indigenous leadership. It also struggled against rivals, enemies, and dissidents: narcotraffickers, indigenous activists and their allies, and the agents of the government and NGOs, who claimed selfless devotion to both development and cultural preservation. The Prefecture found it difficult to rebut critics and embrace change without seeming to deny its primary mission in the region, which was to preach the gospel, which is probably why it embraced the goal of making its message "culturally relevant." For example, the newsletter of the Centro Animación Pastoral Indígena (Center for Missionary Animation in Indigenous Pastoral Work, CAPI), published snippets from mythology called "Narratives," and a warning from a priest that "the radical abandonment of our cultural values . . . will lead to the loss of our identity."[86] *Selva y Río* regularly illustrated scripture lessons with metaphors from Tukanoan everyday life, and contained features titled "Mythology" and "Culture." It was clear to me that the younger priests were interested in multicultural approaches; for example, in a July 1990 letter to me, Father Luis Pinzón wrote about the need to avoid paternalism and of allowing "the Indians to construct their own history."[87]

Having lost its past monopoly over religious and secular education, and in the mission towns, its control of health care and its ability to speak for the state, the Prefecture tried to push its influence over other domains. But it faced competition nearly everywhere. A training program for native leaders was duplicated by an ONIC counterpart. Its youth groups faced competition from programs sponsored by the Office of the Mayor. In 1975 Church-controlled education had been replaced by the government's Regional Education Fund (Fondo Educativo Regional, FER). The Prefecture's development projects competed with numerous NGO equivalents, its health programs with the work of Family Wellbeing and the Ministry of Health.[88]

Along with the Gospel, the Prefecture had always embraced Colombian nationalism, the Spanish language, and "civilization." In its criticism of SIL it implied that sinister foreign agents were importing dangerous doctrines and influences into the region. In fact, however, almost everyone working in the region depended on financial support from international agencies, not least the Prefecture itself, which in 1991 was negotiating with a Catholic diocese in Bavaria for funds to electrify CRIVA's headquarters. As the Prefecture struggled to come to terms with the new multiculturalist regime (and with internal pressure from young left-leaning priests), it began to include *some* anthropological discourses in its proselytizing, and to promote *some* forms of indigenous autonomy and culture. Appropriating some of its rivals' philosophy and methods, however, as the *Selva y Río* excerpts illustrate, produced any number of contradictions, which were apparent in the words and actions of not just the Church but all the change agents in the Vaupés.

Tukanoan Responses

In general Tukanoans wanted to retain their indigenous identity for the simple reason that they continued to value their traditions and autonomy. In addition, those living near Mitú were becoming increasingly aware of indigeneity's symbolic capital. CRIVA leaders worked to validate their authority to act as brokers between Tukanoan communities and the outside world by using the rhetoric of cultural preservation and by making arguments to the effect that they were the appropriate actors to wage political battles with local Whites and outsiders. One of CRIVA's jobs was to introduce ideas about pan-indigeneity. Another was to describe Tukanoan culture and society to outsiders, including Indians from elsewhere in Colombia. Activists needed to refer respectfully to the past and promote progress and development, while avoiding the appearance of buying into assimilationism. They also had to champion Tukanoans' right to a place in the sun in a multiethnic society without appearing to endorse overtly separatist policies.

The difficulties of presenting Tukanoan culture in a way recognizable to outsiders are apparent in CRIVA leaders' referring to Tukanoan language groups as "ethnic groups" in their speeches and publications. Such terminology put the organization in a stronger political position than it would have enjoyed had its leaders spoken of an organization representing a collection of language-affiliated, patrilineal exogamous clans. We saw earlier that in keeping with this ethnic group discourse, Tukanoan language groups were described in a manner that exaggerated the distinctions between them and failed to mention certain crucial similarities. For example, a proposal written in 1989 by a group of Tukanoan schoolteachers refers to "the great indigenous nation" and the "Tukanoan nation," made up of "numerous ethnic groups that inhabited this Colombian territory many millennia before the discovery of America by the Europeans. Each ethnic group had their own way of life, their own social, cultural, political and religious organization, which allowed them to organize and locate themselves in different zones of this territory."[89]

As already noted, as one travels within the region one does find—in addition to differences resulting from geography and degrees of acculturation—linguistic and kinship divisions and differences with respect to ceremonial objects, intangible property, and roles in myths. But apart from these distinctions, no major differences distinguish language groups from one another, and some of the differences work to unify the region into a single "cultural complex." Nor is the actual settlement pattern mirrored in the version offered in the proposal.

This inclination to ethnicize the differences separating the language groups was also evident in the design of a museum CRIVA planned to build in the form of a maloca in Mitú. Each internal compartment along the sides, one leader told me, would represent a different Tukanoan ethnic group "with its distinct culture—Desana, Cubeo, Tukano, and so forth." The rich and complex heritage of the Vaupés region would be displayed in distorted form, very much like the book by Jesús Santacruz mentioned previously. Each language group is identified by supposedly distinctive traits actually characteristic of all of them: Carapana are described as seminomads, though they are no more nomadic than anyone else; Wanano are said to practice "slash-and-burn agriculture in the rainy tropical forest where they dwell,"[90] but this is true for all Tukanoans. The book calls for the Ministry of Education's Experimental Pilot Center to include information about each tribe's history in the school curriculum.[91] Santacruz subsequently describes CRIVA's efforts to unify the region; the organization "has worked to defend the interests of all Tukanoans without distinguishing among the tribes, the castes. In CRIVA's eyes, everyone is the same."[92]

Models borrowed from mainstream society also made an appearance in the way CRIVA came to function as a cabildo (council)—the legal institution governing each community's internal affairs—as happened in 1988, when CRIVA was granted legal authority over the huge Gran Resguardo del Vaupés, with its 3,354,097 hectares,[93] thus ending an administrative vacuum. As noted in Chapter One, a law passed in 1890 recognized the official status of the resguardo and the cabildo, an arrangement confirmed by legislation in the 1960s. However, the cabildo form was completely foreign to Amazonian parts of Colombia, where the maximum political authorities were the headmen of each maloca.[94] Not surprisingly, when organizations like CRIVA were authorized to head newly created or expanded resguardos in those regions, many communities denied them legitimacy, because that control was externally conceived and imposed. As CRIVA insisted on its mandate to control access to the region, acting as intermediary between Tukanoan communities and all outsiders, it provoked resentment and resistance from the communities, and even more from outside change agents. One disgruntled researcher from a Colombian NGO responded to rejection of his proposal:

> With an indigenist discourse they claim recognition as representatives of the communities. The project as such did not interest them, although they expressed their desire to "administer" it. The problem for some was simply economic, and they proposed that we hand over money and equipment. . . . This type of person maintains a pseudo-indigenist discourse, denouncing the critical situation that the indigenous peoples of our country suffer, but are basically interested in negotiating collective interests in exchange for personal profit.[95]

CRIVA activists embraced the culturalist ethos, but in problematic ways, opposing direct access or direct funding by outside organizations. Santacruz's book, for example, demands that "all investigation among the different tribes of the Vaupés ought to consult first with CRIVA, which will communicate with the other sub-regional organizations and the communities"[96]—a demand that others sometimes contested. In one such clash a Canadian filmmaker offered to bankroll development of a school teaching traditional culture in a Makuna community if he could film the project.[97] CRIVA's objections to the project added fuel to complaints already circulating that its officers were corrupt money-grubbers.[98] Santacruz himself characterizes the years 1979 to 1981 as a period of "decadence," during which time CRIVA leaders "did not strictly comply with the statutes" and were "irresponsible and incapable of working as leaders."[99]

The notion of culture and questions of who should study it became hotly contested. A lawyer who had spent a year exhaustively surveying the region told me that, except near Mitú, many Tukanoans rejected the word "culture" as smacking of primitivism and efforts to keep them in loincloths, something priests had accused anthropologists of doing. CRIVA officials might embrace "culture," but local Tukanoans, who had grown suspicious of the word, were more likely to use *lo nuestro* (that which is ours). CRIVA members, although perhaps unsure of precisely what culture consisted of, expressed resentment against anthropologists' supposed claims to know Tukanoan culture better than Tukanoans themselves, an accusation repeatedly voiced by Catholic missionaries. CRIVA, I was told, had in the late 1970s sponsored a book burning that targeted works by Gerardo Reichel-Dolmatoff and Irving Goldman,[100] claiming that they were full of lies and immodest language. As noted, Santacruz demanded that all ethnographic writing be locally vetted prior to publication.[101]

My Tukanoan interlocutors seemed unsure of how one went about studying culture and who should do it. One non-CRIVA Tukanoan asked me whether anthropologists studied customs (*costumbres*) rather than culture itself, for how could you study a culture if you were a foreigner and knew nothing about it? At the same time, at least some Tukanoans looked to outsiders for help with writing proposals and securing funding from international agencies for culturalist projects.

Given the scorn with which most of the nonindigenous world saw tropical forest Indians, CRIVA officials needed to demonstrate, both to outsiders and to their own constituents, the ability to function in that world—at a minimum to speak Spanish and show familiarity with Bogotá and accounting procedures. But CRIVA activists' attempts to sound knowledgeable and authoritative often came across as authoritarian and condescending, much as their local nonindigenous role models did, and the more they demonstrated their sophistication and control, the less they sounded like traditional indigenous leaders.

CRIVA's embrace of pan-indigenous solidarity could also inspire disquiet. In conversation, one of their members claimed that "[t]he people wanted an end to the sense of isolated groups, such as Desana [and] Cubeo, and [wanted to] move toward unity, so that all the groups could reunite like brothers . . . to look for unity." In fact, however, far from embracing homogeneity, as early as my 1968–1970 fieldwork, I heard worries voiced about the erosion of linguistic and settlement exogamy. Aware that prestigious outsiders found the regional system strange or even objectionable, many Tukanoans wanted, nonetheless, to preserve it, expressing worries that increasing reliance on Spanish and Portuguese and the decline of settlement exogamy presaged its collapse. Even the use of "brothers" for Tukanoans as a whole played less well locally than it did for CRIVA activists and Andean Indians who embraced pan-indigenist rhetoric.[102]

The same dissonance appears in descriptions of traditional land tenure. We saw earlier that an article in *Unidad Indígena* asserts that each Tukanoan "tribe" communally controls a clearly bounded territory, but that in actuality even local settlements' territories lack precise boundaries.[103] Furthermore, as any map will show, some settlements' closest neighbors belong to an affinally (in-law) related language group. It is no accident that the generalized image of traditional indigenous culture being attributed to Tukanoans contains notions of communal ownership of land and communal labor, as such assertions, with their anticapitalist overtones, rhetorically buttress territorial claims, an extremely important issue for Andean pueblos. We saw that another article in *Unidad Indígena* states that Tukanoan land is not only owned communally but worked communally as well.[104] While the notion of communal usufruct rights did exist at the settlement level, communal work was limited to a few infrequent activities such as fish-poisoning parties, preparation for ceremonies, and construction of malocas. The article adds that Tukanoans "live from the abundant fruits that the forest gives them spontaneously, and from hunting." The horticulturalist Tukanoans would resent this characterization, which makes them sound like another Vaupés population, the seminomadic Makú, who are discussed in the following chapter.

An image derived from the exterior—simplified and romantic—of Tukanoan society and culture was being constructed, and Tukanoans were increasingly aware of these representations.[105] They read, and some of them wrote for, *Selva y Río*, as well as *La Voz de la Tribu*. I was witness to an emergent process that was in part a case of cultural co-optation, and in part an adaptation to a new social environment. Far from being steamrollered into extinction, as was happening in way too many areas of South America, Tukanoans were being encouraged to celebrate and preserve their culture, but to represent it in ways that outsiders could easily understand and approve of.[106]

CRIVA had three stated objectives. The first, to defend the land, was self-explanatory and for the most part unproblematic—Tukanoans had more than enough territory. The second, to defend the people, involved efforts such as getting rid of the military base that had been established just outside Mitú in 1989. But what, exactly, was the meaning of the third objective, "to defend the culture"? As Handler argues, culture so conceived is a thing to be possessed and defended, something that can be lost, enriched, or stolen—in other words, a commodity, subject to all the processes to which any commodity is subject, a familiar notion in our late-capitalist society.[107] An illustration of culture seen as a thing, a possession that can be alienated, appeared in the report authored by the disgruntled NGO researcher Harold Fernández, cited earlier, who writes about one Tukanoan community that did not want to participate in his investigation because "giving information . . . would contribute to the 'robbery of culture,' which is what the anthropologists did. This ideological argument is very much cultivated by religious and political agents in the zone."[108]

A second, equally revealing example of seeing culture this way came from a CRIVA officer who told me in 1991 about a "cultural exchange" at an event featuring a group of Tukanoans located upriver from Mitú and a dance group from Cali. Each group performed their traditional dances. As it was a balanced exchange of culture—a dance for a dance—there was no risk of being seen as "robbing culture." Of course, the ethnographic record contains many examples of notions about intangible property, where something like a song might be stolen. But the idea that culture in general is able to be possessed and alienated was a new idea in the region.

Tukanoans' increasing embeddedness in the larger society contributed to their changing vision of themselves. In some respects they were rapidly becoming an ethnic group—or in the terminology preferred by the Grupo Investigadores Culturales del Vaupés (a small group of CRIVA activists tasked with raising funds), a nation composed of ethnic groups. To the degree that lowland tropical forest indigenous communities were encouraged, and as a consequence chose, to remain distinctively "ethnic"—while being ever more integrated into an increasingly multiculturalist society—the meaning of that distinctiveness shifted. In 1986 when Mitú celebrated the fiftieth anniversary of its founding, Tukanoan traditions were represented by women dancing bare-breasted, despite having covered their breasts for many years. A maloca was built to house visiting Tukanoans and to serve as a cultural center. Although it looked like a traditional maloca and the artifacts on display were "authentic," their meaning was new. Tukanoan artisans manufacturing artifacts for an emerging crafts market were expressing their identity and validating their culture by using familiar content and form. But of course the objects' meanings were new. We can see Tukanoans, especially those who lived in mission towns or near Mitú, as coming to see themselves as "having" a culture, and learning how to represent themselves in this fashion with input from both Whites and non-Tukanoan Indians.

Conclusions

In the Vaupés during the 1970s and 1980s, some traits were rethought because they had been enlisted in a political project that required deploying a nonlocal imaginary of Amazonian identity and culture. Subsequently they were either retained or cast aside. Since resemblances between certain earlier forms of Tukanoan culture and later ones might be only superficial, I have argued, treating these forms as the same would be mistaken, as would using a quasi-biological model of culture to account for these similarities and differences. When anthropologists and activists (and their nonindigenous allies) talk of culture as an ensemble of traits that endure over time, they might unwittingly be colluding in misrepresenting what is going on. In my earliest work on these issues I suggested that what was needed was to see Tukanoans not as possessing a culture so much as creating and improvising, in Bakhtinian dialogical fashion, the part of their culture they were presenting (and representing) to outsiders.

When the issue of authenticity accompanies assertions about culture (by both natives and authoritative outsiders like anthropologists and government officials), the conversation tends to shift from analytic to normative. If the new cultural forms that native peoples create as part of their political project become part of what they understand to be their tradition, even though these forms are perhaps not historically accurate, they are not spurious culture. They are genuine culture. If every Tukanoan comes to believe that in the past Tukanoans owned and worked the land communally, then this belief will be part of their culture. If Tukanoans come to refer to other Tukanoans (or all Indians) as "brother" and "sister," then this practice will be part of their culture.

When anthropologists create representations of culture that fit their a priori models, both they and native activists may unknowingly reinforce each other's arguments, especially in the many cases today where notions of authentic cultural difference are important. We will see in the following chapters that when highly politicized negotiations about culture occur, authenticity almost invariably becomes a salient issue for the stakeholders. In the 1970s and 1980s CRIVA activists tried to adapt to the changing reality, and as always happens, their actions produced unintended consequences. But if we think of such actions as examples of Tukanoans "inventing" or "manipulating" their culture, we will probably get hung up at the normative level and miss an opportunity to analyze what is going on. When ethnic and national groups speak of their culture as natural and as a *thing* that the group possesses, we need to analyze the reasoning behind such characterizations.

Assertions about land tenure or kinship terminology differ from the actual rules that distribute land or structure kinship relations, just as the construction of a highly self-conscious ideology about practice will be based on a different ontology than the one that underpins the cultural schema informing the practice. But rather than dismiss such constructions as inauthentic and inaccurate, we should focus on understanding these variations in ontological status and their meanings.

In earlier times, a traditional anthropologist's job description valorized studying "pure" and "exotic" cultures, the archetypical image being Bronislaw Malinowski on his island or Margaret Mead on hers. The profession tended to privilege those ethnographers who were willing to venture into "deepest, darkest" fieldwork sites, and it was assumed that only some groups had a "good" culture: intact, and as different from Western culture as possible. Although I have personally benefited from this received wisdom about such differentially valued field sites, I am delighted that today's expectations about fieldwork are based on very different criteria.

One reason negative words appear so often in accounts of culture change is that anthropologists, both as scholars and advocates, do mourn the loss of indigenous cultures and languages. And clearly, some people have more integrated cultures than others, and they benefit from feeling that their lifeways are meaningful, their customs are part of their ancestral inheritance, and their heritage is particularly rich. Other people might not have such a strong sense of who they are and where they come from; for whatever reason they find their material circumstances, their understandings of the world, and their sense of their own value in it greatly diminished, sometimes precipitously so. Exploitation, oppression, cultural imperialism, discrimination, and forced displacement were, and still are, found everywhere, certainly in Colombia. But "culture" is a far more complex concept than phrases like "losing their culture," "enriching their culture," or "preserving their culture" imply.

A final point returns us to the issue of normative terminology and what we might call authorized expertise. In the Vaupés, anthropologists, both those who carry out ethnographic research and those who are involved in advocacy work of various kinds, have always had opinions about what is good and bad about Tukanoan traditional cultural forms, as compared with the values and behaviors intruding from mainstream Colombian society.[109] We might not have liked *at all* how Tukanoans were choosing to adapt to their new conditions. We might see the new patterns of thought and action as indeed counterfeit, less aesthetic, less nutritious, and the like. We might see a high likelihood that the introduced changes pose a danger to Tukanoans' long-term chances for self-sufficiency, autonomy, empowerment, and so forth. Clearly, anthropologists must think about how to behave ethically and about furthering the well-being of their research community. But at the end of the day, indigenous peoples have the right to choose nonnutritious, nonbeautiful, non-"authentic" cultural forms. If the goal is to analyze such choices rather than judge them, an objective and neutral terminology is needed.

3 The State's Presence in the Vaupés Increases

The reader will remember that I began the Introduction by describing what happened to a group of allegedly uncontacted hunter-gatherer Nukak Indians who, in 1988, had suddenly and desperately appeared outside a frontier town in the department of Guaviare. Subsequently flown to Mitú, after spending two very difficult months, they were taken back to their territory. In the media maelstrom that ensued, journalists leapt on this encounter between the West and the primitive Other, asking why the División de Asuntos Indígenas (DAI) had no information at all on these people or their language. Defensive DAI authorities, feeling pressured to respond immediately, struggled to demonstrate command of the situation and commitment to the agency's indigenous constituency. As for Mitú residents, not only did no one have anything good to say about the Nukak, but I was treated to a litany of hoary tropes about "Stone Age" savages—their nudity, disgusting behavior, pathetic language, and mysterious origins.[1] This case, discussed more comprehensively here, illustrates several characteristics of official multiculturalism's entry into the region during the 1980s and early 1990s. It is followed by a second case, one that illustrates an important point made by Tania Li about the way plans and programs mutate as they travel from the metropole to the "out of the way places"[2] where they are to be implemented.[3] The actual end results often depart substantially from those originally envisioned by program designers. In 1983 a "shaman school" was included among the various initiatives taken by the Colombian Ministry of Health that were intended to support and strengthen traditional medical systems in the Vaupés. In actuality it was a kind of workshop designed to teach some aspects of traditional Tukanoan medicine to would-be shaman apprentices. The program's failure, in particular the negative reactions it elicited even ten years later, illustrates the ways in which unwarranted assumptions may be embedded in such projects. The two cases pair nicely to illustrate state intervention processes in the region.

The "Uncontacted"

Because no one spoke their language, the group of Nukak who suddenly appeared in Calamar in April 1988,[4] at this point all of them women and children, represented a total mystery as to who they were, where they came from, and why they had left the forest to make contact in so public a fashion. It gradually became clear that they were by no means untouched by Western society, that they were in fact a subgroup of the Makú, a generic term for nomadic foraging peoples,[5] and that they had stayed deep in the forest as protection against threats to their physical and cultural survival. In addition to periodic exchanges with other indigenous peoples like the Sikuani, Curripaco, and Cubeo, the Nukak had interacted a little with Whites, helping themselves to field crops, or suffering the abduction of Nukak children by *llaneros* (plainsmen, i.e., nonindigenous peasants), supposedly to civilize the children but in fact as a source of cheap servants. Encounters could turn violent: in one instance Nukak killed a llanero they encountered in the forest, and in a 1965 incident three Nukak were killed and a Nukak couple were jailed in the town of Villavicencio.[6]

The language spoken by the Nukak belongs to a family generally known as Makú-Puinave, spoken by traditionally nomadic peoples in Guaviare and in territories to the east, including the Colombian and Brazilian Vaupés. By the time of the encounter narrated here, most Makú peoples living to the east of Guaviare had been sedentarized. However, the Nukak living between the Guaviare and Inírida Rivers, who numbered perhaps seven hundred to a thousand, remained nomadic, moving their camps every three to five days and walking four to eight hours each day.[7]

Media accounts of their dramatic emergence from the forest emphasized the warm welcome Calamar residents extended to the visitors, finding them peaceful, good-natured, curious, sensitive, happy, and amiable.[8] Residents created committees to find lodging and provide food, clothing, and protection. Virtually all the town's civic organizations (communal action committees, labor unions, the Sports Committee, the Prostitutes' Club) became involved, and all of them submitted proposals for dealing with the visitors.

Why the group chose to make themselves known at that moment became clear only later. As it turned out, they had been fleeing punishment meted out by a spirit that had sent a "magical dart" called *gripe* (flu). The spirit had been summoned by llaneros because a Nukak family had kidnapped a two-year-old White child in retaliation for a Nukak kidnapping. As the Nukak saw it, a number of deaths and injuries resulting from an armed encounter between insurgent guerrillas and the army were also part of the punishment.[9] After an epidemic killed many Nukak, especially among the men, the Calamar group, originally eighty in number, decided to travel west.[10]

It was evident that these people were no strangers to violence: two had pieces of shrapnel in their shoulders, and all of them reacted fearfully to aircraft. Both Leonardo Reina, a linguist, and Leslie Wirpsa told me they believed that members of the group had suffered two attacks, one terrestrial and one aerial, the latter probably from a helicopter. The region, far from isolated or safe, was the stopping point for prospectors in search of uranium, gold, and oil, as well as narcotraffickers, right-wing paramilitary squads, left-wing guerrillas, the army, and police antinarcotics teams.[11]

Calamar authorities decided that despite the warm local welcome, the Nukak could not remain. Although remarkably adept at imitating White gestures and speech, they could not communicate with anyone, and some seem depressed, especially the women, who stayed behind in their hammocks as their children went visiting. Town authorities contacted authorities and journalists in Bogotá, who traveled to Calamar.[12] To everyone's surprise, two New Tribes missionaries also showed up, one of whom, Michael Conduff, spoke Nukak, and the other, Daniel Germann, understood it. Germann had worked with a different Nukak subgroup beginning in 1966, and NT had begun its work with them in 1974. Although the missionaries had periodically sent reports to DAI about their activities, they had referred to the people in question as Makú, and as a result the Nukak had not been officially recognized as a distinct pueblo.

The effort to help the visitors called for returning them to their "place of origin," a nonsensical goal, given that, as nomads, they had no place of origin and were, as anthropologist Carlos Zambrano points out, already in their territory.[13] A consensus was reached to send the group to their putative Makú "elder kinsmen" living in Wacará, a Kakwa-speaking community near Mitú where SIL teams had been working since the late sixties. First came a preliminary fact-finding trip, during which DAI, the Consejo Regional Indígena del Vaupés (CRIVA), and the Organización Nacional Indígena de Colombia

(ONIC) arranged for two Kakwa couples to be flown to Calamar. Despite doubts about the voluntary nature of the couples' participation, authorities insisted they were inspired to go by a tape of the Nukak speaking and singing. What was in effect a month-long orientation workshop ensued.

In April 1989, twenty-six Nukak were flown to Mitú. A video shows them being greeted by a crowd at the airport and taken to the hospital, where they were examined and treated. They were then taken to Wacará. What happened there remains a mystery, but after fifteen days they asked to return to Mitú.[14] Authorities in Mitú and Bogotá were at a loss over what to do next. The group stayed there until May 28.

I arrived in July. My initial conversations on the subject, whose negative tone puzzled me, prompted me to begin more systematic interviews. As I learned, the Nukak's return from Wacará had prompted a spate of stories and adverse opinion. No one had anything good to say about them. Some Tukanoans claimed that the Wacará Kakwa had never wanted the Nukak, whom they considered savages, but had been afraid to go against DAI. Others said, to the contrary, that the Wacará people *had* offered a warm welcome, but the Nukak had not wanted to remain. The demographic imbalance between the two groups had definitely created problems and would, everyone felt, continue to do so. The four adult Nukak, all widows and a strain on their hosts' resources, were clearly disappointed by the lack of available men. Wirpsa told me the women were "pleasantly aggressive" in their search for partners. Whatever the effects of this behavior in Wacará, it certainly stirred up gossip in Mitú.

A litany of stories circulated in Mitú about Nukak ignorance and lack of civilization. During their stay in Wacará they were said to have cut down a weathervane at the SIL airstrip for firewood. They neither bathed for real nor willingly accepted clothes. They stole bananas and pineapples from people's gardens. The women refused to help with garden work.[15] It was said that they looked like monkeys. They ate raw meat, even human flesh. One story had a Nukak woman chewing away on a live monkey. Their ability at mimicking Spanish speech and gestures was taken as a sign of low development, indicative of childlike mentality and a lack of proper language. Nukak women supposedly made advances on all kinds of men, even the soldiers from the nearby military base. One anecdote had it that Nukak women thwarted an attempted rape by soldiers by catching their testicles in their teeth, ready to bite them off and eat them. A delegation of Cubeo offered to take the Makusitos (little Makús) back to their village and feed and shelter them in exchange for garden and domestic work, but not surprisingly, the DAI representative declined the proposal.[16] The crisis reached the point that some Tukanoans would pull their children away when a Nukak passed nearby. Concern for the group's safety prompted the authorities to virtually imprison them in the house they had been given. It was clearly an impossible situation.

The anti-Nukak stories, offered even by some of my close Tukanoan friends, appalled me. Even in my earliest fieldwork years before, derogatory talk about Makú had made me extremely uncomfortable. During that time a newsmagazine article I had with photographs of starving Biafrans, victims of the civil war in Nigeria, had elicited howls of laughter and comments that those people must be the Makú of that place, for they clearly could not feed themselves adequately. I on the other hand could hardly contain my anger at their words, which reminded me of my relatives' bigoted remarks about African-Americans during my childhood in Mississippi and Florida.

In late June representatives of DAI flew to the New Tribes Mission station, which consisted of a house for the missionaries, a shelter for visiting Nukak, an airstrip, and a dispensary. A dramatic videotape of the plane's arrival shows at least fifty Nukak running away, the first incontrovertible evidence that there were many more of them in the area than had been claimed. On May 28 the Nukak in Mitú were flown to the station. Upon arriving, they again underwent medical examination and treatment. Videotape footage shows them taking off their clothes, putting on woven fiber arm and leg bands, and sleeping in the forest before they left for good.

Traditional Makú-Tukanoan Relations

That both Tukanoans and Whites despised the Nukak did not completely surprise me. But I was perplexed by Tukanoan vehemence, and by how much more strongly they seemed to feel than the Whites did. Their attitudes were undoubtedly conditioned by ignorance of and aversion to Nukak lifeways, in particular to nomadism and the foraging economy, as well as by near universal ethnocentric attitudes toward difference and alterity.[17] Differences in hygiene, clothing (or its lack), and sexuality are everywhere likely to inspire condemnation, as was certainly the case here. Makú were said to urinate in the river, lack proper body adornment, and disregard what, for Tukanoans, were basic food taboos. Even the name Makú in many of the region's languages simply meant wild, savage people.

But Tukanoan hostility also followed from the traditional subordination of Makú in regional hierarchies. In the past, Makú had sometimes entered into temporary servitude: a brief visit during festivities, in which meat, labor, or various forest products were exchanged for cultivated foods and White trade items, might be extended for longer periods. Makú subordination would be dramatized by, among other things, demands that they light cigars for Tukanoan men. By the late 1980s Makú servitude was a thing of the past, but its memory undoubtedly conditioned negative attitudes toward the Nukak, who were sometimes characterized as "less than Makú." The residents of Wacará, themselves having only recently "overcome" the traditional Makú lifestyle, were perhaps especially sensitive on the subject.

Differences between Makú and Tukanoans, in reality a matter of degree, were often expressed as stark binary oppositions.[18] The fact that Makú took marriage partners from within their linguistic group violated Tukanoan norms, for it meant that they "married their sisters," making them "like animals." Makú-like characters in Tukanoan myths serve as examples of what not to do, stern reminders of what can happen when people become lazy, lustful, selfish, or negligent. Makú also play an important, if implicit, role in clan ranking. Several authors report that characteristics attributed to Makú also describe low-ranking Tukanoan clans,[19] who may be described as formerly naked, speaking incorrectly, and playing a servile role.

Tukanoan explanations of their social order and the position of Makú within it resemble the ideology of many ranked systems: described on the one hand as inherently inferior or even as "not people," such peoples are on the other hand sometimes conceded the possibility of improving, "if only they would . . ." This oscillation between separation and partial acceptance makes for ambivalent, complicated relationships. As a category the Other is treated as completely distinct, even though members of that category are known to have been absorbed into the superior group.

For many Tukanoans the Nukak's arrival exacerbated ambivalence about indigenous identity, reminding them of issues they would have preferred to sublimate. Traditional subordination of the Makú was challenged by new ideas about the nature of indigeneity, especially Tukanoan indigeneity. During a showing of two British films about the region, *War of the Gods* and *Last of the Cuiva* (both from Granada Television), Tukanoan viewers were discomfited by sympathetic depictions of the hunter-gatherer way of life. They joked afterward about what they saw as primitive and crude lifeways. Part of their confusion and uneasiness undoubtedly stemmed from seeming contradictions between positive depictions of nomadic lifeways and their own past experiences with White scorn for all "uncivilized" indigenous lifeways. Tukanoans living in and around Mitú were hearing multiculturalist discourses about a pan-indigenous identity, one that by implication would lump them with the Makú in a seemingly positive way (as opposed to past stigma against all indios). The notion that the Makú were just like other groups in the Vaupés, that they were brothers of Tukanoans, or worse, that foraging and nomadism might be held up for emulation as embodiments of the "ecological native,"[20] inspired confusion and ambivalence among my interlocutors. A young Cubeo man joked that in a research proposal being written by a group of CRIVA members, Makú should head the list of Vaupés ethnic groups "because they are always put last," thus signaling his awareness of the new ethos of equality and perhaps the need to appease potential donors by giving it lip service. Endorsements of dignity and respect for everyone were appearing in the publications of ONIC and progressive nonindigenous organizations, as well as in missionary sermons and texts. But in in the issues of *La Voz de la Tribu* that I examined, I found no mention, let alone praise of the Makú.

Anti-Makú hostility was exacerbated by claims by local Whites that Tukanoans no longer wanted to preserve their culture, which was ironic, given that many Whites had formerly worked hard to suppress it. In the previous continuum of indigenous-White ranking, Makú-Nukak would be at the bottom and Whites at the top, but in the conflicting message now emanating, although Whites stayed at the top of the ladder, in some respects Makú-Nukak epitomized "authentic," "good" indigeneity—consisting of ecological sensitivity, self-sufficiency, egalitarianism, and so forth. In this sense, Makú-Nukak exemplified a kind of *hyperreal* Indian, Alcida Ramos's characterization of an imaginary of The Native suitable for indigenous-rights NGO purposes: that is, a "bureaucratizable Indian." Flesh-and-blood Indians, she writes, would have to be either kept at arm's length or "filtered and tamed, transformed into model Indians."[21]

I believe that these experiences helped generate Tukanoans' remarkably antipathetic reactions to the Nukak visitors. The traditional structures of feeling accompanying Tukanoan views of Makú featured dominance and ambivalence. Such sentiments also characterized Tukanoan-White relations, but there Tukanoans were the subordinates, and the Nukak perhaps represented a kind of fall guy or scapegoat onto whom these upsetting parallels were projected. By 1988 nonindigenous Calamar townspeople, on the one hand, were culturally and socially distant enough from the Nukak to find them unthreatening, almost as pets (easier perhaps, given that they were all women and children). Tukanoans living in Mitú, on the other hand, lacked the distance needed to feel they were not threatened. Just as the Nukak very likely reminded the Wacará Makú of their recent stigmatized past, so they reminded Tukanoans of their inferior status vis-à-vis Whites. The way Nukak were attended to by high-status authorities increased resentment and discomfort. (The commissariat and DAI gave them food and the clinic looked after their health.) Tukanoans knew how far they were from the high-status White lifestyle, and now it seemed that some of what they had understood they needed to discard had suddenly turned into valuable symbolic and cultural capital.

Discussion

The Calamar Nukak's mysterious appearance and their subsequent sojourn in the Vaupés bring up several issues. One is the role played by New Tribes missionaries, who had been in contact with one subgroup of Nukak since 1966. NT had known of at least eight hundred Nukak divided into seven clans,[22] and the two missionaries at the NT station personally knew three hundred and fifty of them. But they had never sent DAI a list of these people or, for that matter, other relevant information about their own operations.[23] Government officials had to learn about the mission and its efforts bit by bit—from airplane schedules, medical services, linguistic work, documents, and photographs. Although a smattering of published information about the Nukak (in which they were called Makú) did surface,[24] they had not received any public recognition. How could scholarly institutions and government agencies not have had information on more than eight hundred Indians? How could a North American missionary group have maintained such a monopoly on access and information for so long?[25] And after it was learned that some information had been sent and it became accessible, why did no one demand that NT comply with the terms of its contract? This issue provoked considerable criticism during two Bogotá conferences on the Nukak that I attended later on in the summer. All the authorities who were involved with the problems the Nukak were experiencing and with whom I spoke believed that at the beginning of the crisis NT had purposely concealed how many other groups of Nukak there were.

The video footage of the Nukak's return to the NT mission station suggested that at least some subgroups would continue to avoid contact with the White world except when needing medical attention. After twenty years NT had failed to either sedentarize the Nukak or convert them to Christianity. Under such circumstances, what should be the role of the state? It had delegated to the Catholic Church the task of educating indigenous children in remote areas, and it had allowed North American missionary groups like SIL and NT to proselytize indigenous communities.[26] The consensus among people working to resolve the crisis was that the Nukak themselves should control access to their territory, and no organization should be given "a carte blanche to do what they want," as one advocate put it. Nonetheless, despite complaints that "Colombia's sovereignty is being compromised!" no detailed alternative proposal emerged. The solution eventually chosen, promoted as a way to allow the Nukak to return to the forest, kept NT on as the intermediary.

Everyone agreed that Colombian officialdom had botched the problem. The decision to fly the group of Nukak women and children to Mitú to live with their "elder Makú kinsmen" had been a rushed and ill-considered response to pressure from the media, ONIC, anthropologists, and left-leaning intellectuals. DAI subsequently was accused of promoting "Nukak tours," and ONIC of grandstanding. Worse, the return of the group to the forest provoked the highest mortality rate (due to respiratory diseases) the Nukak had known until then, because no one thought to quarantine the returning individuals.[27]

The future looked grim for the Nukak. In managing their own affairs, sedentary Tukanoans and other pueblos can call on the mechanism of the cabildo, but there was no Nukak institution that could even begin to play this role. Who would administer the territory? How would it be secured? It was clear that a study was badly needed, but not what kind of study, under whose auspices, or with what goals. How to ensure that the study's results would help rather than harm the Nukak? Yet despite the dangers of intervention, the Nukak could not be left to fend for themselves, given the lawlessness and turmoil in the region. Colonos, guerrillas, narcotraffickers, and antinarcotics police were hardly ideal cultural brokers, which was one reason why NT was allowed to resume its role in the region.

The response to the Nukak crisis and its ultimate outcome show some of the rapid changes in mainstream Colombian society's perceptions of indigeneity. In the past, nomadic groups in the llanos became newsworthy subjects only when they were victims of massacres. Perhaps the most famous case, known as the Planas affair, involved Sikuani (also called Guahibos) living in the department of Meta, who were slaughtered after llaneros invited them to drink whiskey in 1969. When the perpetrators were arrested and tried, the defense argued that they had not known it was illegal to kill Indians.[28] Note that a 1965 violent encounter, known as Charras, between Nukak and llaneros marked the *beginning* of outright hostile attitudes in that area.[29] Peaceful encounters had taken place earlier. For example, the cover of *Los Nikak: Nómadas de la Amazonia colombiana,* a 1999 book by Cabrera, Franky, and Mahecha, displays a photograph of a colono blowing on a musical instrument with a group of eight Nukak standing nearby. The photograph had appeared in 1965 in the daily newspaper *El Espectador.*[30]

By now the Nukak are decidedly well-known.[31] They have survived as a pueblo, though their numbers were reduced by 40 percent during the first five years of contact, and as of 2017 they number around six hundred and fifty.[32] In 1994 the juridical personhood of their self-appointed protector, NT, was revoked by the Constitutional Court, and the mission station was closed down. Though this outcome was celebrated by progressives, it cast the Nukak loose, encouraging migration to urban areas.[33] Not surprisingly, the ongoing violence in the region resulted in massive forced displacement of Nukak.

After their mysterious appearance in 1988 the Nukak began to play the role of poster "primitives." In the Bogotá world of high fashion, a newspaper article from 2003 calls Francy Buitrago, a Nukak, "the model with nomadic blood." Although ostensibly modern and urban, she succeeds in "stealing" the fashion show runway due to her highly exoticized otherness; for example, her completely plucked eyebrows receive serious attention.[34] Another example comes from San José del Guaviare and environs, where the notion of the "ecological native" has been fully exploited by fitting Nukak to this imaginary, in particular as environmental stewards. This "tribe that survived the Paleolithic"[35] fits Whites' preconceptions of "good" indigenous populations; "ideas about innocence, nudity, nobility and docility emerged as indelible marks" of the Nukak's radical Otherness, perceived as characteristic values of "the last green nomads."[36] The development of this notion was helped by UNESCO's designation of Nukak knowledge of nature and their oral tradition as the intangible patrimony of all humankind.[37] The Guaviare region's self-representation as an "eco-ethno-tourist destination" draws on this "last green nomads" construction:

> Nukak iconography is evoked in designs that highlight the exoticism Guaviare offers to its visitors . . . the name and the decorations placed in restaurants, cafés, shops, murals, posters, food products and shoe stores, turning the Nukak into

> a kind of local trademark of an ethnicity that "sells." Indeed, it sells because it folds perfectly into the idyllic and nostalgic views that equate indigeneity with purity, and ahistorical character with traditions.[38]

Unfortunately, this idyllic image is challenged by the presence of displaced Nukak roaming San José streets, begging.[39]

Paradoxically, pueblos like the Nukak that best fit such hyperreal imaginaries tend to encounter the most difficulties in getting their rights recognized. Although representations of the Nukak turned them into hyperreal Indians, in some important respects the state could not "see" them.[40] Carlos del Cairo discusses how Nukak are having to "modernize" in order to be "traditional," needing to transform their political organization structures and abandon nomadism so as to conform "to the normative preconceptions of how indigenous communities must be organized."[41]

Sedentary communities can form cabildos that represent the collectivity to state and para-state actors. In Chapter One I discussed how dispersed populations in lowland areas had to modify their traditional political structures so as to allow their supposedly traditional cabildos and capitanías to play this role. But nomadic foragers, with no traditional institutions that could be molded into such representative bodies, remain outside the state's range of view. In the early 1990s it was very clear that collectively made decisions were not likely to be forthcoming among Nukak subgroups, as each one avoided the others and described them with terms like "garbage, dirty, gross, aggressive, and envious." They were also said to be likely to practice sorcery.[42] Encounters between subgroups are described as tense, some of them including ritualized aggression.[43]

During the 1988 crisis ONIC and CRIVA officials represented their organizations as the best intermediaries for the Nukak because their organizations were indigenous. Twenty-five years later, Guaviare Tukanos[44] claimed that "they, as indigenous people, know how to properly interpret the feelings and the expectations of the Nukak people," because, first, the Nukak were absent in political organizations and discussions; second, they did not have a democratically elected, centralized organization (a capitanía); and third, none of their leaders spoke Spanish.[45]

Today, the sudden appearance of "uncontacted" groups in lowland South America almost inevitably occasions a frenzy of media attention. Reports of such sightings often go viral: videos of near-naked men shooting arrows at airplanes offer a dramatic confirmation of Western conventional wisdom about such radically Other people. However, it is clear that there are no longer any truly "uncontacted" people in the region; rather, groups of what are sometimes called "voluntarily isolated" people are fleeing further contact. Invariably, when we learn the nature of such encounters we understand the group's reluctance to engage further. In some countries today, officially designated "voluntarily isolated tribes" in remote areas are allowed to decline any contact with state authorities, who in turn prohibit any other actor (e.g., loggers, gold prospectors) from entering the territory. Nation-states are supposed to have certain minimal responsibilities toward their citizens: to count and locate them, provide protection, and offer services like health care and education. But given small, nomadic, forest-dwelling populations' vulnerability with respect to diseases against which they have no immunity, voluntary isolation came to be viewed in some quarters as the best means of protection, after conclusive evidence in a number of countries indicated that very vulnerable populations were invariably negatively impacted by any kind of contact with the dominant society. In addition to the threat posed by infectious disease, an inability to remain self-sufficient is often mentioned. Note that when legislated, voluntary isolation brings with it a slew of unintended negative consequences.[46]

As the option of voluntary isolation had not even been conceptualized in the late 1980s, the Nukak's plight provoked many discussions about how much contact, and to what end, should be allowed.[47] While everyone agreed that territory should be set aside for them, and while Colombia was ahead of its neighbors with respect to legislating a collective land tenure regime, the nomadic Nukak posed a set of insurmountable problems. The traditional territory of the thirteen subgroups was enormous. A reserve was established in 1989, followed later by a resguardo that eventually comprised 955,000 hectares—which was not, however, traditional Nukak territory.

The Shaman School

Beginning in the early 1980s the Ministry of Health began to pay serious attention to the negative consequences of bringing Western medicine to indigenous communities. During this period legislation concerned with health care services for the country's pueblos decreed that state-sponsored health care needed to coexist "with the traditional indigenous systems and be compatible with them."[48] The new laws were intended to increase grassroots participation in remote area programs targeting improved nutrition, health education, and other measures. In the local hierarchies established by the laws, *auxiliares de enfermería* (nursing aides) would be supervised by Ministry of Health staff, and *promotores de salud* (health promoters) would link indigenous communities to local clinics.

In 1983 Mitú saw the beginning of a more ambitious program, one aimed at taking an "empirical" approach to gathering and disseminating traditional shamanic knowledge. Referred to as the "first shaman congress" and a "congress of traditional doctors," the program was the creation of anthropologist Juan Guevara, an employee of the Ministry of Health in charge of community health programs. Also referred to as a shaman school,[49] it took the form of a workshop in which shamans would teach some of their knowledge and practices to interested young Tukanoan men. Guevara—a dedicated official who had worked in public health for more than fifteen years, and the author of an anthropology thesis based on fieldwork in the region—was particularly interested in creating programs that recognized and valorized traditional health practices. The author of reports on a wide range of topics concerned with health in indigenous communities, he guided the Vaupés Health Service, in collaboration with local communities, in publishing several illustrated pamphlets in Spanish and two indigenous languages dealing with tuberculosis, stomach diseases, oral health, traditional plant remedies for snake bite, and community health promotion.

A report on the shaman school that Guevara wrote in 1983 fails to mention several problems that emerged during and after the workshop. Privately, he confided to me ten years later[50] that problems had been rife, because the agendas had been over full, and even more, because the shamans involved fought among themselves. Guevara's vision of his work was a complex one. Committed to advocacy anthropology and contemptuous of anthropologists (particularly foreigners) interested only in "collecting data," he said his goal was to recast the hegemonic relationship between the dominant society and Tukanoans, a relationship that was encouraging Tukanoans to despise everything indigenous. Anxious to improve Tukanoan health, he was often stymied by newly introduced problems—pollution, malnutrition, and alcoholism, and diseases like tuberculosis, hepatitis B, and cholera—as well as by the wide dispersal of settlements, minimal access to even the most rudimentary elements of Western medicine, and the way that health workers denigrated traditional medical beliefs and practices.

Guevara had a mixed view of traditional medicine: some practices he thought effective, and others at least had a beneficial placebo effect. More importantly, the loss of shamanism and other traditional practices was creating a vacuum in local authority. If the shaman school inspired Whites' respect for traditional medicine, he felt, Tukanoans would be less inclined to abandon their culture. Many of the specific health problems in the Vaupés would not be affected by this campaign promoting what he preferred to call "ecological medicine." But the shamans, whom he envisioned less as doctors than as naturists or ecological practitioners, safeguarded community well-being and even the cosmos by acting in the natural and spiritual environment.

Guevara wrote about Tukanoan traditional medicine,[51] but he admitted that he found writing extremely difficult, as he felt inferior to the foreign anthropologists with their advanced degrees who had worked in the Vaupés. A radical leftist, he seemed to identify with Tukanoan oppression, comparing it to Colombia's position at the bottom of a ladder whose highest rungs were occupied by multinational interests, most of them North American. Any conversation with him sooner or later ended up in a polemic against the United States and its hold over Colombia. The gringos, he said, had "invented everything by now" and were destroying Colombia by addicting it to the U.S. drug market—diatribes that sometimes left this gringa interlocutor distinctly uncomfortable, though he gave no sign of having me in mind.

The shaman school was held in the mission town of Acaricuara. It was supposed to do two things: first, analyze the problems generated by the encounter between indigenous and White medicine, and second, provide a setting in which shamans (locally called *payés* in Spanish) could pass on their knowledge. The shaman-teachers were paid by the Ministry of Health and by the Convenio Colombo-Holandés de Salud, a public health project receiving funding from The Netherlands.

Although the shaman school was a distinct failure in passing along shamanic knowledge, it nonetheless improved on the ethnocentric and paternalistic public health programs developed for many Latin American indigenous communities. Until multiculturalism appeared in the Vaupés, missionaries, both Catholic and Protestant, had openly denounced shamans as the arch-enemy, and in the case of New Tribes evangelists, as agents of the Devil himself. Secular authorities, no less negative, viewed shamans as the most extreme Other, whose baleful influence on Tukanoan communities depended on "superstition" and other retrograde aspects of local culture. Guevara's initiative was the first official project in the Vaupés, and probably in the country as a whole, to attribute value to shamanic tradition and to present respect for indigenous practice as advisable and even essential. He felt strongly that, given the unavailability of Western health care, health projects in indigenous communities should be designed to fill the gap inevitably left by the disappearance of traditional shamanic medicine.[52]

Of all the change agents I met in the region, Guevara had Tukanoan interests most in mind. Unlike the many anthropologists, such as myself, who involved themselves briefly with development or research projects and then returned home, he was in the Vaupés for the long haul. In addition to working directly with Tukanoans to preserve threatened aspects of their culture, he wrote to sway the opinion of power holders and other influential people. Avoiding the reductionist approaches of some public health projects, he took an expansive vision of Tukanoan health, promoting traditional healing because he felt it could be medically efficacious—if not directly then by increasing patient confidence—and because it might diminish non-Tukanoan dominance. His project was nonetheless doomed, mostly by factors beyond his control, but also by poor project design and by his limited and naïve understanding of traditional medicine.

Tukanoan Schoolteachers' Analysis of the Shaman School

In the summer of 1993, while attending a two-week ethno-education workshop sponsored by the Ministry of Education, I heard thirteen Tukanoan schoolteachers, all men, offer their postmortem on the shaman school project. What they said must be put in the context of ethno-education more generally. The move toward ethno-education began in 1975, when Colombia nationalized primary and secondary education, thus ending the Catholic Church's monopoly on schooling in the national territories. The following year, moving toward decentralization of education policy, the government passed the law that created the Regional Educational Fund (Fondo Educativo Regional, FER).[53] One part of this law established what was called ethno-education, the result of various international treaties on minority rights Colombia had signed, as well as pressure from the indigenous movement.

In a nutshell, *ethno-education* is a "permanent social process, immersed in the culture, which consists of the acquisition of knowledge and values, and in the development of capabilities, in keeping with the needs, interests and aspirations of the community, which will give to it the capacity to fully participate in the cultural control by the ethnic group."[54]

Intended to be flexible, participative, bilingual, intercultural, and systematic, ethno-education became an important component of managed multiculturalism. Colombian anthropologist Axel Rojas considers ethno-education to be a component of the Colombian state's governmentalization of culture, with a mission to define who are considered Others and under which circumstances. Like all pedagogical projects, he says, "ethnoeducation seeks to form a particular type of subject, in this case, the ethnic subject." Ethnic groups must make visible, recover, and strengthen their culture, one that is invariably represented "as incommensurable and always in apparent opposition to that which is considered the dominant, modern, Western, Eurocentric or universal culture; that is to say, a subaltern, traditional, non-Western, non-Eurocentric, and local culture."[55]

Yolanda Bodnar, the director of the Mitú ethno-education team (later she became Minister of Education) told the workshop attendees that ethno-education promotes cultural relativism: although cultures may differ, no culture is inferior or superior to any other. Also, one has to learn about one's culture: one cannot say, "If I'm a member of a culture, then I know it." One also must learn how to criticize one's culture rather than only talk about its "nice" features. She commented to me that ethno-education workshops were intended to convince local teachers that it was possible to control curricular content, that they did not have to passively accept the Ministry's "little packages." Rather, teachers should seek input from the community and fashion a curriculum that was suited to local needs.

The three Mitú team members, who had worked together previously, always in peasant communities, clearly meshed well, but none of them had any experience in indigenous communities. It was apparent that they knew next to nothing about the region, or about indigenous activism, knowledge gaps that would surface repeatedly as issues during the two weeks.[56]

The shaman school project came up again and again during this workshop; team members discovered early on that mentioning it would invariably spark discussion of just what ethno-education was all about. One team member told the participants that although Tukanoans had their traditional healers, getting the best possible health required an exchange of medical traditions: "we have to fill in the spaces"—meaning the gaps in local health-maintaining activities and knowledge—"with proper language and content." She added that if they did not do this for themselves, "then someone—the Summer Institute of Linguistics, for example—*tells* you what to do." Coercive external relationships must stop, she said, but at the same time the community should remain open to suggestions from the outside. It should not "close down completely and say 'no one is permitted to enter here.'"

The shaman school postmortem during the workshop illustrates many of the problems generated by development projects in the Vaupés. Deeply disappointed with the outcome of the project, the schoolteachers worried that some diseases would soon be untreatable because the shaman school had not solved the problem of the older generation's knowledge dying with them. Also, as just one of many failed projects in the region, the shaman school's fate seemed to reflect negatively on Tukanoans as a whole. Although these projects had been poorly conceived, designed, and implemented, the schoolteachers tended to blame themselves. One of them asked, "Is it that we are blockheads? [¿Es que somos brutos?]" "Well, there are a lot of backward people among us," a fellow schoolteacher replied.

The schoolteachers were also frustrated because the shaman school had promised to increase Tukanoan self-sufficiency, symbolize community values, and promote Tukanoans' active participation and intergenerational connection in shaping their future. The government, it seemed, was finally recognizing the value of at least some aspects of traditional Tukanoan culture. For once, Whites were not only interested in an area of Tukanoan knowledge, they were even willing to pay people to help preserve it.

Some of the schoolteachers' negative judgments were directed at the shamans themselves. Several called the shamans egotistical: despite having agreed to participate, the practitioners had been suspicious of one another and unwilling to share their knowledge. One schoolteacher mentioned a shaman in his settlement who had been so possessive of his knowledge that he refused to teach even his own son; rather, "he threw his sacred equipment in the river." Another schoolteacher described a shaman who preferred to die with all of his knowledge—he was not willing to share even a spell against venomous snakes. "They don't want to share the spells . . . we, the young people, are paying for such egotism because when we get sick there's no one to cure us." Rivalry among shamans, often occurring along language group lines, was also criticized.

Predictably, the question of money came up several times. One schoolteacher asserted that, rather than sharing knowledge and putting the community's interests first, a shaman, wanting to create a monopoly, would claim, "only I can do this." Despite the schoolteachers' criticisms, payment is in fact part of traditional shamanic practice: shamans pay their teachers and, in turn, are compensated by clients with items like shirts, cartons of cigarettes, and battery-powered electronics. Ambivalence about the financial aspects of traditional shamanism surfaced again and again. "It's all a business," said one. Shamans were described as unwilling to teach what they knew because they feared their apprentices only wanted to become rich. A Cubeo schoolteacher said that he had been studying traditional medicine with a shaman and that he had learned seventy spells. He also was studying how to write in Cubeo so he could transcribe the spells. But a man said to him, "You are doing this to earn money, which is prohibited."

Another topic concerned Guevara's format and setting for the school. The schoolteachers agreed that many elements had been missing or dubious: its location, the mission town of Acaricuara, was a far cry from the traditional maloca where healing rituals usually took place. Nor were the schoolteachers sure about what "empirical medicine" meant. One man began to explain it by speaking of indigenous science:

> Empiricism . . . this empirical school . . . well, the maloca illustrates it, the maloca is the peak of the culture, of indigenous science. It is like a school, for the young. Including the purgatives. What significance did all of these practices have? We can't know. We believe that bad things enter through the mouth and thus a young man has to maintain himself in a pure state with purgatives. [Traditional shaman apprenticeship] was a true school, everyone with his stomach purified, with his person purified. Then everyone would have the capacity to concentrate on this indigenous science. With *yajé* [a hallucinogenic infusion made from *Banisteriopsis caapi*]. But now, they don't do all of this practice, this self-maintenance, so it will be difficult. The effect of the yajé on the dancer is to be showing him . . . everything. Exactly the same happens with the shaman.

Another teacher agreed that shamans traditionally taught their apprentices under the effects of yajé, noting that although shamans took yajé, chewed coca, and prayed using tobacco, they were never addicts. Even today, he added, prayers are made before allowing a youth to take coca for the first time.

Other conditions had not been met either, and so "the shamans said, 'this isn't permitted. You have to have a special diet, a special preparation, in order to learn.'" In the Vaupés, as in many parts of lowland South America, learning to be a shaman takes a long time and involves sacrifices, such as abstaining from certain foods and activities. The schoolteachers knew this perfectly well.

They also agreed that a great deal of shamanic knowledge could not be taught "empirically," and understood that the shamans would teach only what they were comfortable passing on in such a setting. They had hoped, nonetheless, that some shamanic knowledge could be taught following Western pedagogical models. In order to establish such a shaman school, the shamans "would have to abandon some of their traditions. For example, [in earlier times] the grandfather or the father,[57] when the son was born, would go through a process to turn him into a shaman. They were very strict. And the same continues. . . . Like the requirements for entering a university, there are strict rules."

The schoolteachers also noted that the fate of the shaman school had depended on the overall situation of shamanism in the region. One said that since missionaries had, until recently, opposed all ceremonies—particularly those involving shamanism and consumption of yajé—this part of Tukanoan culture had disappeared almost entirely in certain regions and among certain language groups, most notably the Tukano language group. Another teacher noted that most shamans themselves no longer lived in malocas. Several said that lazy young Tukanoans were reluctant to study shamanism in the proper manner. A teacher jokingly commented that one would-be apprentice expected to learn everything in a single night. Another observed that shamans so feared the inroads of Western medicine into their practice that they had decided to quit. One shaman threw away his paraphernalia when he converted to evangelical Protestantism. Another schoolteacher said he knew of someone who was both learning how to be a community health promoter at the Mitú clinic and continuing to practice as a shaman—but no one in Mitú knew he was a shaman.

The schoolteachers returned insistently to lessons about preserving culture that had emerged from the shaman school experiment. What could one do, for instance, to preserve a practice that could be taught only by specialists, many of whom did not want to teach under what they saw as inappropriate conditions? Was the shaman school format indeed the only way to save shamanic knowledge? Would the culture preserved be authentic if transmitted in an untraditional manner? One schoolteacher noted that even though individuals like himself wanted to preserve Tukanoan culture, what could teachers do with respect to traditional medicine? Although as teachers they could teach a child the names of trees, health promotors could not teach traditional prayers and chants. And although they were all Tukanoans, in a sense traditional medicine was not "their" culture. The whole notion of culture preservation was hard to apply because it was unclear who "owned" these areas of culture; did they belong to everyone, or just the specialists? Judgmental statements surfaced during the conversations: was the shamans' unwillingness to share what they knew justified, or not?

The schoolteachers spoke approvingly of the fact that the shaman school did not involve transmitting "patterns culturally very foreign to us"—which they themselves had to do in the classroom. Indeed, their bitter complaints about having to act as brokers between nonindigenous culture and what Tukanoan children were learning at home might have been the main reason for the schoolteachers' disappointment in the outcome of the shaman school. They complained about feeling caught in a bind, trying to save some elements of traditional Tukanoan culture at risk of disappearing, while at the same time working to ensure that other elements did disappear. One commented that, as schoolteachers, they were products of a formation distant from their own culture (lo nuestro), and their pedagogical mission in the classroom was dictated by that "foreign" formation. He acknowledged that they needed to "promote that which is ours" and challenge the assumption that the only good things came from the outside. But how to do it?

Another schoolteacher responded that he felt himself "in a paradigm [paradox?]" between the house and the maloca. How to resolve the contradictions? Which direction to go in? In fact, he said, teachers continued to find it difficult to talk about "lo nuestro" despite the new multiculturalist discourses, because they had been taught to be ashamed of it. Even though repudiation of Western superiority was in the air, still "it's very hard to go back to the maloca, so I'm in this paradigm." He added that while they were not about to "put on loincloths," putting on loincloths *was* a way of recovering Tukanoan culture. The ethno-education team leader responded, telling him that as time went on this problem would become more and more difficult, and spoke of having to "make culture."

Discussion

Clearly, the shaman school project exemplified some of the traps and difficulties in preserving traditional knowledge and practice, problems analyzed quite comprehensively by the schoolteachers. The first problem, and perhaps the greatest, was the shaman school's exclusive attention to only some aspects of shamanic healing. Guevara chose to break shamanism down into what he understood as its "empirical" component parts, selecting those amenable to Western pedagogical practice. But, just as is the case elsewhere in lowland South America, Tukanoan shamans do more than heal or teach healing. As Guevara himself noted in his comment to me, shamans are charged with keeping the cosmos in equilibrium. The extensive literature on Amazonian shamanism characterizes it as "a globalizing and dynamic social and cultural phenomenon"[58] that expresses central tenets of a culture's worldview. Shamans, notes Robin Wright, not only cure, they advise and guide people in virtually all areas of life.[59] He points out, as do other ethnographers of the Northwest Amazon,[60] that no single myth covers the entire gamut of shamanic powers, as shamanism, in one form or another permeates the mythological cycles of cosmic creation.

In contrast with some lowland South American societies, in the Vaupés, traditional leaders (headmen) are not necessarily shamans—which is not to say that Tukanoan shamans have no political power. Shamans are quintessential mediators: they travel between levels of the cosmos, interceding and negotiating; on earth they help individuals move through the life cycle, and when danger threatens they mediate between individuals and communities. As elsewhere in South America, Tukanoan shamanism works to maintain and restore a correct balance of energy. Illness is a sign of imbalance, a psychosocial and ecological disturbance within the community.[61] In the Vaupés specific cases of illness were always linked to another sphere, one that, although not usually apparent, nonetheless affected daily life.[62]

The schoolteachers did not indicate explicitly that they saw shamanism in these terms, for they had believed the shaman school could succeed at least to some degree. But they did understand the huge gap between traditional shamanic practice and what the shamans were asked to do in the school setting. The schoolteachers' questions about Guevara's notion of "empirical" medicine perhaps stemmed from their awareness that shamanic knowledge and practice did not distinguish between the objective and subjective, or between the somatic, the mental/emotional, and the spiritual.

The schoolteachers' remarks about shamanic formulas reveal their awareness that a great deal of Tukanoan shamanic ritual depended on the performative power of words. Dominique Buchillet provides a detailed discussion of the way Desana shamans' words effect change because they are able to reactivate power already present in the cosmos.[63] The schoolteachers also knew that shamanic language was esoteric, most of it impossible to comprehend even by native speakers. They understandably wondered just how effective a shaman's attempts to teach specific chants could be in the school setting, conducted in Tukano and Spanish.

The failure of the shaman school exemplified as well difficulties inherent in any project targeting cultural preservation and reconstruction. The schoolteachers themselves brought up a number of issues in this vein, one of them being the opposition they perceived between traditional Tukanoan social structure and values and the pan-Tukanoan (and, increasingly, pan-indigenous) ideology being introduced. Regional variations in level of acculturation, along with the complex way Tukanoan language groups mapped onto the landscape, had resulted in a highly uneven distribution of shamanic practitioners and shamanic knowledge, such that what might be thriving in one region could be absent and not easily reintroduced in another. One teacher suggested taking an inventory of shamans in the more acculturated regions downriver, to kickstart revitalization of shamanic knowledge and practices in these areas. But who could carry out such a project? Certainly not a non-Tukanoan, nor even someone who was not a member of the shaman's language group. The schoolteachers' questions about the advisability of such an inventory and whether shamans would agree to be interviewed—and if so, whether they would actually tell the truth—raised the deep and thorny issue of who "owns" shamanic culture. As noted, esoteric shamanic knowledge, much of it secret, was traditionally acquired during a long apprenticeship using a particular Tukanoan language, and the schoolteachers readily perceived the contradiction that preserving this part of culture seemed to require violating the terms under which it was traditionally transmitted.

A related and equally thorny issue had to do with Tukanoan dependence on Whites. The schoolteachers spoke eloquently about the ongoing negative effects of White intervention in the region; we saw earlier that one Cubeo man referred to the abundance of development programs as "the bombardment of our communities." There were so many change agents in the region, he said, that the situation was "ya como deporte" (by now like a game). In fact, so plentiful were the development projects targeted at them that communities close to Mitú had become quasi-experimental sites. And, as noted, when these communities saw program after program fail, their members tended to blame themselves. The schoolteachers also complained about a "collision of authorities" in those communities. Traditional longhouse leadership consisted of a headman and perhaps a shaman. By the early 1990s many settlements were much larger and now included new indigenous authorities like the *catequi-*

sta (catechism instructor), the schoolteacher, the health promoter (and sometimes a nursing aide), and settlement members who represented Communal Action, Family Well-Being, and DAI. Not surprisingly, disputes over turf and influence frequently arose. Health promoters might compete with shamans, and the former's access to medical instruments and drugs, radiotelephones, and outboard motors fostered inequality.[64] Guevara himself criticized the promoter program, saying it had produced hybrid, self-important Tukanoans.

A left-leaning priest commented to me during that same summer that when Tukanoans first mobilized around indigenous rights and cultural preservation, the Prefecture's policy in support of these goals could be characterized as "give us Tukanoans a weapon so that we can defend ourselves from you." He added that a dependency relationship continued because groups like CRIVA continued to use weapons from the oppressors, rather than fashioning ones based on their own traditions. In a way, the shaman school manifested the same sort of dependency, and, more generally, the contradictions deeply embedded in managed multiculturalism that typically surface when programs are implemented.

The contradictions that arise when foreign methods of education and organizing are used to promote indigenous self-sufficiency and preserve Tukanoan culture were mentioned again and again during the workshop. One teacher pointed to political battles still to be won: "Preserve for what? Indians [still] feel inferior to Whites. If we don't organize ourselves, what organization are we going to give to the old people?" The schoolteachers agreed that White pedagogical modes could not be used to transmit some areas of traditional knowledge—about the ancestor cult known as *Yuruparí*, for instance. And they also acknowledged that they themselves were speaking Spanish in the ethno-education workshop, and taught their students in Spanish. At one point they criticized themselves for not teaching their own children about the necessity of preserving Tukanoan languages. They also acknowledged that many facets of the concept of "culture" were foreign to Tukanoan thinking. An example was the way ethno-education team members instructed the schoolteachers about how to think of culture, suggesting that at times Tukanoans would need to "make culture"—which produced quizzical looks. In short, many schoolteachers' comments during the two-week workshop exposed the contradictions that had surfaced. Were White modes of instruction (such as workshops) and technologies (such as tape recorders) appropriate for preserving Tukanoan culture? Yes, no, maybe.

The schoolteachers also discussed the degree to which the project of studying their own culture was already under way. They sometimes disagreed about what "Tukanoan culture" actually consisted of. Some said that because only Tukanoans could study Tukanoan culture, research published by non-Tukanoans was rubbish. Others said that studies had been published that might be useful, but they were in languages Tukanoans could not understand, and that "*we* have to take control of the word." Some schoolteachers agreed with the ethno-education team that Tukanoans *could* learn about their culture from studies done by others, and that outsiders could help Tukanoans study their own culture. Another schoolteacher, who had attended ethnolinguistics courses offered by SIL in order to be able to analyze Tukanoan languages, said that he was only just beginning to understand what investigating his own culture really meant. He thanked the ethno-education team for "showing us the reality" of learning how to investigate one's own culture. But nothing was really resolved during the workshop. Overall, these young men remained confused about ways to systematically study a culture. One source of confusion had to do with knowing what to preserve and what to discard. A schoolteacher's comment that Tukanoans would "save our culture but we're going ahead, and we will adopt new things if they benefit us" reveals the challenge they were facing. Another schoolteacher repeated what team leaders had said about there being good and bad things in all cultures, adding that one should examine different cultures and choose the very best from each. This struck me as a kind of supermarket notion of culture.[65]

These discussions were taking place against a backdrop of very significant changes. One issue that came up had to do with shifts in traditional gender roles. Tukanoan men living near Mitú, unable to hunt and fish, helped their wives in the manioc gardens. The workshop leaders spoke approvingly of this adaptation. But several schoolteachers commented on how members of the older generation would tease them about not setting a good example of the traditional gendered division of labor.

In the Vaupés, two nonindigenous institutions, public schools and public health services, afforded a space within which struggles for rights to culture and cultural revitalization were fought and, to some extent, won. But projects like the shaman school and multicultural school curricula illustrate a pervasive contradiction, for while they provide a way to valorize and pass on indigenous healing traditions, history, language, and culture to the next generation, they are also a means of attaining knowledge and skills that help young Tukanoans attain success in the dominant society. And quite often it is the latter that parents are wanting. In the Vaupés, as in many other places, many parents do not see the value in recovering and promoting native language and culture via bilingual and bicultural education.[66]

Workshop leaders' statements about "inventing" and "creating" culture added to the confusion about just what culture was and how to preserve it. The schoolteachers listened intently to the Mitú team's subversive communication about the need to critically examine the Ministry of Education's curriculum and tailor it to community needs. They seemed attracted to this empowering message; one even said, "We have to invent God." But these ideas *were* confusing, and how to implement them was even more so. What does "making culture" mean in an *indigenous* community? Such empowerment rhetoric perhaps made more sense in the peasant communities where the team had previously worked. Ethno-education's philosophy of community control of government programs, in particular pedagogical curricula, did not easily fit into a plan of action that corresponded with these Tukanoan schoolteachers' goal of finding ways to renew and preserve their culture. How could agents and institutions from a "foreign" culture help rescue a threatened culture before it was irretrievably lost? Might not such efforts actually speed up Tukanoan culture's demise? The schoolteachers were well aware that they themselves embodied the dilemmas.

Conclusions

The Nukak crisis and the shaman school project illustrate some of the ways the Colombian state was responding to its own multiculturalist legislation, developing policies and programs that allowed its agencies to carry on their administrative tasks within the new environment. The cases also illustrate the ongoing evolution of indigeneity, in particular the valorization of alterity, both locally and in the capital.

One cause of the Nukak crisis was terminological: a group of Indians emerging from the forest and from obscurity had been known up to then only by a generic catch-all term rather than by the name they called themselves. As a population they had in fact been mentioned before, in long-forgotten NT and Catholic missionary reports buried in DAI files about Makú Indians in Guaviare. But in an important sense the Nukak could not officially exist until they were named as a distinct pueblo—a telling example of an idea mentioned in the Introduction: Gooding-Williams's notion of "dynamic nominalism," by which "human acts come into being hand in hand with our invention of the categories labeling them."[67] Sensational reports about the emergence of a "previously unknown" Stone Age people resulted in no small part from Nukak invisibility and anonymity.

Unfortunately for the Nukak, they emerged during a period of rapid and disconcerting change in Tukanoan attitudes. Although the Makú had mostly escaped their traditional servant role, long-standing prejudices reemerged with a vengeance. In the context of changing indigenous-White relations and emerging pro-indigenous consciousness in the region, the Nukak's arrival probably aroused exceptionally ambivalent and painful feelings, even (or perhaps especially) in those Tukanoans most interested in claiming indigenous rights. In the recent past Makú had been seen by Tukanoans as not-quite-human, forbidden sexual partners associated with the forest, in effect not very different from White images of Tukanoans. In the light of these disconcerting parallels, hostility to and rejection of Makú could also present a partial and submerged but still painful rejection of self.[68]

The video footage showing Nukak divesting themselves of almost every trace of White culture and returning to the forest illustrates the difficulty state functionaries encounter when trying to do the right thing for nomadic populations. The admittedly depressing lesson to be learned here is that, from the very beginning, all the solutions tried to resolve the Nukak crisis were seriously flawed. Current attempts to establish voluntary isolation policies in countries like Peru and Paraguay pose equally serious challenges.

In the 1983 effort to preserve Tukanoan shamanic healing traditions, three sets of actors were involved: a local public health official, a group of shamans, and a number of would-be shaman apprentices. During a 1993 ethnoeducation workshop led by a team of three Ministry of Education employees, Tukanoan schoolteachers returned repeatedly to the failure of the 1983 effort. Their discussions, as analyzed here, raised difficult questions about efforts to renew culture. First, which parts of traditional culture (and identity) should be preserved? Second, who is to decide? Third, what is "culture?" Fourth, where does authenticity come in? Fifth, who owns culture? And sixth, the schoolteachers wondered, what is this business of "making culture"? Unfortunately, the schoolteachers tended to blame themselves for contradictions and conflicts that were not of their own making and had been imposed on their lives and work, including a guilty feeling that they were betraying their pupils, and indeed their own children, by teaching and speaking in Spanish.

Pedagogical models received from the outside rested on the assumption that many kinds of learning can occur in schoolroom-like settings. In the case of the shaman school, this assumption suggested that the young men taking the classes (female participation, as far as I could tell, was never contemplated) could acquire traditional knowledge usually transmitted in very different settings. But shamanic knowledge is deeply imbricated with the language that expresses and transmits this knowledge, and Vaupés languages are a primary symbol of the exogamous patrilineal clans I call language groups, which stand in a complex, at times rivalrous, relationship with one another. Outsiders, if they even knew of linguistic exogamy, attached little value or importance to it, but Tukanoans still saw it as worth preserving. Thus, as long as the language-group system endures, it will shape and hinder programs to preserve culture, because efforts by individuals from one language group will often be resented and resisted by members of other groups.

Another unwarranted assumption inherent in the shaman school project was that Tukanoan culture belonged to any Tukanoan who wanted to learn it.[69] But shamanic knowledge has traditionally been passed down along patrilineal lines. Long apprenticeships have involved restrictions and purifications of several sorts, which occurred, moreover, within the confines of the multifamily, patrilocal maloca. Remuneration was another sticking point; participants in the ethno-education seminar criticized shamans as money-grubbing, and those Tukanoans interested in learning from the shamans aroused similar suspicions. Further questions were raised about authenticity or its lack, and about the intentions of local change agents, who all voiced the prevailing mantra about valorizing tradition, while at the same time competing furiously with one another. Overall, the events at the shaman school and the ethno-education seminar (and for that matter the actions of CRIVA itself) illustrate how often the goal of preserving indigenous culture is allowed to depend on nonindigenous models and procedures, in this case on a teaching format antithetical to traditional shamanic apprenticeship.

This same entanglement between indigenous patrimony and foreign vehicle is evident in the challenges facing the Nukak in gaining access to resources. In the aftermath of constitutional change, political innovation was forced on the dispersed indigenous populations of lowland areas, who had to create "traditional" cabildos and capitanías that would represent them to the state and other institutions. This task is doubly difficult for nomadic foragers lacking any sort of role or collectivity that could be the basis for such innovation, leaving them outside the state's sustained attention. In the case of the Nukak, it was clear that the different bands, which avoided and denigrated each other, would not soon be reaching consensus. But change was inevitable, and if the Nukak could not learn to represent themselves to the state, brokers from the Tukano language group would do it in their name.

In this respect, the Nukak, who whether they knew it or not desperately needed a mechanism to make their collective wishes known, were like every other pueblo. The myths of primordial indigenous harmony and authenticity envision homogeneous communities able to arrive at a decision by consensus. As already noted, the reality is that indigenous polities, like every other kind of collectivity, are internally heterogeneous, divided by factions and hierarchies, and ruled by decision-making mechanisms that exclude and marginalize some members. Many are riddled with conflicts, some of them overt, others seemingly resolved but still festering. In such circumstances, del Cairo notes, project managers, whether sincere or not, require at least the simulacrum of homogeneous and tractable communities, and their absence in reality is "what makes so many of these projects little more than shell games manipulated by some NGOs, government, and indigenous entrepreneurs."[70] The romance of traditional consensual communities, like the beauty of geese flying across the sky, can only be sustained from a distance. In this respect, the Nukak present acute difficulties, underlining Paul Nadasdy's conclusion that official efforts to make hunting peoples more independent typically tie them more, not less, to the state, a process Bessire calls "bureaucratizing and domesticating valid Indigenous life."[71]

Many Tukanoans share the goals of reclaiming their past, preserving their culture and identity, and enhancing their status and self-esteem. But the means to those goals—political mobilization, resguardo administration, self-conscious preservationist efforts—only tie them ever more closely to representatives of the state, NGOs, and the dominant society. Tukanoans seek a place of their own within the larger polity, a defensible space that does not require complete assimilation or erasure of identity. In the process, however, they find themselves pushed to acquire cultural elements that may be indigenous but do not feel Tukanoan. The Nukak parallel is apparent: the foragers, in order to stay themselves, to preserve difference, must manage their difference and accept modernity. If they fail to do so, middlemen from the Tukano language group will position themselves as spokesmen for the Nukak and prevent them from shaping their own future.[72]

Except in rare cases, official constructions of indigeneity do not allow for internal heterogeneity, something the Vaupés actually has in abundance, both in the ranking of language groups and clans and in the inequality of Makú-Tukanoan relationships.[73] Nor, as Bocarejo points out, do Colombian multiculturalist policies concern themselves with actual relations between indigenous groups; rather, the position taken is that every ethnic group is equal to every other ethnic group.[74] In reality, new hierarchies are added to old ones by the intervention itself, through the external imposition of imaginaries assigning different degrees of indigenous authenticity. The question of "who is more genuinely ethnic," which has challenged the traditional subordination of Makú in the Vaupés, is even more acute in Guaviare, where, as del Cairo points out, local government administrators attend to three groups: Tukanos, Nukak, and Jiw (Guahibo). Officials there tend to see Tukanos as "not indigenous enough," Jiw as indigenous in a negative way (lazy, uncooperative, etc.), and Nukak as possessing the greatest amount of "good" indigenousness. But policies at the national level sweep all such invidious comparisons under the rug, even when those comparisons are made by the bureaucrats themselves. Here we have another example of Nukak constructed as hyperreal Indians. In September 2016, Carlos Franky and Dany Mahecha, who have worked with the Nukak since the mid-1990s, pointed out to me several consequences resulting from such favoritism. When Jiw go to the hospital, they are kicked out, unlike Nukak, who are immediately attended to—and by doctors, not nurses. When Jiw see food being taken to a Nukak neighborhood, "of course" they are going to attack the van and steal the food. One thing that Nukak and Jiw do agree on, however, is that they do *not* want Tukanos as their representatives, for they are mistrusted and seen as opportunists—and not without reason. Mahecha and Franky told me about a Tukano man who not only married a Nukak woman but actually dressed up as one in his efforts to access funds. According to them, Tukanos living in San José and its environs understand the bureaucracy and are more adept at manipulating it because, having grown up in the Vaupés, they were formed in the educational system designed by Bishop Belarmino Correa and so are much more *capacitados* (adept) than Guaviare natives.

What's more, hierarchies based on received notions of authentic indigeneity embody a central paradox: while multiculturalist legislation reproduces an essentialized understanding of indigeneity, the communities that least profit are those whose cultural traits best fit the legal prescriptions. The seemingly most "authentic" communities, lacking the leaders with skills needed to deal with bureaucracy, must compromise their autonomy by relying on cultural and political brokers.[75]

When authenticity determines position within a hierarchy, contradictions ensue. Nonindigenous actors who judge Makú as "better," because they retain more indigenousness, disconcert and upset Tukanoans. The imaginary of nomadic hunter-gatherers at one with their forest habitat permeates Guaviare tourism, despite the reality of Nukak reduced to begging in the streets of San José. In this respect the Nukak case calls to mind Bessire's discussion of the Paraguayan hunter-gatherer Ayoreo, in particular those Ayoreo who do not fit easily into the *middle ground* of politically authorized culture.[76] In 1988 the "uncontacted" Nukak, like the Ayoreo described by Bessire, were shrouded in the mystique of precontact cultural purity. Whereas in fact, both the Nukak and the Ayoreo had already experienced contact, in encounters with outsiders nasty enough to encourage them to stay in the forest and on the move.[77] The nonconforming Ayoreo lie at both extremes of a continuum with semi-isolated, putatively uncontacted "primitive" groups at one end and denigrated urban "ex-primitives," at the other. Similarly, the Nukak imaginary locates them as "the last green nomads" at one end of the "authentic," "pure" continuum, while far too many individual Nukak gravitate toward the other extreme, running the risk of becoming deracinated urban beggars.

Both cases, Nukak emergence and the shaman school, illustrate the ways that understandings and misunderstandings in the minds of dominant outsiders—the tendency to rank degrees of authenticity and indigeneity, and the failure to take into account internal divisions, oppositions, hierarchies, and antagonisms—affect the people subject to those stereotypes and imaginings, at times in major ways.

4 The Indigenous Movement and Rights

After 1993, when I could no longer return safely to the Vaupés, I expanded my approach to indigenous rights and the indigenous movement, taking Bogotá (and occasionally other cities) as research sites and returning to Colombia every two or three years. Of necessity, my research methodology changed as well, with an emphasis on formal interviewing and on documents: for example, I was making use of Organización Nacional Indígena de Colombia (ONIC) publications and División de Asuntos Indígenas (DAI) archives. To get a sense of how the country's pueblos were being represented in the two national newspapers, *El Tiempo* and *El Espectador*, I assembled a complete archive of articles about indigenous matters from 1991 to 1999. The cases discussed in this chapter, which focuses on indigenous rights discourses and mobilizing, reflect these shifts in focus and methodology.

From the beginnings of the indigenous movement its leaders employed rights-claiming language to achieve several key goals. The first of these goals, the "right to have rights," is a demand made by previously excluded minority populations to be included in the national polity. While some mobilizations targeted abuses perpetrated by the state, others protested minority exclusion from participation and protection, especially in the case of remote communities lacking public order, either because police garrisons were absent or because national security forces were present but colluding with right-wing militias.[1] These communities found themselves, in effect, noncitizens, with few if any rights, because illegal armed actors did what they wished with total impunity.[2] As Gow notes, for many indigenous communities, resistance is not so much placing themselves "in opposition to [the state]; rather, it is the demand to be recognized as indigenous and be treated as citizens; to become a vital part of it. . . . While the quest for justice is a demand for respect and dignity, it is also a request that the state be more inclusive, more democratic, that it treat *all* of its citizens better and allow *all* of them to contribute to the national well-being."[3]

A second goal, a derivative of the first, is the right to run for public office. A third goal, less straightforward than the first two, is recognition of the right to culture: although guaranteed by the Colombian constitution, cultural rights continue to need a great deal of legislative and judicial action if they are to have a significant presence in Colombians' everyday lives.

The platform of the Consejo Regional Indígena del Cauca (CRIC) included the right to culture, and the claims-making of Autoridades Indígenas de Colombia (AICO) with respect to rights to autonomy and securing ancestral territory was justified on the basis of being indigenous—autochthonous "authentic Americans."[4] Guambiano notions of Derecho Mayor (Greater Right), and Pensamiento Propio (Our Own Thought), signal this pueblo's own form of differentiated citizenship. According to the Guambiano Manifesto, "we all have rights but not everything is equal" (*pero no todo es igual*[5]). The manifesto contains within it many of the sticking points around the right to cultural difference that would emerge in the postconstitutional period.

Intrinsic to the notion of cultural rights is the existence of a collectivity to which those rights attach. As Rodolfo Stavenhagen notes, cultural rights must be collective, "since some of these rights can only be enjoyed by individuals in community with others, and such a community must have the possibility to preserve, protect and develop its common culture."[6] The notion of collective rights, however, has generally been resisted by Western nation-states, which have almost invariably identified the individual as the bearer of rights and obligations.[7] The United Nations Universal Declaration of Human Rights emerged from the unspeakable suffering many peoples underwent during the first half of the twentieth century; ironically, although that document located human rights in the individual, in fact many of those atrocities were inflicted collectively on members of culture-bearing communities.

In Latin America over the past four decades, culture as a collective right has received increasingly robust protections, but this change has revealed a series of contradictions. As Jane Cowan notes, there are "complex and contradictory consequences of being granted rights on the basis of having a culture and a cultural identity."[8] Complexity can also grow as rights discourse penetrates even remote locales, where it undergoes change (or "vernacularization," as Sally Merry puts it[9]), and subsequently returns in new guise to the metropole.

This chapter addresses these issues in three sections. The first examines a series of occupations by indigenous activists of government buildings throughout Colombia during the summer of 1996. Demonstrators were protesting actions taken by DAI during a confrontation with an indigenous NGO of the Guajira peninsula in the northeast of the country, and more generally the dire situation of all the country's pueblos. My 2002 analysis of this dispute and its participants and grievances[10] revealed several core tensions, including some that had been developing even before the constitutional reforms. Prominent among them was the question of who has the right to represent Colombia's pueblos in their dealings with the government. The protests also revealed changes in how indigeneity and indigenous authority were being asserted and performed.

The second section explores the question of special indigenous jurisdiction as illustrated by two cases in which prominent indigenous leaders were accused of misconduct. The cases illustrate how indigenous participants understood what was at stake for them when claims were made to local indigenous jurisprudence as an aspect of indigenous autonomy, and—since both cases received considerable media attention—how sectors of mainstream society reacted to those claims. I first wrote about these cases in 2007.[11]

The third section examines a conflict that erupted between the government and an indigenous manufacturing company, Coca Nasa, when it sought to distribute foods and beverages containing coca. The controversy illustrates the contradictions that can arise when rights are asserted in an expansive fashion in response to state efforts to foster indigenous economic development projects. While growing and consuming coca is legal within resguardos, Coca Nasa's attempts to market its products throughout the country ran up against the international antinarcotic treaties Colombia had signed. This case also illustrates the very dissimilar treatment an indigenous development project may receive from different government agencies. I explored these issues in a paper I presented in 2011.[12]

The 1996 Occupations of Government Offices

The Origins of the Dispute

The 1996 dispute began when representatives of a Wayuu[13] NGO petitioned the local mayor's office to release government funds for a project, and Gladys Jimeno, DAI's director, refused, insisting that the petitioners had to show that the community, and in particular its traditional authorities, were involved in the project. In angry response members of the NGO traveled to Bogotá and occupied DAI's offices. Numerous other government buildings were subsequently taken over by indigenous activists brandishing long lists of grievances. The most salient point of contention concerned what qualifications should be required of intermediaries between indigenous communities and the state, and the appropriate role for traditional local authorities. On DAI's side Jimeno insisted that in any mediation those local authorities should take the lead, and that DAI's mandate was to strengthen these local institutions. On the other side the leaders of ONIC and other national and regional groups fought to maintain their near-monopoly as intermediaries.

The Organizations Involved in the Dispute

When the dispute erupted, four indigenous political organizations were asserting a national presence, the first of which was ONIC. The second, AICO, emerged out of alliances a predecessor organization, AISO, had forged with the Arhuacos of the Sierra Nevada de Santa Marta in the north of Colombia, and with other pueblos like the Emberá, who are located in the Chocó and several other departments. AICO, however, had difficulty acting as a truly national movement, since its cultural ties and its claims to legitimacy are heavily linked to one pueblo, the Guambiano (although in fact not all Guambiano cabildos are AICO members). AICO criticized ONIC as authoritarian, vertically structured, and dismissive of traditional authorities.[14] The third organization, Alianza Social Indígena (ASI, Indigenous Social Alliance), a political party created by CRIC, was criticized by some activists for including nonindigenous members and therefore not being, strictly speaking, an "indigenous organization." The fourth organization, the Movimiento Indígena de Colombia (MIC, Indigenous Movement of Colombia), also a political party, came on the scene in 1994 to run senator Gabriel Muyuy's reelection campaign following a decision by ONIC (until then Muyuy's sponsor) to get out of electoral politics. MIC was primarily allied with the Inga people of Putumayo, in southern Colombia.

AICO had hived off from CRIC over the same issue that subsequently emerged in the dispute between ONIC and DAI during the 1996 standoff: the role of traditional authorities. ONIC's organizational model, resembling that of a labor union, without ties to a particular territory or pueblo, freed it to represent the nation's pueblos much more inclusively. Many of its thirty-five regional affiliates represented more than one pueblo, having been created along regional rather than ethnic lines. Some pueblos had ties to more than one regional ONIC affiliate. But ONIC's structure also held disadvantages, as became apparent during the 1990s as indigenous rights discourses became increasingly culturalist. Both ONIC and AICO, their rhetoric heavily influenced by Western essentialisms, tailored their claims about indigenous cultural difference to make them "more palatable for outside observers."[15] ONIC used a "trait list" that essentialized indigenous identity "in much the same way that national legislation and social science had done for a century, by identifying native culture with discrete cultural traits such as language, social organization, and traditions, or with expanses of land."[16] AICO, taking a different tack, avoided such "outmoded anthropological criteria," by romanticizing indigenous resistance, appealing to history as the prime definer of native identity.[17]

As noted in Chapter One, Colombia's indigenous movement first emerged out of a situation of exploitation that encompassed both indigenous and non-indigenous sharecroppers in the departments of Cauca and Tolima. The first step toward ethnic-based mobilizing came with the founding of CRIC. From the beginning, two contrary tendencies emerged concerning culture. One conceded the importance of culture but did not put it at the center of the struggle: demands for cultural rights, from this perspective, should form part of a more general eradication of social inequalities, building a just world for all oppressed people.[18] The other tendency stressed the need for a strategic foregrounding of cultural and ethnic difference. This emerging culturalist position (sometimes termed *indianista*) asserted that indigenous rights differed significantly from other movement goals, because the struggle was necessarily grounded in a pueblo's history and in its divergence from the national society. Other goals—political, material, and territorial—should be grounded in those ethnic and cultural claims. Defense of indigenous land, for instance, would be justified through the discourse of territory, spelling out the differences between capitalist commodification and indigenous conceptions of the land as a "source of life and a prolongation of existence."[19] Although Indians and campesinos both worked the land, their relationship to it, according to culturalist arguments, diverged significantly, in both historical and cultural terms. Campesinos saw land as private property, a means of production for subsistence and the market—a guarantee of the peasant family's survival now and in the future. Pueblos, in contrast, were repossessing their traditional territories in order to expand resguardos and strengthen cabildos, in no small part through studies of the pre-Columbian roots of their communal land tenure systems. If struggles in the 1970s were about land, pure and simple, by the 1980s land was inextricably tied to political authority: a territory must be governed by a cabildo whose members are elected by community members. As AICO saw it, all of CRIC's complicated organizational chart—cooperatives, committees, executive committee, and assessors—was based on a Western model alien to traditional forms of organization. AICO feared, moreover, that traditional authorities, one of the great moral strengths of the pueblos, were in danger of being forgotten.[20]

In internal discussions, first AISO and then AICO sought ways to organize on an indigenous rather than Western model. New ideas and slogans, like Pensamiento Propio, were advanced. Encounters with representatives of the state, even the President of the Republic, were to be structured as meetings between co-equal leaders. Indigenous authority was characterized as Derecho Mayor, which the pueblos enjoyed by right of their priority as the first "authentic Americans": "Our rights are born right here [*aquí mismo*], from the land and the community from before Columbus, from the epoch of the great leaders [*caciques*] nominated by the communities . . . by reconstructing, recovering and strengthening the authentic authorities of each pueblo . . . not only the concepts but also all of the practical work in the communities will change."[21] These claims were elaborated in other AICO documents, spelling out the basic concepts and looking for distinctively indigenous ways of thinking about authenticity, autonomy, and sovereignty.

ONIC, in contrast, employed a discourse much like CRIC's, valorizing indigenous culture, but only in a general way, in terms familiar from Western ideology. When I spoke with Abadio Green, at that time president of ONIC, about the summer's mobilizations, he said: "We spoke with a single voice. The advantage we have is that we speak of our culture, our language, and our Mother Earth." The cultural difference he was claiming was generic and vague, without grounding in any particular indigenous lifeway.

Over the course of the 1990s, leaders of ONIC, ASI, and MIC stepped up their displays of indigenous alterity before metropolitan audiences, for instance by bookending their oral statements with a few sentences from their native languages, a practice increasingly used by indigenous activists all across the Americas.[22] Indigenous-themed clothing became commonplace: Green (a Guna originally from Panama) wore a *mola* panel (reverse-appliqué work sewn and worn by Guna women) on the back of his denim jacket, and Gabriel Muyuy wore the wool poncho associated with the Inga people.[23] A number of leaders wore their hair long.

The Occupations

On June 24, 1996, forty-five Wayuu (a pueblo formerly known as Guajiro) occupied DAI headquarters in Bogotá. A Wayuu NGO had earlier submitted a proposal to the mayor of the local municipality[24] outlining a project requesting three million pesos, at the time about three thousand U.S. dollars, a not-inconsiderable sum for a rural Colombian community. The mayor wrote DAI asking for advice about how to proceed. DAI also received letters from adjacent Wayuu communities complaining that they knew nothing about the project. DAI wrote the NGO that the community had to be involved. The occupation of DAI headquarters attracted media attention throughout the country. Two weeks later sixty activists occupied the Episcopal Palace in Bogotá, which, because it occurred during an annual meeting of the bishops, gained even more publicity. The Minister of the Interior and the president of the Episcopal Conference met with indigenous leaders, who presented a list of demands focused on the critical situation of the nation's pueblos. Additional occupations took place around the country, in support of those in the capital and to protest local problems.

A month after the initial Wayuu occupation, it was clear that the actions had triggered an outpouring of indigenous anger against the state's failure to respond to a wide range of grievances. The depth of that frustration was evident just in the fact that various competing segments of the movement had come together. The two indigenous senators, Lorenzo Muelas and Gabriel Muyuy, joined the occupiers, who were mostly from ONIC and its regional affiliates. Muelas, a leader of AICO and nationally known as a former Asamblea Nacional Constituyente (ANC) delegate, was highly respected by both pueblo members and many in mainstream society, and Muyuy, head of MIC, was in his second term as senator. Other leaders included Jesús Piñacué, president of CRIC, and Francisco Rojas Birry, at that time a Bogotá city council member and an Emberá who had also served on the ANC. According to Victor Jacanamejoy, vice director of MIC, the occupiers agreed to avoid mentioning by name the separate indigenous organizations involved, which might have appeared divisive when in fact they shared the same goal—an end to the oppression of the country's indigenous citizens. As Green put it, "We are united with respect to life, because we are being killed; we are also united around the issue of our territories. Mother Earth summons us, she convenes her children."[25] The activists insisted that the occupations would end only after the government agreed to a procedure for definitively establishing indigenous territories (i.e., the indigenous territorial units [ETIs] mandated in the constitution as discussed in Chapter One).

Support for the occupations also surged among some nonindigenous Colombians. Many were deeply troubled by what seemed a blatant effort to undermine the constitution. Old and new problems had indeed emerged in the aftermath of the constitutional reforms, some of them unintended consequences of the reform itself: ethnic conflict, for example, was erupting in areas where pueblos, Afro-Colombians, and colonos had previously coexisted peacefully. National NGOs and human rights groups placed manifestos in the national press highlighting the lack of progress since the signing of the constitution; although multiple agreements had been signed, nothing concrete had ensued. Campesino organizations also declared solidarity, joining the occupation of regional Instituto Colombiano de Reforma Agraria (INCORA) offices because "hundreds of us are being killed too!" Many religious and international organizations sent letters to the country's president, Ernesto Samper.

The turning point came on August 1, when more than three thousand members of Cauca pueblos and their campesino allies blocked the Pan-American Highway, forcing the government to yield.[26] A week later, two decrees were signed that upheld "the fundamental rights of Colombian indigenous people."[27] The decrees and the Cauca agreement established several official bodies: a committee on human rights, a national commission for lands, and a permanent inter-institutional *mesa de concertación* (consultation roundtable) at which government and indigenous leaders would meet periodically. The Inter-American Commission on Human Rights, the International Labor Organization, and the Episcopal Conference were charged with making sure that promises were kept.

Indigenous Grievances

During the occupations, Gabriel Muyuy assessed the indigenous movement's progress up to that point: "In some respects we have advanced a little bit, but not in the fundamental themes. For example, we have made zero progress with respect to territory. Human rights abuses grow more serious each day. In some places we have gained ground in social investment, but most indigenous communities remain poor, marginalized, and victimized by land invasions."[28] Contentious issues mentioned during the occupations included (1) land (the constitutionally-mandated territorial ordination process), so far stalled; (2) mega-development; (3) transfer of resources; and (4) human rights violations, in particular repression of indigenous leaders. Muyuy claimed that attention to indigenous issues under the Samper administration had declined by 90 percent since the Gaviria administration.[29] The most serious complaint concerned the state's failure to promote legislation implementing the fundamental ("organic") law regarding territorial ordination.[30] Once the ETIs were legislated, cabildos would receive funds (known as transfers) directly from the state, but until then funds would continue to be administered by local mayoral offices—the arrangement that triggered the initial Wayuu occupation of DAI headquarters. This issue fueled the debates about traditional authorities and autonomy.

Many of the occupations occurring elsewhere in the country took place in the offices of INCORA. The agricultural reform agency's opposition to indigenous demands, its lackluster record in places where problems were most acute, and its unmitigated failures in the most violent regions of the country effectively guaranteed the endemic problems that provoked condemnation that summer. Funds assigned to INCORA for land acquisitions were often inadequate, institutional infrastructure was lacking, and obstructions typically appeared during acquisition and titling phases. The paltry amounts offered to landowners ensured that only lands of marginal quality were offered for sale. INCORA agents, it was said, saw the land crisis as something for indigenous, peasant, and Afro-Colombian communities to resolve among themselves. Worst of all, critics claimed, INCORA's policies and actions were completely compromised by links to multinational corporations and their Colombian affiliates.[31]

More generally, the occupations were motivated by Colombia's national crisis, which included the deepest recession in seventy years and a drastic reduction in living standards caused by neoliberal policies adopted in the early 1990s, which left more than 50 percent of the population in dire poverty.[32]

In the ongoing violence, indigenous, peasant, and Afro-descendant communities were periodically caught in the crossfire between government security forces and paramilitaries and guerillas.[33] Criminals escaped prosecution with impunity, and government repression caused more than thirty-five thousand deaths and drove more than a million people from their homes—a shocking number of internally displaced persons out of a total population at that time of forty million.[34] The homicide rate was the highest in the world, and indigenous communities were assailed not just by the police and army, but, as Jacanamejoy put it in our interview, "everything below them—kidnappers, assassins, paramilitaries, guerrillas." And in all of the pueblos' encounters with officialdom, locally or nationally, neglect and corruption were the norm.

The DAI View of the Dispute

Gladys Jimeno, the focal point for the initial occupation, branded the members of the original Wayuu delegation as merely corrupt: their lack of a valid political agenda was blatantly obvious in the wording of the "ridiculous" agreement they wanted her to sign, which, according to her, was entirely concerned with money. A lawyer familiar with the case told me that in his opinion the Wayuu had not anticipated the protracted conflict that ensued. They behaved in a "very ugly" way during the occupation of the offices, he said. Although accustomed to highly politicized discussions, he had never heard petitioners insult their adversaries in such an offensive way. He deplored the ripped-out telephones and vandalized offices, adding that ONIC had also condemned this behavior.

Among the many grievances aired during that summer, complaints about Director Jimeno herself headed the list. She was attacked for stating publicly that leaders of the indigenous organizations disregarded and looked down on traditional authorities, and for denying that the national leaders were authorized to represent the nation's indigenous communities. While almost everyone had similar criticisms—movement leaders had lost their roots, had become too much at home in the city, and increasingly acted like bureaucrats—it was felt that Jimeno, as a government official, had no business making such statements on the record. Trained as a psychologist, she had virtually no previous experience in indigenous affairs or, according to her critics, sufficient knowledge of DAI history and policymaking.

When I asked her about policymaking, Jimeno spoke of "political projects" and "ethnic projects." DAI's responsibilities, she continued, included assisting cabildos, which meant supporting traditional authorities. Another responsibility was to deal with regional and national organizations. By no means, she said, would DAI exclude as intermediaries the leaders of such organizations or indigenous individuals who had achieved positions in the government. But in the case of a small-scale local effort—what she called a "micro project"—DAI should work directly with community leaders: "we simply want to support the traditional authorities and reduce corruption." Should a pueblo choose ONIC as its representative, there would be no problem, but few had chosen that option. She added that ONIC, despite its rhetoric, undercut indigenous autonomy at the community level: it was ONIC, for example, who invented the notion that traditional leaders had jurisdiction only over internal matters. After the occupations began, she said, "secrets" had come out during discussions, revealing ONIC's unwillingness to talk about local autonomy and an insistence on monopolizing interactions between the communities and national organizations. As she saw it, ONIC's labor union structure prevented it from valuing the diversity found in the pueblos. And the supposed naïveté and gullibility of traditional authorities on which ONIC harped were illusory: "Give them time to think and confer with community members, and even those who are very traditional will make sensible decisions."

Like DAI, other government agencies increasingly saw traditional leaders as the real authority, and the most remote communities as the holders of real indigenous culture. Other, less traditional actors claiming jurisdiction or influence, whether indigenous NGOS or activists at the national level, were increasingly mistrusted. This attitude was motivated in part by neoliberal attempts at reforming the corrupt, clientelistic two-party political system, and by laws requiring that multinational companies interested in oil and other natural resources obtain permission to work in indigenous territories. Both the corporations themselves and the government agencies supporting their work preferred dealing at the local level rather than with the national organizations.

Valorizations of indigenous culture (and much less often, of Afro-Colombian culture) were now appearing in the media, in sermons, and in school festivals, and so ONIC found itself caught on the horns of a dilemma. Although drawing at first on universalizing Western notions like social justice, law and order, human rights, and minority rights, ONIC increasingly took on at least a veneer of culturalism. Culturalist language was increasingly prominent in its statements, but only in vague formulaic language, in part because Colombian pueblos are culturally quite heterogeneous. What the pueblos share is not a common culture but a common history of exploitation, dispossession, and victimization, a history that also characterizes indigenous experience in other countries. When concrete illustrations of indigenous lifeways were required, one or another of the pueblos would be invoked, very often the peoples of the Sierra Nevada de Santa Marta. And so ONIC was stymied when it tried to represent or to offer thoughts about a shared pan-indigenous culture.

In other contexts Green and other leaders made telling use of generic culturalist discourses, notably when portraying pueblos as guardians of Mother Earth, guarantors of biodiversity, and practitioners of sustainable development, echoing the eco-rhetoric being promulgated by international NGOs[35] and, at times, by the Colombian government. But generic environmentalist discourse of this sort was of little use to ONIC in its struggles with government agencies over who was to represent the pueblos to the state.

As Jimeno saw it, the Wayuu occupation of her offices revealed the vested interests behind the action. Interested parties included NGOs (external as well as local, and indigenous as well as not), ethnic fence-straddlers (like the non-indigenous husbands of some Wayuu women), and especially mayors. Jimeno characterized the latter as *politiqueros* (totally self-interested politicians) and thieves, who, soon after passage of Law 60 of 1993, recognized the necessity of including indigenous partners when stealing large sums of money: "Finding corruptible Wayuu is not difficult; local NGOs are set up, and the money disappears." Law 60 specifies how direct cash transfers (*transferencias*) from the central government to the communities are to be distributed (e.g., what proportion to direct to education or health).[36] Thus, applications for project funds required more than evidence of indigenous identity: collective backing also had to be demonstrated. "And, especially in the Wayuu case, the authorities should be truly *traditional*, and their right to represent clearly validated."

Given the very public and sensitive nature of the dispute and its focus on Jimeno herself, I wondered why she had agreed to talk with me. One clue emerged in a passing mention of a crisis among the Guambiano caused by an alliance between some authorities and narcotraffickers: "Being the state, *we* can't accuse them of corruption. Because they are minorities they deserve their lands, they deserve to have their human rights respected; their cultures are fragile." As a state functionary she could not point the finger at their corruption, but *I* could. (I asked her sister, anthropologist Myriam Jimeno, who had arranged my first meeting with Gladys, about this. Her answer was, "In Colombia, the only thing that works is family.")

ONIC's View of the Dispute

The occupations delighted national indigenous leaders. More than a platform for airing long-standing grievances, the unity demonstrated in the protests, the participation of all sectors, including traditional authorities, belied accusations of indigenous factionalism. Jacanamejoy commented: "The occupation of the Episcopal Palace was an example of acting together . . . rather than thinking that each one only works for their own benefit. Such a path would be very easy for the senators [Muelas and Muyuy] to take, but to work unilaterally is not the idea. Everyone felt the unity. There are specific problems, but we have a lot in common." Green commented: "Although now everyone wants to be a senator or a mayor, the *compañeros* Muelas, Muyuy were with us, as well as [Francisco] Rojas. No one thought it, but all of a sudden, there it was! We spoke with one voice. The solidarity was a very good thing, more important than obtaining the decree. No one spoke about individuals, it was "the indigenous peoples of Colombia."[37] Green felt that the evidence of support from far-flung communities had been especially significant, in particular he appreciated the traditional authorities who joined local protests. He continued: "An old U'wa shaman was with us . . . those from the Sierra said . . . they were praying for us—and we do not have a tight relationship with them. So we *had* support. So the government found out that we were not just a group in Bogotá with no representation . . . we can have our advisors—anthropologists, lawyers—and participate." He ominously referred to "interests attempting to separate us," and complained about government attempts to introduce divisions into communities, which happens when, capitalizing on the food crisis present in almost all communities, agents recognize only some of the elderly authorities to be recipients of material aid. In this way, he said, resentment is fostered and paternalism and dependence are promoted.[38]

Green scorned the DAI argument that it should target strengthening cultural institutions in the communities: the current DAI administration knew nothing of the thirty-year history of struggle waged by indigenous organizations. "The traditional authorities are the focus of conflict. Gladys doesn't like the indigenous organizations. She pays attention to the traditional authorities and ignores us. We are also authorities, but not traditional ones." DAI, he said, was continuing assimilationist policies that had been created in Mexico in the 1940s. One lawyer I interviewed felt that DAI did lack policies suitable for the 1990s, and that it was wedded to the antiquated indigenist principles contained in its founding charter, evident, for instance, when it spoke of "the indigenous problem."

ONIC, however, shared in the criticism. A young Ika woman told me, "One has to criticize ONIC. [When mobilizing the occupations] they just called the organizations, not the traditional authorities, who are more respected." She denied that ONIC represented the nation's pueblos, in part because its leaders failed to travel to the communities to consult with them. AICO worked with the communities and hence was more representative.

When speaking off the record, nonindigenous allies of the movement criticized the indigenous organizations and their leadership, including ONIC's behavior during the occupations. Interviewees generally agreed that the organizations were partly to blame for the obstacles Colombia's indigenous people were encountering. In spite of the positive tenor of many of my conversations about the takeovers, speakers were aware of deep splits in the movement. Green, for example, commented: "We have advanced but we also have regressed. Indians now can be governors, deputies, and senators, but a chaos has come that divides us. Instead of building solidarity, there are more divisions." He blamed the politiqueros and the government—and noted, somewhat defensively, that factions and divisions happened frequently in other organizations. It was ironic, he said, that Jimeno's behavior had produced the movement's unification: "even if the various organizations could agree on nothing else, everyone agreed that she had to be opposed."

Discussion

As official multiculturalism gained hold during the late 1980s and 1990s, concerns about identity, culture, and authenticity grew apace. Government agencies and international NGOs increasingly identified traditional authorities and their communities as appropriate targets for development projects. Of course individual communities had previously made many decisions; what was new was state-sanctioned authority being granted to traditional authorities who, because they were selected according to each pueblos' *usos y costumbres* (uses and customs) were seen to embody authentic cultural difference. The state had to respect these processes, for the constitution mandated it. Although the state had also designated ONIC and the regional organizations as the pueblos' legal representatives, these bodies were increasingly being evaluated negatively according to culturalist criteria. In the early 1980s, no one had paid much attention to whether movement leaders themselves embodied cultural difference, or whether traditional authorities approved of their activities. Now all that had changed.

The Wayuu controversy vividly exposes some of the difficulties in the state's move to interact more directly with traditional pueblo authorities. Traditional Wayuu leadership was narrowly confined to the local settlement and matrilineage; beyond that very restricted domestic sphere, representational political institutions were entirely absent; there was thus no way to ascertain what the Wayuu thought as a collectivity. Though the Wayuu crisis had occurred for a number of reasons, it was not irrelevant that local authority consisted of thousands of maternal uncles. Under these circumstances, the government had tremendous difficulties in finding local traditional authority structures to respect and consult, just as was also happening with the Nukak.

Both ONIC and DAI struggled to adapt to the changing times, each trying to secure what political advantages it could. But knowledgeable people told me that both institutions were indeed stuck in an earlier era, often failing to see the implications of current events, and operating with outdated assumptions and authority structures. One lawyer contemplated possible solutions: What about a federation of pueblos? Or perhaps something totally new, an empowered organization of professional indigenous leaders. But where would the political will come from to explore such reforms? Green conceded that some of the difficulties indigenous people faced were internally generated:

> The situation of Colombia's Indians is more uncertain than before. If we speak about the year 1600, it was the Spaniards and the Indians. Our forefathers knew who they were and what their culture was. But the years have passed and more actors opposed to the pueblos appeared. Not only Spaniards but even mestizos opposed to pueblos. . . . There are Protestant sectors wiping out cultures. Some NGOs don't have close relationships with the pueblos, and the money that comes serves to divide them.

In a nutshell, Indians themselves could be the enemy. Protestant converts could be against indigenous empowerment. Mestizos, even those who self-identified as indigenous, could be the enemy. Indigenous politiqueros were often the enemy. Indigenous NGOs were the enemy if they were corrupt or unresponsive to the needs of indigenous communities. Sometimes enemies could be recognized only in hindsight, and sometimes people argued about who was an enemy and who an ally.

ONIC was facing serious challenges. As a political organization, some of its difficulties resulted from structural problems inherent in its relationship with state actors like DAI, not to mention a built-in rivalry with the other national organizations. It also suffered from a dual role, both in and out of the government. Expected to champion indigenous rights, to increase state responsiveness to the pueblos. and to oppose oppression, its official standing meant it was also called on regularly as an official actor to help with difficult situations. The stark opposition with DAI so apparent during the summer of 1996 had not always been so clear. The absence of truly secure financial backing also created problems. Both Green and Jacanamejoy mentioned that, whereas earlier international support had helped build indigenous organizations, "currently the European countries are abandoning us." One nonindigenous activist I spoke with, although quite critical of ONIC, felt that such an organization was necessary, and that 1 percent of state funds designated for indigenous communities should be earmarked for it.

Finally, some of ONIC's problems were internal, and had to do with interpersonal struggles and, at times, very poor choices about how to behave. One lawyer's sharp criticism said that the internal problems had resulted in a decline in the organization's authority and legitimacy so precipitous that when ONIC called a meeting, the regional organizations did not attend. Another example of dysfunction was the expulsion of ONIC from an Emberá-Katío resguardo whose members complained about an "indigenous elite" who did nothing except personally profit from their position, and nonindigenous ONIC consultants who "ignored our highest authorities" and made decisions without consulting with the communities.[39]

Clearly, ONIC's internal divisions and its difficult interactions with the pueblos and MIC, AICO, and ASI contributed significantly to the problems it was facing, many of which derived from the fact that, being an institution, it behaved like one, working to expand its influence, protect itself, and decrease competition. Despite the rhetoric of unification, during that summer's events ONIC made many attempts to discredit its rivals, notably in the signing of the decrees ending the crisis, an event from which AICO was absent, with the result that it was not represented in the permanent *mesa de concertación*. During the negotiations ONIC tried to have language inserted favoring indigenous organizations over traditional authorities. A lawyer who participated in the discussions said that DAI refused to budge on this issue and in the end prevailed.

ONIC resisted the increasing prominence of traditional leaders because the culturalist turn represented a threat. Its officers and activists were increasingly being asked to substantiate and perform a culturally distinct identity, and traditional leaders, when given the opportunity to perform, put on a better show. As Green observed, "We are authorities, but not traditional ones." His argument that ONIC was entitled to represent Colombia's indigenous peoples because of its long fight on their behalf was dismissed by Jimeno, who said the movement began in the 1970s during a racist era characterized by powerful capitalist interests that opposed land repossessions. The movement's mobilizations and the repression that followed (assassinations, prison terms) had given leaders a particular political perspective, she said, noting that the nonindigenous consultants in organizations like CRIC had been Marxists who championed socialist, revolutionary solutions. "Given that ONIC comes out of this experience and this perspective, what *is* the relationship between it and these sixty-four or sixty-five languages and eighty-five pueblos? ONIC emerges from all of this history and cannot reflect all of the diversities that characterize the pueblos." She listed a number of pueblos that opposed such militant politics and chose not to follow the labor union model of ONIC and its affiliates, adding that while AICO's political project aimed at supporting and strengthening the traditional authorities, because it played a part on the national stage, it also had come to occupy a "joint position," and was thus open to some of the criticism being levelled at ONIC.

A knowledgeable lawyer said that one reason why ONIC decided, despite the risk, to support the occupation of DAI headquarters was precisely because of its shaky position. Being a political organization, some of the actions ONIC took to be maximally effective (such as attempts to reduce the influence of rival organizations) risked censure. Also, its efforts to build and sustain a professional administrative structure were criticized for adhering to a "White model." The organization's clout (and that of its regional affiliates) derived in considerable part from nonindigenous institutions such as the state and international actors like the European Community. The youth of its personnel, and the university educations some enjoyed fueled comments that of course traditional authorities would be excluded. ONIC was supposed to represent a diverse constituency, but a substantial number of its members denied that it spoke for them. A restructuring was not likely to happen, since such a destabilizing undertaking would further reduce the organization's influence. Confronted with judgmental government officials, financial worries, and challenges from indigenous leaders and local communities, it had a propensity to engage in behavior that only fueled the criticism.[40]

Green affirmed that ONIC's project included strengthening the traditional authorities (he added, "because we'll *have* to") and improving relations with "the old ones." Jacanamejoy also spoke of MIC's need to come up with ways to include traditional authorities in decision making at the national level. But ONIC was quite aware that it needed to regularly demonstrate that under certain conditions only it could represent the country's pueblos. Green recounted examples of multinational corporations "tricking" cabildo elders into giving permission for undertakings like seismic exploration for oil. He said that such projects had strong backing from government bureaus like the National Agency of Mining, which prefer to work directly with local leaders "who don't know the dangers." Such statements could be interpreted as implying that traditional authorities were naïve and incompetent.

That summer many concerned Colombians paid attention to the opening up of a space in which the actors in the indigenous movement were able to engage in serious dialogue. The crisis alerted many citizens to the glacially slow implementation of legislative reforms. There *had* been advances; Jacanamejoy commented, "It's not the same as during the 1960s and 1970s when the policy was 'hit them on the head.' Now the government listens to indigenous officials." He also confirmed the movement's accomplishments: "There are others as well—Afro-Colombians, campesinos, workers. At times we are better off than these other sectors, so we have to make claims for them as well." But ONIC's modicum of de jure (state-sanctioned) and de facto authority that resulted from official recognition was being eroded through changes in the rules of the game. The events of 1996 brought out into the open the ways such claims to authority were, on the one hand, being challenged and, on the other, being supported by sectors of civil society.[41]

The conflict between communities' traditional authorities and ONIC and its regional affiliates was growing more acute because of the structural changes brought about by the new constitution and subsequent legislation. With the apportioning of significant power to traditional authorities, the stakes for the winner of the struggle were raised considerably. Indigenous activists increasingly spoke of the right to cultural difference, and increased their demonstrations of indigenousness.

But as already noted, the more activists were prepared to deal with the White world by speaking Spanish fluently, receiving a university education, and living in Bogotá or other urban sites, the less authentic they appeared in both indigenous and nonindigenous eyes. The difference between ONIC and AICO illustrates this issue at the level of indigenous organizations. The turn to culturalist criteria led to a championing of a kind of very visible alterity that had not been necessary earlier on. CRIC's own history of its birth and development illustrates an early version of this process, its members only gradually coming to recognize and valorize their culture and identity.[42] Clearly both indigenousness and political and administrative skills were needed to ensure that movement leaders would be taken seriously by nonindigenous power brokers (some of whom, of course, did everything they could to undermine this authority). Hence, ONIC faced a significant and growing challenge. Its claim to the right to represent the nation's indigenous peoples rested on its indigenous identity and the movement's past history of fighting for indigenous rights. But Green's statement that "we are authorities, but not traditional ones" was being increasingly repudiated by certain actors, both indigenous and not, because a person who spoke for a pueblo increasingly needed authorization linked to traditions that had sedimented over a long time in a rural community. That the traditional, the local, and the culturally different were increasingly important meant that both ONIC and DAI had to jump on this discursive bandwagon. Each accused the other of not really supporting the traditional authorities, and in fact both accusations were true, at least in part, because, Jimeno's and Green's avowals to the contrary, this trend advanced their institutional interests only some of the time.

Two, at times contradictory, characterizations of the indigenous population of Colombia can be identified: they could be seen as members of pueblos and also as a sector of the nation's citizenry. The state's growing propensity to conceive of its official indigenous intermediaries as "leaders of a pueblo" rather than "representatives of indigenous Colombians," posed problems for ONIC. As noted, collectively, Colombian pueblos possess no shared cultural characteristics other than those deriving from colonial and neocolonial history. Leaders like Green did attempt to construct generic cultural alterity discourses about Colombia's indigenous people as a whole,[43] but although references to this whole abounded, language characterizing the collectivity's shared culture was a work in progress. When speaking of a common culture, indigenous activists appropriated images from the international indigenous movement or else narrowed the focus to a specific pueblo's culture, treating it implicitly as representative of the whole. And in some contexts it *was* advantageous to point out the rich cultural diversity of indigenous Colombia. Overall, however, ONIC officers and activists, most of them educated young men, could not easily avail themselves of traditional authority symbols, because those symbols could be acquired only over a period of years spent in an isolated community with the acquiescence of its leaders.

The explosion of takeovers of government offices throughout the country brought many grievances to light, an important one being the need to address, and hopefully resolve, the question of who has the right to represent Colombia's indigenous peoples. Leaders in the regional and national organizations understood that if they were to ensure that Colombian citizens and their government, along with international participants, were going to continue to consider their organizations as the legitimate representatives of the nation's indigenous citizens, their leaders would have to earn this privilege by performing and embodying a culturally distinct indigenousness to a much greater degree than the previous era had required.

Such moves were occurring throughout Latin America. For example, at a meeting in Ecuador in April 1999, "an emerging consensus in CONAIE [Confederation of Indigenous Nationalities of Ecuador] held that the indigenous movement should move from representation by organization toward representation by 'nationality and pueblo.'"[44] And in Bolivia during this time, a push was under way to move from union-based structures to *ayllu*-based[45] ones; here the shift was from a top-down government-imposed structure to one seen as more authentically indigenous. Both examples illustrate an overall movement from Western-derived organizational structures to ones derived from a particular country's indigenous traditions.

Unfortunately, the most problematic part of the negotiation, the creation of ETIs, was not resolved, and indigenous representatives, complaining about bad faith on the part of government representatives and overall lack of political will, eventually refused to participate in the roundtable discussions, returning only in 2007.

Rights to Special Indigenous Jurisdiction

If indigenous communities are to enjoy true autonomy, it would seem that the ability to adjudicate offenses and disputes locally, according to indigenous rules and procedures, should be fundamental. Such a rights regime, however, when applied to real cases, can have unwanted, unintended, and often completely unforeseen consequences, as happened in the two cases considered in this section. The cases illustrate the problematic relationship between two equally fundamental notions—the collective right to culture and fundamental human rights, meaning protection against being killed, tortured, or forcibly exiled. The latter are seen as inhering in individuals and applying equally to all; the former represent an ideology that Will Kymlicka calls *liberal culturalism.*[46] The two kinds of rights have different origins: human rights are a basic tenet of liberal philosophy, whereas culturally specific collective rights emerged in nineteenth-century European nationalism. The intellectual and moral footings of these two concepts only partially overlap. The clash between these ideologies in the two controversies examined in the following cases derived in no small part from the different circumstances and contexts within which human rights and the right to culture were articulated. I first wrote about these cases in 2007.[47]

The Case of Francisco Gembuel

The constitution's recognition of the special jurisdiction to be enjoyed by indigenous communities, which produced the greatest degree of juridical autonomy found anywhere in Latin America,[48] seriously challenged cabildo authorities, who then found themselves having to deal with serious crime that occurred within their jurisdictions. In earlier periods traditional authorities had in fact dealt with such cases, but in recent years the local legal machinery had been neglected because the state had taken over the adjudication of major crimes. The cabildos were on the whole eager to meet the challenge of reviving their legal jurisdiction, reasoning that if they could succeed in this area, they could reinforce the gains secured in other areas. The stakes were high, and the task was difficult. Among other things, the judicial process employed demanded adherence both to traditional usos y costumbres (some of which, as noted, had fallen into disuse) and to the fundamental law of the land.

These issues came to a head in the case of Francisco Gembuel, which received considerable attention in the media and scholarly literature.[49] In such cases, with real situations and multiple stakeholders, adjudication will necessarily become politicized, especially when, as in this case, the sentences handed down are bitterly contested, and the laws are being revised during their application or even created on the spot. During these difficult and messy proceedings, it became clear that the pueblos saw special jurisdiction as a crucial element in their recently recognized and still fragile legal status—crucial in the eyes of their fellow Colombians, the eyes of international observers, and even their own.

The Colombian national media regularly feature sensationalized stories about "traditional" punishments being handed out in indigenous communities. A story in *El Tiempo* from the year 2000 covers a decision by a cabildo's female governor to sentence men who neglect their wives and children to hang by the ankles for a short—but very painful—period in the community's stocks.[50] The story comments that traditionally stocks were used to punish people found guilty of homicide and theft; punishing irresponsible fathers this way is an innovation. Another story describes the former governor of a cabildo who, upon being found guilty of adultery and neglect, was sentenced to fourteen lashes (administered with a cattle whip on legs covered by trousers).[51] Another article describes an adulterous Nasa pair receiving seventeen lashes each. The mother of the woman says, "I'm sorry, daughter, but this is our law and we have to follow it."[52]

In the case at hand, on August 19, 1996, the Nasa cabildo of Jambaló, Cauca, found Francisco Gembuel, a Guambiano leader, and several of his companions guilty of the murder of Marden Betancur, a Nasa leader. Gembuel was sentenced to fifteen minutes in the stocks, sixty whip lashes, and banishment from Nasa territory; the others received the same or lesser sentences. Gembuel challenged the verdict and sentence: while he did not disapprove of these punishments in general, and had in fact used them during his tenure as president of CRIC, in his own case he alleged procedural irregularities and insufficient evidence for a judgment. Some Jambaló residents felt the case should have gone to the state judicial system.[53]

Both Gembuel and Betancur were well-known as leaders; Gembuel had been a member of Jambaló's cabildo as well as president of CRIC, and Betancur was Jambaló's mayor when he was killed. Gembuel and his allies, who belonged to a rival CRIC faction, had openly charged that Betancur was a *pájaro*—a paramilitary spy—and although the murder had been carried out by members of the guerrilla army ELN, the men were convicted as the intellectual authors of the crime. Gembuel's motive was allegedly anger over Betancur's winning Jambaló's highly contested 1994 mayoral election.

Gembuel's sentence was imposed on December 24, but after he received eight lashes his daughter and others physically prevented further punishment.[54] The Public Defender of Cauca (Defensor del Pueblo de Cauca), a kind of ombudsman, advised Gembuel to bring an acción de tutela to avoid further punishment, which he did. The judge found whipping to be torture, and an appellate court upheld the decision. During this period numerous protests, national and international, were voiced; Amnesty International insisted that the sentence be suspended, and it called on the civil authorities to ban any kind of corporal punishment.[55]

On January 11, 1997, an assembly of approximately one thousand Nasa met and voted to reopen the investigation. The punishment was postponed to February 20, and cabildo governors asserted that, come what may, the sentence would be carried out on that date.[56] ELN sent a communique to the cabildos saying that Betancur had not been a pájaro, and his assassination had been in error.[57] A protracted debate over many issues began, one of them being the pernicious influence of "White law" on indigenous law.[58] The case progressed to the Constitutional Court, which ruled that concepts like human rights, due process, and torture were not universal, but, rather, context-dependent, and that the use of the whip "accorded with Nasa cosmovision and was, therefore, not an instrument of torture."[59] But Gembuel had by then left Nasa territory and was never punished.

The media fixed a great deal of attention on the case. The way journalists framed the issues varied, but a surprising number of sympathetic treatments appeared. One columnist wrote about stocks' deterrent effect and concluded that, "although Colombian law does not understand, these sanctions enable the person's rehabilitation. Because everyone witnesses the punishment being carried out, a lesson is learned by all."[60] In another fairly sympathetic article, subtitled, "White law does not wash away the blame," the Jambaló governor is quoted saying that while White law is respected, they *have* to carry out sentences their own judicial authorities have handed down.[61]

Nasa authorities explained to journalists the aims embedded in their customary law. Whereas White law sentences criminals to long prison terms, Nasa punishments permit the offender's reintegration into society immediately after the sentence is carried out. The Jambaló governor told a reporter that, although the wrongdoer might prefer the penitentiary, "indigenous law considers prisons to be cruel punishments that fill the accused with vices and separate him from his family."[62] Anatolio Quirá, a well-known leader and former senator, said that the sixty-three Indians currently in Colombian prisons should be working on behalf of their communities, and that the punishment Gembuel and his associates would undergo would serve to rehabilitate and reincorporate them.[63] Rappaport notes that the offender and the community become reconciled not only by carrying out the punishment but also through the accompanying four hours of ritual, during which some cabildo officials briefly put themselves in the stocks.[64] Shamans perform a ceremony, the wrongdoer is given advice, and at the end women ritually wash the wounds.

Nasa authorities insisted that none of their traditional punishments were torture; on the contrary, handing down and carrying out such sentences worked to secure community harmony.[65] Reporters were told of Nasa fears that further bloodshed would accompany the inevitable intensification of factionalism should the sentences not be carried out. One leader said, "this [punishment] might be seen by Western culture as a rejection of the tutela and ordinary law, but we are convinced that it is this other law that threatens our indigenous social equilibrium."[66] Remarkably, even one of the accused, Alirio Pitto—who would not be whipped but would lose his political rights and be forcibly exiled—affirmed that carrying out the sentences was crucial to achieving the main goal of ending "the opposition that questions the work of the governor."[67]

It was also argued that were Gembuel to win his tutela, the pueblo's hard-won autonomy would be threatened. The outcome of the case would probably establish definitively whether indigenous or nonindigenous authorities would adjudicate cases when both sorts of jurisprudence were involved. Nasa authorities wanted to avoid any process that determined once and for all the degree of pueblo autonomy in this domain. Interviewees stressed the importance of the constitutional guarantee of special indigenous jurisdiction. The incommensurability between the two legal systems was also mentioned: Jesús Piñacué, at the time president of CRIC, said that Amnesty International's protests had "created a confusion about laws because Westerners don't understand indigenous law."

Interviewees also argued that Nasa authorities' actions had reduced ELN's influence. Cristóbal Secué, a Nasa leader, said that if a man was found guilty of committing a serious crime and not punished, "guerrilla justice" would step in and kill him, which would once again demonstrate illegal armed groups' power in indigenous territories.[68] A major motivation driving Nasa efforts to define and implement legal jurisdiction, according to Rappaport, was "to establish a legitimate local authority in the face of the threat of guerrilla, paramilitary, and army hegemony, in the absence of efforts on the part of the Colombian state to contain armed actors."[69]

The Gembuel case throws into stark relief the built-in contradiction between the hope that usos y costumbres would "ultimately supplant Colombian legal usages in the resguardos" and the insistence that indigenous people's individual rights as Colombian citizens entitled them to due process and to fair and reasonable punishment.[70] Disputes over jurisdiction occur regularly whenever traditional and state authorities both intervene, either when a case draws in indigenous and nonindigenous actors, or when indigenous individuals appeal cabildo court rulings.[71] Indigenous tribunals have been criticized as discriminatory, authoritarian, or overly intrusive, and their fact-finding procedures and rulings have been found incompatible with foundational premises of Western law—in the Gembuel case, with habeas corpus.

Rappaport notes that the Constitutional Court did not define special indigenous jurisdiction in terms of age-old traditions and customs that needed to be recovered and put into practice.[72] Special jurisdiction, she argues, is best understood as a form of "counter-modernity," which will vary from pueblo to pueblo and evolve over time. Clarifying the relationship between indigenous special jurisdiction and Western law is very much an ongoing project that takes place in many venues—not only appellate courts and the Constitutional Court but also grassroots legal committees and cabildo meetings. Regardless of the outcome of Colombia's experiment in legal pluralism, the relationship between special indigenous jurisdiction and Western positive law will always be strained and subject to periodic crises, which Jane Cowan, Marie Dembour, and Richard Wilson call "explosions."[73]

Special jurisdiction, it turns out, is a dynamic institution. It is not at all clear to what extent pueblos will be permitted to *generate* their own laws, as opposed to discovering abandoned laws and traditions from the past.[74] The criteria imposed by magistrates have differed widely. Some have tried to assess a plaintiff community's cultural "purity" in terms of its degree of acculturation.[75] The Jambaló decision received so much attention in part because Magistrate Carlos Gaviria Díaz did *not* zero in on such questions. Informed by *amicus curiae* briefs from legal anthropologist Esther Sánchez, who had worked with the Nasa, he asked Nasa authorities to describe the intention behind their laws, which led to the finding that whipping was not equivalent to torture because its purpose was to ritually purify the violator, welcome him or her back into the community, and restore harmony. Gaviria maintained that "only a high degree of autonomy would ensure cultural survival."[76]

This case also illustrates a tension between two strategies. On the one hand Nasa authorities became increasingly conscious of the need to translate their legal and moral reasoning into a language dominant society institutions could understand. On the other hand it was at times politically useful to insist on radical difference, to assert that their reasoning was so radically Other that translation was impossible. Rappaport calls this assertion of incommensurability "the expression of sovereignty through cultural difference," deployed to reinforce claims of authentic indigenousness when they are under threat.[77] The distinct Nasa worldview, their *cosmovision*, undergirds this incommensurability by providing the framing for Nasa legal procedures.[78] Not only is there at times no compelling reason for pueblos to translate their cosmologies or social practices into the Westernized rights language, but at times pueblos will have strategic reasons to present their cosmologies and traditional usos y costumbres as simply untranslatable. Adopting this position helps pueblos to establish and maintain claims to sovereignty, especially during disputes involving the interface between customary law and Western law.[79]

The Case of Jesús Piñacué

A second special jurisdiction case parallels the Gembuel one in several respects. While it did not receive nearly as much international attention, it was widely covered in the national media due to the prominence of its protagonist, Jesús Enrique Piñacué, a Nasa senator in the Colombian Congress. Despite a promise to Nasa authorities and ASI (one of the two political parties supporting him) that he would not publicly support any candidate during the 1997 presidential campaign, he subsequently declared on television that he would vote for Horacio Serpa, the Liberal party candidate. The president of ASI accused Piñacué of "high treason" and of violating Nasa customary law. In response to these charges, Piñacué said he would postpone occupying the senate seat to which he had just been elected until the matter could be resolved, adding that he would prefer losing his seat to losing his *patria* (fatherland; i.e., the Nasa pueblo).[80]

Cabildo governors and members of ASI assembled to debate the issue, along with more general questions about juridical authority.[81] Much of the discussion was devoted to deciding on an appropriate punishment, both its "physical" (whipping) and "moral" components; the latter would involve denying Piñacué permission to assume his senate seat.[82] A lot of political jockeying followed, but in the end Piñacué received the punishment he requested: to be cast into the sacred lake of Juan Tama in the eastern part of Cauca, a traditional ritual that had been revived in 1983 after having fallen into disuse at the beginning of the twentieth century.[83] This "sacred wash," a ritual of *refrescamiento* (cooling), would be preceded by deep, secret, and silent meditation.[84]

Although the outcomes of the two cases differed, and electoral politics played a major role in the Piñacué case, there are a number of similarities. Both men had been president of CRIC. Both cases inspired debates about whether special jurisdiction could be a legitimate part of Colombia's jurisprudence. As indicated earlier, the customary laws enlisted in the decision making were a work in progress. Having been passed down orally from generation to generation, these laws were missing the kind of documentation that typically accompanies judicial decision making in the West. Both cases illustrated the felt need to punish in an expedient manner in order to get past the matter of wrongdoing, rehabilitate the offender, and restore order. Like the punishment handed down to Gembuel and his companions, Piñacué's sentence involved rituals. In his case the participants would need to walk more than six hours to reach the lake, and after spending the night in the freezing cold (at 4,400 meters), ten shamans would throw the nude Piñacué into the water, which would allow him "to begin to walk the road back"—to be reincorporated into the Nasa community and able to occupy his senate seat. He would also have to acknowledge his wrongdoing to the governors, and visit every resguardo to renew his commitments with his fellow Nasa.[85] Both cases also illustrated concerns at some remove from the specific matters at hand; for example, shamanic and other rituals would work to confirm to the community that cabildo authority was being upheld. Participants also hoped to minimize the likelihood of negative consequences such as political factionalism, which in the Gembuel case might incite revenge killings and strengthen guerrilla power in Nasa territory. In both cases pueblo members—even some of the accused—praised the superiority of customary law. Finally, both cases illustrate how a diverse set of complications may appear when dominant society institutions become entangled with the application of traditional justice. Nasa leaders were insistent in both cases that traditional jurisprudence had jurisdiction, but displayed an uneasy defensiveness following the negative publicity generated about procedures that were poorly understood by mainstream society, in particular punishments that seemed to violate Western notions of basic human rights.

The role played by whips, stocks, and coerced exile in both cases resonates with Elizabeth Povinelli's discussion of "repugnance" in her examination of Australia's multiculturalist laws and government policies.[86] Such "repugnant" behaviors threaten to "shatter the skeletal structure" of state law. When this happens, mainstream society's experience of "fundamental alterity" transforms the subaltern into something so profoundly "not-us" that an impasse is reached. Nasa customary law not only needed to be seen by the dominant society as a "real acknowledgment of traditional law and real observance of traditional customs," the laws also had to be acceptable—in Povinelli's terms, they could contain no "repugnant" features.

The Piñacué case inspired some journalists to offer critiques of the larger society by pointing out certain "constructive" lessons Nasa traditions and special indigenous jurisprudence could provide. Newspaper columnist Manuel Hernández begins his discussion of the case by pointing out that Colombia's pueblos, having suffered from discrimination, abandonment, and great hardship, were working hard to maintain the vitality of indigenous customs.[87] Unlike what happens in Colombian society, he writes, Piñacué and those accompanying him to Juan Tama Lake had joked together during the long walk, and all accepted that the punishment was just—a substantial contrast with the antagonism and ill will found so frequently in the judicial proceedings of the "so-called 'civilized' sectors."

In both cases Western liberal notions about human rights conflicted with, in the Gembuel case, a "repugnant" sentence handed down by resguardo authorities, and in the Piñacué case, the possibility that Nasa governors would choose a similarly unacceptable punishment. The Gembuel case illustrates Cowan, Dembour, and Wilson's point about the tensions and periodic "explosions" that will inevitably occur with the growth of rights discourses, and the linking up (sometimes so awkwardly that we should perhaps say "lashing up") of indigenous, culture-specific, collective rights regimes (e.g., rights to culture regimes) with universal basic human rights ones.[88] Both cases show the important role played by struggles for autonomy and sovereignty, in many cases involving special indigenous jurisdiction.

These cases provide support for Goodale's proposition that "social practice is, in part, constitutive of the idea of human rights, rather than simply the testing ground on which the idea of universal human [rights] encounters actual ethical or legal systems."[89] Authorities like Constitutional Court magistrate Carlos Gaviria provide clear evidence of this constitutive capacity, as Gaviria did with his ruling on the Gembuel case. And while we cannot conclude that the concept of basic human rights lost any of its power subsequent to the ruling, a heterodoxy was introduced in a very visible manner. That the heterodoxy was taken seriously by an authoritative state institution occasioned a great deal of discussion and controversy, both inside Colombia and in the broader world. The case supports Goodale's argument that the concept of transcultural universal human rights is "itself a product of particular histories and cultural imperatives, so that it is simply not possible to consider the idea of human rights 'in the abstract.'"[90]

The Gembuel case involved a variety of actors with a range of interests in its outcome: Jambaló residents, other Nasa resguardos, other pueblos, indigenous organizations and their allies, government officials, armed combatants, a curious public, and international organizations like Amnesty International. Examining rights-claiming practices in cases like this reveals the dynamic mutual influence between international rights discourses and what happens on the ground. That transnational human rights regimes imported into the country have had powerful effects is clear: their premises and language have deeply influenced indigenous decision making about what kinds of demands to make and how best to articulate them. But we also see how rights-claiming practices can produce effects in the other direction—in the Gembuel case, for example, on the state apparatus via the Constitutional Court, and in the court of public opinion, as evidenced by the sympathetic media accounts.

Debates about special indigenous jurisprudence like the ones discussed here open up spaces for citizens, indigenous and not, to rethink, and at times contest, the parameters of state and civil institutions. Following adoption of the constitution, Colombian citizens found themselves confronting new forms of governmentality that involved dispersed and graduated sovereignties. If a diverse citizenry with differentiated rights is recognized by the most fundamental law of the land, and upheld by multiple state institutions, what, in fact, does citizenship consist of? Achieving the constitutional and legislative goals of strengthening indigenous customary legal institutions worked to redefine the identity of the state itself.

The two cases illustrate how indigenous movements, like all social movements, challenge "the boundaries of cultural and political representation and social practice,"[91] and illustrate the need to see culture as first, a dimension of all institutions, and, second, a set of *material* practices that constitute meanings, values, and subjectivities.[92] When customary law is used to safeguard cultural alterity, unanticipated material practices will occur that at times radically diverge from the national and legal multiculturalist imaginary. The reforms transformed Colombia into a "multicultural and pluriethnic" state, which did constitute a radical change, but only at the discursive level. A subsequent and quite powerful example of a material instantiation of this new discursive regime was a state institution's ruling that torture, as defined in the West, could be interpreted as not torture if the trial took place under special indigenous jurisdiction. In the Piñacué case, had the governors chosen whipping, the state might very well have allowed the sentence to be carried out, which would have been another powerful instantiation of the new regime.

Special jurisdiction is granted when a community is officially recognized as indigenous, a recognition that depends in part on the belief that its members share a culture distinct from mainstream society's. Both cases, the Gembuel one in particular, vividly illustrate Cowan's point regarding "the complex and contradictory consequences of being granted rights on the basis of having a culture and a cultural identity."[93] Because autonomy depends on a community's having a distinct culture, if that community is to ensure that their special status remains in good standing—in their own eyes as well as the eyes of outsiders—it needs to reach a consensus about conceptions of, and proper performance of, their Otherness. "Culture" is not the same as autonomy, but the two are deeply imbricated in multiculturalist regimes, and the two cases reveal a concern on the part of both the Colombian state and the country's indigenous citizenry that increased participation in modern life can restrict or otherwise diminish a pueblo's culture. We have seen many examples of pueblo members struggling to ensure that their culture not be diminished in a way that would threaten their special status.[94] Some Colombian Constitutional Court magistrates work hard to respect the constitution's intent, aware of the threat posed by "a rigid federalism that seeks to create a homogeneous community via the force of a sovereign mandate."[95] Of course, given that the constitution was framed within the context of Western democratic ideals and practices, the court's mandate to respect the country's pluriethnic and multicultural character extends only so far.[96] But we have seen that at times the parameters of decision making have taken extraordinarily divergent visions of justice into consideration.

In a country with a dysfunctional legal system, rife with immunity and impunity, these decisions might seem especially paradoxical. But magistrates' receptivity to the challenges posed by special indigenous jurisdiction might in fact be due to the fact that ordinarily judges operate in a situation where the vast majority of crimes go unpunished and court schedules are massively backlogged. The country's judicial apparatus, along with the numerous state and civil institutions involved in the case, might have been especially responsive to a case that *presumed* a well-intentioned and reasonably functional judicial system. Some authors, like the journalist Manuel Hernández, suggest that such judicial processes, albeit unfamiliar, are nonetheless providing an alternative vision of a just state and civil society.

Pueblos know that they must performatively index alterity if they are to ensure that their communities continue to qualify for the benefits to which they are entitled as possessors of an authorized culture. The two cases show Nasa authorities engaged in precisely such self-authenticating performances by enacting their traditional jurisprudence, and by so doing subverting federal and municipal law. Trouble arises when mainstream society deems the cultural content of such performances "inappropriate," or even "repugnant." Povinelli argues that indigenous people face an impossible demand: "that they desire and identify with their cultural traditions in a way that just so happens, in an uncanny convergence of interests, to fit the national and legal imaginary of multiculturalism."[97] She believes that flesh-and-blood indigenous people will never manage to get it "just right," and will invariably fail to qualify for inclusion in the nation's imaginary of indigeneity. The hegemonic domination characteristic of postcolonial multicultural societies, she argues, "works primarily by inspiring in the indigenous subject a desire to identify with a lost indeterminable object—indeed, to be the melancholic subject of traditions." For her, indigenous persons are "'always already' failures of indigeneity as such."[98] Although the Colombian and Australian cases differ profoundly, Povinelli's points about what happens when an unanticipated "repugnance" is evoked in a multiculturalist environment that, in general, celebrates difference and works to increase tolerance are well taken. Pueblo authorities are charged to come up with forms of cultural difference that are sufficiently Other to convince mainstream society that a pueblo's claims-making should not be dismissed out of hand—but not too Other, which would summon "repugnant" responses.

Both cases, particularly the Gembuel one, show what can happen when indigenous authorities in an out-of-the-way place productively engage liberal multiculturalism's logics and adopt "pluralizing strategies . . . that employ the deceptively novel language of human rights."[99] The cases provide a telling example of human rights theories being shaped and conceptualized "outside the centers of elite discourse."[100] The cases also demonstrate Merry's argument that the notion of "local" is "deeply problematic," as well as Goodale's contention that "the sites where human rights unfold in practice do matter, and these sites are not simply nodes in a virtual network, but actual *places* in social space."[101]

A final point relates to Richard Wilson's recommendation to pay attention to "human rights according to the actions and the intentions of the social actors, within the wider historical constraints of institutionalized power."[102] A major factor in the Gembuel case was a weak and negligent state, one that by no means had a monopoly on violence. This kind of situation permits horrendous violence to occur with impunity, which of course threatens further violence, here in the form of either a revenge killing by a pueblo member or an extrajudicial assassination by illegal armed actors. In such situations, vulnerable indigenous populations, working to secure and maintain stability, enlist particular traditions and authorize particular actors to carry out actions that challenge assumptions contained within the West's putatively transcultural human rights regime. In the two Nasa cases stakeholders participated in a variety of ways: some actors (cabildo governors) handed down sentences that other actors defended, or challenged, during a sequence of appeals. A multitude of bystanders discussed the proceedings and their ramifications. If the opposite of vulnerability is stability, we need to keep in mind that in Colombia indigenous communities have been anything but stable, and that the armed conflict was a backdrop to every single event that led to the various packages of legislation, treaty-signings, and government policy proclamations that gave pueblos collective territory, degrees of autonomy, and other benefits.

Coca Rights: Manufacturing and Marketing Indigenous Tradition

The questions about rights that I have been exploring in this chapter, in particular the state's evolving definition of indigenous autonomy, surface again in quite a different context, an effort by a group of Nasa to manufacture and sell coca-based products.[103] Their decision to develop such products grew out of legislation allowing small amounts of coca to be grown in the country's resguardos. In a discussion of these issues, anthropologist Marta Zambrano describes coca as occupying a "gray zone, ambiguous and contradictory" in state policies.[104] This convergence of ethnic identity, managed multiculturalism, and capitalism, in which state promotion of indigenous arts and crafts came up against antidrug legislation, produced a number of telling contradictions.

Beginning in 1999, a company called Coca Nasa, located in the resguardo of Calderas in Tierradentro, Cauca, developed a coca tea called Coca Nasa, Nasa Esh's (Figure 2), and a coca soft drink (*gaseosa*) called Coca-Sek. Coca Nasa also manufactured coca cookies and had plans to develop coca toothpaste, soap, chewing gum, bread, *tortas* (cakes), and wine.[105] The Huila branch of the Yanacona pueblo (most Yanaconas live in Cauca) also began to market a coca tea called Kokasana.

Coca tea is drunk throughout the Andes, and packaged coca tea had been

Figure 2. Coca Nasa, Nasa Esh's tea.

on Colombian store shelves for some time. But a coca-based gaseosa was something new. The question was, what rights and protections were to be extended to Coca Nasa's plan to market its products beyond Nasa resguardos? The quite considerable debate that erupted over this question illustrates in a revealing way what happens when state efforts to institutionalize multiculturalism encourage expansive assertions of rights, in this case leading the state to rein in such assertions and work to confine indigenous difference to specific locations—resguardos—and to an imaginary of "tradition" that is rooted in the past.

Coca is intimately linked to indigenous culture: it is used for medicinal and ritual purposes throughout Colombia's highlands and in parts of Amazonia, including the Vaupés. The packaging for Coca Nasa, Nasa Esh's states: "This delicious infusion is produced and commercialized by Nasa Indians of Tierradentro, Cauca. It comes from the coca leaf of life, EXs [*Erythroxylum coca*], and has an important significance for the Nasa people. We want to show part of our millenarian wisdom to the *Musxkcas* [nonindigenous person]. The coca leaf comes from coca cultivations authorized by law. Indigenous industry of Cauca (www.cocanasa.org)." The packaging for Kokasana is similar:

an indigenous, "100% natural" product that comes out of ten thousand years of tradition, Kokasana is

> the essence of the coca leaf, a plant cultivated in indigenous family plots in Colombia. Its leaves are selected following ancestral wisdom, harvested during the most propitious lunar stage, and subsequently dried in a natural manner. . . . This tea has an aroma of both the Andes and the jungle. . . . The product is manufactured with the support of Autoridades Ancestrales Indígenas in concordance with the National Constitution Sent. No. C-176/94, Constitutional Court. A project directed by members of Aboriginal Cultures of Colombia, with the support of the Indigenous Foundation Sol y Serpiente de América. . . . The proper use of coca brings life, essence of the spirit and bodily strength. Coca is one of the most prodigious ancestral plants of America because of its nutritive and preventive properties. For centuries it has been used by indigenous science and is recognized today by present-day science (www.kokasana.com).

Promotors have pointed out that not only are Kokasana and Coca Nasa, Nasa Esh's pure and medically valuable, the teas are manufactured in Colombia by Colombian companies—and profits remain in the country. An added value for some people was that these products avoid being a part of controversial treaties, like the free trade agreement Colombia signed with the United States.

Coca represents an extremely interesting—and rare—kind of polyvalence. In Colombia, it is seen as indigenous, traditional, pure, healthy, natural, and (within resguardos) entirely legal. But as the source of cocaine, coca conjures up an immense illegal economy characterized by drug cartels, monstrous violence, addiction, and prison terms. In my experience very few people in the United States know about coca's "good" side—no one has been interested in drinking the tea I brought back. But for the most part the Colombian media have supported Coca Nasa's efforts, in part out of nationalism: coca is Colombian, cocaine a foreigner's vice.

At the first public tasting of Coca-Sek in November 2005, attendees said they liked its taste. Journalist Adriana Espinel writes that Coca-Sek clearly has the earthy (*terroso*) flavor of coca.[106] Its color, a translucent yellow, made it totally distinct from other gaseosas. Another journalist likened its color to apple cider, its taste to ginger ale.[107] Coca Nasa representatives said that while indigenous approval of the gaseosa was important, the trick was to get potential nonindigenous consumers to accept Coca-Sek's flavor: six years had been spent testing the product on mestizos, Whites, and foreigners. The formula had not yet been patented because, representatives said, it was the shared heritage of all Latin American peoples. Coca-Sek's formula, nonetheless, like Coca-Cola's famously top-secret formula, was "the most closely guarded secret in this zone."[108] The press was also on hand for the launch of Coca-Sek at a festival the next month. Coca Nasa's co-director, David Curtidor, is quoted as saying, "We thought a lot about how to penetrate the Western market and we realized that the ideal product would be a gaseosa." Espinel writes that the manufacturers hoped that Coca-Sek would prove popular enough to compete with "the big ones" in a "war of the colas"—national gaseosas and, of course, Coca-Cola.

Like coca tea, Coca-Sek's marketing drew heavily on an indigenous imaginary. The manufacturers were quoted as saying that Coca-Sek tastes best "when the Sun God shines with all of his splendor and it is hot." Promotional rhetoric also drew on tropes relating to the natural and the healthy. Curtidor said that they wanted to demonstrate that the coca leaf can have a healthy use, and hoped that "people buy our product rather than others because this one comes out of the true earth." Co-director Fabiola Piñacué said that, during her student days, she realized she wanted to work to "de-Satanize" the plant's reputation.[109] Above all, Curtidor emphasized, Coca-Sek was national.

But Coca-Sek lost the cola war. On January 29, 2007, the Instituto Nacional de Vigilancia de Medicamentos and Alimentos (INVIMA, National Institute of Vigilance with Respect to Medicines and Foods) sent a circular to the secretaries of health in thirty departments, requiring that all commercial establishments remove "products derived from coca" from their shelves if they were being sold outside of indigenous territories. INVIMA's director explained that although "the Indians had been requesting a health license for their products for five years," the agency had not granted one, and that, furthermore, the Ministry of Social Protection had told the company in 2005 that the "derivatives of coca are a monopoly of the State." The National Directorate of Narcotics had also sent a letter saying that the production of these products violated the United Nations Single Convention on Narcotic Drugs (*Estupefacientes*), issued in 1961. For these reasons, said INVIMA's director, it was not possible to issue a health license for these products: "I respect the rights of indigenous pueblos, but as an institution we need to act within the frame of the international conventions, as well as certain current legal regulations."[110] Curtidor and Piñacué responded on behalf of Coka-Sek that they had received permission in a letter signed by INVIMA's director, telling them that the resguardo of Calderas in Cauca's Tierradentro zone had permission to utilize coca leaves in the production of infusions. Curtidor said that the denial of permission smacked of retaliation by Coca-Cola, because in 2006 the Nasa had won a suit brought by that company trying to prevent Coca-Sek from using the word *coca* because it was a trademark. Curtidor suggested that Coca-Cola had bought off INVIMA: "We haven't seen the check, nor do we know its amount." He asked, "Who can call himself owner of the word 'coca' when this plant is endemic throughout the Andes and Amazonia?"

The decision received considerable media attention, most of it sympathetic to Coca Nasa's side.[111] One article points out that INVIMA's ruling carried serious consequences—the damage was substantial for an economy as small as that of Calderas. For example, five thousand boxes of coca tea had recently been sent to Puerto Rico and another three thousand to Canada. With annual sales of over 300 million pesos and a total investment of 500 million pesos, Coca Nasa was described as having undertaken the reactivation of eastern Cauca's subsistence economy. More than two thousand indigenous families had taken charge of providing dried coca leaf to the company.

Coca Nasa subsequently brought a tutela against the ruling, alleging violation of the pueblo's right to life, subsistence, identity, and ethnic and cultural integrity, not to mention equality and due process. In addition to the lawsuit, ONIC took the measure as an affront to all the country's pueblos. The previous week ONIC had denounced the case to U.S. Congressman James McGovern: "We cannot speak of the Free Trade Act in a country where we are not even at liberty to market products throughout national territory." They also alleged that the action violated Convention 169 of the International Labor Organization, which protects the work rights of indigenous peoples.

Coca Nasa leaders also announced that they would go to the Inter-American Commission on Human Rights. As reported in an *El Tiempo* article, Curtidor argued that "the state ought to combat narcotrafficking, but it also ought to defend the patrimony of the nation, which coca is." He was referring to Article 7 of the constitution, which says the coca leaf "is cultural patrimony of the Colombian Nation." In addition, co-director Piñacué complained of a paradox: "in the resguardos we consume commercialized foods with preservatives that damage health—they're poison, rubbish—whereas our products, which are healthy, ought to be in the national market."[112]

INVIMA director Julio César Aldana responded to Curtidor and Piñacué by saying that if his accusers' claim about "hidden interests" was backed up by evidence, they should denounce him to the Attorney General; the one time he spoke with Coca-Cola representatives was to talk about the content of their ingredients and review their health licenses. Also, while coca tea did not appear to be injurious to health, INVIMA had not supervised the production of the gaseosa and so could not affirm anything. Resolution of the issue, he said, would require the participation of many government agencies.[113]

The article also quotes Arahugo Gañán, ONIC's Counselor of Peace, who said that "these medicinal plants" had been used by the narco-mafiosos for purposes that hurt the country, and now that a way had been discovered to provide another use that was favorable to the resguardo, "they come up with this." He blamed the national gaseosa companies, who, he said, fearful of inroads to their profits, had pressured INVIMA. He also complained about the government's "poisonous" aerial spraying of coca plants. He contended that the government *could* authorize Coca Nasa because the Single Convention on Narcotic Drugs, which Colombia signed on March 30, 1961, established that some parties were permitted to authorize the use of coca leaves in the preparation of soporific agents if they did not have any alkaloid—provided that such projects were communicated to the United Nations International Narcotics Control Board (INCB). Gañán also complained about the National Narcotics Council's reason for turning down the company's request, saying that it could not approve a manufacturing project whose purpose did not protect the usos y costumbres of the nation's indigenous communities. Commercially manufacturing these products appeared to threaten Nasa culture.[114]

An even more sympathetic article reports on a meeting on March 18, 2007, that lasted three and a half hours. Arguments were "thrown back and forth" by the participants, who exhibited, according to the journalist, "some fine displays of bureaucratic posturing." The National Narcotics Council held that products such as Coca-Sek did not fit the national identity of Colombian indigeneity; others disagreed. The director of the Office of Ethnic Groups (formerly DAI) "emphatically" told the attendees that while the government respected the traditional uses of coca, "to market gaseosas made out of coca is another matter." Curtidor responded by pointing out that the Constitutional Court had ruled that "cultural identity transcends indigenous territories," such that to allow coca use "only within an indigenous territory is segregation, and coca is national patrimony."[115]

After asking "Why Coca-Cola yes and Coca-Sek no?," the journalist provides an interesting summary of a discussion about whether the amount of active agent in Coca-Sek was legal. Curtidor said an analysis of Coca-Cola would reveal traces of some components of coca. INVIMA's director said that that would have to be looked into, because "there ought to be equality of conditions." According to Curtidor, each gram of Coca-Sek had a percentage of 1 in 10,000 (i.e., 0.01%) of egnonina, the active agent, which meant that the alkaloid that could be extracted from these soft drinks was legal, because such substances were only illegal after reaching 1 percent—which probably left some *El Tiempo* readers wondering to what extent claims made for the drink's benefits were valid.[116]

The journalist points out that "perhaps what is most disconcerting to the Indians is that when Coca-Sek was launched . . . President Alvaro Uribe sent them a message congratulating them on the product and the company."[117] Uribe's letter congratulated Coca Nasa because the Coca-Sek project had been selected as a finalist in a contest for the best business plan. A similar sort of recognition was issued by the Office of the President in 2003 to the Fundación Sol y Tierra, praising the initiative behind Kokasana tea as a laudable example of entrepreneurship, sustainable agriculture, and respect for culture.[118]

An Op-Ed appeared two days later that came out strongly in favor of the Nasa project, beginning with, "How many times have I taken a coca tea for a headache or accumulated fatigue?" The author continues: "indigenous communities have woven complex cultural constructions . . . around the plant, which serves as a key element in the perpetuation of their identity," an identity protected by the constitution. He adds that the distance "between this case and the 'supposed' arguments about [the need to] prevent drug trafficking" is "huge . . . and I say 'supposed,' because, at bottom, apart from a whiff of racism, it would seem that what bothers those who have taken . . . this decision is that the indigenous communities are no longer on those post cards, good for tourism." When, he continues, the Indians dedicated themselves to constructing options for the future that were market-based, they apparently represented a threat, even to great multinational companies. Apparently the country was already uneasy with "these Indians who want to leave the borders of their resguardo and participate as citizens in the construction of the nation." He asks, who was going to compensate the indigenous communities that took out microcredits in order to build these companies? Who was going to assume the costs of the lost jobs? Was this the right way to activate the economy of the region so as to help the poorest populations? He ends by saying, "sad news, whose bitter taste only a good coca tea can fix."[119]

Another Op-Ed, from 2008, makes many of the same points, arguing that INVIMA's actions threatened Indians' ability to modernize a pre-Columbian custom, which meant that "we are not facing a policing problem, but a cultural one."[120] The article ends by pointing out that although cocaine is indeed a dangerous drug, it wasn't the Incas who synthesized cocaine but the Europeans.

A lot more could be said about the background of this case (e.g., the international community was gearing up to protest the coca policies of Bolivian president Evo Morales[121]), and about the various positions taken in the dispute. Arguments keyed to development not only pointed to Coca Nasa as a sustainable alternative project targeting one of the poorest regions of the country, but also claimed that support for this sort of coca cultivation would divert Indians from growing coca for narcotraffickers.[122] A related argument, in favor of projects that would develop Colombia as a nation, invoked official multiculturalism's insistence on inclusivity—on democratic processes made available to all sectors of the country, no matter how small or remote. Curtidor stated that because Coca-Sek "is a symbiosis of the indigenous and mestizo worlds," it represents informed and tolerant coexistence. And nationalism (as previously noted) appeared frequently: coca, it was argued, is patrimony of the nation, and profits from these products would stay within the country's borders.

It would seem that both the Nasa entrepreneurs and coca itself, once outside an isolated resguardo, lose their special protected status, the Nasa as *indio permitido*[123] and the plant as *hoja permitida*. Coca-Sek attracted attention not only from prospective clients and supporters, but also from critics, most of them in the government, who took issue either with Indians engaging in nontraditional projects, or with coca products leaving the resguardos for the mestizo world, where they were subjected to the crossfire of contradictory discourses. On the one hand, official multiculturalism, which was most obvious in the actions of the Constitutional Court, favored the expansion of the kinds of rights claimed by companies like Coca Nasa. On the other, the liberal juridical regime, as both Marta Zambrano and Juliana Iglesias point out, was focused on upholding antinarcotics covenants and policies.[124]

Conclusions

Rights are often seen as inhering naturally in individuals and collectivities, but, sociologically speaking, rights exist only when they are claimed or recognized.

In this chapter, the implications and contradictions of rights-claiming have been examined in four cases, which fall into three general categories: (1) demands that officially recognized rights be enforced; (2) crises that occur when two rights systems come into open conflict; and (3) disagreements about the legitimacy of resguardo-originated commercial endeavors engaging mainstream society.

Indigenous communities struggle for recognition of their civil and political rights (what are sometimes known as "negative" rights), as well as recognition of certain "positive" rights to such things as education and health services. These communities also struggle to have their collective right to difference recognized and enforced. Indigenous Colombian citizens belong to two polities, each with its own rights system. In effect, they exercise two distinct sets of rights, the first embodying the "negative" and "positive" rights of national citizenship, and the second embodying rights—often labelled "special" rights—enjoyed by members of a pueblo.[125] The arguments marshalled by the participants in the two cases concerned with special jurisdiction hinge on "the relative weight and merits of universalist and particularist claims."[126] As these cases demonstrate, contradictions often appear when rights inhering in the individual and rights inhering in the community are put into play at the same time.[127]

Rights-claiming activities may take the form of public demonstrations demanding enforcement of rights officially recognized but so far not activated or supported. Protests may include civil disobedience, notably takeovers of government buildings or highway blockades. Or claimants may decide to work entirely within the system, by circulating petitions, writing Op-Eds, and appealing to various institutions, national and international. This last approach, sometimes termed the "politics of embarrassment," is evident in Coca Nasa's efforts to counteract the government's refusal to approve marketing of their product.

Despite the contending parties' disparate amounts of power, rights-claiming is a two-way street. Tania Li notes the constraints felt by those trying to assert themselves in national arenas: "Those who demand that their rights be acknowledged must fill the places of recognition that others provide, using dominant languages and demanding a voice in bureaucratic and other power-saturated encounters, even as they seek to stretch, reshape, or even invert the meanings implied."[128] Such stretching and reshaping do sometimes happen, as the 1996 takeovers illustrate: in their encounters with state functionaries, indigenous leaders extracted concessions like the agreement to set up the consultation roundtable and to commission nonstate authorities to monitor future proceedings.

Official recognition of the right to difference can lead to subsequent unanticipated meaning construction, and novel, often expanding, demands. The Gembuel case in particular illustrates how, in a democratizing polity, "rights are not just what the law provides, but are created through the process of governmentality as well as in the process of their pursuit."[129] In the Coca Nasa case, actors took a development project based on the right to culture and on each pueblo's right to work toward a better future (as spelled out in the constitutionally mandated Life Plans[130]) in an unforeseen direction. In the light of coca's status as part of the national patrimony, the state's interest in patrimonialization became tangled in the controversy. However, even though at times the state appears to be forced to cede power, or faces the threat of that happening in the future, many examples show the state benefiting in some way from a decision to recognize rights more robustly or to take a more hands-off stance. For example, by allowing indigenous communities to deal directly with multinational companies seeking permission for intrusions like seismic testing, the state sidesteps any accusations that it helped multinationals at the expense of small, vulnerable communities it is supposed to protect.

In multiculturalist regimes the right to culture underpins other kinds of demands, such as political and territorial claims. Advancing such claims, however, may have costs and unforeseen consequences, as is evident in the four cases making up this chapter (as well as in other cases considered in the next chapter). In such struggles, "culture" almost inevitably ends up essentialized in a simplified imaginary, forcing indigenous actors and pueblos to demonstrate their authenticity.[131] Karen Engle writes of the "dark sides and unintended consequences" of such moves, including the alienation and commodification of culture and the burden of performing it more or less continuously.[132] Faudree takes this argument one step further: "claims to rights within polyethnic, postcolonial nation-states such as Mexico become necessarily linked to a peculiar form of cultural violence, in which notions of culture and tradition must be codified and thereby fundamentally altered in the process of presenting them to national audiences."[133] As Povinelli puts it, indigenous communities must produce "a detailed account of the content of their traditions and the force with which they identify with them," an account congruent with mainstream society's imaginary of "real" indigeneity.[134] Official multiculturalism, in her opinion, requires subaltern and minority subjects "to identify with the impossible object of an authentic self-identity . . . a domesticated nonconflictual 'traditional' form of sociality and (inter) subjectivity."[135]

The right to difference is always linked to the question of authorization: how is the rights-claiming actor, whether an individual or community, whether authorized (or not), to mount a case? Who determines which actors have which ethnic rights? In the Gembuel case, Magistrate Gaviria argued in favor of supporting Nasa usos y costumbres even when the punishment involved whips and coerced exile, citing the need to strengthen pueblo autonomy "to ensure cultural survival." Although Engle argues that recognition of the right to culture in fact leads to its being sidelined from political debate—"utilized as a celebratory form of (limited) recognition, it enables visibility and autonomy over certain aspects of indigenous worlds but is not allowed to be a charter for governance that might compete with the sovereignty of the nation-state"[136]—Gaviria's decision and its rationale seem to suggest that this is not always the case.

The four cases also illustrate the coexistence of the right to culture with other rationales for rights. In her interviews with me, Gladys Jimeno mentioned the state's obligation to support the country's pueblos: first, in order to right past wrongs, and second, because of the pueblos' current vulnerability. I noticed that she did not use multiculturalist rhetoric about the value of indigenous culture, but, rather, focused entirely on pueblos' suffering in the past, present, and future. Niezen provides an interesting discussion of claims-making based on the right to culture versus claims-making based on suffering.[137] He is interested in the way a community's quest for cultural justice can lead to a "rediscovered" collective self. For him, cultural justice is concerned with "the extent to which indigenous claims must be made on the terrain of cultural difference to gain recognition by nonindigenous publics . . . and the tendency of such claims to be made on the basis of suffering."[138]

One can see, in the way that culture is invoked, a diverse set of rationales and even a continuum of differential valorizations of difference. Indigenousness just by itself is valuable: a product containing coca has added value if it is manufactured by indigenous people because they harness nature, the sun, and so forth, in the process. Indigenous culture, if seen as part of a national or universal patrimony, also adds value. And, of course, culture may support or attract tourism, evident in Guaviare's self-designation as an "eco-ethno-tourist destination" because of the Nukak residing within its borders. Indigenous actors benefit if they submit the best business plan or the best menu using local ingredients. Authenticity produces added value—"real Indians" and "real indigenous communities" are preferable to hybrid ones.

A final positive value of culture is alterity itself, which is enshrined in many forms of multiculturalism. As is evident in this chapter, pueblos that successfully argue for the incommensurability between the basic premises of their justice system and national law demonstrate the attraction and valorization of the Other. When this value is in play, we have the curious situation of the state denying its own capacity to gather information and evidence in order to determine the appropriate course of action.

The right to culture, however, often comes up against distinct limits, as happened when critics argued that activities linked to coca must accord with conventional understandings of usos y costumbres. Coca-Sek lost the cola war in part because of its unacceptably loose "lashing up" of the gaseosa with authentic Nasa culture and, more broadly, with the hyperreal indigenousness found in official multiculturalism.[139] The controversy also revealed the geographic limits of official multiculturalism: coca is fine in the resguardo but not outside it. Bocarejo argues that this presupposition that "minority rights seem to be limited and attached to a territory" turns up in a great many other cases.[140]

Given the lack of content in much multiculturalism, and given the lack of comprehensive knowledge about indigenous cultures, when assertions of cultural rights reveal previously unseen practices considered repugnant or barbaric, they may be seen as betrayals of the national imaginary of usos y costumbres. Colorful costumes, slightly strange cuisine, or flamboyant rituals may be acceptable, but not whipping, stocks, and banishment. The Gembuel case in particular illustrates what can happen when the dominant society encounters behaviors that deeply disturb its moral sensibilities.

Interestingly, that reaction was not unanimous. Both the Gembuel and Piñacué cases received sympathetic treatment in some of the mass media. Perhaps the cases prompted commentators to rethink and revalorize diversity. More important perhaps, the Nasa pueblo's judicial procedure offered alternative role models in the midst of the national breakdown of law and order resulting in 98 percent impunity, rampant corruption, a half century of armed conflict, and uncontrolled narcotrafficking. Despite a general abhorrence of whipping, stocks, and coerced exile, some journalists looked for ways to treat the Gembuel and Piñacué cases at least somewhat sympathetically.[141] Similarly, despite the contested value of Coca-Sek's coca, the vast majority of articles about the product were favorable. Colombian journalists were well aware of pueblos' stances of neutrality and vows of noninvolvement with respect to the panoply of armed actors, despite the at times great price to be paid. The pueblos offered a rhetorical resource, the same one invoked centuries before by Rousseau and Montaigne, to critique the flaws of the national society.[142]

Perhaps another source of sympathy arises from an awareness of the ways in which activating the right to political participation damaged the indigenous movement; my interview with Green poignantly outlined some of them. As Colombian anthropologist Roberto Pineda noted in 1997 about the national indigenous movement, "the competition for accessing the offices of political representation has generated some rivalries that, for the moment, do not seem the most convenient for achieving certain goals."[143]

In sum, the four cases take us beyond the simple dichotomy of individual human rights versus culture-specific collective rights. They offer a broader and more nuanced view of the contested fields of struggle over mandated rights, cultural practices, and political positioning. Rights are first transformed in struggles in the courts, in the media, and on blocked highways—and then transformed again in such forums as mandated roundtables in which they are discussed, negotiated, and instantiated or refuted. While rights are defined by the laws, regulations, and accords that put them on paper, they become real only in the field of action.[144]

5 Reindigenization and Its Discontents

What happens when a community tries to reconstitute itself as an indigenous pueblo, when its members set out to recover their indigenous identity and culture? As it turns out, the process is contentious and difficult, and success depends on the acquiescence of others. Although self-determination is championed in numerous multiculturalist-informed policies and rhetorics, and self-identification suffices in some identity-ascertaining practices (e.g., census-taking), a community cannot simply assert an identity; it must persuade others—existing pueblos, government agencies, the media, the public at large—to accept those claims. When demands for official recognition are turned down, the rejection raises further questions about who should have the right to make such decisions. Even when a community surmounts that first hurdle of gaining official acquiescence, more hurdles await, as established actors contest community members' new or old identity and the claims they make based on that identity.

On a 2006 trip to a world-famous UNESCO archaeological site in the department of Huila, I encountered a reindigenizing community so at odds with local authorities that at one point two truckloads of SWAT forces had been called in to bring them to heel. Community members had begun to cut a road through a corner of the park, in part to get the state to pay attention to their demands. Over the following two days I witnessed heated accusations and responses, followed by negotiations and some concessions on the part of the authorities. The community supported their assertions that they were indeed indigenous and deserved the respect they had been denied with demonstrations of indigenousness. Not being overly impressed with these performances,

I had to ask myself, why not? The following pages continue our exploration of culture, identity, descent, and performance by examining several examples of the reindigenization process and my evolving reactions to direct encounters with it.

Throughout the Western Hemisphere, the process of reindigenization has grown rapidly, posing challenges for bureaucrats, indigenous activists, anthropologists, and already established pueblos. Some of the most compelling anthropological work coming out of Colombia in recent decades examines that process, considering how and why the state accepts some claims and rejects others, and how the criteria for evaluating reindigenization have evolved. In recent decades several communities—of indigenous descent but with only remnants of past native identities—have succeeded in reinvigorating their culture and gaining official recognition, in most cases with the help of anthropologists. In the 1980s the successful pueblos included the Zenú in Córdoba, the Kankuamo in the Sierra Nevada de Santa Marta, the Pastos in Nariño, and the Yanacona in Cauca.[1]

Previously, recognition as an indigenous pueblo required little more than certification by a local authority that a cabildo governor had been installed.[2] But during the year following passage of Law 60 of 1993, which made it easier for indigenous authorities to pry economic resources out of the Colombian state, 80.4 percent of the country's resguardos presented projects to be funded.[3] This led to a stiffening of official requirements, which forced petitioners to demonstrate the validity of their cultural claims. In 2001, for example, would-be reindigenizers first had to organize a cabildo, then petition municipal authorities to recognize it, and finally undergo an ethnographic assessment to verify that they had "a common history as well as group cohesion, a deep-rooted affiliation with the ancestral territory, worldview, traditional medicine, [and] kinship ties," as well as a distinct value system.[4]

A newspaper article from 2001 about what it calls the "proliferation of Indians" illustrates the problematics of reindigenization.[5] The director of DAI (by then called the Office of Ethnic Groups) cast doubt on applicants, asserting that "indigenous pueblos that disappeared before the Spaniards arrived cannot reappear now." This remark provoked a retort from ONIC leaders:

> Communities that weren't indigenous are now recognizing themselves as such because for 500 years they were told that to be indio was a shame. But they now realize that this is not so and they are recovering their dignity. Nevertheless,

> this process is being delegitimized by the government. . . . We do not agree that the Ministry of the Interior should be the one to recognize who is and is not indigenous. The community ought to define itself. What is really going on is a dispute over resources and lands.[6]

My own visits to the agency confirmed that officials there, deluged by applications (150 petitions received in 2006, with 250 more in the pipeline), were struggling with the issue.

Contested Indigeneity in Putumayo

Several very interesting and significant cases were documented in long-term ethnographic research by anthropologist Margarita Chaves in the department of Putumayo.[7] She focused on campesino colono communities seeking official recognition from the government for a revived indigeneity. After the invariable denial of each petition the community would make changes to meet the criteria imposed by DAI, only to have the agency once more move the goalposts and alter the criteria, and thus ensure another failure. Chaves's work documents the shifts in the functionaries' notions of indigeneity, demonstrating the mutability and ad hoc manipulation of supposedly stable, principled requirements.

The communities petitioning DAI were composed of families from heterogeneous ethnic backgrounds who had arrived in Putumayo over the previous eighty-odd years in several waves of immigration from other parts of the country, many of them during La Violencia, the two-decade period of violent confrontations between the Liberal and the Conservative political parties. A series of censuses in Putumayo had documented rapid growth among both indigenous individuals and cabildos, to the dismay of regional and national DAI officials. The new petitions for indigenous status also inspired opposition from established pueblos in the region, who feared that official recognition for new pueblos would increase competition for scarce state resources.

These efforts to recover and "re-create" indigeneity, according to Chaves, could not be reduced to purely instrumental motives. Over the previous quarter century, the well-established ideology of *blanqueamiento* (whitening) had begun to shift toward valorization of indigenous identity, exerting a powerful influence, both symbolic and emotional, on reindigenizing communities.[8] Discourses of indigeneity taking place at national and international levels were penetrating peripheral regions like Putumayo via diverse routes. As one result, officials tried to establish a "qualitative scale" by which to judge the "quality" or "grade" of indigenousness in a given community, closely resembling the efforts of several of the Constitutional Court magistrates discussed in Chapter Four, who in their decisions tried to take into account levels of cultural "purity," meaning, in effect, degree of acculturation.

Although colonos in Putumayo had always resisted state marginalization, in this new effort they were for the first time embracing indigenous identity as a vehicle of resistance. In response to the government's increasingly stringent criteria for official recognition, the petitioning communities churned out improved documentation to establish the "objective reality" of their indigeneity. But state functionaries responded by setting standards that could not be met. DAI demanded "purification" of the censuses for already existing cabildos: every member had to meet strict criteria in terms of language and usos y costumbres.[9] Although these demands assumed that colono and indígena were mutually exclusive categories, many of the petitioning families claimed indigenous descent on the grounds that their parents or grandparents had migrated from highland pueblos like the Nasa, seeking land and respite from the terrors of La Violencia.

When the regional DAI director (herself a member of the Inga pueblo, one of several in the area dead-set against the formation of new cabildos) ruled against the possibility of multi-ethnic cabildos, the petitioners contested her ruling, demanding to know the grounds for the rejection. In response DAI imposed even more exacting criteria, which the communities then met in their re-applications. They also played up the physical features and usos y costumbres that displayed their ethnic uniqueness, both to DAI representatives and to neighboring pueblos. One petitioner community rediscovered an origin myth that located its original homeland in Putumayo; according to the story, their ancestors had long ago migrated from Putumayo to Cauca, with the implication that their ultimate arrival in Putumayo constituted a return to their roots.[10] During just one three-month period, DAI emitted four *circulares* and *ordenanzas* (policy statements), with increasingly strict and precise specification of requirements. Rather than stopping the creation of cabildos, however, the circulars and ordinances had the unintended consequence of helping petitioners fine-tune their discourse and behavior. The communities also discovered genealogical "footprints" in shared patronyms, and they began renaming their cabildos, sometimes more than once. One of them, the Cabildo Multiétnico Urbano de Puerto Caicedo (Multiethnic Urban Cabildo of Puerto Caicedo), whose membership encompassed Nasa, Awa, and Inga peoples and even Afro-Colombians, was renamed the Cabildo Páez de la Zona Urbana de Puerto Caicedo, Páez being another name for Nasa. Later, the cabildo was renamed once again, this time as Nasa Ku'esh Tata Wala, an appellation signaling the successful "purification" of the cabildo.[11] Another cabildo fashioned an acronymic name, QUIYAINPA, combining the first syllables of its component ethnicities (Quillacingas, Yanaconas, Ingas, and Pastos). Since the name sounds like an Inga word, the cabildo received legal recognition from the municipal authorities.[12] Exchanges of this sort, in which the state's demand for increasing "purification" and "cleansing" sent petitioners back to authorized sources, including published ethnographies, generated ever-greater and more ingenious self-camouflage and mimicry. In Chaves's work on these cases, she portrays cabildo formation as a challenge to colonial discourses about rights, a "profound and disturbing" subversion of state authority precisely because petitioners' performative strategies were imperfect—they "almost convinced themselves" and others that they were indigenous. She observes that such subversion in particular disturbs state officials, regional elites, and those academics who champion "the idea of alterity at all costs," which they see to be embodied in Amazonian Indians.[13] The communities countered government rejection by hoisting the state on its own petard, revealing in stark terms just how flexible, contextual, and politicized the criteria for official recognition of the "right to indigenous rights" could be.

As James Scott, Begoña Aretxaga, and others have indicated, states are neither unitary nor consistent in their policies and actions; although displaying a (misleading) façade of a unitary polity, they are in fact heterogeneous congeries of institutions such as legislatures and judiciaries within which discourses and practices of power are produced.[14] In the cases discussed here the various actors included, on the one side, the petitioning communities, and on the other, regional and national officials of DAI, along with their allies, municipal officials, and the local pueblos that already enjoyed official recognition. They all contended within the context of the discourses about indigenous identity being promoted by the transnational indigenous movement and its various allied NGOs. Chaves draws attention to a hybridity discernible in the representations put forward by reindigenized communities, which drew on cultural images of widely diverse origin that were circulating at the regional, national, and international level.[15] These images included the "indigenous defender of the tropical forest" and the "wise *curandero*" (shaman). In the end, the reindigenized cabildos, having accumulated evidence of their alterity, restructured their political and cultural institutions, and recovered traditional festivals and origin myths (in sum, having met the putatively stable criteria for official recognition), could clinch the case for bias and discrimination. Chaves notes that cases of this sort reveal the inherently political and ideological nature of all definitions of indigeneity, as well as the essentialisms embodied in the state's version of those definitions.[16]

The Putumayo cases fit Povinelli's notion of cultural difference that members of mainstream society find not different enough, identities "too hauntingly similar to [their own] to warrant social entitlements."[17] In this instance the petitioning cabildos did not at first seem sufficiently different or authentic, either to neighboring pueblos or to the national society (represented in these processes by DAI). But over time, through an extended series of interactions, for most intents and purposes the new pueblos did become indigenous, providing a telling example of subjects creatively engaging "the slippages, dispersions, and ambivalences of discursive and moral formations that make up their lives."[18] The petitioners' struggle and ultimate success underlines Cowan's point that "the recent revision of political and legal structures to recognize 'culture' and 'multiculturalism' has its own transformative effects, shaping and at times creating that which it purports merely to recognize."[19]

We can chortle at the spectacle of communities besting state agencies, but their example has important lessons. Chaves stresses the complex changes that community members undergo during the process of reindigenization; in their efforts to win recognition from the state and acceptance from neighbors, both individuals and the communities are transformed. Sara Schneiderman perceived a similar process among the Thangmi, a people on the border between India and Nepal, whose ritual performances target a heterogeneous audience including both state agents and divine beings. Deploying ethnicity

> for political purposes can have important affective results, transforming both the content of ethnic consciousness itself and its subsequent political expressions. . . . Beyond simply serving as a means of crass cultural commodification—becoming "living signs of themselves"—performances can allow people to objectify their own self-consciousness in a manner that has deep affective results. Through such self-replicating action, they generate a reflective awareness of these processes of subjectification and alienation, allowing "double selves" to stand without contradiction.[20]

French makes a similar point concerning a community of sharecroppers in northeast Brazil that split in two.[21] One of the factions embraced indigenous identity, whereas the other received official recognition (and its entitlements) as a *quilombo* community, that is, as descendants of fugitive slaves. French notes that the interpretation of laws changed over time, and these changes brought with them changes in the meaning of both communities' cultural practices. Dances reconfigured for the sake of legal recognition expressed at the same time yearnings for social acceptance and for ties to the land.

The Huila Yanacona and San Agustín Archaeological Park

A second illuminating example of reindigenization and the reactions it may provoke from others comes from a Yanacona community located near the town of San Agustín in the department of Huila in southern Colombia. San Agustín is also the name of an archaeological park, a UNESCO World Heritage site that abuts the Yanacona resguardo, which is an offshoot of the Yanacona pueblo in neighboring Cauca.[22] As can happen in reindigenizing projects, the community in question contended both with regional, national, and international organizations and with neighboring campesino families and residents of the town.

The Yanacona of Cauca were reindigenized during the 1980s and 1990s, with help from anthropologist Carlos Vladimir Zambrano and his students.[23] In the 1980s such cultural projects went hand in hand with land repossession, occurring most often in places with acute land shortages. The cluster of communities in Cauca that would gain the name Yanacona had previously been known simply as the "indigenous communities of the Massif"; their members, although they considered themselves indigenous, had so far lacked motivation to embrace a particular indigenous identity.[24] In the 1980s, however, frustrated by the "invisibility" that impeded their land reclamation efforts, they adopted the ethnonym Yanacona.[25] Through the 1980s and 1990s, they regained title to four of their colonial resguardos, as well as, eventually, recognition of their cabildos, but it was not until the national census of 2001 that they were first listed as a pueblo, and began to appear on maps and receive assistance from government agencies and NGOs.[26]

Acute land shortage led a group of Yanacona families in Cauca to petition the Instituto Colombiano de Reforma Agraria (INCORA) for relocation. In December 2000 they received a parcel of land abutting San Agustín, and in September 2001, their cabildo was officially recognized and their territory designated a resguardo. People with last names said to indicate Yanacona descent were invited to join the community, and some did. After settling in, the community turned its attention to reindigenization, holding workshops in 2003 and 2004 to recover usos y costumbres, assisted by their *asesor*, Fredy Chikangana, a member of the Cauca pueblo.[27] Chikangana was head of a Bogotá-based NGO, Fundación Indígena Sol y Serpiente de América (Sun and Serpent Indigenous Foundation of America), which was providing considerable amounts of funding for the community's projects. These included construction of a schoolhouse, a communal meeting house, a "House of Thought" (Figure 3), and a bullfight ring. Their efforts encountered resistance from neighbors and town residents, who accused the Yanacona of inauthenticity, portraying them as upstarts not even native to the area who lacked language and culture—ethnic opportunists with designs on acquiring even more land.

For their part, the Yanacona lost patience with the Instituto Colombiano de Antropología e Historia (ICANH), which administered all national archaeological sites, including San Agustín, because, they said, it ignored the many petitions they had sent following their relocation. The alleged neglect ended definitively in February of 2006, when the Yanacona cut a road through a corner of the park, in order to connect their headquarters (*sede*) with the state highway. Dr. María Clemencia Ramírez, who had just taken over the directorship of ICANH, found herself and her institution the subject of newspaper headlines and television reports.

Over the next nine months, numerous exchanges and confrontations ensued. In May, following a visit by Ramírez to the park, the Ministry of Culture sent a letter to the director of UNESCO's World Heritage Center (WHC) requesting a technical examination of the area of the new road. The WHC official in charge of Latin America and the Caribbean scheduled a trip to Colombia for the following November. Arrangements were also made to send an independent consultant from the International Council for Monuments and Sites (ICOMOS), which provides technical expertise concerning the condition of monuments, buildings, and sites to archeologists and architects. On November 6, 2006, Ramírez, accompanied by an ICANH archaeologist and myself (as a guest of ICANH—I was not formally involved) traveled to San Agustín and met the WHC and ICOMOS consultants. We were greeted by the cabildo governor and invited to attend a lunch and a meeting at the sede. More informal discussions took place later that day and the following morning.

In a 2009 article I co-authored with Ramírez about the episode,[28] we characterized the encounter as an instance of what Sally Falk Moore calls a diagnostic event: one that reveals ongoing contests, conflicts, and competition, as

Figure 3. Ongoing construction of the San Augustín Yanacona "House of Thought."

well as efforts to prevent, suppress, or repress such interactions.[29] Local stakeholders at the day's events included park staff and representatives from the Church, municipality, and police, as well as local campesinos and townspeople. All of them worried about the potential impact of the discord on tourism. In a memo Ramírez declared that if the Yanacona impeded ICANH's efforts to resolve the crisis, the park would be shut down "until the situation normalizes." That announcement triggered worries that UNESCO might revoke the park's status as a World Heritage site, and a letter to Ramirez from Huila's secretary of culture and tourism pleaded with her to maintain a "low profile," because ICANH's threat to close the park had generated "minor outbreaks" and "ethnic confrontations."

Members of the Yanacona community argued that their unauthorized road-building had been motivated by frustration with existing access to the resguardo, a dangerous and poorly maintained dirt road, quite steep in places and impassable in heavy rain. Repeated requests to the mayor of the town of San Agustín for repairs to the road, they said, had been ignored. The new road cut distances dramatically, allowing them to reach the highway in just five minutes. Neighboring campesinos chimed in, stating that a paved road would also help them get their products to market. Although various parties continued to plead with the mayor to repair the old road, it was obvious to everyone that he was sending a very clear message about his priorities—and by extension, his opinion of the Yanacona.

The bad blood between townspeople and the Yanacona sprang from a number of disagreements and provocations. Recognition as indigenous people had freed the Yanacona from some aspects of municipal authority, and it opened access to government funds not available to the town. Townspeople also resented Chikangana's NGO, Sol y Serpiente, and in particular its policy of seeking funding only for resguardo projects. Generous donations to the resguardo from sources in the Netherlands only served to confirm in the eyes of townspeople the instrumental nature of Yanacona motives. Another complaint had to do with growing and selling illicit drugs. We were told that young people would come to town asking to be put in contact with "the Indians who sold marijuana." Pollution of the town's water supply due to the community's location near its source was another problem. Other complaints had to do with cabildo decisions about judging and sentencing wrongdoers—townspeople felt the punishments were sometimes too lenient.

Yanacona authenticity was cast in doubt, on the grounds that their reindigenization had been politically and economically motivated. One town official branded the cultural recovery project as "artificial," a ploy to acquire land and official recognition for a resguardo and cabildo, and so "of course they are not going to admit that they don't have a culture." The Yanacona, for their part, offered their own complaints, mostly about contemptuous treatment by townspeople—snubbed and laughed at, kicked out of town meetings by the police, refused entry into the council room, forced to travel on a dangerous dirt road. Over the last seven years, they said, no one—not local residents and authorities, not the national government—had shown them any respect.

Although the November meeting did not produce a solution, important shifts did occur.[30] Clearly, the motives and results of cutting the new road transcended practicality: at a minimum this action had made the government pay attention. The Yanacona were obviously proud to host an event attended by international officials and authorities, who possessed far more clout and prestige than mere local officials and park personnel (see Figures 4 and 5). Moreover, some of those high-status officials actually expressed sympathy for some aspects of the Yanaconas' dilemmas; Ramírez, for one, acknowledged that the government had indeed been negligent.

Figure 4. Yanacona procession beginning the meeting.

The Yanacona also appreciated the attention they received from various indigenous authorities following the road incursion. At a meeting the previous April, consultants from the Organización Nacional Indígena de Colombia (ONIC), the Regional Indigenous Council of Huila (CRIHU), and the Regional Indigenous Organization of Valle del Cauca (ORIVAC) had advised the Yanacona about tactics and engagement style. Perhaps as a result of that advice, a discourse of "speaking truth to power" that linked current problems to past abuses appears in several of the case documents. Although the part played by these organizations was minor, it is worth noting because, as happened in the Putumayo case discussed earlier in this chapter, when the Cauca Yanacona began their reindigenization efforts, neighboring indigenous communities had snubbed them. When the highest-ranking Yanacona cabildo (the *cabildo mayor*, which represents the entire pueblo) petitioned to join CRIC (the Consejo Regional Indígena del Cauca), CRIC refused—although later, in 1997, it relented.

For the Cauca Yanacona, on the one hand, reindigenization ultimately worked fairly well, allowing them to "cleanse" (*sanear*) much of their territory of nonindigenous people. Their San Agustín relatives, on the other hand,

Figure 5. Musicians playing the Yanacona hymn.

found themselves opposed by nearly everyone in their new home. In both locations Yanacona had to struggle against doubts about their indigeneity, but those in Cauca at least had land rights in the form of titles to four colonial resguardos. The San Agustín Yanacona struggled with a double invisibility: recent immigrants to their Huila resguardo, their only claim to blood ties in their new home consisted of Yanacona surnames shared with some of the locals.

The November meeting revealed that the Yanacona had carefully mapped out their arguments. Speakers asserted that the area in dispute no longer had archaeological value—"it's just weeds." By working "to enclose and protect the territory . . . as a form of celebrating our spirit of cooperation," the Yanacona insisted that they had in fact done everyone a favor, carrying out improvements that should have been carried out by ICANH. The road had been cut across "abandoned" terrain that "represented a danger to the community because people went there to engage in improper activities" (i.e., do drugs). Speakers pointed out that while town residents had benefited substantially from the park in their restaurants and craft stores, the resguardo and the campesinos who owned land abutting the park had not. Once the reindigenization project was complete, the entire region would benefit: "When we have recovered everything from the ancestors, when the tourists visit us here in the resguardo and we show them all the culture we have, not only will they come to buy crafts and attend our ceremonies, they will also spend money in the town—we Yanacona don't have restaurants or hotels, we don't have anything. This way the town will benefit as a consequence of our activities." Those anticipated tourist visits, and the possibility of visiting the sede and seeing the Yanaconas' "total identity" would be greatly facilitated by the road.

Beyond their specific criticism of ICANH, speakers lambasted the state as neglectful at best, and abusive at worst, because it had done nothing during previous occasions, for instance when that part of the park was being damaged by a police station built during a period of crisis with the FARC. *Guaqueros* (pot-hunters) had despoiled many archaeological sites, but the government "did nothing." Environmentalist discourses were also invoked: at the previous meeting in May, a CRIHU representative had argued that, given the widely admired capacity of indigenous people to protect and sustain natural resources within their territories, Yanacona should be made guardians of the park. Another discourse about "indigenous consciousness" emerged during the November meeting when the Yanacona governor stated that "as indigenous persons we are very conscious of the proposal we are making, and we know very well that we would be doing something very bad if we were to put our own history in jeopardy." Covering all the bases, speakers also invoked anticolonial discourses, as when the resguardo governor connected the present situation of the Yanacona with pueblo experiences of being "targets" over the past five hundred years.

Some of the arguments fell on deaf ears. The worries expressed about damage—to the park and to the nation—and about threats posed to townspeople's livelihoods if ICANH were to close down the park (or UNESCO revoke the site's World Heritage status) trumped Yanacona discourses about "cleaning," "protecting," "reforesting," and "beautifying" the area for the good of all.

Taken together, the Yanacona and Putumayo cases illustrate key features of reindigenization. In both, cultural recovery was seen as a means to receiving land and support, as well as less tangible benefits like self-esteem and community solidarity. In both, anthropologists played important roles, most obviously in the Yanacona case, first of all in official roles in government agencies (although their intervention was not always appreciated). Carlos Zambrano and his students worked to establish links between present-day Cauca Yanacona and earlier populations: "It's the voice of the Yanacona pueblo, which after 3,000 years of silence and invisibility authoritatively informs us about its own horizon." Zambrano responded emphatically to expressions of doubt about Yanacona indigeneity: "Their rights are called into question and unjustly denied because today in Colombia, you practically have to put on a loincloth to be considered indigenous."[31] Archaeologists have in various cases also played a role, in this instance in a book from 1944 by Juan Friede, which provided the ethnonym chosen by the pueblo.[32] Indigenous consultants and intervenors also played roles in both cases; one of them, Chikangana, also an anthropologist, had a degree from the Universidad de los Andes.

Both cases also illustrate how a community, in the process of mobilizing, can advance and even create an indigenous identity. Both cases also show in dramatic form how much claims to identity depend on acceptance by others. They illustrate as well the variety of discursive maneuvers to which reindigenizing pueblos resort when interacting with the state apparatus, in particular when disputes are involved. The governor of the cabildo, in a letter to the Director of Municipal Justice, got around the inconvenient fact that the San Agustín Yanacona had no historical claim to their territory by invoking an article in the constitution that stipulates that ethnic groups living in archaeologically rich areas have special rights with respect to these sites.

In the Yanacona case one also sees benefits that can accrue from copious media coverage: authorities, in attempting to calm the situation, will meet with disputants, point out shared understandings and goals, and make concessions. Following the crisis provoked by the initial incursion into the park, a number of changes were proposed. Plans were quickly made to celebrate the eleventh anniversary of the park's designation as a UNESCO World Heritage site, even though eleven-year spans are not typical celebration choices. At the November meeting the ICANH archaeologist suggested that a large cake, to be provided for the celebration by the mayor's office, would symbolize San Agustín culture: "we will be symbolically taking in our culture . . . so that you will love your park." ICANH also proposed building a *vivienda* (dwelling) on what would be an exclusively pedestrian path leading to the sede: a reconstruction of a prehispanic house and an exhibit that would link past inhabitants with present-day ones, thus encouraging tourists to include the Yanacona as part of their park visit. The proposal included a poster with a photograph of three children captioned "The Yanacona Community: Guardians of Archaeological Patrimony."

Whereas earlier reindigenizing efforts in Colombia were motivated by a

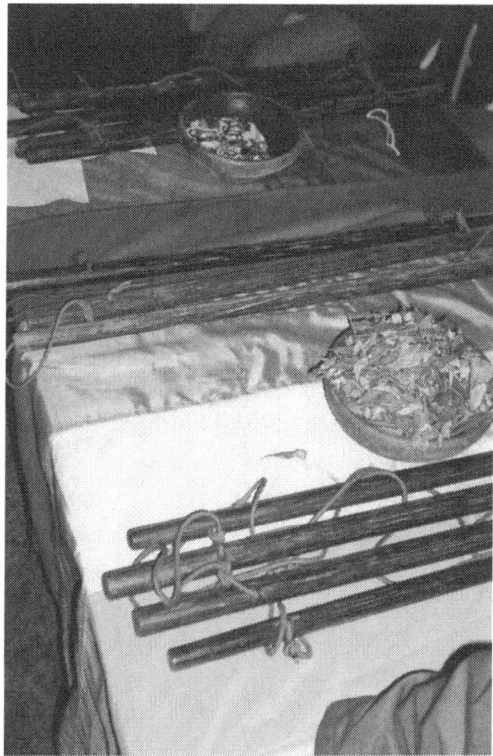

Figure 6. Yanacona staffs of office.

need to regain territory and defend collective land rights, the San Agustín Yanacona case illustrates additional concerns. The community had already acquired ample land; what was at stake was the practical problem of the near-impassable road, and the challenges to the community's legitimacy—their right to be in their new home and to call themselves indigenous. Whether or not the road became a reality, their action moved them toward those goals. During the months of negotiations and crisis, the Yanacona asserted and performed their indigeneity whenever they could. Yanacona staffs of office were displayed (see Figure 6), both in meetings and in an earlier standoff with anti-riot national police summoned by the park director. At that confrontation, adolescent Yanacona girls, armed with these staffs of office, formed a human fence between the adults cutting the road and two truckloads of SWAT teams, who as it turned out, did not challenge them.

In another assertion of indigeneity, Chikangana pointed out at the November meeting that the school would be a place "where children will be taught about traditional medicine—traditional in the anthropological sense. Weaving, dances, we're pursuing our goal in a comprehensive way, not along a single path." Claims were also made to kinship ties with the ancient San Agustín communities that had produced the spectacular archaeological artifacts. During the April meeting Chikangana contrasted Yanacona links to the park's original inhabitants to the illegal and reprehensible behavior of townspeople who made their living as guaqueros. The story of the migration from Cauca to San Agustín was motivated, he said, by not just a need for land, but also by an authentic and difficult quest: "The spirits were jealous at our crossing the *páramo*" [the mountainous region separating Cauca Yanacona territory and San Agustín] . . . we maintained and reconstructed our usos y costumbres. With our governor we came, working, and our spirits, our gods, came with us and sustained us. We also have our traditional medicine and know how to conserve our lands." With this discourse, the Yanacona linked themselves both to a World Heritage site—a "sacred" indigenous space—and to a culture from the distant past, arguing that, simply by being from a neighboring pueblo, they were descendants of the park's earlier inhabitants and therefore had resided there longer than their nonindigenous neighbors. While acknowledging their recent transfer from Cauca, they saw their reindigenizing project as grounds for asserting, "We are not recent arrivals [*no somos de ahora*], we have existed for 5,000 years."

State laws and UNESCO policies regarding indigenous heritage and patrimony were also invoked. The UNESCO consultant pointed out many times that San Agustín was not only a park of great natural beauty and an important historical site, but also a sanctuary—and "as members of a resguardo, you need to save this sanctuary." The Yanacona subsequently argued that UNESCO should take into consideration immaterial patrimony, "which involves customs, traditions, values," and given that present-day pueblos were part of the nation's patrimony, they had special rights with respect to patrimony like the park—as ICANH itself had recently baptized them, they were "Guardians of Archaeological Patrimony." By associating themselves with the UNESCO consultant, the Yanacona were linking themselves with symbols of distant and powerful authority in a way that challenged townspeople's rejection of Yanacona legitimacy.

The claim to be qualified as guardians of the park extended assertions by the Cauca Yanacona that they had been long-term stewards of their territory. The San Agustín Yanacona indicated a deep respect for their antecedents who had inhabited the park's lands. This reasoning—because we are indigenous, we have a special investment in "conserving and being guardians of the nation's cultural patrimony"—bolstered their claim to indigeneity, albeit with some circularity.

Were the Yanacona to win their case, their connection to the land would not hold just for páramos and mountains, as is the case for their Cauca counterparts, but would link them to a sanctuary containing the remains and remarkable material culture of ancient indigenous peoples. Strengthening these connections would, in a sense, transform the Yanacona into quasi-patrimonial subjects themselves. Their status would doubtlessly improve in light of their increased ability to play certain roles: first, the role of descendants of these forebearers; second, the role of still-vulnerable survivors of colonial and neocolonial oppression and erasure; and third, the role of participants in the park project, offering themselves and their living culture as objects for the tourist gaze alongside their artisanal production. The apparent weakness of any conventional "blood and soil" claims notwithstanding, the Yanacona linked themselves both to a World Heritage site—a "sacred" indigenous space—and to a culture from the distant past by using the unique argument that their indigeneity meant that they were native to the territory and thus had resided in the territory longer than their nonindigenous neighbors. Mary Louise Pratt argues that indigeneity and similar descriptors that are "used to refer to indigenous peoples . . . all refer etymologically to prior-ity in time and place."[33] The San Agustín Yanacona, by making claims both to land and history, endeavored to convince others that this "prior-ity" extended to them, despite their having lived there only seven years.

The San Agustín Yanacona crisis was my first encounter, up close and personal, with reindigenization. I was staying with María Clemencia Ramírez, my friend and former student, in her Bogotá home when it became clear to her that she would have to make a second trip to San Agustín. When a trip I had been planning fell through, she invited me to accompany her. To prepare myself I began going through her voluminous documentation on the case and became, as Alice experiencing Wonderland puts it, "curiouser and curiouser" about the crisis. By the time we reached the sede, I was asking lots of questions and taking notes and photographs. My fieldnotes reveal a fascination with the way the various stakeholders were making legal and moral claims. The notes also reveal doubts about Yanacona claims. For example, I was not overly impressed with Chikangana's comment about schoolchildren being taught about traditional medicine and dances. And where did that incense-wafting ritual come from? It looked rather Catholic to me. Also, what was with that plastic mustard container sprinkling perfumed water on the floor? The funding pouring into the community was indeed very impressive, and the two men who took me on a tour of the construction efforts were clearly very proud of how far along they had come. But one of the projects was a bullfight ring! How did they square *that* with indigenous tradition? I was applying fairly standard criteria for indigenousness. San Agustín Yanacona seemed pretty indigenous in terms of physiognomy, at least through gringa eyes—but then the majority of Colombians look either mestizo or Afro-descendant. But when I considered the cultural evidence, especially when I compared Yanacona to Tukanoans—which was unfair—I just didn't see it. My confusion was not, as I had hoped, resolved by the work Ramírez and I did on our 2009 article. The trip to San Agustín marked the beginning of a serious promise to myself to delve more deeply into the question of reindigenization, along with the larger issue of just what indigeneity consisted of.

Urban Cabildos: The Muisca

A third example of reindigenization, this one urban, comes from communities in Bogotá and adjacent areas who self-identify as Muisca (sometimes spelled Muiska), who assert a connection with a famous pre-Columbian people who figure prominently in books and websites about Colombian history. The original Muisca inhabited the areas today known as the departments of Boyacá and Cundinamarca, which include Bogotá and its highly urbanized surrounds. Colonial archives contain a great deal of documentation on the Muisca, some of it on their language, Muiscubbun, which belongs to the Chibcha language family. Although the Muisca had lost recognition as a distinct people by the eighteenth century, the members of the five present-day Muisca cabildos in this area assert a direct connection back to Muisca ancestors.

It was in the 1990s that five communities in and around Bogotá, in the towns of Bosa, Chía, Cota, Suba, and Sesquilé, formed cabildos as Muisca and sought official recognition.[34] In March 2007 I was introduced to the Sesquilé community by Victoria Neuta, a Muisca woman active in ONIC. She invited me to attend one of the community's monthly gatherings, held on Sundays, which were open to all Muiscas and their guests. Victoria told members of

Figure 7. The Sesquilé community welcome message.

the community that I was an anthropologist interested in cultural recovery projects.

On the day of the gathering, after taking a bus from the city, Victoria, her husband, and I began a difficult uphill walk to the resguardo, which sits on a rather steep slope. At the entrance a sign containing an image of a four-legged animal announced: "Prepare the land, plant the seed, thought/wisdom is the path in the universe. Be born to live, live in order to be, be in order to die, die in order to be born. Live in equilibrium, observe things from all sides of your thought, walk cultivating your spirit—Muisca Community of Sesquilé" (Figure 7).

Entering, I saw a school, a terraced garden (Figure 8), a *temazcal* (sweat house, the word is thought to be Nahuatl, shown in Figure 9), a communal kitchen, and a *chuszua*, or meeting house (Figure 10), which was also referred to, in Spanish, as a "temple." The chuszua's round shape and thatched conical roof contrasted with the rectangular shape and zinc roofs of the other buildings. The school, meeting house, and temazcal were decorated with various images—serpents, cornstalks, fruit trees, mythic animals, and culture heroes. The day's activities included a ceremony inside the chuszua (Figure 11), a lunch, a speech and subsequent discussion, and a puppet show put on by children about the history of indigenous Colombians. About forty people were in

Figure 8. The Sesquilé gardens.

attendance. Children were dressed in everyday clothes, but many adults wore white tunics modelled after Muisca clothing depicted in the archives.

The seriousness with which the Sesquilé Muisca had investigated colonial-era Muisca culture and language—using both scholarly publications and more personal, experiential interaction—was clear from the outset. A political and religious leader named Carlos Mamanché had spent extended periods in various reindigenizing efforts, including eight years apprenticed to shamans. He traveled to the several centers of Colombia's "magic indigenous world" that make up the "national magic geography," visiting wise men and healers in the Sierra Nevada de Santa Marta, the Amazon, the Colombian Massif (Cauca and Huila), and the Sibundoy Valley (Putumayo), whose Inga shamans are known as the masters of *yajé* (*Banisteriopsis caapi*, also mentioned in Chapter Three), a powerful hallucinogenic infusion.[35] Also present was an Arhuaco man from the Sierra Nevada de Santa Marta, serving as an expert guide in the recovery efforts. This man's role somewhat resembled that of Fredy Chikangana, with the significant difference that Fredy was Yanacona, whereas the Arhuaco guide was from a pueblo located near the Caribbean coast. Colombians consider the four Sierra pueblos (Arhuaco, Kankuamo, Kogi, and Wiwa) to be

Figure 9. The Sesquilé temazcal.

the country's ur-Indians, the very epitome of indigeneity, and deeply respectful depictions of their lives, clothing, architecture, and artifacts frequently appear in coffee-table books, tourist posters, textbooks, and environmentalist publications.[36] Their word *bunchi*, meaning "younger brother" and, more generally, nonindigenous person, has been adopted in newspaper articles. *Mochilas* (in this context, shoulder bags woven from virgin wool) from Sierra peoples are worn throughout the country. No one at the gathering revealed any concern about what I perceived as the incongruity, in a project dedicated to adopting authentic Muisca culture, of distinctly non-Muisca elements, which in addition to the Arhuaco guide, included various Sierra artifacts such as implements for chewing (*mambear*) coca, and Sierra mochilas with designs from a variety of sources, only some of them indigenous.

At the beginning of our visit, upon entering the chuszua, we sat on benches along the wall. Mamanché began with a kind of homily about indigenous wisdom, spirituality, living a balanced life and relying on medicinal plants as much as possible. He also addressed issues relating to the reorganization project, at times somewhat defensively: "do not pay attention to people who question what you are doing. What's important is what's on the inside, not

Figure 10. The Sesquilé chuszua.

the outside." At the end of his talk he circled the room and, accompanied by two assistants, shot a very potent tobacco snuff called *rapé* (mixed with ashes of the Yarumo tree [*Pourouma cecropiaefolia*]) deep into each adult attendee's nasal passages with a snuff-blower constructed of two small bones attached together in a V shape. One end is inserted into the recipient's nostril, and the other is inserted into the mouth of the person administering the substance, who then blows through it. (Figure 12 shows a Vaupés version.) After delivering the snuff, an assistant handed toilet paper to each recipient, who was invariably coughing and spitting. I did not experience the temporary altered state of consciousness some participants reported, perhaps because I was physically bigger than the others. However, the snuff certainly hit me hard.

The rapé inhalation was the peak spiritual moment of the gathering, in which everyone experienced a powerfully enhanced embodied state associated with an Otherness that was highly, even exclusively, indigenized—an indigenous substance delivered by an indigenous shaman blowing through an indigenous artifact, during an indigenous ritual. This activity was followed by music, played on traditional instruments, and dancing in pairs.

Subsequently, in 2016, I had a chance to visit the Urban Muisca Cabildo

Figure 11. A ritual inside the chuszua.

Figure 12. A snuffblower (Vaupés version).

Figure 13. The Bosa Cabildo headquarters.

of Bosa (Figure 13), at the invitation, again, of Victoria Neuta, a member of that cabildo. The history of how the Bosa cabildo was organized offers a well-documented example of Muisca organizing. The town of Bosa, which was founded in the sixteenth century, was eventually swallowed up by the city of Bogotá, and in 1954, it was designated as the Localidad Séptima (Seventh District).[37] A lawyer who was working in the archives on the history of an indigenous resguardo attached to a hacienda there that was dissolved in the nineteenth century, suggested to residents of the district who self-identified as indigenous that they organize themselves and petition to be officially recognized.[38] Members' last names, some in Muiscubbun, others in Spanish, provided them with evidence of their descent from original inhabitants of the resguardo. The petition was approved and the cabildo certified in 1999.

I spent the day touring the community's buildings and environment, attending an assembly, and eating lunch at a Muisca-owned restaurant with Victoria and another cabildo member, who, like Victoria, is an activist. The main agenda at the assembly was to inform the audience about the work that the governor was doing on the community's behalf, in particular her efforts to induce the district government to adhere to protective legislation, such as that requiring "free, prior and informed consent." The assembly also included

Figure 14. Bosa Muisca officers at the General Assembly.

opening and closing rituals, entertainment, a raffle run by a group of Muisca youth seeking to paint the outside walls of the chuszua, a contest involving four elderly women telling stories about the past, and a performance of the Muisca hymn (see Figures 14 through 18).

From my readings and from previous correspondence with Victoria, I knew of the cabildo's many problems, but the visit brought them home in dramatic form. I saw a polluted river, illegal invasions in the form of jerry-built buildings, and sewage overflows trickling from a large building into community gardens. I heard about the ways that the district and the city ignored Muisca demands and petitions by delaying action and throwing up bureaucratic roadblocks. I also heard about insecurity—the presence of both paramilitaries and FARC members who, along with common criminals, haunted the night hours. I heard about community members who had sold out and were collaborating with developers. The neighboring district of San José is even worse off: the residents, all of them refugees from rural violence, have no legal claim to the lands on which they squat and thus no access to city services. Public transportation and ambulances cannot navigate the torn-up streets.

Despite this sad, desperate situation, despite all the challenges facing the Bosa community, there were impressive signs of self-organization: communal

Figure 15. A Bosa Muisca official with a staff of office.

Figure 16. A performance of the Muisca hymn.

economic efforts (vegetable and medicinal gardens, two restaurants, artisanal production), shared beliefs and practices (evidenced by the chuszua), and, overall, community spirit and solidarity. Many people welcomed me warmly, inspired, I thought, by the respect they felt for my companion, who was about to receive her law degree. And all events were accompanied by delicious *chicha* (home brew made with corn). Several individuals wore Muisca dress (see photographs), and staffs of office were on view. I was moved by it all, just I had been during my 2007 visit to Sesquilé. The opportunity to experience the similarities and differences between the Sesquilé and Bosa communities increased my understanding of what Muisca reindigenization is all about.

In Sesquilé it seemed to me that the participants were trying to attain a generic indigenous identity, an indigenous way of being-in-the-world. While they were definitely searching for ways to link themselves with the ancient Muisca, they were also taking on a much broader pan-Colombian indigenousness, drawn from heterogeneous sources. Their clothing, ritual practice, plant-based medicine, and recitation of indigenous history displayed a yearning for a way of life radically different from what the West offered. The Muisca connection mattered deeply to them, but not so much the specifics of Muisca culture. Having lived in an urban commune for four years, and having taught

Figure 17. The end of the General Assembly.

a course on nineteenth- and twentieth-century communal movements in the United States, I could not help but perceive similarities between Sesquilé Muisca efforts and the North American hippie communes of the 1960s and 1970s, with their spiritual, natural, and antimaterialist ethos.[39]

My reactions to what I saw at Sesquilé in 2007 were mixed: fascination and a desire to know more, and reservations about what I had witnessed. I remembered accounts of nonindigenous wannabees in the United States imitating what they thought were authentic practices.[40] As it turned out, my ambivalence echoed similar feelings on the part of Santiago Martínez Medina, a physician-anthropologist who participated in the reorganization efforts of the Bosa Muisca community, contributed to their publications, and wrote an ethnography about them. He describes his initial doubts frankly. While participating in a healing ceremony, his questions were "intensifying and multiplying incessantly . . . the ethnographer . . . in the presence of something inauthentic . . . charlatanism, neo-shamanism, superstition, pantomime."[41] The explanations that came to him while observing Muisca healers in action ran the gamut from placebo, suggestion, and psychosomatic response to hysteria. Later, however, following an apprenticeship with two healers, he moved from an attitude of "shadow and discredit" to admiration.[42]

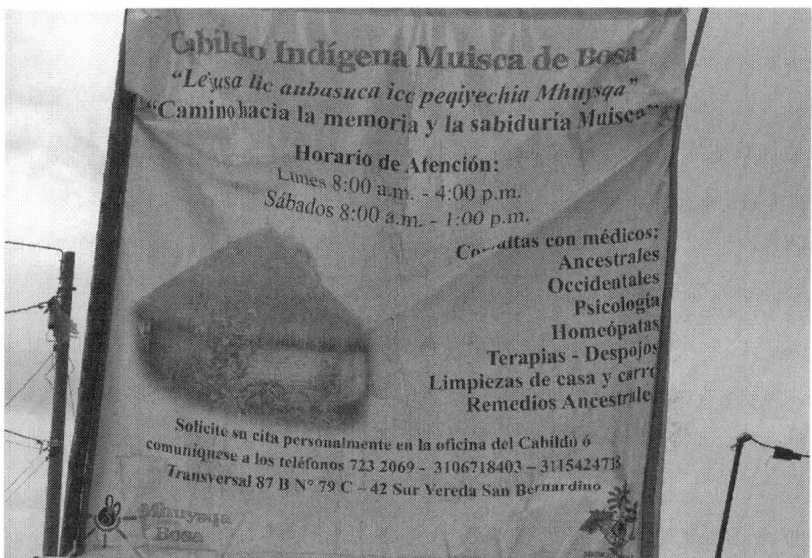

Figure 18. Therapies offered by Bosa Muisca healers.

Like Martínez Medina, I now have a different view of the urban Muisca. They, along with the Putumayo and Yanacona cases, call into question the possibility of a clear-cut divide that can be applied everywhere between indigenous and nonindigenous, and suggest various complexities and contradictions in the very notion of indigeneity itself. Martínez Medina argues that indigeneity is "a colonial stereotype, *fixed* in the *first contact* and continually verifiable by means of the act of seeing . . . a *prefiguration* that precedes that which is represented."[43] Constructed and reconstructed each day, indigeneity is "above all a fiction."[44]

There is more to Martínez Medina's analysis than can be engaged here in the light of my own brief visits, and some of his claims inspired disagreement or puzzlement. We do agree, however, on the basic conclusion that the Muisca case reveals much more than simple "manifestation of difference in order to obtain economic and political benefits from the dominant society."[45]

Muisca have marshalled several kinds of evidence in support of their claims, working to meet requirements discussed by legislative and policymaking bodies, and embodied in official rules. In so doing they have achieved partial success. Although the state has so far recognized only two of their cabildos, the communities are composed of highly motivated people, all of indigenous descent—although phenotype matters less in Latin America, where most people have some native blood, than it does in North America. Muisca have been intently developing a vision of themselves, an ontology, and practices for decision making and community-building.

Muisca cabildos occupy lands that, at one and the same time, are urban—decidedly nonindigenous sites as conventionally understood—and are also ancestral territory. Bosa cabildo members reported that their grandparents were known as "the indios of Bosa." Victoria Neuta observed that even though the Bosa community had remained on the land of their ancestors, the invading city had nonetheless dispossessed them.[46] All of the urban Muisca communities have ancestors buried in nearby cemeteries, as well as umbilical cords buried nearby. In short, the fundamental requirements of ethnic claims—blood and soil—have been met. In some ways the urban Muisca resemble some of the reindigenized Putumayo cabildos discussed previously, because both base their claims on connections with indigenous antecedents, the Putumayo Nasa on forebearers geographically distant, the Bosa on ones temporally distant.

The problem, as most analysts see it, is that the Muisca are *urban*. Although the San Agustín Yanacona did not meet the requirements, narrowly defined, of either blood or soil, at least they were rural, as are the members of most of the reindigenized Putumayo cabildos. In 2005 the National Office of Ethnic Groups (DAI) issued a statement that "'urban communities should not be recognized . . .' because once indigenous people leave their traditional land, their 'social relations, relations of production, . . . their relationship to the land and [their] cultural traits, customs, and traditional knowledge, are slowly lost or modified.'"[47] Martínez Medina offers numerous examples of how urban living has impeded the recovery project of the Bosa Muisca.[48] At one public event the mayor of Bogotá demanded, "Where are your loincloths, feathers, and face paint?" although he and everyone else knew that the vast majority of Colombian Indians sport none of these. Many indigenous Colombians lack pueblo-specific attire, and some no longer speak an indigenous language. But the great majority *are* rural, and this is basically why the Muisca are asked to respond to questions like "Where are your feathers?" It also appears that Bosa Muisca were imposing similar demands on one another, straining to demonstrate their indigenousness. Martínez Medina argues that the modern Muisca are the victims of a long-lasting ideology of colonial origin that requires lo indígena to manifest a specific kind of *otredad*, "otherness," which disqualifies Muisca because they—like indigenous Australians discussed by Povinelli, "dress, act, and sound like the suburban neighbors they are."[49] Martínez Medina argues that Bosa Muisca face such challenges because their claims, which he himself finds persuasive, are discursive in nature, and, citing Michael Taussig, he adds that recognition based only on discourse is "impossible."[50] Muisca find themselves having to perform "stereotypes of indigeneity" that, over time, performatively transform them so that both they and others accept their claims. Following Taussig, Martínez Medina labels such performance as *mimesis*, which is "the theatrical manifestation of difference."[51] Such performances permit construction of "a new form of being in the world that allows them to confront situations that affect them as a collectivity."[52] Given the relational character of indigeneity, reindigenizing individuals and collectivities must perform such "stereotypes of indigeneity" in their recovery process to induce recognition from nonindigenous actors. Muisca put up a brave show, with such statements as these: "I AM indigenous because I FEEL indigenous"; "We recognize ourselves. No one has to tell us if we are or are not indigenous"; "We do not need them to give us permission to feel ourselves indigenous."[53] In their hearts, however, they know that they need to win acceptance, that "one must be identified as Other by someone who is not recognized as indigenous," and that one must do it through *performances* (Martínez Medina uses the English word) of indigenous culture.[54] Hence, among other things, the adoption of artifacts associated with the Sierra peoples, who are seen as the very essence of alterity.

Taussig argues that such performances of stereotypical indigeneity are crucial, even if they are episodic.[55] And it is the case that Indians throughout the hemisphere, many living in urban areas, go for long periods of time without displaying overtly "indigenous" behavior. But through periodic displays (e.g., the pow-wows of North American Indians), they can reassert their identities. The crucial issue under discussion here is whether they succeed in persuading nonindigenous skeptics.

My experience with the Sesquilé Muisca in 2007 disturbed as well as fascinated me, because it called into question some of anthropology's basic precepts. Anthropology has been stuck with a number of rigid categories, some of the most rigid bequeathed by the colonial encounter. True, our ethnographic inquiries are constantly confounding these categorizations, and although this sort of fieldwork-derived challenge to received anthropological wisdom has always attracted me, in this case, nonetheless, I was stumped, because analysis does require some form of classification. How can performances of what are obviously cherry-picked indigenous behaviors, and displays of a cherry-picked indigenous semiotics, do the trick? The answer hides perhaps in indigeneity's prerequisite of relationality, a paradox Martínez Medina addresses: "We are . . . before people who call themselves Indians and do not appear to be Indians, because their difference, according to the investigator who observes them, is not 'substantial' or 'essential.'"[56] He continues: "So a true form of being exists, alongside one that is not true. This seems to be the point of departure taken by many observers who find themselves in front of the multiple paradoxes that occur in these processes of 'resurgence.' Immense paradox, if we take into account that [these observers] precisely are trying to overcome the 'essentialist postulates of classic ethnology.'"[57] Another author who has written about the Muisca, Carlos Andrés Durán, feels that the judgment "made about this phenomenon depends on how essentialist and burdened by stereotypes the observer might be."[58]

The uphill path climbed by the urban Muisca is especially steep because of the major role allocated to the colonial era Muisca in the triumphalist narrative of the birth of the Colombian nation through cataclysmic colonial encounter; as a consequence, the Muisca are fixed in the past more than most other pueblos. Pratt's argument that the descriptors used to refer to indigenous peoples "all refer etymologically to prior-ity in time and place" is relevant here.[59] Muisca words are found throughout the city, but they are names of streets and of stores in upscale malls. In contrast, actual people who bear Muisca last names are discriminated against, and Martínez Medina provides some upsetting examples. Nelsy Chiguasuque recounts: "the teachers asked me to spell my name, 'You are Chigua . . . Chigua what?' A teacher said to me, 'Are you one of those Indians that makes a little hole in the earth and puts the food in there, makes your meals there and eats from that?'"[60] In short, urban Muisca tell familiar sad stories about the painful consequences of poverty and having indigenous looks and strange surnames, stories that reveal the scars acquired in early childhood, lacerations from the stigma of indigenous inferiority.

Not surprisingly, phenotype plays a contradictory yet crucial part of the Muisca reindigenization story, illustrating Chaves's points about the effects of a reversal from whitening discourses to indigenizing ones.[61] A Muisca woman, talking about another cabildo, says, "even the governor doesn't look indigenous . . . and that is why they have to put on feathers and things. Whereas anyone looking at Reinel [a member of the Bosa cabildo], just looking at his face one can tell that he is indigenous."[62]

Reading Martínez Medina's book allowed me to at least partially reconcile the disturbing inconsistencies I encountered during my visit to the Sesquilé resguardo—for example, the mandala pictographs on women's tunics, or the sweat bath's Mesoamerican origin and its pictographs. Muisca mochilas only resemble Sierra ones "because if it is effective as a mimetic object it is because it looks like the mochila of the Sierra without being it."[63] The Muisca mochila represents many other transformations that together work to bring about a "new form of being in the world." In this way mimesis, playing its "game between the same and the other," achieves its purpose.[64]

Martínez Medina's main example of mimesis is the *chuszua*, for him, a "central image of academic doubt."[65] The word, from Muiscubbun, means "house." A chuszua was constructed in Bosa in 2003, using modern materials, including plastic and rubber. Yet it achieved its objective because "it seems and is recognized as rustic and natural (read indigenous)."[66] Although the chuszua is made of modern materials, at the point of naming it a chuszua it becomes authentic, because this name comes from Muisca ancestors. Choosing a mimetic word that enlists Muiscubbun, rather than going with, as Martínez Medina suggests, *kiosco*, *little house*, or *maloca*, allows the structure to achieve its purpose, one that is highly constrained and limited to the specific context of the community.[67] The chuszua is thus an instrument that does not only *represent* difference in front of the dominant society; in addition, its plastic and rubber construction materials permit the construction of an identity, because what is produced is an *almost exact* copy, and thus a denunciation of the stereotypical "first contact" requirement, a denunciation of the "necessity of primitivism and nostalgia over its loss"—a denunciation of the demand for feathers and face paint.[68] The chuszua is a response to a double, interconnected proposition: achieving a proper, workable, acceptable type of difference allows one to convincingly manifest an alterity through which one makes oneself *Other*: an Other that is not just any Other but a specific indigenous Other, yet one living in the present rather than the "first contact" past.[69]

Both the Muisca mochila and the chuszua are mimetic objects that are "irremediably" located between the *Same* and the *Other*, between *falsification* and *identical imitation* (which would posit an authentic chuszua being constructed by authentic Indians who use authentic materials in conditions of pure authenticity).[70] A space of ambiguity is left that allows the creative construction of an appropriate way of being a Bosa Indian, a *raizal* (a "rooted" person), a Muisca.[71] The chuszua, like Muisca identity itself, is an achievement that functions in the present: cabildo members want to feel and demonstrate Muisca culture and to benefit from it. Present-day communicating and legitimating resources are enlisted to this end: a book and a video were produced.[72]

An aspect of the story I cannot go into deeply is the role Muisca reindigenization plays as a social movement. As noted, Bosa is plagued with problems: among districts in Bogotá it has the second highest number of internally displaced people fleeing the half century of violence; its river is horribly polluted; artisanal electronic recycling activities wreak havoc with the soils, water, and air; and the city's scheme to thwart rampant real estate speculation is itself a mega land grab. As has happened in many other places in the hemisphere, reindigenization efforts have taken place under the banner of "organize to survive," where survival by no means refers only to recovering and maintaining a collective identity.

Like most of my contemporaries I started out as a positivist anthropologist. There was truth out there, and my job was to look for it. After having acquired the appropriate scholarly armamentarium via my graduate studies, I was supposed to gather data, analyze it, and deliver my findings to academic audiences in the accepted ethnographic forms: a PhD thesis, followed by articles and books. My multiple trips to Colombia were dedicated to this type of discovery and analysis. Such efforts also fostered self-discovery—the hermeneutic cliché that one discovers oneself via an exploration of the Other. But ethnographic fieldwork, which can take the form of a quest, may involve walking through the mirror like Alice in *Through the Looking-Glass* and discovering that one has, in the process, become Othered. Yes, doing ethnographic research allows one to mature as a scholar and gain wisdom about life in general. But with some of us there is a greater transformation, and in my case, the topic of identity was always a major part of this quest. At first I was challenged to understand identity as it pertained to Tukanoan social structure: if these people could not be described as members of tribes, what kind of unit did they belong to? Looking at this and other identity issues over the following forty-odd years, I managed to better understand all sorts of things, including anthropological charter myths, most of which emerged from colonial charter myths (e.g., Amazonian Indians are organized into tribes). It never occurred to me to wonder whether Tukanoans were Indians—they just *were*—and I did not begin to look closely at this particular bit of received wisdom until the mid-1980s, when I began to ponder just what "being indigenous" consisted of. Today, nearing the end of my scholarly journey, I find that my field research and reading have in some respects made such questions even more intractable. But I also find I am OK with this—a reconciliation I was able to pull off while on the other side of the mirror.

I cannot imagine a better ending to the parts of this book that discuss my own scholarly journey than to provide these comments on what I saw and felt during, and after, my visits to the Sesquilé and Bosa cabildos. I do not have a comprehensive or clear set of answers on how to analyze reindigenization. Clearly mimesis is involved. Clearly reindigenization's evolution has been influenced by the state and other stakeholder institutions in the dominant society. Clearly many participants do experience what they are seeking: for example, cures. But many questions remain. For example, what to do about indigenous communities that do not accept other communities' assertions and performances? During a visit to Boston the Guambiano Floro Tunubalá, a former governor of Cauca, wanted to visit an indigenous organization, and I accompanied him to one that represents New England Indians. During our chat with the director she began to harshly criticize a New England tribe, saying they were fake Indians. I was very uncomfortable translating her rant, and he seemed seriously taken aback. The director's critique illustrates Barker's point about tribal membership criteria being "a politic of relationship (un)making, as Native peoples negotiate the terms of their legal status and rights in relation to one another as 'Indian members.'" Such processes of identification "involve multiple mirrorings of what it means to be Native."[73] In similar fashion, Martínez Medina notes Bosa Muisca members' criticisms of other cabildos' dances, which, they say, are not "authentic."[74] But I am mostly at peace with this lack of closure, analytic rigor, and certainty. Because normativity hovers so close to any definitive conclusions I might attempt to draw about these often vexed issues, I find myself most comfortable quoting Pope Francis: "Who am I to judge?"

The Urban Cabildo Tubú Hummurimasa

During that 2016 trip to Colombia I visited another urban cabildo, Tubú Hummurimasa,[75] which had been established by about forty Siriano (Tubú) refugees from the Vaupés. The Tubú language group is one of the Tukanoan language groups. Their experience also sheds a revealing light on reindigenization: although no one has as yet expressed doubts that the Tubú are indigenous, if they are to avoid being swallowed up by the city, assimilated, and relegated to the residual category "of indigenous descent," they must continue to find ways to perform indigeneity in new and radically different surroundings.

Although indigenous Colombians have lived in Bogotá for a very long time—the Muisca, as we saw, say they have been there all along—today the vast majority are recent refugees from the at times catastrophic violence in rural areas.[76] Many of them have formed cabildos,[77] some of them under an umbrella organization called Asociación de Cabildos Indígenas de Bogotá (ASCAI, Association of Indigenous Cabildos of Bogotá). Others initially belonged to that organization, but broke away to form another group, Organización Nacional de Cabildos Indígenas de Ciudad (ONCIDEC, National Organization of Indigenous Urban Cabildos). The Tubú live high up on a ridge overlooking the city, on the periphery of the district of San Cristóbal, southeast of the city center. My visit was arranged by the cabildo's *asesor*, Germán McAllister, who had been working with them for two years.[78] Germán informed cabildo members that a North American anthropologist who had carried out research in the Vaupés wanted to pay a visit. They agreed to meet with me and requested that I bring a carton of cigarettes, beer, and a "collaboration," meaning a donation. Our party consisted of Germán, my research assistant Juliana Sánchez, Mauricio Romero (a young anthropologist working in Putumayo), and myself. Upon hearing the address the taxi driver was not *at all* happy about taking us there, but as we had already entered the car, what could he do?

The community owns a meeting house, the inside of which was nicely painted and decorated with several photographs and traditional musical instruments like maracas and panpipes. (Also their bathroom, unlike many, many others in Colombia, came equipped with toilet paper.) We sat on low wooden benches positioned along three walls. After Germán introduced us and described why I was there, the eldest man present, Sebastián Uribe, who is both a payé (shaman) and a *kumú*,[79] as well as head of the Diákara clan (which occupies the second position in the Tubú language group ranking), spoke for a while. His Tukano wife, Etelvina Sierra, spoke next, followed by their son, Ramiro, the cabildo governor. Ramiro wore a felt cowboy hat; long, loose hair; and a jaguar-tooth necklace. Otherwise his clothes were unremarkable, as were his father's, with the exception of flip-flops on his feet (Bogotá is *cold*). Etelvina, from the Tiquié River area, was dressed more colorfully, with a long skirt and woolen Andean cap. Upon hearing that I had been in the Papurí-Paca drainage area in the late 1960s, she was sure we had known some of the same people, and began listing names and their settlements. I do not speak Tukano and her Spanish was very poor. I was elated at hearing a Tukanoan language, but also quite anxious during this exchange. We finally agreed that we both had known Manuel, the headman of a maloca on the Inambú River. Remembering Manuel, and the Bará name for the river, *bóaya*, came as a relief.

The Uribe family came to Bogotá in 2002, victims, like so many others, of intimidation and violence. In their case, a visitor to their house (located fifty kilometers from Mitú at a place called Bogotá Cachivera), was killed by FARC guerrillas, but the family escaped by running downhill to their kitchen building. Afterward they traveled to Mitú and later decided to migrate permanently to Bogotá.

Like clans occupying second rank in all other Tukanoan language groups, these Tubú are dancers and chanters. They have participated in organized dance competitions in both Mitú and Bogotá. The group has been able to pay their asesor's salary and buy the impressive meeting house using prizes won through dance performances and money earned by Sebastián and Ramiro, who refer to themselves as coca healers.[80] Indigenous curers in the city who advertise themselves as Amazonian healers practice what is sometimes referred to as neo-shamanism, often using yajé. They attract many clients.[81] In the Vaupés, Sebastián had undergone the traditional shamanic apprenticeship with his father, and Ramiro had been interested from an early age in following in his father's footsteps.

The meeting I attended lasted four hours. It had been a long time since I had sat with Tukanoans in this kind of encounter, and it affected me deeply. As in a meeting of the Society of Friends (Quakers) in North America, silence ruled throughout, broken only when someone was moved to speak. Otherwise people looked at the ground, kept their movements to a minimum, and waited. I had forgotten the feel of such evening gatherings, the atmosphere, the bodily praxis, and, above all, the quiet and the sense that time simply did not matter. Even in a Bogotá slum, with buses passing by periodically on the broken-up road, a feeling of calm and tranquility prevailed, achieved by long periods of silence and almost motionless bodies. As usual my height and my gringa looks marked me out, but I remembered long periods of time in the Vaupés sitting on hard benches and chewing coca. I knew how to insert coca powder into my cheek without embarrassing myself (and I knew how to drink beer). I passed up the opportunity, however, to snort rapé when it was passed around, having experienced its effects in Sesquilé. And I was the only one not to smoke. As the others consumed cigarette after cigarette, the clouds of tobacco smoke brought back memories of low-ceilinged music clubs from the 1970s in the United States. I found out later that my Tubú hosts had expected us to stay longer, which pleased me (as had my ability to sit still for four straight hours). At one point we asked if we could take photographs and were met with silence. I was disappointed, but we did not ask again.

The Tubú visit provided a Tukanoan critique of the indigenous movement. Sebastián and Ramiro sounded very different from previous indigenous interviewees I had spoken with, most of them young activists from highland regions. Ramiro spoke frankly about deep disagreements and schisms within the urban indigenous community, in particular between lowland and highland segments, something I knew about but had not heard expressed so directly by an indigenous speaker. Ramiro added that the Tubú community "had not asked help from anyone, nor had anyone offered help"—which was not entirely accurate, since they *had* sought help from ONIC, an effort that had convinced Ramiro that "it is easier to gain access to a senator than to ONIC officers."

What the Tubú professed as their goal in their new environment was to continue, as much as they were able, with Tukanoan practices. Germán said that the core of these activities consisted of evening gatherings in which people drank chicha and chanted and danced, or else sat and talked as we were doing. According to Germán, the Tubú approach consists of "working within the *entorno* [structure or environment] of Our Own Thought [Pensamiento Propio], and traditional culture, through dances, coca-chewing [*mambear*], rapé, and traditional medicine."

Ramiro's assessment of their current situation was bleak. According to him, the attack on their house in Bogotá Cachivera had been provoked by envy on the part of in-laws and Tubú kinsmen who were spreading gossip that the family had money. Other antagonists included state functionaries, followed by Catholic priests (the Tubú are evangelical Protestants), the *muchachos* (boys, i.e., the FARC), and then, when they moved to Mitú, the army. He criticized government and NGO policies, which, he said, destabilized traditional political structures. He deplored the "incentivizing" by Gaia Foundation, an NGO, to create administrative zones within the eastern section of the Gran Resguardo of the Vaupés, as well as the policy of favoring bilingual young men as leaders over older authorities rooted in tradition. This favoritism, he said, promoted an indigenous bureaucracy that displaced traditional structures, generating disorder and confusion in "the proper forms of organization."

Ramiro's terminology was interesting. He consistently used the word *indio* rather than *indígena* because, Germán said, Ramiro considers the latter a euphemism: the derogatory epithet *indio* traditionally denotes beings who are "almost animals" and who lack souls and religion. *Indígena* cushions the impact of this semantic "heavy burden," offering the appearance of humanity. But even if *indígena* confers rights, it still relegates those it designates to a position of inferiority. Ultimately, said Germán, the attempt to erase the semantic burden of *indio* ends up folkloricizing *indígena*. In his discourse, Ramiro also repeatedly used the word *nación* (nation), rather than the much more common term *ethnic group*, a usage common in North American activist circles but seldom invoked in Colombia—neither Germán nor I had heard it before.[82]

Ramiro's dissatisfaction with the indigenous movement also surfaced in a throwaway passing comment that "earlier they disrespected us, but later on they came to adopt our concepts"—"they" presumably being highland activists. As an example of such appropriation, he mentioned the *Círculo de la Palabra* (Speaking Circle), a Spanish term referring to the traditional practice of sitting quietly in a circle, chewing coca, smoking, and sharing conversation—in short, following traditional lowland models for evening gatherings. Germán told me that a number of urban indigenous groups, particularly those interested in revitalizing lo indígena, now use the term Círculo de la Palabra, and that some groups have also adopted Tubú words for rapé (*murudi*) and cannabis (*yémuru*).

So far, it seems that the urban Tubú have managed to adapt without assimilating; despite their many problems they have retained their notions of who they are and are living their lives according to certain basic Tukanoan principles, while managing to earn a living on some of the meanest streets in Latin America. They face the daunting task of performing indigenous lifeways in a modern, globalizing society, something particularly challenging for lowland indigenous refugees in urban spaces. The Tubú rejection of "White" organization models is reminiscent of AICO's criticisms of CRIC, which were mentioned in Chapter One. Tubú authenticity, however, is grounded in traditions that differ much more radically from mainstream society than do those of highland pueblos, increasing the difficulty of deciding what to retain and what to discard. These men actually do wear feathers, at least in their performance attire (which, being minimal, is not at all suited to Bogotá's climate).[83] The parts of their lives that are specifically Tukanoan are already so reduced that in the future they will very likely be viewed as "folkloric" remnants of their forebearers. However much or little they retain of lowland authenticity, they still face disregard and disrespect from their highland counterparts. Ramiro's young son will be the chief of the Diákara clan, but in one video he looks like any other child in Bogotá's Plaza Bolívar, walking with his nonindigenous mother and eating store-bought snacks.

Discussion

Authenticity challenges are a worldwide phenomenon. Writing about Australia, Francesca Merlan notes that once presumably progressive, well-intentioned legal and administrative processes of granting native land titles were established, an "insufficiency according to traditionalist criteria" was revealed for many communities, and they were deemed inauthentic.[84] Barker goes so far as to say that "cultural authenticity for Native peoples exists only in a pre-colonial—indeed pre-historical—moment that has been forever lost to the natural, inevitable, compromised, or tragic ends of colonialism and imperialism."[85]

In general we find few examples in present-day Colombia of cases where indigenous identity is disclaimed by populations the rest of us would call indigenous, although in earlier eras such cases definitely occurred. Carmen Martínez Novo describes a group of migrant Mixtec laborers in Baja, California, who did not wish to be classified as indigenous. But in a kind of perverse multiculturalist move, the agribusiness company employing them justified paying them less than other laborers and providing substandard benefits by claiming that, as they were indios, they did not need better treatment.[86] Bogotá residents with indigenous last names who deny any indigenousness would be the Colombian equivalent to these laborers and their denial of ethnic identity. But in parts of Andean Bolivia and Peru, entire communities that we see as indigenous see themselves in terms of their geographical identity—as members of their communities—and have not adopted the indígena label.[87] In Bolivia, writes Canessa, being indio means being "poor, backward, and culturally retarded." He also notes that although a wide variety of actors self-label as indígena, "who would want to be an indio?"[88] While these two points about the term *indio* hold for Colombia as well, Canessa's overall account does not characterize the current Colombian situation. Part of the explanation for the differences in the two countries is demographic: Colombia is 3.5 percent indigenous, whereas in Bolivia Indians are in the majority. But historical conjunctures and current politics also play a role. In Colombia *indígena* may be a euphemism, but it is current parlance, whereas *indio* today is a rarely heard slur. Although Aymara leader Felipe Quispe "loathed" the term *indígena* and proclaimed that "as indians [*sic*] [indios] they oppressed us and as indians we will liberate ourselves."[89] His rhetoric is an example of subordinate appropriation of a dominant society epithet, whereby its sting is lessened and with which political points are made. This is not to say that indigenous Colombians are not sometimes seen as dirty, lazy, and stupid; subjected to all sorts of discrimination; and sometimes called indios. It is to say that the majority of people we would label indigenous Colombians would also label themselves as such. And as we have seen, there are many wannabees.

In Colombia successful reindigenization demands performances that powerfully index symbols of indigeneity often treated as negative—isolation, social and geographic marginality, and a stubborn rootedness in the past. This same dilemma confronts native North Americans when confronted with the assumption that "social change is eroding the core of Indian ethnicity, implying that American Indians will retain their place in society only by living as their ancestors did in the nineteenth [or some earlier] century"[90] an epistemology that Jack Forbes argues is applied only to Indians.[91] Reindigenization challenges this "vanishing race" view and its underlying evolutionary premises. Analyzing reindigenization thus constitutes a special problem for social scientists, who, happily, have risen to the challenge in significant numbers. Rappaport's analysis of Nasa constructions of a "counter-modernity," a notable example of such work, discredits, once and for all, the "tradition/modern" dichotomy that, vampire-like, stubbornly lives on despite repeated attempts to kill it off.[92]

Throughout the Americas, whether ethnic identity is resurgent or emergent, similar processes of group formation and political mobilization occur when economic or political advantages are linked to ethnicity.[93] But more is going on than reaching for opportunity. The examples offered here suggest additional, less pragmatic motives driving cultural recovery projects. The San Agustín Yanacona had agendas and motives of several sorts, some of which responded to friction with neighbors and authorities—local, national, and international. The Sesquilé Muisca's project mostly met needs for personal fulfillment and sociality rather than political or economic gain—they had their land, but no one was actually living on the site. They seemed engaged in a quest to find a better, more meaningful life, one that explicitly rejected many aspects of modernity.

In North America the well-known case of the Mashantucket Pequot in

Connecticut displays some of the same goals. Nagel writes: "History and tradition, excavated and renovated, are the foundation and cement of these ethnic construction projects."[94] The Pequots have relearned native traditions: "We're just looking back into our traditions and finding our way like the birth of a new nation. And we're working with other tribes in the area to learn from them how to do things like dancing and bringing back our culture."[95] Among the cases examined here, the Sesquilé Muisca illustrate this tactic of "working with other tribes"; the Arhauco man helping them recover their culture is an example. In similar fashion the San Agustín Yanacona were aided by a member of the Cauca Yanacona community, Fredy Chikangana.

But not everything echoes North American examples: we can discern additional incentives to reindigenize that are unique to Colombia. Alongside the valorized generic characteristics of indigeneity (spirituality, etc.) can be found some specific and instructive examples of Indians getting it right when nonindigenous Colombians get it wrong. As discussed in Chapter Four, horrific national violence and a weak, corrupt state helped create an imaginary of Colombian pueblos whose values, community structure, and practices, while certainly not ideal, at times pointed to how much better things could be in certain respects.

Any investigation of reindigenization can lead the analyst into a quagmire, parts of it veritable quicksand. Reindigenization projects reveal dynamic processes of appropriation, contestation, and refashioning of Western meanings, in particular those of culture, and scholars have been problematizing the notion of culture to better understand these processes. Clearly one kind of problematization involves examining the ways in which indigenous movements, like all social movements, challenge "the boundaries of cultural and political representation and social practice."[96] Deconstructing the culture concept often generates controversy. Native activists often object to deconstructive anthropological analysis, fearing quite reasonably that it may provide ammunition to their opponents and critics. In particular, in the United States and Canada, critics have argued that social scientists should focus on "the machinery of power" rather than on vulnerable indigenous communities that do not deserve the negative consequences that can sometimes follow from publication of constructionist analyses.[97] A great deal can ride on establishing the authenticity of identity and culture, and specific cases sometimes do not stand up to a social science gaze. As pointed out in Chapter Two, part of the problem comes with lexical connotations—even *reconstruction* can be problematic, not to mention *invention*. However, it is also abundantly clear that new cultural practices and newly formed institutions that have been developed by disadvantaged, threatened, and exploited communities have helped them withstand the onslaught of acculturative forces and far worse threats.

Part of the problem comes from the historical evolution of anthropology's vision. We have discarded (mostly, not entirely) our past fixations on tradition and authenticity. If a community comes up with a new or borrowed costume; if it adopts a practice like the sweat lodge, unknown to the ancestors; if it devises a new ritual or dance or founding narrative; or if its members claim descent from somebody's else's ancestors, we may feel uncomfortable, but mostly we analyze what's going on and try to help in any way we can. We have come to realize that even those seemingly stable, self-made traditional cultures once taken as models of authenticity necessarily had *their* beginnings in creative innovation, cultural borrowing, and even human inventiveness and mendacity. But that accepting point of view has not reached the enemies and critics of those communities, nor, at least on the surface, some of these communities' erstwhile allies. The concept of ethnogenesis does not dovetail with many varieties of cultural politics.

For Colombianists who are theorizing ethnoracial identities and movements and struggling to develop a multifactorial approach, a comparison of Afro-descendant communities and indigenous pueblos is in order. As scholars like Arocha, Escobar, Ng'weno, and Wade have pointed out, Afro-Colombians insist that they, too, have ethnicity. Their ethnicity, however, has different boundaries: moving from racialized blackness to Afro-descendant ethnicity is a different process from moving from mestizo identity to indigeneity. Although indigenous identity is racialized more in North America than it is in Latin America, by and large, in both places being indigenous is a largely cultural category. Forbes contrasts the purely genetic "one drop" rule that applies to Blacks—however mixed their actual ancestry—with the historical and cultural criteria applied to Indians, criteria that put tremendous pressure on Native Americans either to remain unchanged or to deny and obfuscate the changes.[98] Under what circumstances could someone reasonably say "there aren't any *real* Blacks left," similar to "there aren't any *real* Indians left"? Despite significant differences in racializing practices between the United States and Canada and Latin America, this thought experiment works in both North and Latin America, and for that matter in Hawaii and other places.

Conclusions

The explosion of reindigenization efforts in Colombia and elsewhere can usefully be seen as an unforeseen consequence of official multiculturalism. The decline of the corporatist state, the opening up of spaces for parastatal entities, the signing of international covenants and treaties, the development of neoliberalism as an ideology and cultural project telling people to participate in civil society—all these events have contributed to the process, as has rights-based discourse. Official multiculturalism holds that discrimination on the basis of ethnoracial identity is unacceptable (which may not, of course, tell us much about what actually happens on the ground). The San Agustín Yanacona succeeded to some degree by creatively combining two kinds of discourses, one featuring rural, marginalized, and traditional alterity, the other a cosmopolitan, environmentalist, and developmentalist vision. The Yanacona, the reindigenized Putumayo communities, and the Muisca clearly fit Marisol de la Cadena and Orin Starn's characterization of the "essence of indigeneity": these communities—and, I would posit, other successfully reindigenized ones—all illustrate efforts to share "a view of mixture, eclecticism, and dynamism as opposed to a falling off or 'corruption' of some original state of purity."[99]

Conclusion

Indigeneity's Ironies and Contradictions

In these pages, I have examined four concepts fundamental to indigenous struggles across the Western Hemisphere: multiculturalism, culture, rights, and indigeneity. I have considered those concepts as they have worked themselves out in one particular country, in one particular era of transformative change, and as seen and understood by one particular ethnographer. I come to terms with this history and with these key concepts in two ways: through a series of ethnographic cases, each one the subject of historical and theoretical commentary; and through a reflexive look back at my own fieldwork and scholarship—the fifty-year career trajectory of an anthropologist working to make sense of what she observed in a country she came to love deeply.

Given that I am addressing four quite complex and even self-contradictory concepts, and given that the ethnographic cases occurred in a variety of sites and at various moments over a substantial span of time, I cannot provide comprehensive conclusions here. What I do offer in this final chapter is a brief summary of the major changes that fundamentally affected the Colombian indigenous movement, followed by a discussion of a number of lessons taken from the ethnographic cases, points that seem especially worth highlighting.

Key Changes

The contradictory nature of multiculturalism, defined as the legal and normative recognition of cultural and ethnic difference (and therefore as one form of governmentality), has been a recurrent theme in this book. Multiculturalism, according to Partha Chatterjee,[1] emerged from the tensions between the project of universal citizenship and demands for differential recognition. In the abstract, multiculturalism celebrates diversity, but official multiculturalism seeks to define and dissect that diversity, to specify who will receive official juridicopolitical recognition and who will not. In Colombia, as elsewhere in Latin America, indigeneity emerged as an important way to claim citizenship, rights, and justice. In addition to official multiculturalism (which began to appear in legislation and policymaking a number of years before being consolidated in the 1991 constitution), we have looked at the varieties embraced by a wide range of individuals, ethnicities, and organizations. As I have tried throughout this book to show, Colombian multiculturalism emerged in a complex and unstable historical context, one that combined neoliberalism, widespread armed conflict, indigenous activism and government response, and donor agendas favoring grassroots initiatives, and in which outcomes were heavily influenced by nonindigenous stakeholders that included the Catholic Church and foreign and national NGOs.

The Colombian state's multiculturalist policies were subsequently joined by environmentalist ones that characterized pueblo members as "ecological natives," a doctrine first articulated in the late 1980s by then-president Virgilio Barco. The state's generic construction of *lo indígena* was reconfigured to portray the pueblos as stewards of the environment, a gaze just as essentializing and homogenizing as what preceded it, and one that refers mainly to Sierra Nevada and lowland pueblos.[2]

Why did indigenous mobilization become the most vocal and powerful popular social movement in Colombia? Among a variety of causes were the failures and contradictions of class-based politics, which opened space for alternatives. Some state actors, notably DAI, tolerated and even at times encouraged ethnic-based mobilizations in an effort to repress others based on class, and to counter the expansion of guerrilla movements into indigenous areas.[3] Foreign actors and international social movements also played a part, offering external partnerships, new ideas, funding, and a number of international covenants beneficial to the indigenous cause. Among the agreements signed by Colombia, ILO Convention 169, which gave indigenous peoples standing in international law, and the 2007 United Nations Declaration on the Rights of Indigenous Peoples, which recognized indigenous peoples' collective rights to self-determination and autonomy, were crucially important.

The material, economic, and political realities of indigenous life in Colombia have changed radically, due in no small part to the de jure changes initiated in the 1980s. To be sure, indigenous communities are still poor and oppressed. But together they now collectively own almost 30 percent of the national territory. Although shocking numbers of indigenous and Afro-descendant leaders are still being assassinated,[4] kidnappings and massacres have decreased, in part due to the negotiations that led to the 2016 peace accords.[5] Pueblo members' livelihoods cannot as easily be taken from them as happened in the past, often with total impunity. On the question of who is or is not considered indigenous, even if non-Indians continue to dominate the discussion, pueblo voices matter more than they once did. And those voices are heard more often now, as numerous claims to rights and benefits are advanced, indigeneity is displayed rather than concealed, and being indigenous transcends the earlier categorical definition of indigeneity as residence in a resguardo.[6]

Even the very concept of indigeneity (expressed in Colombia as *lo indígena*, *indianidad*, or *indigeneidad*) has been transformed. An array of determinants produced these semantic shifts, a major one being the emergence and impressive impact of the indigenous movement, both nationally and internationally. In the multiculturalist context, belonging to an indigenous community occurs at several levels, from the very local to something much broader, as indigenous people also belong to a global community—which gives indigeneity a unique global currency. As Pratt notes, indigeneity "enables historically and geographically separated peoples to recognize each other and collaborate."[7] While members of many ethnic groups also belong to much larger, at times global, communities (e.g., the Chinese community), the notion of indigenous belonging articulates the local and the global, and everything in between, in a unique fashion. Yes, there are huge numbers of overseas Chinese, but they all relate, in admittedly complicated ways, to China, whereas the global indigenous community lacks an equivalent geographical anchor. Anchored they indeed are, but to a vague and abstract imaginary that locates them in a temporal and spatial prior-ity. However one wants to characterize this notion, in Colombia, the initial entry and spread of the idea of a nationwide (which grew to a hemisphere-wide and then worldwide) belonging powerfully influenced the way Colombia's indigenous people today see themselves, analyze their situation, and make decisions about how to act. Part of that newly received wisdom is, as Canessa points out, realizing that indigeneity is about a sense of historical injustice.[8] A pueblo's understanding of their own history of injustice becomes enriched by knowledge about past and present colonialisms in other places.

Beginnings: The Vaupés and CRIVA

I witnessed the earliest signs of multiculturalism and indigenous mobilization in the Vaupés, with the appearance and growth of the Consejo Regional Indígena del Vaupés (CRIVA). The organization was midwifed by Catholic priests in Mitú, who sought to end debt peonage and to rid the Vaupés of their Protestant North American rivals by encouraging young Tukanoan men, most of them teachers, to organize. What happened to CRIVA illustrates the myriad ways state and nonstate actors can influence the evolution of a local indigenous organization. The sudden appearance of substantial amounts of international funding intended for multiculturalist-themed projects was an important factor, as was the part played by the national indigenous movement. Rivalry between local stakeholders like state officials and Catholic and evangelical missionaries played an important role as well.

After 1991, with a national constitution offering recognition to "traditional authorities" in the Orinoco and Amazon territories, CRIVA underwent a major shift in its legal status, becoming an official intermediary between local communities and the government. While remaining dependent on the Catholic Prefecture in some ways, most of them unhelpful, CRIVA distanced itself from the Catholic Church, veering off in an ill-advised, hyper-political direction.

As the politics of culture entered the Vaupés region, Tukanoan identity was reconfigured in certain respects. Linguistic exogamy was a particularly sticky issue. Although the Catholic Prefecture seems to have been the only organization that had actively opposed this traditional system, given that its complexities confounded received wisdom about Amazonian native life, no one apart from a few anthropologists saw it as an institution worth preserving. In response to the new political spaces that recognized the right to difference, CRIVA activists worked to shape an imaginary of their culture that would meet with outsider approval. Publications appeared containing information that the authors undoubtedly knew was incorrect.

Tukanoan linguistic exogamy continues today to confound received wisdom about the Amazonian variety of lo indígena. By causing endless confusion among government officials, missionaries, academics, and members of pueblos living outside the region, it embodies perfectly the dilemmas of cultural representation. Any effort to represent an indigenous culture as deserving some form of redistributive justice must convince its intended audience of that culture's authenticity, which depends in turn on representing it in a form that outsiders can understand and endorse.[9] Through the processes of managed multiculturalism, groups once fairly independent and culturally distinct end up as enclaved ethnic groups, whose cultural distinctiveness depends on a dialogic relationship with national culture, and on received stereotypes of indigeneity.[10] CRIVA's efforts illustrate the circularity embedded in the notion of culture as a right but also as the site from which to claim rights, because an authentic culture must fit into an imaginary already in existence.

In my own efforts to understand this process, I found myself critiquing CRIVA authors because I saw linguistic exogamy not only as a basic building block of Tukanoan social structure but also as a magnificent example of ethnogenesis—collective cultural creativity during an era of great change. In the past, Tukanoan marriage was probably based on direct exchange *within* monolingual communities or blocks of communities, as is the case in several other Amazonian societies.[11] As the region became a refuge area and the local population dropped sharply (and with it the supply of potential partners), Tukanoan communities began to accept spouses from immigrant groups speaking different languages. With time, the notion grew that potential spouses *should* speak different primary languages. Partner groups even reshaped their dialects in order to be able to consider them mutually unintelligible. "We marry our enemies," a phrase found in anthropology textbooks to describe a number of direct-marital-exchange kinship systems, succinctly describes what the transformation probably looked like, and in a more literal fashion than is usually the case.

Given my own intellectual investment in the institution of linguistic exogamy, I took offense when I watched this remarkable institution being thrown into the dustbin of (invented) history. My reaction sharpened my focus on questions of representation more generally, in particular on indigenous self-representation, and on ethical issues in ethnography raised by my own involvement. In commenting on the efforts of Tukanoan activists to shape their cultural accounts to fit outsiders' expectations, I was unsure how to handle the errors and distortions they produced. I searched for an analytic framework that would neither endorse nor discredit their revisionist auto-ethnography.

In one essay, I drew on the emerging literature on pidgin and creole languages (discussed in Chapter Two), which I hoped would help me make sense of CRIVA's novel representations, seeing them as one example of a response to colonialism and other kinds of change. But despite my efforts in this and other early essays to avoid giving the impression that I was judging CRIVA's representations of Tukanoan culture in an entirely negative manner, the essays provoked clashes, first with anthropologists and then with indigenous activists. I learned the hard way about the complexities of writing about indigenous self-representation—the difficulty of finding a balance somewhere between passive acceptance of every activist assertion and heedless criticism that could be picked up and exploited by outsiders hungry for indigenous territory and resources. I learned that one must anticipate all the ways that one's writing might be interpreted (or misinterpreted), that one must always keep in mind the deeply asymmetrical power relations inherent in ethnography, and that to write about such topics one must have a thick skin.

I would have benefited from two concepts proposed since I wrote. One is Anna Tsing's notion of "indigenous voice . . . the genre conventions with which public affirmations of identity are articulated."[12] Tsing, in effect, focuses attention on the power of genres rather than the power of those who use them, with the implication that even a total stranger who knows those conventions, who speaks in ways an audience can hear, might appropriate indigenous power. CRIVA activists were learning and deploying these conventions to reach their intended audiences.

The literature on performativity offers another analytic resource. If writing can be glossed as a kind of performance, even if it does not include embodied movement, then the CRIVA authors could be understood as performing Amazonian indigeneity: in James Clifford's terms, they were being "'called' or 'hailed' to perform themselves as authentic cultural subjects."[13] Although Clifford had in mind heritage performances, his conclusion, that "[c]ultural subjects discover themselves and make themselves legible," applies with equal force to CRIVA auto-ethnography, designed as it is to reach "powerful audiences that dispose of attractive resources and coercive power."[14] Those audiences, the Tukanoan and non-Tukanoan readers of the articles and pamphlets in the national publication *Unidad Indígena* and the local *La Voz de la Tribu*, became consumers of alterity.

The questions raised about Tukanoan social identity, language, and culture were inevitably projected onto a larger screen, as the struggles taking place throughout Colombia increasingly foregrounded cultural issues. It became clear to me that anthropologists approaching such issues, either as scholars or as advocates, must tread carefully, trying to avoid the pitfalls I walked into in the Vaupés. As Tsing's notion of friction captures, contradictions often arise between policies and projects emanating from the metropole and their implementation in the hinterland.[15] Dramatic interactions—often clashes—can occur between Western models and traditional patterns of authority, knowledge production, and collective decision making. Well-meaning NGO personnel and agents of the state may not recognize the arrogance, condescension, and unthinking assumptions inherent in their own attitudes and actions, as was apparent in the traditional medicine and ethno-education projects discussed in Chapter Three. Change agents also trip over their assumptions about the egalitarian harmony and consensual decision making they expect to find in all indigenous communities—expectations that a community will "act as a singular and unified political entity, making decisions on behalf of its population and managing those who live within its borders."[16] They fail to recognize that, as often as not, those stereotypes first appeared, not through serious engagement with the Other, but as critiques of the West through its imagined and idealized antithesis.

Another important issue to consider has to do with occasions when pueblos display values and actions that are anything but fair, democratic, or egalitarian, as these concepts are defined and valorized in the West. The evolving imaginary of lo indígena as it played out in the Vaupés in the late 1980s and 1990s complicated received wisdom about "the good Indian," who in that setting basically was an acculturated Tukanoan who somehow had managed to steer clear of dominant society failings so prevalent in the region (e.g., alcoholism). Whites agreed with Tukanoans that they were superior to Makú (and when the Nukak were brought in, a third position, "less than Makú" emerged), but challenges to that ranking were beginning to appear. Although during their stay in Mitú the Nukak were subjected to appalling treatment, notions were entering the region about the "ecological native" and the value of truly authentic, radically indigenous Others like the Makú and Nukak. This new perspective caused confusion among Tukanoans, as well as, very probably, many local Whites. However, the overall hierarchy remained, and to this day Makú are scorned and laughed at.

The Makú-Nukak case illustrates how government officials and other change agents, when caught in a humanitarian crisis, feel pressure to come up with a narrative that will appeal to the media and to skeptical left-wing critics of their efforts. But such narratives often lead to short-term, shortsighted, and failure-prone solutions. This case also reveals a recurrent clash between multiculturalist support for tradition and the oft-inconvenient facts of that tradition. Traditional Tukanoan society is anything but egalitarian.

In all language groups clans are ranked, and members of high-ranking clans look down their noses at those further down the ladder, who in turn despise the Makú at the very bottom. Although the particulars of other cases in other regions may differ, change agents—with their reluctance to acknowledge diversity, hierarchy, conflict, and other sticking points—often bring the same half-baked assumptions and predispositions to each one.

The Nukak imaginary, constructed in terms of homogeneity, docility, innocence, nobility, and naïveté, led to unfortunate official actions. Del Cairo describes one case where two Nukak subgroups were merged into one, and since Nukak bands' subgroups do *not* live in harmony with one another, the merger inevitably produced conflict.[17] As Francis Nyamnjoh argues, bureaucratic assumptions that indigenous communities are all alike run up against the "hierarchies and relationships of inclusion and exclusion informed by race, ethnicity, class, gender, and geography that determine indigeneity in real terms."[18]

Assumptions about egalitarian values are not the only problem. Although the official government position is that all pueblos are equally indigenous, in practice state agents make invidious distinctions when dealing with more than one pueblo in a given locale. In Guaviare, del Cairo found that state agents and local nonindigenous actors often attributed different degrees of indigenousness and worthiness to the three populations (Nukak, Tukanoans, and Jiw) living near the regional capital of San José, judgments that resulted in different treatment when the three competed for scarce state resources.[19] The Nukak's value as ecologically Noble Savages stands in stark contrast with the Jiw, who are constructed to represent many of the "bad" characteristics associated with indigenous people: lazy, dirty, and so forth. (To round out the triad, Guaviare Tukanos are seen as too acculturated to be considered "real" Indians.) It is thus not surprising that angry Jiw sacked a van carrying supplies to the Nukak.[20] Clearly, official multiculturalism's focus on ethno-development benefits some indigenous communities, but disadvantages others.

The move to adopt concepts and practices associated with ethno-development has been trenchantly critiqued by Dorothy Hodgson who, citing Arundhati Roy, bewails the dampening effects that "NGO-ization" can have on political action and other forms of resistance.[21] Her concern speaks to the larger one voiced by Hale, which holds that multicultural neoliberalism may be "little more than a strategy of management, containment, and global capitalist expansion" without long-term changes in how ethnic minorities articulate with dominant society structures, in particular racial hierarchy and economic inequality.[22]

The fight for territorial rights has been at the forefront of indigenous rights-claiming in Latin America from the beginning; thousands of activists have struggled to make sure boundaries are demarcated, and titles, preferably collective and inalienable, securely gained. But what happens when indigenous people no longer reside in the territory assigned to them? In the case of the Nukak, FARC threatened violence because, commanders asserted, they could not trust the Nukak not to give information to the army and paramilitaries. The irony is telling: whereas earlier on, territories inhabited by indigenous people were declared *baldíos*—terra nullius—because such inhabitants were seen to be incapable of "improving" the land (i.e., clearing it and engaging in agriculture), we now have land that in effect has become a terra nullius even though it was designated specifically for an indigenous forager people. Margarita Chaves has described members of a pueblo in Guainía, to the north of the Vaupés, leaving for urban areas to find work, and anthropologists and lawyers who had fought hard to secure their territory trying to convince them to stay put.[23] Such are the disconnects that arise between living communities' realities and the juridicopolitical assemblages that have been created to protect them in official multiculturalist regimes.

The National Level

Beginning with Chapter Four, we left the Vaupés and looked at cases of managed multiculturalism occurring elsewhere in the country. The 1996 crisis that involved takeovers of DAI offices throughout the country revealed shifts in that agency's agenda that led it to prefer "traditional authorities" living in the pueblos over national leaders as the appropriate pueblo representatives to the state. The dispute between AICO and CRIC discussed in Chapters One and Four presaged the one between ONIC and DAI with respect to rights-claiming based on discourses of generic indigenous militancy versus ones stressing local, culture-specific difference and traditional forms of leadership.

During this latter standoff, both DAI and ONIC revealed an inability to keep up with the changing times, in which definitions and imaginaries of indigeneity were evolving rather quickly. Both organizations accused each other of being out of step with the times, and in fact both were, neither one finding some of the changes to its liking. ONIC's leaders were well aware of their declining prestige and its causes, but feeling beleaguered, they hunkered down and engaged in actions that, in the long term, only worsened their situation. And DAI's self-interested institutional agendas impeded its ability to properly carry out its mandate to serve the country's pueblos. The way the crisis unfolded and was eventually resolved illustrates many of the issues that have arisen throughout Latin America in standoffs between the state and indigenous activists who attempt to engage the government in a politics of recognition. In the long run, institutions' tendency to engage in self-protective behavior and foot-dragging can seriously undermine their ability to function optimally.

Chapter Four also points out that the differences between the experiences of indigenous activist leaders, who tend to be young, educated, bilingual, and knowledgeable about official procedures, and the lives of those they represent, can lead to serious problems. Postero notes that in most indigenous communities leaders are tied to those they represent through carefully regulated rituals of social control.[24] When they move to the national stage they continue to represent their constituents, but the social control erodes and the differences increase. The corruption and lack of real democracy that often result when this happens should not surprise anyone.

Clearly a sweeping change in Colombian indigenous politics has been the shift from an emphasis on demands that repression and discrimination cease and differential citizenship be legislated to an emphasis on demands more focused on the right to be culturally autonomous. Through constitutional reform and subsequent decisions handed down by the Constitutional Court, the state increasingly offered protections to indigenous populations within a regime of rights and entitlements that included a substantial degree of autonomy and self-determination. Paradoxes abound here because, as Joanne Rappaport points out, when a pueblo wins its argument that some of its traditional knowledge simply cannot be translated into concepts and rules that fit into the state's juridicopolitical regime, a principle of incommensurability is incorporated into the state apparatus.[25] The state must relinquish its demands for full commensurability precisely because it previously ceded an important amount of power to indigenous "traditional authority," and that authority is legitimated by authentic difference. Rappaport's discussion of the benefits of incommensurability as opposed to those of legibility points up the paradox of a state that embraces multiculturalism and follows its logic.

Disputes arising from certain decisions taken by Constitutional Court magistrates also reveal interesting aspects of official multiculturalism's conceptualization of indigeneity. The court's ruling on Nasa sentences that involve whipping offenders illustrates particularly interesting and thorny unintended consequences. These cases also illustrate the phenomenon of the Hermeneutical Indian: a representation that helps us to understand ourselves via an exploration of the Other, or more specifically, leads us to a critique of mainstream ways of doing things achieved via scrutiny of pueblos and their members that reveals a superior indigenous way. Some Colombian newspaper editorials found Colombian society to not measure up in domains such as peacekeeping and judicial institutions, community values, and respect for authorities. These critiques were all the more dramatic because, in the two cases discussed here, the "superior" indigenous way involved sentences that mandated whipping. We also saw court rulings that, despite being remarkably progressive, demonstrate the juridicopolitical propensity to specify and limit indigenous difference. Diana Bocarejo documents ways in which binaries that appear and reappear—in court decisions, expert opinions voiced in academe, and state edicts—starkly distinguish between indigenous and peasant, and between peasant territory and indigenous territory. She also documents the court's reliance on a concept of gradations of indigenousness when ruling on the cases brought before it.[26]

Reindigenization, "the production of new and the reproduction of old native social groupings and identities," would seem to have been destined to happen in multicultural regimes.[27] One reason to study cases where reindigenization is contested stems from the general rule that researchers who want to learn about a given institution should focus on its margins and instances where things don't work. Interested in the dynamics of indigeneity in Colombia? Study the Pasto, Yanacona, Zenú, Kankuamo, or Muisca. Indigenous communities engage concepts like culture and indigenousness to advance their rights-claiming activities, because at some point all communities need official recognition from authoritative others. But given that an association is often made between instrumental motives—political intentions—and inauthenticity, such efforts are suspect almost from the start, particularly once culturalist criteria become a key means for evaluating communities' claims and petitions. For the most part, Tukanoan communities have experienced this process only indirectly, because no one doubts they are indigenous. In contrast, the Yanacona, the Muisca, and the members of the new cabildos in Putumayo faced challenges concerning their legitimacy and authenticity from the beginning.

Pratt states that "one can imagine indigeneity as a bundle of generative possibilities, some of which will be activated or apparent at a given time and place while others will not."[28] The San Agustín Yanacona case in Chapter Five illustrates ways in which the context can determine whether an asserted indigeneity, with its generative capacities, successfully articulates authenticity and legibility—or not. Reindigenization efforts by the Putumayo groups studied by Chaves, along with the other communities discussed in Chapter Five, illustrate important points about how indigenousness is made manifest. Linda Tuhiwai Smith notes that the process of becoming indigenous does not end when one acquires the label—rather, it begins there. Indigeneity for her names an "ongoing, nonteleological process of becoming, self-creation and self-determination, the living out of a collective's being in time and place."[29] We saw with the San Agustín Yanacona that when a pueblo's indigenousness is limited to official action (their cabildo and resguardo have been recognized), establishing authentic indigenous identity recognized by the rest of their world will take considerable amounts of time and effort. And the Yanacona were well aware that any performance of indigeneity runs the risk of providing countervailing evidence that the members of a reindigenizing group are indeed only *de ahora* (recent arrivals).

The Yanacona case also demonstrates how, at times, government-set limits must be transgressed to enable marginalized communities to get their rights-claiming efforts heard and attended to. The way officialdom reacted to Yanacona transgression, which produced a major crisis leading to a multipronged response, illustrates how regional, national, and international institutions at times respond to such crises by crafting new policies that they hope will be acceptable to everyone. In this case the state's very active response to the crisis starkly contrasted with state officials' previous dismissive inattention. Sometimes one has to break the law in a very visible and mediagenic way if one wants to be heard.

Reindigenization efforts also demonstrate the significant role played by anthropologists, many of whom are called upon to arbitrate disputes of various kinds over authenticity, especially if they are enlisted in their capacity as state employees to assess petitioners' assertions of indigenousness. Such anthropologists serve as gatekeepers because of a presumption of expertise. Their decisions to shut the gate and deny certain petitioners' demands are sometimes accompanied by an equal unwillingness on the part of nearby indigenous communities who have a perceived stake in the negative outcome of a given negotiation. This is a hemisphere-wide phenomenon.[30] Things get more interesting when the state functionaries themselves are indigenous, as happened in one of the cases analyzed by Chaves.[31]

The topic of reindigenization returns us to the issue of how a liberal cultural politics of inclusion is always "tied to culturally based conceptions of Otherness, which inevitably lead to exclusion."[32] In Chapter Four we saw discomfort with the idea of an indigenous coca-based gaseosa, even though the company had won accolades from the Office of the President for developing the best business plan. Although scholars often analyze indigeneity from a political perspective, pointing out, for instance, the key definitional criteria of a colonial legacy and marginalization, the "purest" imaginary of indigeneity requires that the construct, and the people so constructed, be apolitical, because of their prior-ity, spirituality, closeness to nature, and so forth. Authentic leaders are traditional authorities—shamans, governors, and councils of wise elders. That such local leaders *govern*, and hence are doing politics, does not matter so long as the governing is traditional and internal to the community. But when a community politically engages the outside in a way that necessitates assertions of their indigenousness, they often find they must deal with a prerequisite of apolitical purity that neither they nor any other community can live up to. Carlos del Cairo points out that the communities that best fit essentialized perceptions, such as the Nukak, are the ones that face the most difficulties in gaining access to multicultural rights.[33]

It is interesting that other kinds of ethnic and racial categorizations do not have an equivalent built-in requirement to disprove inauthenticity. Yes, there are "wannabee" Irish-Americans (and even wannabee African Americans) who are found to have no legitimate claim to the identity, but such imposters are an occasion for laughter (and sometimes bewilderment), whereas when an individual or community is seen to be faking indigenousness in order to benefit in some way, while there may be laughter, it is often seen as a serious matter.[34] Assertions of indigenousness, when linked to actions seen as politically motivated, are open to being challenged as illegitimate and inauthentic. Politics and (indigenous) culture do not make good bedfellows; an uneasy sleep is guaranteed.

More than is usually the case for other identity categories (e.g., children), indigenousness—which at least in the Western Hemisphere can initially seem such a solid identity category—when approached and closely examined, to paraphrase Marx, melts into air. This occurs because indigeneity is flexible;

as Nyamnjoh points out, in many areas of the world broader and more flexible regimes of indigeneity are being sought and established.[35] Olaf Kaltmeier and Sebastian Thies note that cultural identities are today "experienced and voiced in a much more flexible, fluid, strategic and self-reflexive manner," making the "homogeneous, quasi-ontological group identities" of early multiculturalism obsolete.[36] Sara Latorre notes that scholars have followed suit, recognizing the flexibility of indigeneity by deploying "concepts such as 'articulation,' 'self-positioning,' or 'emergent indigeneities'" precisely to get away from essentializations.[37]

Heritage and patrimonialization processes raise additional questions. In 2003 UNESCO recognized the Nukak-Makú and their "knowledge of nature and the oral tradition" as Patrimony of Humanity, and in 2004 Colombia designated the Nukak "of National Cultural Interest." We saw that the Nukak are being turned into a kind of local trademark of an ethnicity that "sells"; as del Cairo points out, "good ethnicities are those that help produce capital."[38] Although such patrimonialization makes vulnerable pueblos more visible, it hardly helps solve their very grave problems.

Another negative effect occurs when a community sells its birthright, so to speak, for a mess of pottage by adopting practices members do not want to engage in but that will please tourists—of the culture-philiac, eco-, or New Age variety. When carried to an extreme (and the intended audience might also include NGO personnel or state functionaries), we have an example of what Alcida Ramos calls "the hyperreal Indian."[39] Note that, however, because such performances might be examples of an indigeneity that is unfolding along as yet undetermined pathways, at a later point in time community members might be quite content with how those performances represent their indigenous culture. There are many well-documented examples of communities borrowing practices that were completely foreign to their ancestors. As I point out in Chapter Two, in the future, Tukanoans might agree with Jesús Santacruz's characterizations of their culture in the booklet he authored, even though these descriptions are currently inappropriate.

The indigeneity paradox has to do with the fact that to be indigenous is to be different in specific ways. It carries with it the burden of needing not only internal agreement as to what a people's particular indigenousness consists of but also acceptance by a range of outsiders, many of them nonindigenous. As Marisol de la Cadena and Orin Starn note, "[r]eckoning with indigeneity demands recognizing it as a relational field of governance, subjectivities, and knowledges that involves us all—indigenous and nonindigenous—in the making and remaking of its structures of power and imagination."[40] Being indigenous is not like being a Hutterite, a member of one of the Anabaptist sects who fled religious persecution in Europe. Hutterites depend far less on what non-Hutterites propound about Hutterite identity, authenticity, raison d'être and so forth, than do many indigenous communities, their statements to the effect that "we know who we are" (i.e., we alone determine our identity) notwithstanding. Hutterites can authoritatively say who they are, where they came from, and why they have not assimilated into mainstream U.S. and Canadian society. An indigenous community can also state who they are, where they came from, and why they choose to remain different, but their narratives must have the ring of truth, and—because the concept of indigeneity itself is so vague and ambiguous—the truth depends on context, history, and politics, oftentimes both local and national. The Bosa Muisca's insistence that their chuszua, despite the construction materials used, is authentically Muisca is a telling example of creative attempts by a reindigenizing community to meet this challenge.

If a community can lose its indigenousness, why can't it transform back into an indigenous state—why can't the arrow go in both directions? Because indigenous culture should not be intentionally acquired. Many other kinds of culture can be intentionally acquired—for instance, when immigrants arrive in their new home they are often encouraged to do precisely this. But, as the Yanacona learned, intentionally acquiring indigenous culture required them to confront their neighbor naysayers, which turned out to be a formidable challenge.

It is true that, over time, the seemingly static, tradition-obsessed Hutterites have changed, but they have done so in a dialogic relationship with the changes happening in the mainstream society in a way that, at any particular point in time, maintained the appearance of a German-speaking subculture stuck in the past. When reindigenizing communities succeed at becoming accepted as indigenous, despite initial disapproval, we can see some similarities with the Hutterites, for both groups locate themselves in an imagined traditional past. But the comparison takes us only so far. While abstractly, indigeneity can be described in terms relating to prior-ity in time and space, actual indigenous communities have to work with this static and vague imaginary in the local context to figure out how best to represent themselves. Individual pueblos operate within the confines of their history, present-day surroundings, semiotics, and future goals. Those goals articulate with what members understand to be possible in their current situation, which they explicitly analyze during activities like writing a pueblo Life Plan, consulting with the local DAI/National Office of Ethnic Groups representative (or with elders or national movement leaders), negotiating with an international NGO, or discussing among themselves whether to incorporate some aspect of a representation of indigeneity seen on television. A CRIVA proposal mentioned in Chapter Two for an indigenous group's ethno-development project included a narrative of the group's collective identity that reflected what they believed the funders wanted to hear about their unique indigenousness. Hence, an individual community's "dense web of symbols, fantasies, and meanings" is what makes sense to them as a particular indigenous people living at a particular time and in a particular place.[41] As Tania Li's oft-quoted characterization has it, a group's self-identification "is not natural or inevitable, but neither is it simply invented, adopted, or imposed. It is, rather, a *positioning* which draws upon historically sedimented practices, landscapes, and repertoires of meaning, and emerges through particular patterns of engagement and struggle."[42] Shane Greene uses the idea of "customized" to characterize this kind of local fashioning of indigeneity: the vernacularization of national and international indigenous discourses that penetrate into even very remote regions.[43] The San Agustín Yanacona case provides an example of a transnational indigenous culture discourse penetrating into, and in turn being modified and transmitted out of, a very isolated and marginalized locale.

Urban indigenous communities bring into stark relief familiar assumptions about indigenous people being linked to indigenous territory. Being Other, they belong in Other places, preferably the most authentic ones, which means rural and remote. If, as Bocarejo cogently argues, authentic Indians are seen as necessarily residing in the remote lands that have been their home for eons, then the Tubú group currently living in Bogotá, and members of many other unrecognized urban cabildos have a serious representational problem. Although Amazonian peoples like the Tubú are seen as indisputably indigenous, at least for the time being, they definitely do not belong in a San Cristóbal slum. All urban Indians are seen to be "out of place," as Mary Douglas puts it,[44] and their very attempts to survive and adapt to city life, by doing wage work and dressing for a cold climate, further challenge their assertions of authentic Otherness. The Muisca, too, are "out of place," even though some of their cabildos have been officially recognized. Despite their assertions that they are living on the land they have always lived on, they still face the challenge of demonstrating that they are not simply residents of one of the many poor neighborhoods in a modern megapolis. Worse, in order to successfully claim their rights, they must engage in what appear to be extremely nonindigenous activities, like studying for law degrees and attending numerous district council meetings—and to ensure the highest probability of success at these meetings, leaders must persuade their fellow Muisca to attend as well, despite the fact that everyone is poor and needs to spend that time looking for what is often very impermanent and exploitative daily wage labor. Muisca also must deal with the sellouts in their midst, and confront ever-present dangers in the form of drug trafficking, extortion, and threats from ex-paramilitaries, ex-guerrillas, and standard-issue criminals. How can a people manifest indigenous Otherness, lo indígena, and authentic culture, under such circumstances? The chuszua example illustrates one attempt; the traditional practices of Muisca shamans and midwives another. The requirement to produce acceptable evidence of authentic cultural difference before any rights-claiming activities will be taken seriously leads to efforts to learn how to perform the *right kind* of indigeneity. We have seen a number of creative attempts by Muisca to learn how to do this; for example, the Sesquilé Muisca enlisted an Arhuaco teacher. And all five Muisca cabildos learn from one another, even while, at times, disparaging one another's authenticity.

We can agree with analyses by scholars like James Clifford, who states that "to grasp the active, unfinished, processes at work in various articulated sites of indigeneity it helps to open up, or at least 'loosen' . . . common understandings of key terms like native, autochthonous, and sovereign."[45] Culture is dynamic; ethnogenesis is always occurring, and to a greater or lesser extent it is always political, especially when cultural politics are at play. As Laura Graham and H. Glenn Penny note, indigeneity itself is a "second-order identity" because "local—and sometimes even borrowed—behaviors and other semiotic phenomena become resignified to index Indigeneity."[46] This is fine for scholars. But governments, in particular their legislative and judicial bodies, presume a stasis and require definitive definitions and fixed boundaries. It is the case that over time the official criteria for indigeneity change. The Colombian Constitutional Court plays an active role in this regard, illustrating de la Cadena and Starn's comment about "the changing boundary politics and epistemologies of blood and culture, time, and place that define who will or will not count as indigenous in the first place."[47]

The problem facing Andean peasant communities like the Pasto in the south of the country, who have lost their language and distinctive clothing, or urban cabildos whose members are "too hauntingly similar . . . to warrant social entitlements" because such people "dress, act, and sound like the . . . neighbors they are," is that "thickly sedimented stereotypes" that traffic in timeless tribal cultures whose members wear feathers and lack knowledge about cell phones, simply do not allow for such "self-positioning," nor permit "emergent indigeneities."[48]

When multiculturalism becomes managed, that is, turned into policies and projects, the quest for recognition of indigenous rights will always involve "defining in particular terms who is the beneficiary of those rights and who is not."[49] Efforts to protect human rights and achieve redistributive justice through constitutional guarantees, when sovereignty is located in an idea of "people" conceived of as diverse, will inevitably encounter problems when defining and operationalizing cultural difference, and will struggle mightily with the fact that cultures, no matter how defined, change. Cultures are used by people to adapt to changing social conditions, and are adapted in turn, particularly in situations demanding rapid change.

My final point is a request that the reader consider what the Colombian case contributes to our understandings of indigeneity globally. Countries with much larger percentages of indigenous citizens (e.g., Mexico, Guatemala, Peru, Bolivia) tend to dominate the literature on indigenous peoples in Latin America. But I hope I have demonstrated that looking at interactions between indigenous communities, indigenous organizations, and mainstream society in countries with very small numbers of indigenous people is also a very worthwhile effort. Of course each country's demography, history, geography, and so forth are different, and Colombia is unique in many respects, in particular in its fifty-year internal conflict that has colored every aspect of indigenous organizing and state responses to it. But we still can learn important and broadly applicable lessons about the larger processes of social movement formation and evolution. Surely we can agree that understanding the processes that led to such small numbers of citizens becoming collective owners of almost 30 percent of national territory, that led to some indigenous leaders becoming the equivalent of rock stars during the period of constitutional reform, and that led to dominant society imaginaries of pueblo values and practices going from an extremely negative to a very positive valence in a relatively short period of time is a valuable, productive endeavor.

Notes

Acknowledgments

1. See Jackson 2001.

Introduction

1. A department (*departamento*) is the equivalent of a U.S. state.

2. See Sieder 2002, 4–5; and Yashar 1996 and 2005.

3. Multiple mobilizations and other forms of protest also took place earlier in the century; see, for example, Becker 2008.

4. Note that Colombia, a democracy, did not go through this process.

5. *Neoliberal* refers to the notion that limiting government interference in the marketplace enhances personal liberty.

6. Argentina, Bolivia, Brazil, Chile, Colombia, Costa Rica, Ecuador, Guatemala, Honduras, Mexico, Nicaragua, Panama, Paraguay, Peru, and Venezuela. See Hooker 2005, 285.

7. *Discourse* refers to Foucault's notion of modes of representation that are seen to construct social realities. People's "ways of thinking the world, themselves and others around them are constituted—rather than simply constrained—by discursive formations . . . coherent ways of representation of a given realm of activity and experience" (Wade 1997, 80).

8. A third took place in Rio de Janeiro in 1993.

9. A number of authors have analyzed this linkage: for example, Varese 1996; Brysk 2000; Conklin and Graham 1995; Conklin 1997 and 2002; Ramos 1998; and

Ulloa 2005.

10. See "Los 82 pueblos indígenas de Colombia: Por la autonomía, la cultura y el territorio" 1996, 25. For example, in 1997 the Universidad Javeriana's blood-sampling project was harshly criticized as bio-piracy ("No patentamos genes: U. Javeriana" 1997).

11. A corporatist state negotiates with interest groups like labor unions and business to manage a national political economy. It is significantly more interventionist than a neoliberal state and works to achieve a homogeneous national identity through assimilation; see Yashar 2005.

12. See, for example, Warren 1998.

13. See Hooker 2005, 285.

14. Subsequent agreements include the 2007 United Nations' Declaration on the Rights of Indigenous Peoples.

15. Van Cott 2000.

16. Postero 2013, 108.

17. Turner 1999, 69.

18. I use *pueblo*, a word that can mean both "people" and "town" in Spanish, to indicate both a local indigenous community and an officially recognized larger group. This term is recognized internationally; see Lucero 2006, 41.

19. "Ojo a los indígenas" 2004.

20. See Bergquist, Peñaranda, and Sánchez 2001.

21. See Jackson 2005; Villa and Houghton 2005; and Mercado 1993.

22. The conventions for using the term *Indian* in Latin American scholarship vary. Many authors avoid the word because its cognates in Spanish and Portuguese remain highly derogatory. Nevertheless, because the term *indigene* is not really English, *native* can be equally problematic, and Native American is not used in the Latin American context, the best translation for *indígena* is Indian, which is the ethnonym of choice in much of the scholarship on indigenous people in North America. I always choose *indigenous* except when a noun must be used. Canessa uses *indian* (which he does not capitalize) precisely to remind readers of a long history of colonial oppression; he argues that while *indigenous* may increasingly take on symbolic value, many people cannot access it and remain *indios* (2012, 7). The last word comes from Clifford: "there is no universally satisfactory name: indigenous, native, aboriginal, tribal, Indian, Native American, First Nation. . . . Depending on where one is and who is paying attention, one risks giving offense, or sounding tone deaf" (2013, 10).

23. Rathgeber 2004, 115; "Resguardo indígena cierra sus puertas a los violentos" 1999.

24. Organización Nacional Indígena de Colombia, founded in 1982.

25. "Tregua indígena con 'paras'" 1998.

26. Unless otherwise indicated, all translations are my own.

27. Kirk 2003.

28. At that time the Colombian Vaupés was a *comisaría* (precinct) with a state-appointed local government. It is now a department.

29. Not for lack of trying; see de Friedemann 1984b, 412–414.

30. Counterattacks by anthropologists criticizing the Native American cultural recovery movement can also be found in, for instance, Clifton 1990.

31. Note that anthropologists have also aided indigenous people in many long and bloody fights for rights to land and self-determination. William Sturtevant testified on behalf of the Wampanoag at a trial discussed by Clifford (1988). And sometimes the historian or ethnographer is also a member of the group being studied. The problematic and complex nature of the opposition between the concepts *native* and *anthropologist* is often best explored by looking at instances where the two overlap; see, for instance, Sanjek 1983.

32. Westerman 1969.

33. Deloria 1969.

34. Clifford 1988. James Howe addresses this issue in a volume about the many outsiders (and, more recently, insiders) who have written about the Guna of Panama (2009, 238–251).

35. Friedman 1994, 140.

36. Field 1999.

37. Some scholars, Ruth Benedict and Margaret Mead among them, who belonged to a U.S.-based school of thought known as *culture and personality*, addressed certain identity issues, but under the rubric of personality.

38. See Lawler 2008, 7.

39. Lawler 2008, 2.

40. Brubaker and Cooper 2000.

41. Bucholtz and Hall 2004, 374.

42. Brubaker and Cooper 2000, 8.

43. Clifford 1997, 46.

44. See Hall 1996, 4.

45. Lawler 2008, 3.

46. See Wade 1997, 80.

47. These systems order the social world by creating standardized categories that designate relevant others, both individuals and groups. Along with their underlying principles of inclusion and exclusion they reflect the larger social system, and almost always express power disparities. See Eriksen 2010, 73.

48. Gooding-Williams 1998, 23.

49. Brubaker and Cooper 2000, 25.

50. Collins 2001, 687.

51. Kaltmeier and Thies 2012, 237.

52. Latorre 2013, 68.

53. See Faudree's discussion of the distinction between indigeneity and indigenousness (2013, 103).

54. Chatterjee 2004.

55. Both Faudree 2013 (31) and Clifford 2007 (211) use the phrase "managed multiculturalism."

56. Povinelli 2002, 25.

57. Kapila 2008, 118.

58. Niezen 2009, 40.

59. *Civil society* refers to a country's nongovernmental and nonbusiness institutions, including the family.

60. Note Mehta's very astute point that political systems based in liberalism include everyone as citizens but exclude those the dominant classes do not consider capable of governing themselves (1999).

61. See Rajagopal 2003, 264. Although Eriksen sees "the 'responsible, bounded, autonomous, maximizing individual,' who is simultaneously a moral agent and a rational person, but fully accountable for his or her actions" to be neoliberalism's subject formation project, he is in fact characterizing liberalism's goal (2015, 917).

62. Bocarejo 2011, 98.

63. Eriksen 2015, 914.

64. See Nash 2001; and Stephen 2002.

65. See, for example, Bessire 2014, 187.

66. McCormack 2011, 282.

67. See Ong 2006.

68. Burman 2014, 253.

69. Goodale 2010, 493.

70. Liberalism holds that protecting and enhancing individual freedom should be the central concern of politics.

71. Goodale 2009, 29.

72. See Bonner 2014.

73. Many, but not all, of my points apply to Afro-descendant mobilizing as well.

74. Orta 2013, 109–110.

75. Orta 2013, 110.

76. Radcliffe 2010, 302.

77. Hale 2006, 219.

78. Larson 2014, 241.

79. Orta 2013, 118.

80. Eriksen 2015, 916.

81. Hale 2011, 198.

82. See Martínez Novo 2009, 120–121.

83. Eriksen 2015, 915.

84. Hale 2002, 491.

85. Bessire 2014, 177.

86. Martínez Novo 2009, 22.

87. Larson 2014, 241.

88. Postero 2006, 18, 225.

89. French 2009.

90. Sujatha Fernandes, *Who Can Stop the Drums?*, 23 (as cited in Gustafson and Fabricant 2011, 7).

91. Postero 2006, 8.

92. Eriksen 2015, 916.

93. Hale 2002, 493.

94. Kroeber and Kluckhohn 1952.

95. Dressler 2015, 20; also see Hippert 2011, 91.

96. Collins 2001, 687.

97. Yúdice 2003.

98. Kapila 2008, 120–121.

99. See Rojas 2011, 191.

100. Escárcega 2012, 207.

101. Barker 2011.

102. See Briggs 1996; Veber 1998; and Jackson 1999.

103. Stephen 2007, 322. Also see Hale and Stephen 2013; Hale 1997; Fabian 1999; and Escobar 2008. For a very instructive discussion of these issues as they played out in an actual research situation in Cauca, see Gow 2008, 21–58.

104. While the term *indigenous* and its cognates have been around for quite a while, *indigeneity* emerged as a legal and juridical category during the Cold War era; see Graham and Penny 2014, 4. As already noted, my use of a third word, *indigenousness*, also recently coined, refers to quality and amount.

105. Deloria 1998.

106. For example, see Merry's discussion of native Hawaiians (1998).

107. That there were no "indigenous people" prior to the arrival of the Europeans demonstrates the constructedness of the concept.

108. See Lucero 2006; and Canessa 2007.

109. For example, the United Nations Subcommission on Prevention of Discrimination and Protection of Minorities defines "indigenous" as follows: "Indigenous communities, peoples, and nations are those which, having a historical continuity with pre-invasion and pre-colonial societies that developed on their own territories, considered themselves distinct from other sectors of the societies now prevailing in those territories, or parts of them. They form at present non-dominant sectors of society and are determined to preserve, develop, and transmit to future generations their

ancestral territories, and their ethnic identity, as the basis of their continued existence as peoples, in accordance with their own cultural patterns, social institutions, and legal systems" ("Study of the Problem of Discrimination Against Indigenous Populations," UN Doc. E/Cn.4/Sub.2/1986/7Add.4,para.379[1986], as cited in Van Cott 1994, 23).

110. See Canessa 2012.

111. See Berkhofer 1979.

112. See Bodley 1990.

113. An excellent example is Rappaport's discussion of "de-Indianization" in Cumbal, Colombia (1994). The literature on Native Americans with respect to this issue is vast; see, for example, Barker 2011; Lomawaima 1993; Sturm 2002; and Strong and Van Winkle 1996.

114. Handler 1988, 51.

115. Handler 1988, 154.

116. Rappaport and Dover 1996, 27–30. Note that indigenousness sometimes had value in earlier periods as well. In addition to Deloria's discussion of Whites "playing Indian" (1998), the title character in the musical *Annie Get Your Gun* sings, "I'm an Indian too!" Basso writes about tourists in Indian country in the United States talking about their great-great-grandmother having been a Cherokee princess (1979, 61).

117. Gros 1991, 206–214.

118. Speed 2006, 72–73. Also see Occipinti 2003.

119. The U.S. Native American Graves Protection and Repatriation Act of 1990 is an example.

120. Cadena 1988; Henríquez 1988.

121. See del Cairo 2012. Cf. Conklin 2006 on the issue of the relationship between environmentalism and indigenous communities.

122. See Hooker 2005, 294; and Beyerlin 2015, 343.

123. Howe 1998.

124. See Bodley 1990; and Maybury-Lewis 2002.

125. Cowan, Dembour, and Wilson 2001, 11.

126. Tsing 2005.

127. Merry 2006.

128. Comaroff and Comaroff 2009.

129. See Nagel's classification of kinds of culture revitalization: renewal, revision, revival, recovery, restoration (1997, 46). Which ones would fall under the rubric of "reindigenization" is an interesting question.

130. Bocarejo 2012, 669.

131. Sahlins 1999.

Chapter 1

1. The U'wa (also known as Tunebo) received a great deal of publicity in 1995 and after when they stated they were at the point of committing collective suicide as a result of the government granting a license to Occidental Petroleum to conduct seismic testing in their territory. Located in the departments of Boyacá, Arauca, and Norte de Santander, prior to this crisis the U'wa were virtually unknown nationally; see Osborne 1995; and Kolter 1998.

2. "Los 82 pueblos indígenas de Colombia" 1996, 23. Green also noted that "[i]f the constitution is not applied as it ought to be, they are going to finish us off not only with bullets but with highways, with oil exploration, hydro-electric dams, interoceanic canals. The indigenous person is not consulted as to whether the project should be undertaken, but to negotiate reimbursements after the decision has been made" (as cited in Navia 1996).

3. Departamento Administrativo Nacional de Estadística 2005; Jimeno 2014, 29–30. The number of pueblos varies according to author.

4. See Rappaport 1990; Triana 1993, 101–106; and Dover and Rappaport 1996, 5.

5. Laurent 2005.

6. Troyan 2015, 15.

7. See Arango and Sánchez 2004.

8. Roberto Pineda, personal communication, 1991.

9. Pineda 1995, 12; Gros 1996, 255.

10. Although this bureau's name has changed several times, it is called DAI throughout this book.

11. Note that in Spanish and Portuguese, the cognates for *indigenism* have two well-established and potentially confusing meanings. The first, most often used in reference to the policies of a state toward its indigenous peoples, indicates an integrationist position, while the second meaning refers to support of indigenous rights. No ambiguity attaches to Ronald Niezen's choice of indigenism for the title of his 2003 book, *The Origins of Indigenism*, because, first, the term is not used in U.S. or Canadian government documents, and second, the title makes it clear which meaning is intended. For Niezen, indigenism identifies the social movement of those indigenous groups who deliberately built translocal and transnational alliances with other indigenous groups to achieve their own goals. In Ramos's 1998 book title, *Indigenism: Ethnic Politics in Brazil*, the word can be read as signaling both meanings.

12. Jimeno and Triana 1985.

13. Stoll 1982.

14. Jimeno and Triana 1985, 102.

15. Pineda 1995, 31.

16. Pablo Morillo, "El ILV y nuestras comunidades nativas," a 1978 *El Tiempo* ar-

ticle (quoted in Stoll 1982, 183).

17. *Latin America* 1975, 371.

18. Jimeno 1979.

19. Arboleda 1983, 118.

20. Pineda 1997, 112.

21. Pineda 1997, 112.

22. Findji 1992, 113.

23. Dietz 2004, 38.

24. Dietz 2004, 41.

25. Brading discussing Manuel Gamio, director of the Instituto Indigenista Interamericano (Inter-American Indigenist Institute) (1988, 83–85).

26. Sánchez, Roldán, and Sánchez 1993a.

27. Whitten 1985 and Wade 1993 discuss mestizaje. Genocidal policies were implemented in some countries: for example, Argentina's "Conquest of the Desert."

28. A Peruvian example of this politics is this statement, from independence hero José San Martín: "in the future the aborigines shall not be called Indians or natives; they are children *and citizens* of Peru and they shall be known as Peruvians" (as cited in Anderson 1983, 52).

29. Stepan 1991; Smith 1996; Wade 1993.

30. Pineda 1997, 114. Wade provides a nice analysis of how mestizaje "coexists easily alongside multiculturalist representations of difference" (2016, 333).

31. For example: "porque indio es el nombre por el cual nos sometieron, indio será el nombre con el cual nos levantaremos" (because indio is the name they forced on us, indio will be the name with which we raise ourselves up). Quoted by Laurent 2005, 69, from Yvon Le Bot's "Revendications d'identité ou luttes de libération?," a chapter in *L'idéologie politique latinoaméricaine et la question indienne*, by Gros and Le Bot, 1982.

32. Gros 1991, 179; Troyan 2015, 21.

33. Lame 1981; Castillo 2007, 129–136.

34. Gow 2008, 217.

35. See Espinosa 2009.

36. See Nelson 2001; Speed, Hernández Castillo, and Stephen 2006; and Hernández Castillo 2010.

37. Pineda 1984, 211–212.

38. In the colonial era, *criollo* (creole) referred to people of Hispanic ancestry born in the Americas.

39. Castillo 2007, 145–147.

40. See Gros 1991, 158; and Castillo 2007, 279.

41. Christine and Stephen Hugh-Jones, Bernard Arcand, and Peter Silverwood-Cope.

42. Gros 1991, 160.

43. For a Mexican example of this position, see Collier with Lowery Quaratiello 2008, 67. Also see Conklin and Graham 1995.

44. See Gros 1991, 132–133.

45. Troyan 2015, 4, 136.

46. Troyan 2015, 148.

47. Rappaport 1994, 9.

48. Troyan 2015, 127, 129, 170.

49. Jimeno and Triana 1985, 92.

50. Jimeno and Triana 1985, 91.

51. Von Hildebrand worked for the government in various capacities in the Alfonso López (1974–1978), Belisario Betancur (1982–1986), Virgilio Barco (1986–1992), and César Gaviria (1992–1996) administrations. For example, influenced by von Hildebrand, Barco added five million additional hectares to the Predio Putumayo, a resguardo in the department of Amazonas—a gesture that led to very good publicity for Colombia. Note that Barco was by no means a progressive politician. Von Hildebrand was awarded two prestigious environmentalist awards for his work (Nieto de Samper 2005). Roque Roldán, another director of DAI, also worked tirelessly on behalf of the country's pueblos. He and von Hildebrand co-authored the first official document espousing indigenous rights, a synthesis of many petitions from indigenous communities throughout the country.

52. Zamosc 1986.

53. Gros 1991, 217.

54. See Findji 1992, 119–121; Jimeno and Triana 1985; and Laurent 2005.

55. Pineda 1995, 31.

56. Jimeno and Triana 1985, 118.

57. Rappaport and Gow 1997; Gros 1996, 254.

58. Jimeno 1985.

59. Findji 1992, 118.

60. Rappaport 2005, 2.

61. Consejo Regional Indígena del Cauca–CRIC 1981, 12.

62. Consejo Regional Indígena del Cauca–CRIC 1981, 11.

63. See Autoridades Tradicionales Indígenas de Colombia, n.d.

64. Pineda 1997, 115.

65. Castillo 2007, 142.

66. Castillo 2007, 147.

67. See Triana 1978.

68. Avirama and Márquez 1995, 84.

69. Paschel gives a figure of 29.8 percent of Colombia's territory (2010, 735). Also see Roldán 2000.

70. See Archila 2003; Castillo 2007; and Jimeno 2014.

71. See Troyan 2015, 153.

72. Fuerzas Armadas Revolucionarias de Colombia (FARC), Ejército de Liberación Nacional (ELN), Movimiento 19 de Abril (ADM-19), Ejército Popular de Liberación (EPL), Movimiento Armado Quintín Lame (MAQL), and Partido Revolucionario de Trabajadores (PRT).

73. Sengupta 2016.

74. Findji 1992, 122.

75. Anderson 1983.

76. Jimeno discusses the extensive meaning of *territorio* in Colombia (1996, 51).

77. Grueso, Rosero, and Escobar 1998, 210.

78. Barker 2011, 97.

79. Jimeno 1993; Sánchez, Roldán, and Sánchez 1993b.

80. See Chernick 2005; and Green 2005. And in fact, serious levels of violence in many areas of the country followed the 2016 peace accords.

81. Dugas 2012, 205. Estimates of numbers of victims of the violence (tortured, killed, disappeared, displaced) vary considerably. Green provides an estimate of more than 350,000 lives (2005, 139). García-Godos and Lid provide an estimated total of 674,000 homicides between 1964 and 2007, 94,000 of them directly attributable to the conflict (2010, 487–516, 490–491); also see Tate 2007. Jimeno estimates the number of deaths at almost 300,000 (2017).

82. Forero 2011.

83. "Más que neutrales, autónomos." 2000.

84. Rappaport 2003; Valencia 2001.

85. Rappaport 2003, 41.

86. "Colombia: FARC Releases Indigenous Leaders" (2004) is a culturalsurvival.org report describing how 400 Nasa obtained the release of Arquímedes Vitonás, mayor of Toribío, in September 2003. Also see "Indígenas rescatan su alcalde" 2003.

87. Forero 2005; Dudley 2005.

88. Also referred to as *repertoires of contention* (in Doug McAdam et al., *Dynamics of Contention*, 2001; as cited in Wolff 2007, 17). These occur when illegal actions are undertaken to pressure governments to begin negotiating about previously ignored demands.

89. Padilla 1996.

90. Avirama and Márquez 1995, 85; Van Cott 2000, 46.

91. See Tate 2015.

92. Ramírez 2011, 54.

93. Associated Press 2015.

94. See Organización Nacional Indígena de Colombia 2011.

95. Gow and Rappaport 2002, 70–72.

96. Van Cott 2000, 48.

97. Van Cott 2000, 51.

98. Pineda 1997, 112–115.

99. Van Cott 2000, 50.

100. Van Cott 2000, 20.

101. Van Cott 2000, 20.

102. ADM-19, EPL (which had changed its name to Esperanza, Paz y Libertad [Hope, Peace and Liberty]), MAQL, and PRT. Van Cott 2000, 62; Cepeda Espinosa 2006, 73.

103. Van Cott 2000, 20.

104. De la Calle 1994, 9.

105. Including, for example, the Universal Declaration of Human Rights (1948), and also Convention 169 of the International Labor Organization (1989) regarding the rights of indigenous, tribal, and semi-tribal populations.

106. Van Cott 2000, 32.

107. Rappaport 2005; Rojas 1997.

108. Stavenhagen 2002, 33.

109. See Yrigoyen 2002.

110. Cepeda Espinosa 2006, 97.

111. Hunt 2006, 100.

112. Van Cott 2000, 74, 112–116.

113. The indigenous councils would perform these functions:

> 1. Oversee the application of legal norms regarding use of the land.
>
> 2. Design the political programs and plans for economic and social development within the territory, in accordance with the National Plan of Development.
>
> 3. Promote public investment in the territory and oversee its implementation.
>
> 4. Identify and distribute resources.
>
> 5. Safeguard natural resources.
>
> 6. Coordinate the programs and projects promoted by the different communities in the territory.
>
> 7. Collaborate in the maintenance of public order within the territory in keeping with the instructions and dispositions of the national government.
>
> 8. Represent the territory to the national government and other entities.
>
> 9. Perform other functions indicated by the Constitution and the Law.

Also see Padilla 1993, 18.

114. ETIs are to be defined by indigenous communities and organizations, the Territorial Ordinance Commission (Comisión de Ordenamiento Territorial), and the Colombian Congress. The ETI process (and the territorial ordinance as a whole) conceives of territory as material, social, and cultural space. The constitution arranges for follow-up legislation, called the Organic Law for Territorial Demarcation, to specify

the actual distribution of territorial entities and define in detail these units' actual responsibilities. This law would also regulate dispute settlement between the national government and the territorial entities. See Betancourt and Rodríguez 1994, 22–23.

115. Rappaport (personal communication, 2016) spoke with a lawyer from CRIC who said that the organization was in the process of submitting the documents necessary for establishing an ETI.

116. Cepeda Espinosa 2006, 75.

117. Cepeda Espinosa 2006, 75.

118. See Laurent 2005; and Correa 1993a.

119. See Stavenhagen 2002, 39. See Sierra 1995 for a Mexican example.

120. Van Cott 2000, 33.

121. Cepeda Espinosa 2006, 73–74.

122. Van Cott 2000, 33.

123. Cepeda Espinosa 2006, 75.

124. Cepeda Espinosa 2006, 54.

125. Cepeda Espinosa 2006, 75.

126. Cepeda Espinosa 2006, 90.

127. Jaramillo 2012, 316.

128. Padilla 1995, 5.

129. Cepeda Espinosa 2006, 91.

130. Cepeda Espinosa 2006, 94.

131. See Instituto Colombiano de Antropología, 1993, 5.

132. See Rappaport 2005, 239–240.

133. See Rappaport 2005.

134. See, for example, cases dealing with abandonment of newborn twins among the U'wa, and required abandonment of disabled children among the nomadic Nukak (Sánchez 2006, 217–279).

135. Wilson 1997, 16.

136. Merry 1997, 45.

137. Wade 1993, 29; also see de Friedemann 1984a.

138. Paschel 2010, 733.

139. Mestizaje is usually understood to refer to the mixing of European and indigenous populations; Black populations were ignored for the most part. Paschel notes that some Colombian official state discourses do "actually include blackness in the concept of *mestizaje*, producing a language of a harmonious triethnic nation" (2010, 737). Also see Pineda 1997, 114.

140. Van Cott 2000, 43.

141. Anthony Marx, *Making Race and Nation*, 1998 (as quoted in Paschel 2010, 733).

142. Paschel 2010, 733, 736.

143. Van Cott 2000, 43. Wade gives a figure of 26 percent (2006, 61).

144. Sánchez, Roldán, and Sánchez 1993b, 116–120.

145. Rojas 2011, 188.

146. As noted earlier, such territories were not actually vacant. The *baldío* classification constituted a convenient fiction that facilitated state projects, such as homesteading (*colonización*).

147. Pineda 1997, 117.

148. Pineda 1997, 115. On Afro-Colombian organizing in the Pacific zone, see Escobar 2008.

149. Van Cott 2000, 44; Hooker 2005.

150. These refuges, some of them fortified, were known as *palenques*. Wade 1993, 53–54, 87–89.

151. Van Cott 2000, 43. Also see Arocha 1999; and Losonczy 2006.

152. See Latorre and Farrell 2014, 298.

153. Note that while Colombia, Nicaragua, Honduras, and Ecuador emphasize "ethnic difference, autonomy, and culture expressed in land rights and multicultural policies," legislation for Black populations in Brazil "has focused on racial equality and integration expressed in affirmative action and the creation of the Ministry for the Promotion of Racial Equality" (Paschel 2010, 735).

154. Farfán-Santos 2015, 112.

155. Rojas 2011, 187.

156. Ng'weno 2007, 418.

157. Wade 2009, 6.

158. Nina S. de Friedemann "Ética y política del antropólogo," a chapter in *Un siglo de investigación social*, edited by Arocha and de Friedemann (cited in Restrepo 1998, 341). Also see Restrepo 1997.

159. Pineda 1997, 117.

160. Latorre and Farrell 2014, 298.

161. Pineda 1997, 117.

162. Hunt argues that Black and indigenous Colombians "are therefore by definition rural and poor, as any change in social or spatial status simultaneously connotes a change in race/ethnicity that would likely negate them not only access to identity-based rights, but access to said identity per se" (2006, 96).

163. Hooker 2005, 307.

164. Greene 2007, 345.

165. Ng'weno 2007, 418.

166. Ng'weno 2007, 418, 432. Analyses of the ways in which rootedness is associated with culture do appear in the literature: see, for example, Pratt 2007; and Malkki 1992.

167. Van Cott 2000, 43, 44; also see Leiva 2004. Note that the San Andrés and Prov-

idencia population previously had no collective name. Given that an ethnic label is needed for official recognition, these communities were designated Raizales (Roots), because of their desire to recuperate their roots (Pineda 1997, 117). As the Raizales are named for a quest they are engaged in, in effect their name points to a lack.

168. Ng'weno 2007, 432.

169. Personal communication, April 2016.

170. Arocha 1992; also see Arocha 2015.

171. Wade 1997, 19.

172. See Ng'weno 2007, 418.

173. Wade 1997, 30.

174. Rahier 2013, 155.

175. Paschel 2010, 734; Wade 1993, 357.

176. See Blackburn 2009, 66.

177. Hale 2004; Rivera Cusicanqui 2003.

178. For an interesting Ecuadorian case, see Sawyer 2004.

Chapter 2

1. Briggs 1996, 448.

2. As characterized by Segal 1996, 431.

3. Segal 1996.

4. Jackson 1989.

5. And to other critiques, for instance, Veber 1998.

6. Wade 1997, 81.

7. I take the situation as I encountered it then as the baseline for the descriptions that follow, despite agreement with Johannes Fabian's critique of our discipline's use of the ethnographic present (1983). I resort to this device for reasons of expediency—to avoid having to note repeatedly "that was then, but things have changed"—and because my brief follow-up trips to the Vaupés, which ended in 1993, do not allow authoritative statements about the situation there today.

8. Scholars differ on the exact number of language groups.

9. Ethnographies on the Colombian Vaupés include Århem 1981; C. Hugh-Jones 1979; S. Hugh-Jones 1979; Correa 1996; Goldman 1963 and 2004; Jackson 1983; and Reichel-Dolmatoff 1968. Authors focusing on the linguistic side of things include Gomez-Imbert 1996; Gomez-Imbert and Hugh-Jones 2000; and Sorensen 1967. Fleming 2016 and Shulist 2018 discuss multilingualism in the city of São Gabriel, Brazil.

10. Language groups could conceivably be called super-clans (the "super" would avoid confusion with the clans that make up each group). Note that the Makuna and Cubeo do not practice language group exogamy (Århem 2000).

11. Cf. Gros's characterization of the Vaupés: "the Vaupés, compared with other regions of the Amazon, seems an island of relative tranquility. It has escaped . . . that

which in other places is the most decisive and dramatic element in the recent history of Indian populations: the massive arrival of homesteaders and the loss of land" (1991, 16).

12. Twice during my 1968–1970 fieldwork, I was asked if I wanted to "buy" an Indian, which was how the debt peonage system was talked about. A man would come to "own" a Tukanoan when he sold him trade goods or gasoline, with the understanding that the debt would be paid with labor. A second person could "buy" the Tukanoan by paying off his debts. Both times I declined.

13. See Goldman 1981; Jackson 1984; and Stoll 1982.

14. Some sources estimate the Vaupés to be 95 percent indigenous.

15. See Rappaport and Dover 1996, 33.

16. Cf. Lee's assessment of a conference in Cape Town, South Africa, attended by two very different stakeholders. One group was composed mostly of San from rural parts of Namibia and Botswana, who "had claims to cultural legitimacy that were impeccable, but whose political leverage and media savvy were weak," whereas the other group, composed mostly of Khoi revivalists, "had political and media clout, but, by reason of land and language loss, had claims to legitimacy that were far more tenuous" (2006, 467).

17. Organización Nacional Indígena de Colombia 1998, 25.

18. Godoy 1988; "Renunció ayer el alcalde de Mitú" 1994. Del Cairo provides similar examples (2010, 207–208).

19. *Asesores* are not members of the organization. Full-time nonindigenous supporters are often called *colaboradores*. The equivalent positions for AICO are referred to as *solidarios*. Rappaport discusses the differences between the two roles (2005, 65–66).

20. Cf. Erazo 2013.

21. Various authors write about the issue of legitimacy of leadership: see, for instance, Brown 1995; and Chaumeil 1990. Brown wrote to me in 1996 that indigenous federations throughout lowland South America grappled with problems of legitimacy; unlike tribal governments in the United States and Canada, these federations' assertions were at times backed up neither by law nor by the sentiments of their constituencies.

22. See Hugh-Jones 1988, 80–81.

23. Santacruz 1985.

24. "El Vaupés: Geografía" 1976, 6–7.

25. "Las comunidades indígenas en Colombia" 1976, 11.

26. The distinction between culture and "culture" was made early on in Roger Keesing's work on *kastom* (1989); also see Carneiro da Cunha 2009.

27. One of the earliest treatments is Moerman 1965. Other sources I found useful include the seminal collection edited by Barth 1969a, and also Clifford 1988; Handler

1988; Keyes 1976 and 1981; Nagata 1974; O'Brien 1986; and Williams 1989.

28. See Cohen 1978, 399.

29. Lévi-Strauss 1966, 234.

30. Wolf 1982.

31. Kroeber 1961; also see Starn 2005.

32. See Barker 2011, 16.

33. Bourgois 1988, 329.

34. Barth 1969b, 13, emphasis added.

35. Cohen 1978, 388.

36. Vincent 1974, 377, emphasis added.

37. Kahn 1981, 49; Bourgois 1988, 329, emphasis added.

38. Isaacs 1975; Devereux 1975; Wirth 1961. Also see Kahn 1981, 49.

39. Cohen 1978, 397, emphasis added.

40. Cohen 1978, 385–386.

41. Vincent 1974, 376.

42. Vincent 1971, 10.

43. Clifford 1988, 290.

44. Wolf 1982, 387.

45. In addition to the already cited 1999 essay by Field are works detailing similar processes, in which a people over time have found themselves defined by, and have defined themselves in line with, ethnographic writings. Also see Simpson 2014.

46. Jimeno 2014, 68.

47. See Penny 2014.

48. Jackson 1991a.

49. Carrier 1995; Said 1978.

50. See Schneiderman 2014.

51. Collins 2001, 687.

52. See Wade 1997, 91; and Hill 1991.

53. Garrett 2004.

54. See DeGraff 1999.

55. DeGraff 2005.

56. Todd 1974.

57. Cohen 1978, 380. Brubaker characterizes ethnographers who reify indigenous communities as ethnic groups as "ethnopolitical entrepreneurs" (2004, 10). Also see Hymes 1968; and Morton Fried's comprehensive deconstruction of the concept of "tribe" (1975). See Wolf 1988 on the invention of "society."

58. Bakhtin 1981, 276.

59. Cf. Clifford 1988, 60, 337–339.

60. Geertz 1973, 5.

61. See Labov 1966.

62. See Hill 1996. Also see Eriksen's discussion of the divergence between the account of their history provided by the Quebec Huron (Wyandot) and versions in historical monographs (2010, 83–84).

63. Gros 1993.

64. Handler and Linnekin 1984.

65. See Friedman 1992, 848, 852. For my essay, see Jackson 1995a. Some people who wrote letters said they approved of the position they inferred I was taking about "fake" indigenous culture, putting me in the same camp as authors like Clifton 1990.

66. For example, the article was reprinted in Moore and Sanders 2006.

67. See Jackson 1992 and 1996a. Note that settlement exogamy has broken down in many places.

68. See Escobar 1992, xvii–xix.

69. Ministerio de Educación Nacional, Comisión de Asuntos Indígenas del Vaupés 1987, 4, 7.

70. Programa Colombo/Holandés de Atención Primaria en Salud 1980, 3.

71. Instituto Colombiano de Bienestar Familiar 1988, 13–14.

72. See Jackson 2002a and 2005.

73. León Restrepo 1998.

74. Moser 1975.

75. Ministerio de Gobierno, División de Asuntos Indígenas, Mitú, 1987 letter to the director of DAI, titled "Informe de los labores de la Comisión de Asuntos Indígenas del Vaupés."

76. Ministerio de Gobierno, División de Asuntos Indígenas, Mitú, 1987 letter to the director of DAI, titled "Programación General Año 1987."

77. See Jimeno 1979.

78. "Testimonios: Entrevisa a Lorenzo Muelas" 1991, 10.

79. "Noticias" 1992, 15.

80. *Selva y Río* 1992.

81. "Noticias: El cultivo de la coca" 1991, 16.

82. "Noticias: El cultivo de la coca" 1991, 8.

83. "Editorial: Frente al evangelio y la cultura" 1990, 2.

84. "La voz del pastor: ¡Bienvenidos al futuro!" 1991, 3.

85. "Testimonios: Nuestro Obispo habla en favor de los indígenas ante el presidente de la república" 1991, 11.

86. "El güío domesticado" 1989, 9.

87. Luís Pinzón Vélez, July 12, 1990, letter to Jean Jackson, sent from Trinidad, Tiquié, Vaupés.

88. David Stoll, reporting on his investigation of SIL/WBT in Latin America, writes that in the region "[indigenous rights] organizing was sometimes difficult to distinguish from patronage battles between rival brokers" (1982, 166).

89. Grupo Investigadores Culturales del Vaupés 1989, 2.

90. Santacruz 1985, 28–29.

91. Santacruz 1985, 109.

92. Santacruz 1985, 79.

93. Zuluaga 2009, 41.

94. In periods of extended violence, military leaders would lead larger confederations of communities.

95. Fernández 1990, 3.

96. Santacruz 1985, 114.

97. Århem 1993.

98. ACAIPI (Asociación de capitanes indígenas del Pirá Paraná), the organization in the Pirá-Paraná region, later separated from CRIVA (Borrero and Pérez 2004, 312).

99. Santacruz 1985, 80–81.

100. Reichel-Dolmatoff 1968; Goldman 1968.

101. Santacruz 1985, 114.

102. The fact that many CRIVA leaders were Cubeo, who do practice clan, but not language group, exogamy, might have played a role in CRIVA's promotion of the "brotherhood" discourse.

103. "El Vaupés: Geografía" 1976. This statement recalls Bocarejo's point about an imaginary that locates *one* indigenous group in *one* place (2015). Borrero and Pérez provide a map locating each Tukanoan "ethnic group" in a specific site (2004, 26). Also see Franky's and Mahecha's discussion of this imaginary in terms of a state strategy (2010, 124, 137).

104. "Las comunidades indígenas en Colombia" 1976.

105. Clearly I cannot know the impact that creating and reading about such images had on individual Tukanoans' self-image and notions about Tukanoan society. The many settlements at some remove from Mitú experienced less impact.

106. Del Cairo discusses the degree to which Colombia's multicultural reforms respond to the demands and expectations of Andean pueblos, whose sociohistoric and political processes differ profoundly from those of Amazonian ones (2010, 205).

107. Handler 1988.

108. Fernández 1990, 4.

109. See Jimeno 1995.

Chapter 3

1. I wrote about this case at the time; see Jackson 1991b.

2. Tsing 2005.

3. Li 2005.

4. See Wirpsa 1988; Wirpsa and Mondragón 1988; and Chaves and Wirpsa 1988.

5. Makú is a generic and pejorative name, used since the seventeenth century by

travelers to the Northwest Amazon to refer to people (and groups) that were captured for labor, some of whom were nomads (Mahecha et al. 1996–1997, 90–95). Makú is also a generic name for two languages found in the Vaupés and the populations speaking them: Kakua (also spelled Cacua), which includes the dialect spoken by the Nukak, and Hup and Yuhup (and others). See Epps and Bolaños 2017, who recommend abandoning the name "Makú." The information available on Makú groups and languages at the time the Nukak appeared (e.g., Cathcart 1973; Correa 1987; and Reid 1978 and 1979) was confusing: first, because authors were not always clear about whether they were talking about a social or linguistic unit; second, because of many gaps in the ethnographic information; and third, because authors did not agree on either terminology or classification schema. Other early publications that mention Makú include Koch-Grunberg (1906) 2010 and Van Emst (1966) 2010; both can be found in Cabrera 2010.

6. Cabrera et al. 1999, 72–75; Cabrera 2002b, 113.

7. See Torres 1994, 220; and Politis 1995, 13.

8. Wirpsa and Mondragón 1988, 38; Chaves and Wirpsa 1988, v. Townspeople angrily protested an inaccurate and sensationalistic report suggesting the visitors were cannibals, which appeared in *VEA*, a regional newspaper.

9. Cabrera et al. 1999, 80; Cabrera 2002b, 115.

10. See Zambrano 1994, 179, 183, who states that the rest of the group continued their journey westward.

11. See Molano 1987.

12. Representatives came from DAI, the National University of Colombia, the Universidad del Valle in Cauca, and the Corporación de Araracuara, an agency concerned with environmental and indigenous development in the Colombian Amazon.

13. Zambrano 1994, 185.

14. Wirpsa and Mondragón speculated that SIL representatives convinced the Wacará Kakwa that they *had* to accept the Nukak, which contributed to the problems the Nukak encountered when they arrived (personal communication, July 1989).

15. Hector Mondragón was told that Tukanoans said the only thing worse than a Makú was a Makú who did not want to be a servant (personal communication, July 1989).

16. Elsa Gómez, personal communication, July 1989.

17. See Trouillot 1991.

18. Makú also used Tukanoans as symbolic vehicles; see Silverwood-Cope 1972; and Cabrera 2010.

19. For example, Goldman describes Cubeo characterizations of low-ranking sibs in Makú-like terms (1963, 75–103). Also see Jackson 1983, 148–163.

20. During the 1970s indigenous people in many areas of the world were recognized as admirable figures in many kinds of environmental discourses and policy-

making. By the early 1990s these notions had thoroughly penetrated Colombia (see Ulloa 2005, in particular pp. 169–191). International lending agencies like the World Bank often simply equated indigenous issues with environmental ones.

21. This imaginary involves "the fabrication of the perfect Indian whose virtues, sufferings and untiring stoicism have won for him the right to be defended by the professionals of indigenous rights. That Indian is more real than the real Indian. He is the hyperreal Indian" (Ramos 1994, 9; and 1998, 159–161).

22. Mahecha and Franky report thirteen local groups, with populations varying between fifteen and fifty-four people (2017).

23. Zambrano 1994, 179.

24. In 1967 Reichel-Dolmatoff reported the possibility of approximately 1,000 Makú living in the Guaviare area. Kaj Århem (personal communication, October 1989) noted that bloody encounters between Nukak and Whites were occasionally mentioned in the regional press. Århem himself was offered a chance in 1971 when he was in the area to "go and see some wild Indians" (he declined).

25. In fact, beginning in 1974, NT periodically sent reports about "the Makú tribe" to DAI's Bogotá office, where they were archived. But, writes Cabrera, in 1988 no one knew anything about these reports, one of many lapses of institutional memory illustrating the state's long tradition of "subvalorizing" the Amazon (2002b, 117). Mahecha (personal communication, September 2017) notes that Catholic missionaries also sent bulletins about the Nukak beginning in 1974, but no one in Bogotá had read them. They, too, are available in DAI archives.

26. See Cabrera 2002b and 2007.

27. Franky and Mahecha, personal communication, October 2017.

28. Pérez 1971. Pérez also wrote a book cataloguing the appallingly long list of massacres of natives. Several local terms refer to hunting Indians: *guahibiar* (hunt Guahibos), and *cuibiar* (hunt Cuiba). In December 1967, eight llaneros lured sixteen Cuiba (also spelled Cuiva) to a dinner and murdered them ("Colombia Trial Reveals Life ('Everyone Kills Indians') on Plains" 1972; del Cairo 2012, 273).

29. Cabrera 2002b, 114.

30. Mahecha and Franky 2011, 9.

31. See work by Cabrera et al. 1999; Cárdenas and Politis 2000; Politis 1995; and Franky 2011. Note that some Nukak did engage in horticulture, and would visit the fields on their circuits.

32. Mahecha and Franky 2017, 165.

33. Cabrera et al. 1999; del Cairo 2012.

34. Perilla 2003.

35. Margarita Serje, *El revés de la nación: Territorios salvajes, fronteras y tierras de nadie*, 2005 (as cited in del Cairo 2012, 268).

36. Del Cairo 2012, 268; also see Franky 2011, 11–12, 144–146.

37. Del Cairo 2012, 275.

38. Del Cairo 2012, 277; also see Mahecha and Franky 2017, 171.

39. Del Cairo 2012, 275.

40. See Scott 1998.

41. Del Cairo 2012, 288–289. See Mahecha and Franky on why Nukak avoid creating state-required roles and institutions such as *capitán* (headman) or "indigenous cabildo" (2017, 164).

42. Hector Mondragón, "La defensa del territorio Nukak," 1992 (quoted in Zambrano 1994, 190).

43. Torres 1994, 215.

44. One of the sixteen-plus Tukanoan language groups.

45. Del Cairo 2012, 285.

46. See Bessire 2014; and Shepard 2017.

47. Recommendations are found in Zambrano 1994; Torres 1994; Cabrera et al. 1999; and Mahecha and Franky 2011.

48. Ministerio de Gobierno, Departamento Nacional de Planeación 1984, 14.

49. I wrote about the shaman school in 1995 (see Jackson 1995b).

50. I did not witness the shaman school project itself because I did not return to the Vaupés until 1987. I had planned on carrying out additional fieldwork, but a 1974 resolution (Resolución 626 bis) that regulated research by foreign investigators, required that 30 percent of the research funds be used to buy equipment that would stay in the country. During a 1975 trip to Bogotá I was informed by the head of ICANH that he planned to buy a small airplane with the funds I was to hand over, should my NSF grant proposal be funded. With one exception, no foreign cultural anthropologist carried out research in the country until the resolution was rescinded in 1982 (see de Friedemann 1984b, 412–414).

51. Guevara, n.d.

52. Jackson 1996b discusses this issue.

53. See Gros 1993, 16; and Correa 1993b, 170.

54. Ministerio de Educación Nacional 1986, 49.

55. Rojas 2011, 191.

56. Two reports had been written about ethno-education programs in the Vaupés prior to the workshop: Bodnar 1986, 59–62; and Ministerio de Gobierno, Departamento Nacional de Planeación 1987. Both documents reveal considerable politicization of the educational programs targeted for Tukanoans. Also see Jimeno 1979; and Alfonso et al. 1988.

57. Buchillet discusses Desana shamans' efforts to keep their knowledge within a single clan (1992).

58. Langdon 1992, 4.

59. Wright 1998; and 2013.

60. Especially S. Hugh-Jones 1979; and C. Hugh-Jones 1979; also see Cayón 2002; 2013.

61. See Langdon 1992, 16.

62. Obviously there is a lot more to say about Tukanoan shamanism. For one thing, shamans are born with the potential to become shamans—not everyone can become one. Also, Luís Cayón disputes the notion that the cosmic "life force" (*fuerza vital*) is contained in a closed system (2002 and 2013), which challenges the notion that shamans work to maintain an equilibrium. Cayón also identifies two kinds of Tukanoan shamans, *kumú* and *yai*, terms he translates as "protective shaman" and "healer-sorcerer" (2002).

63. Buchillet 1992, 211; also see S. Hugh-Jones 1979; and Cayón 2002; 2013.

64. See Correa 1993b, 180.

65. Cf. Correa's characterization of the goals of the Ministry of Education for its ethno-education program: "The education sector considers that participation by the community, using resources from its own culture, will foment its socio-cultural patrimony and capacitate its members to select knowledge and technologies from other cultures for their development" (1992, 101).

66. For example, Bastos writes that when indigenous Guatemalan parents want a pedagogical program that helps their children eliminate or modify the traits "that will prevent them from 'progressing,' a standoff between the parents and the proponents of the Mayanist project may result, because activists maintain that 'education in native languages is a right that must be demanded as well as a way to inculcate and reinforce identity and culture'" (2012, 159).

67. Gooding-Williams 1998, 23.

68. See del Cairo's discussion of colonos' notions about savagery (2012, 98–99). An extensive literature deals with this theme; see, for instance, Dudley and Novak 1972.

69. See Whiteley's 2003 analysis of the issue of "ownership" of culture in a Hopi project.

70. Del Cairo 2012, 290.

71. Nadasdy 2003; Bessire 2014, 210.

72. Del Cairo 2012, 292–293.

73. See Lasmar and Gordon's interview of Stephen Hugh-Jones (2015, 631).

74. Bocarejo 2015.

75. Del Cairo 2012, 299–300.

76. Bessire 2014. In his *The Middle Ground: Indians, Empires, and Republics in the Great Lakes Region, 1650–1815*, historian Richard White employs the term *middle ground* to refer to the "construction of a mutually comprehensible world characterized by new systems of meaning and exchange" (quoted in Conklin and Graham 1995, 695).

77. Bessire argues that policies of voluntary isolation are premised on the valoriza-

tion of a kind of alterity that can only be legitimate to the degree that it remains outside of history, the market, and social relation itself. He argues that in fact, "isolated life is inseparable from pure nature, as well as pure culture" and is not a human right at all, but a "legal slot reserved for the latest reincarnation of natural man" (2014, 204). Shepard 2017 also provides a critique.

Chapter 4

1. See Romero 2003.

2. See Ramírez 2011.

3. Gow 2008, 253. U.S. and Canadian indigenous politics tend to be more concerned with sovereignty and autonomy issues than with inclusion. Of course, I am speaking only about officially recognized communities; communities petitioning to be recognized are obviously very concerned with this right.

4. See van Cott 2005, 235, 179–182.

5. As cited in Castillo 2007, 153.

6. Stavenhagen 2008, 34.

7. See Rosen 1997.

8. Cowan 2006, 18.

9. Merry 2006.

10. Jackson 2002b.

11. Jackson 2007.

12. Jackson 2011.

13. The Wayuu live in the northeast and their territory straddles the Colombia-Venezuela border.

14. See Muyuy 1992, 52.

15. Rappaport and Dover 1996, 25.

16. Rappaport and Dover 1996, 28.

17. Rappaport and Dover 1996, 25, 28.

18. Castillo 2007, 144.

19. Quoted in Castillo 2007, 145, from Autoridades Indígenas de Colombia (AICO), "Elementos de evaluación de lo que ha sido y es el Movimiento de Autoridades Indígenas de Colombia," mimeographed, 2003.

20. Castillo 2007, 147.

21. Castillo 2007, 152–153.

22. Authors writing on discourses of generic indigenousness include Graham 2002; Conklin and Graham 1995; and Gros 2013.

23. See "De mochila en la Asamblea Constituyente" 1991.

24. The NGO had submitted the proposal to the mayor because Law 60, passed in 1993, which established direct transfer of state funds to pueblo communities, required local mayoral offices to administer this kind of funding.

25. Navia 1996.

26. Several people I interviewed said that what was happening in Bogotá should be seen as supporting the Cauca action, rather than the reverse. Green would not have agreed: "One week CRIC blockaded the Pan-American Highway, and it had an impact. I had to go there to support them."

27. "Nuevo amanecer indígena: Desalojada la conferencia Episcopal, cuya mediación fué decisiva" 1996.

28. Cited in Navia 1996.

29. "Nuevo amanecer indígena" 1996.

30. See "Los 82 pueblos indígenas de Colombia" 1996, 23.

31. See Organización Nacional Indígena de Colombia 1998, 335–336.

32. Van Cott 2000, 49.

33. See Jackson 2002a.

34. By 2016, 5 million had been displaced and 220,000 people had lost their lives (Casey 2016).

35. See Conklin and Graham 1995; Albert 1997; and del Cairo 2012.

36. Cabildos could obtain these cash transfers only after submitting detailed development plans, in accordance with their *usos y costumbres*. See Gow 2008, 98.

37. Several knowledgeable people commented that in signing the decree, the national indigenous movement had settled for too little, revealing that it had, once again, been co-opted by the government. What had been won was merely promises written "on two pieces of paper." One lawyer remarked that a considerable amount of the text basically said "that the government carry out such-and-such decree." However, once a decree is signed, it *has* to be carried out. Writing decrees that mandated carrying out previous decrees was a pointless exercise because the problem was one of political will.

38. "Los 82 pueblos indígenas de Colombia" 1996, 24.

39. Guzmán 1998.

40. ONIC was by no means unique in this respect. Michael Brown notes that indigenous federations throughout lowland South American grapple with this problem (1995): unlike tribal governments in the United States and Canada, these federations at times make assertions backed up neither by law nor by the sentiments of their constituencies. Also see del Cairo 2010.

41. The problems associated with creating indigenous supra-community organizations that articulate with state structures, yet maintain autonomy and, as much as possible, traditional authority structures, were being experienced in other Latin American countries during the 1990s. For Brazilian examples see Ramos 1998; and Albert 1997. Stephen (1997) discusses the peace negotiations following the San Andrés Accords in Mexico: single-ethnicity organizations were preferred by some, and multiethnic ones (that would include local mestizos) by others.

42. Consejo Regional Indígena del Cauca–CRIC 1981.

43. See Albert 1997 (194–198) for an insightful discussion of the "dialectic" between generic ethnicity and specific tradition during the successful Kayapó-organized Altamira protests in 1989 and later "eco-indigenist" projects.

44. Lucero 2006, 42.

45. The *ayllu* is an Andean authority structure linked by kinship ties and communal modes of production (Lucero 2006, 33).

46. Kymlicka 2001, 42.

47. Jackson 2007.

48. Stavenhagen 2002, 33. Note that indigenous "customary law" by no means implies a unitary and coherent corpus of law; see Sieder 2002, 39; also see Santos 2001.

49. Rappaport provides a much fuller discussion of this case (2005, ch. 7). Also see Sánchez 2004; Van Cott 2000, 114–116; Assies 2003; and Castillo 2007.

50. "Cepo, a padres irresponsables: mujeres paeces no tolerán el abandono" 2000. Stocks were introduced by the Spaniards: see Rappaport 2005, 250; and "Siempre he obrado de manera limpia" 1998b.

51. "Fuete a gobernador indígena" 2000.

52. "Castigan pareja indígena paez por infidelidad" 2000.

53. Mompotes 1997b.

54. "Protestan por pena de látigo a indígenas" 1997.

55. "Amnistía rechaza latigazos a paeces" 1997.

56. Melo García 1997c.

57. "Aplazan latigazos contra cinco indígenas paeces" 1997.

58. Melo García 1997a.

59. Rappaport 2005, 249.

60. Mompotes 1997a.

61. "Paeces levantarán 300 veces el látigo" 1997.

62. Mompotes 1997b.

63. Melo García 1997d.

64. Rappaport 2005, 241.

65. Melo García 1997b.

66. Melo García 1997b.

67. Melo García 1997b.

68. Rappaport 2005, 258.

69. Rappaport 2005, 244.

70. Rappaport 2005, 229.

71. See E. Sánchez 2010.

72. Rappaport 2005, 235.

73. Cowan, Dembour, and Wilson 2001, 10.

74. Rappaport 2005, 240.

75. Van Cott 2000, 113–116; Bocarejo 2012, 671.

76. Van Cott 2000, 115.

77. Rappaport 2005, 236.

78. Gow and Rappaport 2002, 58.

79. A fascinating discussion of ontological incommensurabilities and partial coordination between indigenous and Western "world-making agendas" can be found in de la Cadena 2015.

80. "Piñacué no se posesionará como senador" 1998; Mompotes 1998a.

81. "Juicio 'politico' indígena" 1998.

82. "Una justicia de dolor y leyenda" 1998.

83. Mompotes 1998a; Campo 1998.

84. Melo García 1998.

85. Mompotes 1998b.

86. Povinelli 2002, 17, 34, 39, 45.

87. Hernández 1998.

88. Cowan, Dembour, and Wilson 2001, 10; Li 2005.

89. Goodale 2007, 8–9.

90. Goodale 2007, 25; also see Speed 2007.

91. Alvarez, Dagnino, and Escobar 1998, 8.

92. As discussed by Glenn Jordan and Chris Weedon in *Cultural Politics: Class, Gender, Race, and the Postmodern World*, 1995 (as cited in Alvarez, Dagnino, and Escobar 1998, 3).

93. Cowan 2006, 18.

94. See Trouillot's concept of the "savage slot" (1991), and Castañeda's discussion of the Yucatec Maya's unwillingness to occupy this "slot" (2004). Also see Merry 2001.

95. Gaviria Díaz 2000, 15.

96. Benavides 2004.

97. Povinelli 2002, 7–8.

98. Povinelli 2002, 39.

99. Wilson 2006, 79.

100. Goodale 2007, 25.

101. Merry 2006, 39; Goodale 2007, 13.

102. Wilson 1997, 4.

103. I presented some of this material at the 2011 American Anthropological Association annual meeting in the session "Investigating the 'Identity Industry'" (see Jackson 2011).

104. Zambrano 2014.

105. "'Erradicación' del té de coca perjudica a 2,000 familias del Cauca" 2007.

106. Espinel 2005.

107. de León 2007.

108. Espinel 2005.

109. Iglesias 2012, 9–10.

110. "'Erradicación' del té de coca perjudica a 2,000 familias del Cauca" 2007.

111. Zambrano notes that between 2000 and 2010, twenty articles were published in *El Tiempo* on the marketing of coca-based products, and sixteen of them adopted a positive position (2014, 448).

112. "'Erradicación' del té de coca perjudica a 2,000 familias del Cauca" 2007.

113. "'Erradicación' del té de coca perjudica a 2,000 familias del Cauca" 2007.

114. "'Erradicación' del té de coca perjudica a 2,000 familias del Cauca" 2007.

115. "Gobierno e indígenas no llegaron a acuerdo por productos a base de coca" 2007.

116. "Gobierno e indígenas no llegaron a acuerdo por productos a base de coca" 2007. De León (2007) reports that at a session of the UN General Assembly in 2006, Bolivian president Evo Morales asked why the coca leaf was legal for Coca-Cola but illegal for medicinal purposes throughout the world.

117. "Gobierno e indígenas no llegaron a acuerdo por productos a base de coca" 2007.

118. As cited in Zambrano 2014, 460. Even more ironic was that a recipe for a *tortilla de coca* (coca cake) won the 2011 National Prize of Gastronomy. The recipe was submitted by a group of investigators, pseudonymously calling themselves Misak May, as an example of Guambiano tradition. Guambía is too high to allow cultivation of coca and its use there is infrequent (Zambrano 2014, 454–455).

119. "De coca, papa y género" 2007.

120. "La coca, macartizada" 2008.

121. See Iglesias 2012, 4–5.

122. Rather abstract neoliberal commentaries about indigenous initiatives, citizen responsibility, and self-actualization also appeared ("'Erradicación' del té de coca perjudica a 2,000 familias del Cauca" 2007; "La coca, macartizada" 2008).

123. Hale 2006.

124. Zambrano 2014; Iglesias 2012.

125. I speak of two "rights systems," but recall that each pueblo's distinct usos y costumbres are the source of its "special rights"; see Perafán 1995.

126. Brubaker and Cooper 2000, 32.

127. Gow 2008, 253.

128. Li 2001, 653.

129. French 2009, 12.

130. Article 330 specifies that indigenous territories will be "governed by the councils formed and regulated according to the uses and customs of their communities." Each community is required to "design the policies, plans and programs of economic and social development within their territory, in accordance with the National Development Plan." These documents are called Life Plans.

131. See Escárcega 2012, 213.

132. Karen Engle, *The Elusive Promise of Indigenous Development*, 2010 (as cited in Geismar 2013, 338).

133. Faudree 2013, 29.

134. Povinelli 2002, 39.

135. Povinelli 2002, 6.

136. Karen Engle, *The Elusive Promise of Indigenous Development*, 2010 (as cited by Geismar 2013, 338).

137. Niezen 2009; also see Zeiderman 2013.

138. As characterized by Cattelino 2010, 334.

139. Li 2005, 386; Ramos 1994.

140. Bocarejo 2012, 669; also see Deloria 2004; and Gupta and Ferguson 1997.

141. Gow and Rappaport write of the romanticization and orientalization in journalists' enthusiastic documentation of "the charismatic and photogenic Piñacué's calvary" (2002, 65).

142. See Howe for a vivid example of North American criticism of official Panamanian policies directed at Guna [Kuna] traditions (2009, 107–114). Deloria provides examples of what we might term the Hermeneutical Indian, a concept that allows us to examine ourselves via a detour through Indian country (1998).

143. Pineda 1997, 126.

144. "When rights are declared by universal transnational agencies, such as the United Nations, they are, by definition, acultural and ahistorical. They anticipate an undiversified human condition" (Schaft 2012, 461).

Chapter 5

1. Pardo 1993; Rappaport 1994; Zambrano 1993, 1995, and 2000.

2. Ramírez 2002, 143, 161.

3. Laurent 2005, 342–343.

4. Chaves and Zambrano 2009, 235.

5. Linares 2001.

6. Cf. "The governor of the Quillacinga-Pasto said that from that time on, indigenous rights would be fully exercised because they were no longer 'ignorant Indians,' meaning that an identity suppressed and hidden for centuries had re-emerged" (Ramírez 2002, 147).

7. Chaves 2001a, 2002, 2003, 2005, and 2010.

8. See Chaves and Zambrano 2006.

9. Chaves 2003, 126.

10. Chaves 2003, 132.

11. Chaves 2003, 129. According to Joanne Rappaport (who discussed this with Abelardo Ramos, a Nasa linguist), the name has no meaning in Nasa (personal com-

munication, February 2006).

12. Chaves 2003, 129.

13. Chaves 2005, 147.

14. Scott 1990; Aretxaga 2003.

15. Chaves 2001b, 242.

16. Chaves 2003, 134.

17. Povinelli 2002, 13.

18. Povinelli 2002, 29.

19. Cowan 2006, 17–18.

20. Schneiderman 2014, 290.

21. French 2009, 14.

22. This entire area is known as the Central Massif, where the Central Cordillera mountain range and the Magdalena, Caquetá, Cauca, and Patía rivers begin.

23. See Zambrano 1993, 1995, and 2000.

24. Zambrano 2000, 207.

25. Juan Gregorio Palechor (see Jimeno 2014), a Yanacona activist and leader, found the term in a 1944 publication by Juan Friede, an ethnohistorian-archaeologist working in the region (Zambrano 2000, 213). The term's meaning shifted radically with the adoption: in Incaic times, *yanacona*, a Quechua word meaning "servitor," was applied to "a servant class of full-time retainers alienated from local ayllus and communities" (Stern 1982, 22; also see Salomon 1986).

26. Zambrano 2000, 206.

27. See *Resguardo Yanacona de San Agustín*, n.d.

28. Jackson and Ramírez 2009.

29. Moore 1987, 730.

30. Despite repeated attempts, the Yanacona were never able to build a vehicular road. But after the highway was repaired they accepted a pedestrian walkway (Margarita Reyes and María Clemencia Ramírez, personal communication, June 2018).

31. Zambrano 1993, 21.

32. Zambrano 2000, 213.

33. Pratt 2007, 398.

34. The cabildos of Suba and Bosa have been officially recognized. Cabildos within city limits cannot form resguardos. The Chia, Sesquilé, and Cota cabildos are located outside Bogotá; recognition proceedings are ongoing. A number of authors have written about Muisca cabildos, among them Sánchez 2008; Chaves and Zambrano 2009 (about the Suba Muisca); and Bocarejo 2015. Chaves writes very perceptively about indigenous urban neighborhoods in Putumayo (2010). Also see Sevilla and Sevilla-Casas 2013 on an urban Yanacona cabildo in Popayán, Cauca.

35. See Martínez Medina 2009, 45, 70.

36. Note that such respect is not forthcoming from all quarters: Sierra leaders have

been assassinated, by paramilitary thugs (hired by agricultural interests) and by leftist guerrillas.

37. Martínez Medina 2009, 19, 30.

38. In Carlos Andrés Durán, "Ser un muisca hoy: La identidad muisca como proyecto colectivo de organización política y cultural en la Localidad de Bosa," a chapter in *Muiscas*, edited by A. M. Gómez, 2005 (as cited in Martínez Medina 2009, 23).

39. The Muisca projects also reminded me of reindigenization efforts in the United States and Canada, about which an abundant literature exists (e.g., Nagel 1997).

40. I also was reminded of films about wannabees I have used in teaching. One, *Seeking the Spirit: Plains Indians in Russia*, deals with Russians holding gatherings in rural settings at which they display the Native American costumes that they have carefully constructed (Medicine and Baskauskas, 1999). Another, *White Shamans and Plastic Medicine Men*, deals with New Age appropriations of Native American culture, in particular rituals (Native Voices Public Television, 1996).

41. Martínez Medina 2009, 51–52, 57.

42. Martínez Medina 2009, 11.

43. Martínez Medina 2009, 106–107.

44. Martínez Medina 2009, 108.

45. Martínez Medina 2009, 57.

46. Martínez Medina 2009, 26, 29.

47. As cited in Bocarejo 2012, 663.

48. Martínez Medina 2009, 19.

49. Martínez Medina 2009, 13; Povinelli 2002, 13.

50. Martínez Medina 2009, 22; Taussig 1993.

51. Martínez Medina 2009, 14; Taussig 1993.

52. Martínez Medina 2009, 6.

53. Martínez Medina 2009, 25, 26, 43.

54. Martínez Medina 2009, 106.

55. Taussig 1993.

56. Martínez Medina 2009, 14.

57. Martínez Medina 2009, 14.

58. Durán, "Ser un muisca hoy" (as cited in Martínez Medina 2009, 15).

59. Pratt 2007, 398.

60. Martínez Medina 2009, 27.

61. Chaves 2002, 195.

62. Martínez Medina 2009, 17; also see L. Sánchez 2010, 144–145. An article in the daily *El Tiempo* ("Resguardo de avivatos" 2001) labels one reindigenizing Muisca group *avivatos* (wise guys) because, although they say they are descendants of the Muisca, their physical appearance "shows otherwise." The article finds it "incredible"

that the state has allowed the group to receive funds, "as if they were a real, legally recognized resguardo." Also see Conklin 1997.

63. Martínez Medina 2009, 22.

64. Martínez Medina 2009, 22.

65. Martínez Medina 2009, 52.

66. Martínez Medina 2009, 15, 21.

67. Martínez Medina 2009, 21.

68. Martínez Medina 2009, 21.

69. Martínez Medina 2009, 16.

70. Martínez Medina 2009, 15: the mochila and chuszua do not comply with the requirements that a trained observer (read: anthropologist) would expect to find in a "museum of difference."

71. Martínez Medina 2009, 107.

72. Reported in Durán, "Ser un muisca hoy" (as cited in Martínez Medina 2009, 15).

73. Barker 2011, 22; also cf. Forte 2013.

74. Martínez Medina 2009, 17. Cf. "Similarly, illegitimation, or the process of removing or denying power, may operate either to support or to undermine hegemonic authority. In so far as every establishment of a standard or official language strips authority from those languages or varieties classified as non-standard or non-official, such language planning is an act of illegitimation as well as authorization" (Bucholtz and Hall 2004, 387).

75. This cabildo has its own web page (http://cabildoTubuhummurimasa.blogspot.com) and a YouTube presentation (https://www.youtube.com/user/cabildoTububogota?app=desktop). The cabildo is officially unrecognized, but appears on lists of urban indigenous communities in various official documents.

76. See L. Sánchez 2010.

77. The groups with recognized cabildos are the Suba, Bosa, Kichwa, Inga, and Pijao. The groups with as yet unrecognized cabildos are the Nasa, Pasto, Yanacona, Eperara-Siapidara, Wounaan, Misak, Uitoto, Kamentsá Biya, and Tubú.

78. As noted previously, asesores serve as intermediaries between a community and the state; what they actually do, and the amount of time they spend on this function, varies a great deal.

79. Sometimes translated as "priest"; the role of a *kumú* is to protect the community, for example, through divination.

80. There is no traditional Tukanoan healing practice based specifically on coca. Germán explained that, in fact, their healing practices are based on chants and prayers, as happens in the Vaupés.

81. See Caicedo-Fernández 2015.

82. See Jackson 1993.

83. See https://www.youtube.com/watch?v=VcAeI7oEJJk, and https://www.youtube.com/watch?v=T_slFI3ZISs.

84. Merlan 2007, 141.

85. Barker 2011, 16. For an even more critical analysis of the politics of recognition and reconciliation, see Coulthard 2014.

86. Martínez Novo 2006. A kind of collusion between the company, government agents interested in attracting global capital, and local ranchers emerged: if transient workers are indigenous, they need only minimal medical services, for they prefer their own traditional medicine. Child laborers? Not a problem, it is part of their culture. And indios are used to living in huts with dirt floors and no running water. Docile and irrational, they will not protest, and so any organized disruptions that occur have obviously been organized by "outside agitators."

87. This was true in Colombia as well before the 1960s, when highland indigenous petitioners identified themselves by their geographical location (*parcialidad*) (Troyan 2015, 8).

88. Canessa 2012, 6, 10.

89. Fausto Reinaga, *La Revolución India*, 1969 (as cited in Canessa 2012, 9).

90. C. Matthew Snipp, *American Indians*, 1989 (as cited in Nagel 1997, 62).

91. Forbes 2001.

92. Rappaport 2005.

93. Nagel 1997, 31.

94. Nagel 1997, 60.

95. Becky Miller. *Early Edition*, Christian Science Monitor Radio, October 11, 1993 (as quoted in Nagel 1997, 53).

96. Alvarez, Dagnino, and Escobar 1998, 8.

97. Nagel 1997, 62. Cf. Rappaport's comment about neither wanting to be relegated to the role of a "CRIC cheerleader," nor wanting "to undermine CRIC with ultracritical observations" (2005, 273).

98. Forbes 2001.

99. De la Cadena and Starn 2007, 3.

Conclusion

1. Chatterjee 2004.

2. Del Cairo 2012; Ulloa 2005.

3. Troyan 2015; Rappaport 1994, 9.

4. Unfortunately, the numbers increased after the signing of the peace accords. See Gruner 2017; and Gruner et al. 2016.

5. The FARC demobilized and formed a new political party (with, it should be noted, the same acronym), and ELN, the other guerrilla army, entered into negotiations ("Alternative Communal Revolutionary Forces" 2017). Five dissident FARC fac-

tions remain, however (Gruner 2017, 179).

6. Cf. Gros 1991, 206–214.

7. Pratt 2007, 399.

8. Canessa 2012, 32.

9. Kapila 2008, 120.

10. See Carrier 1992, 196.

11. Note, however, that displaying various forms of linguistic diversity is a characteristic of Northwestern Amazonia; see Epps and Stenzel 2013.

12. Tsing 2007, 38.

13. Clifford 2013, 47. See Huarcaya 2015 on the role of performance and performativity in the development of ethnic consciousness in Peru, Bolivia, and Ecuador.

14. Clifford 2013, 47.

15. Tsing 2005; see also Walley 2004.

16. Erazo 2013, 1.

17. Del Cairo 2012, 251.

18. Nyamnjoh 2007, 324.

19. Del Cairo 2012.

20. Dany Maheca, personal communication, September 2016.

21. Arundhati Roy, *Public Power in the Age of Empire*, 2004 (as cited in Hodgson 2011, 11).

22. De la Cadena and Starn's characterization (2007, 8) of Hale's argument (2006).

23. Margarita Chaves, personal communication, September 2016.

24. Postero 2006, 162.

25. Rappaport 2005.

26. Bocarejo 2015.

27. Nagel 1997, 12.

28. Pratt 2007, 402.

29. As characterized by Pratt 2007, 399.

30. See, for example, Jarvis 2017.

31. Chaves 2005.

32. Uday Mehta, "Liberal Strategies of Exclusion," a chapter in *Tensions of Empire: Colonial Cultures in a Bourgeois World*, edited by Cooper and Stoler (as cited in Postero 2006, 147).

33. Del Cairo 2012, 250.

34. See Comaroff and Comaroff 2009.

35. Nyamnjoh 2007, 325.

36. Kaltmeier and Thies 2012, 223.

37. Latorre 2013, 68.

38. del Cairo 2012, 277.

39. Ramos 1994.

40. De la Cadena and Starn 2007, 3.
41. De la Cadena and Starn 2007, 2.
42. Li 2000, 151.
43. Greene 2009.
44. Douglas 1966.
45. Clifford 2007, 198.
46. Graham and Penny 2014, 21.
47. De la Cadena and Starn 2007, 3.
48. Rappaport 1994; Povinelli 2002, 13; de la Cadena and Starn 2007, 3.
49. Niezen 2009, 10.

References Cited

Albert, Bruce. 1997. "Territorialité, ethnopolitique et développement: À propos du mouvement Indien en Amazonie brésilienne." *Cahiers des Amériques Latines* 23, 177–201.

Alfonso, Luís Alberto, Theo Oltheten, Jan Ooijens, and Anton Thybergin. 1988. *Educación, participación e identidad cultural: Una experiencia educativa con las comunidades indígenas del Nordeste [sic] Amazónico.* The Hague: Centro para el Estudio de la Educación en Países en Desarrollo (CESO).

"Alternative Communal Revolutionary Forces. Former Colombian Rebels Change Their Name . . . To FARC?" 2017. *New York Times* (AP), August 31.

Alvarez, Sonia E., Evelina Dagnino, and Arturo Escobar, eds. 1998. *Cultures of Politics, Politics of Cultures: Re-visioning Latin American Social Movements.* Boulder: Westview Press.

"Amnistía rechaza latigazos a paeces." 1997. *El Tiempo,* January 8.

Anderson, Benedict. 1983. *Imagined Communities: Reflections on the Origin and Spread of Nationalism.* London: Verso.

"Aplazan latigazos contra cinco indígenas paeces: ELN dice que fue un error asesinato del alcalde." 1997. *El Tiempo,* January 11.

Arango, Raúl, and Enrique Sánchez. 2004. *Los pueblos indígenas de Colombia en el umbral del nuevo milenio.* Bogotá: Departamento Nacional de Planeación.

Arboleda, José Rafael. 1983. "El conflicto entre indígenas en la obra misionera Colombiana." *Revista de Misiones* 613, 118–119.

Archila, Mauricio. 2003. *Idas y venidas vueltas y revueltas: Protestas sociales en Colombia 1958–1990.* Bogotá: Instituto Colombiano de Antropología e Historia, Centro de Investigación y Educación Popular.

Aretxaga, Begoña. 2003. "Maddening States." In *States of Terror: Begoña Aretxaga's Essays,* edited by Joseba Zulaika, 255–268. Reno: Center for Basque Studies, University of Nevada.

Århem, Kaj. 1981. *Makuna Social Organization: A Study in Descent, Alliance and the Formation of Corporate Groups in the North-Western Amazon.* Uppsala: Acta Academiae Upsaliensis.

———. 1993. "Millennium Among the Makuna: An Anthropological Film Adventure in the Northwest Amazon." *Anthropology Today* 9, no. 3, 3–8.

———. 2000. *Ethnographic Puzzles: Essays on Social Organization, Symbolism and Change.* London: Athlone Press.

Arocha, Jaime. 1992. "Los negros recrean su mundo: África en América." *Crónicas del Nuevo Mundo,* 18: 274–288. Medellín: *El Colombiano,* Centro de Investigación y Educación Popular, and Instituto Colombiano de Antropología.

———. 1999. *Ombligados de Ananse: Hilos ancestrales y modernos en el Pacífico colombiano.* Bogotá: Centro de Estudios Sociales, Universidad Nacional de Colombia.

———. 2015. "Etnia y guerra: Relación ausente en los estudios sobre las violencias colombianas." In *Debates sobre conflictos raciales y construcciones afrolibertarias,* edited by Melquiceded Blandón Mena and Ramón Emilio Perea Lemos, 205–235. Medellín: Ediciones Poder Negro; Centro Popular Afrodescendiente, Corporación Afrocolombiana de Desarrollo Social y Cultural, and Proceso de Comunidades Negras.

Assies, Willem. 2003. "Indian Justice in the Andes: Re-rooting or Re-routing?" In *Imaging the Andes: Shifting Margins of a Marginal World,* edited by Ton Salman and Annelies Zoomers, 167–186. Amsterdam: CEDLA.

Associated Press. 2015. "Popular Weed Killer Deemed Probable Carcinogen by UN." March 20.

Autoridades Tradicionales Indígenas de Colombia: Gobierno Major. n.d. [Website.] http://gobiernomayor.org.

Avirama, Jesús, and Rayda Márquez. 1995. "The Indigenous Movement in Colombia." In *Indigenous Peoples and Democracy in Latin America,* edited by Donna Lee Van Cott, 83–105. New York: St. Martin's Press.

Bakhtin, Mikhail. (1975) 1981. *The Dialogic Imagination: Four Essays.* Edited by Michael Holquist. Reprint, Austin: University of Texas Press.

Barker, Joanne. 2011. *Native Acts: Law, Recognition, and Cultural Authenticity.* Durham: Duke University Press.

Barth, Fredrik, ed. 1969a. *Ethnic Groups and Boundaries: The Social Organization of Culture Difference.* Boston: Little, Brown.

———. 1969b. "Introduction." In *Ethnic Groups and Boundaries: The Social Organization of Culture Difference,* edited by Fredrik Barth, 9–38. Boston: Little, Brown.

Basso, Keith. 1979. *Portraits of "The Whiteman": Linguistic Play and Cultural Symbols among the Western Apache.* Cambridge: Cambridge University Press.

Bastos, Santiago. 2012. "Multicultural Projects in Guatemala: Identity Tensions and Everyday Ideologies." *Latin American and Caribbean Ethnic Studies* 7, no. 2, 155–172.

Becker, Marc. 2008. *Indians and Leftists in the Making of Ecuador's Modern Indigenous Movements*. Durham: Duke University Press.

Benavides, Farid Samir. 2004. "Hermeneutical Violence: Human Rights, Law, and the Constitution of a Global Identity." *International Journal for the Semiotics of Law* 17, no. 4, 391–418.

Bergquist, Charles, Ricardo Peñaranda, and Gonzalo Sánchez. 2001. *Violence in Colombia 1990–2000: Waging War and Negotiating Peace*. Wilmington: Scholarly Resources.

Berkhofer, Robert F. 1979. *The White Man's Indian: Images of the American Indian from Columbus to the Present*. New York: Random House.

Bessire, Lucas. 2014. *Behold the Black Caiman: A Chronicle of Ayoreo Life*. Chicago: University of Chicago Press.

Betancourt, Ana Cecilia, and Hernán Rodríguez. 1994. "After the Constitution: Indigenous Proposals for Territorial Demarcation in Colombia." *Abya Yala News: Journal of the South and Meso American Indian Information Center* 8, no. 1&2, 22–23.

Beyerlin, Ulrich. 2015. "Aligning International Environmental Governance with the 'Aarhus Principles' and Participatory Human Rights." In *Research Handbook on Human Rights and the Environment*, edited by Anna Grear and Louis J. Kotzé, 333–352. Cheltenham: Edward Elgar.

Blackburn, Carol. 2009. "Differentiating Indigenous Citizenship: Seeking Multiplicity in Rights, Identity, and Sovereignty in Canada." *American Ethnologist* 36, no. 1, 66–78.

Bocarejo, Diana. 2011. "Dos paradojas del multiculturalismo Colombiano: La espacialización de la diferencia indígena y su aislamiento político." *Revista Colombiana de Antropología* 47, no. 2, 97–121.

———. 2012. "Emancipation or Enclosement? The Spatialization of Difference and Urban Ethnic Contestation in Colombia." *Antipode* 44, no, 3, 663–683.

———. 2015. *Tipologías y topologías indígenas en el multiculturalismo colombiano*. Bogotá: Instituto Colombiano de Antropología e Historia, Pontífica Universidad Javeriana, and Universidad del Rosario.

Bodnar, Yolanda. 1986. *Etnoeducación: Política educativa indígena nacional y algunas experiencias bilingües-interculturales adelantadas en el país*. Bogotá: Ministerio de Educación Nacional.

Bodley, John H. 1990. *Victims of Progress*. 3rd ed. Mountain View: Mayfield.

Bonner, Michelle D. 2014. "Violence, Policing, and Citizen Insecurity." *Latin American Research Review* 49, no. 1, 261–269.

Borrero, Milciades, and Marleny Pérez. 2004. *Vaupés: Mito y realidad*. Bogotá: Ediciones Desde Abajo.

Bourgois, Philippe. 1988. "Conjugated Oppression: Class and Ethnicity Among Guaymi and Kuna Banana Workers." *American Ethnologist* 15, no. 2, 328–348.

Brading, David A. 1988. "Manuel Gamio and Official Indigenismo in Mexico." *Bulletin of Latin American Research*, 7, no. 1, 75–89.

Briggs, Charles. 1996. "The Politics of Discursive Authority in Research on the 'Invention of Tradition.'" *Cultural Anthropology* 11, no. 4, 435–469.

Brown, Michael. 1995. "Facing the State, Facing the World: Amazonia's Native Leaders and the New Politics of Identity." *L'Homme* 33, no. 2–4, 307–326.

Brubaker, Rogers. 2004. *Ethnicity Without Groups*. Cambridge, MA: Harvard University Press.

Brubaker, Rogers, and Frederick Cooper. 2000. "Beyond 'Identity.'" *Theory and Society* 29, no. 1, 1–47.

Brysk, Allison. 2000. *From Tribal Village to Global Village: Indian Rights and International Relations in Latin America*. Stanford: Stanford University Press.

Buchillet, Dominique. 1992. "Nobody Is There to Hear: Desana Therapeutic Incantations." In *Portals of Power: Shamanism in South America*, edited by E. J. Matteson Langdon and G. Baer, 211–230. Albuquerque: University of New Mexico Press.

Bucholtz, Mary, and Kira Hall. 2004. "Language and Identity." In *A Companion to Linguistic Anthropology*, edited by Alessandro Duranti, 369–394. Malden: Blackwell.

Burman, Anders. 2014. "'Now We Are Indígenas': Hegemony and Indigeneity in the Bolivian Andes." *Latin American and Caribbean Ethnic Studies* 9, no. 3, 247–271.

Cabrera, Gabriel. 2002a. *La Iglesia en la frontera: Misiones católicas en el Vaupés 1850–1950*. Bogotá: Universidad Nacional de Colombia.

———. 2002b. "Los Nukak: De caníbales a indígenas: Itinerario de una exclusión." *Palimpsetus*, no. 2, 112–118.

———. 2007. *Las nuevas tribus y los indígenas de la Amazonia: Historia de una presencia protestante*. Bogotá: LitoCamargo.

———, ed. 2010. *Viviendo en el bosque: Un siglo de investigaciones sobre los Makú del Noroeste Amazónico*. Medellín: Universidad Nacional de Colombia.

Cabrera, Gabriel, Carlos Franky, and Dany Maheca. 1999. *Los Nikak: Nómadas de la Amazonia colombiana*. Bogotá: Universidad Nacional de Colombia.

Cadena, Edgar. 1988. "Colombia; Líder de la cuenca amazónica?" *El Tiempo*, May 15.

Caicedo-Fernández, Alhena. 2015. *La alteridad radical que cura: Neochamanismos yajeceros en Colombia*. Bogotá: Ediciones Uniandes.

Campo, Carlos. 1998. "Misterioso baño de Piñacué: El camino hacia la laguna sagrada de Juan Tama solo está trazado en la memoria de los paeces más viejos." *El Tiempo*, July 19.

Canessa, Andrew. 2007. "Who Is Indigenous? Self-identification, Indigeneity, and Claims to Justice in Contemporary Bolivia." *Urban Anthropology* 36, no. 3, 195–237.

———. 2012. *Intimate Indigeneities: Race, Sex, and History in the Small Spaces of Andean Life.* Durham: Duke University Press.

Cárdenas, Darion, and Gustavo G. Politis. 2000. *Territorio, movilidad, etnobotánica y manejo del bosque de los Nukak orientales: Amazonia colombiana.* Bogotá: Ediciones Uniandes.

Carneiro da Cunha, Manuela. 2009. *"Culture" and Culture: Traditional Knowledge and Intellectual Rights.* Chicago: Prickly Paradigm Press.

Carrier, James G. 1992. "Occidentalism: The World Turned Upside-down." *American Ethnologist* 19, no. 2, 195–212.

———. 1995. "Introduction." In *Occidentalism: Images of the West*, edited by James G. Carrier, 1–32. New York: Oxford University Press.

Casey, Nicholas. 2016. "After 5 Decades of War, Colombia Signs Peace Agreement with Rebels." *New York Times*, September 27.

Castañeda, Quetzil E. 2004. "'We Are Not Indigenous!': The Maya Identity of Yucatán, an Introduction." *Journal of Latin American Anthropology* 9, no. 1, 36–63.

"Castigan pareja indígena paez por infidelidad." 2000. *El Espectador*, June 5.

Castillo, Luis Carlos. 2007. *Etnicidad y nación: El desafío de la diversidad en Colombia.* Cali: Universidad del Valle.

Cathcart, Marilyn. 1973. "Cacua." In *Aspectos de la cultura material de grupos étnicos de Colombia*, edited by Stanley Schauer et al., 101–133. Bogotá: Ministerio de Gobierno and Instituto Lingüístico de Verano.

Cattelino, Jessica. 2010. Review of *The Rediscovered Self: Indigenous Identity and Cultural Justice*, by Ronald Niezen. *American Anthropologist* 112, no. 2, 334.

Cayón, Luis. 2002. *En las aguas de Yuruparí: Cosmología y chamanismo Makuna.* Bogotá: Ediciones Uniandes.

———. 2013. *Pienso, luego creo: La teoría Makuna del mundo.* Bogotá: Instituto Colombiano de Antropología e Historia.

Cepeda Espinosa, Manuel José. 2006. "The Judicialization of Politics in Colombia: The Old and the New." In *The Judicialization of Politics in Latin America*, edited by Rachel Sieder, Line Schjolden, and Alan Angell, 67–103. New York: Palgrave Macmillan.

"Cepo, a padres irresponsables: mujeres paeces no tolerán el abandono." 2000. *El Tiempo*, May 10.

Chatterjee, Partha. 2004. *The Politics of the Governed: Reflections on Popular Politics in Most of the World.* New York: Columbia University Press.

Chaumeil, Jean-Pierre. 1990. "'Les nouveaux chefs . . .': Pratiques politiques et organisations indigènes en Amazonie péruvienne." *Problèmes d'Amérique Latine* 96, 93–113.

Chaves, Margarita. 2001a. "Conflictos territoriales o la política de la ubicación: Actores étnicos, re-etnizados y no étnicos en disputa por un territorio en el Putumayo." In

Memorias. II seminario internacional sobre territorio y cultura: Territorios de conflicto y cambio sociocultural, edited by Beatriz Nates, 167–186. Manizales: Universidad de Caldas.

———. 2001b. "Discursos subalternos de identidad y movimiento indígena en el Putumayo." In *Movimientos sociales, estado y democracia en Colombia*, edited by Mauricio Archila and Mauricio Pardo, 234–259. Bogotá: Centro de Estudios Sociales de la Universidad Nacional de Colombia and Instituto Colombiano de Antropología e Historia.

———. 2002. "Jerarquías de color y mestizaje en la Amazonía occidental colombiana." *Revista Colombiana de Antropología* 38, 189–216.

———. 2003. "Cabildos multiétnicos e identidades depuradas." In *Fronteras: Territorios y metáforas*, compiled by Clara Inés García, 121–135. Medellín: Hombre Nuevo Editores.

———. 2005. "'¿Qué va a pasar con los Indios Cuando Todos Seamos Indios?': Ethnic Rights and Reindianization in Southwestern Colombian Amazonia." PhD diss., Department of Anthropology, University of Illinois at Urbana-Champaign.

———. 2010. "Normative Views, Strategic Views: The Geopolitical Maps in the Ethnic Territorialities of Putumayo." In *Editing Eden: A Reconsideration of Identity, Politics, and Place in Amazonia*, edited by Frank Hutchins and Patrick C. Wilson, 191–217. Lincoln: University of Nebraska Press.

Chaves, Margarita, and Leslie Wirpsa. 1988. "Aparecen los Nukak." *Noticias Antropológicas*, 89 (June–July), 1, 5.

Chaves, Margarita, and Marta Zambrano. 2006. "From *Blanqueamiento* to *Reindigenización*: Paradoxes of *Mestizaje* and Multiculturalism in Contemporary Colombia." *Revista Europea de Estudios Latinoamericanos y del Caribe* 80 (April), 5–23.

———. 2009. "Desafíos a la nación multicultural. Una mirada comparativa sobre la reindianización y el mestizaje en Colombia." In *Repensando los Movimientos Indígenas*, edited by Carmen Martínez Novo, 215–245. Quito: FLACSO and Ministerio de Cultura del Ecuador.

Chernick, Marc. 2005. "Economic Resources and Internal Armed Conflicts: Lessons from the Colombian Case." In *Rethinking the Economics of War: The Intersection of Need, Creed, and Greed*, edited by Cynthia J. Arnson and I. William. Zartman, 178–205. Washington, DC: Woodrow Wilson Center Press and Johns Hopkins University Press.

Clifford, James. 1988. "Identity in Mashpee." In *The Predicament of Culture: Twentieth-Century Ethnography, Literature, and Art*, 277–348. Cambridge, MA: Harvard University Press.

———. 1997. *Routes: Travel and Translation in the Late Twentieth Century.* Cambridge, MA: Harvard University Press.

———. 2007. "Varieties of Indigenous Experience: Diasporas, Homelands, Sovereignties." In *Indigenous Experience Today*, edited by Marisol de la Cadena and Orin Starn, 197–224. Oxford: Berg.

———. 2013. *Returns: Becoming Indigenous in the Twenty-First Century*. Cambridge, MA: Harvard University Press.

Clifton, James A., ed. 1990. *The Invented Indian: Cultural Fictions and Government Policies*. New Brunswick: Transaction.

"La coca, macartizada." 2008. *El Tiempo*, May 21.

Cohen, Ronald. 1978. "Ethnicity: Problem and Focus in Anthropology." *Annual Review of Anthropology* 7, 379–404.

Collier, George A., with Elizabeth Lowery Quaratiello. 2008. *Basta! Land and the Zapatista Rebellion in Chiapas*. 3rd ed. Oakland: Food First Books.

Collins, John. 2001. "Melted Gold and National Bodies: The Hermeneutics of Depth and the Value of History in Brazilian Racial Politics." *American Ethnologist* 38, no. 4, 683–700.

"Colombia: FARC Releases Indigenous Leaders." 2004. *Weekly Indigenous News*, September 27.

"Colombia Trial Reveals Life ('Everyone Kills Indians') on Plains." 1972. *New York Times*, July 9.

Comaroff, John L., and Jean Comaroff. 2009. *Ethnicity, Inc.* Chicago: University of Chicago Press.

"Las comunidades indígenas en Colombia: Comunidades de la selva." 1976. *Unidad Indígena* (June).

Conklin, Beth A. 1997. Body Paint, Feathers, and VCRs: Aesthetics and Authenticity in Amazonian Activism. *American Ethnologist* 24, no. 4, 695–721.

———. 2002. "Shamans Versus Pirates in the Amazonian Treasure Chest." *American Anthropologist* 104, no. 4, 1050–1061.

———. 2006. "Environmentalism, Global Community, and the New Indigenism." In *Inclusion and Exclusion in the Global Arena*, edited by Max Kirsch, 161–176. New York: Routledge.

Conklin, Beth A., and Laura Graham. 1995. "The Shifting Middle Ground: Amazonian Indians and Eco-politics." *American Anthropologist* 97, no. 4, 695–710.

Consejo Regional Indígena del Cauca–CRIC. 1981. *Diez años de lucha: Historia y documentos*. Bogotá: Centro de Investigación y Educación Popular.

Correa, François. 1987. "Makú." In *Introducción a la Colombia Amerindia*, edited by François Correa and Ximena Pachón, 123–134. Bogotá: Instituto Colombiano de Antropología.

———. 1992. "Lo 'indígena' ante el estado Colombiano: Reflejo jurídico de su conceptualización política." In *Antropología Jurídica: Normas Formales: Costumbres Legales en Colombia*, edited by Esther Sánchez, 71–102. Bogotá: Sociedad Antropológica de Colombia.

———. 1993a. "A manera de epílogo. Derechos étnicos: Derechos humanos." In *Encrucijadas de Colombia Amerindia*, edited by François Correa, 319–334. Bogotá: Instituto Colombiano de Antropología, Colcultura.

———. 1993b. "Mercancías y aldeas de misión en la Amazonia." In *Encrucijadas de Colombia Amerindia*, edited by François Correa, 161–182. Bogotá: Instituto Colombiano de Antropología, Colcultura.

———. 1996. *Por el camino de la Anaconda Remedio: Dinámica de la organización social entre los taiwano del Vaupés*. Bogotá: Universidad Nacional de Colombia.

Coulthard, Glen Sean. 2014. *Red Skin, White Masks: Rejecting the Colonial Politics of Recognition*. Minneapolis: University of Minnesota Press.

Cowan, Jane K. 2006. "Culture and Rights after *Culture and Rights*." *American Anthropologist* 108, no. 1, 9–24.

Cowan, Jane K., Marie Bénédicte Dembour, and Richard A. Wilson. 2001. "Introduction." In *Culture and Rights: Anthropological Perspectives*, edited by Jane K. Cowan, Marie Bénédicte Dembour, and Richard A. Wilson, 1–26. Cambridge: Cambridge University Press.

Departamento Administrativo Nacional de Estadística. 2005. Censo General de 2005. https://www.dane.gov.co/index.php/estadisticas-por-tema/demografia-y-poblacion/censo-general-2005-1.

"De coca, papa y género." 2007. *El Tiempo*, March 21.

de Friedemann, Nina S. de. 1984a. "Estudios de negros en la antropología colombiana." In *Un siglo de investigación social: Antropología en Colombia*, edited by Jaime Arocha and Nina S. de Friedemann, 507–572. Bogotá: Etno.

———. 1984b. "Ética y política del antropólogo: Compromiso profesional." In *Un siglo de investigación social: Antropología en Colombia*, edited by Jaime Arocha and Nina S. de Friedemann, 381–428. Bogotá: Etno.

De la Cadena, Marisol. 2000. *Indigenous Mestizos: The Politics of Race and Culture in Cuzco, Peru, 1919–1991*. Durham, Duke University Press.

———. 2015. *Earth Beings: Ecologies of Practice Across Andean Worlds*. Durham: Duke University Press.

De la Cadena, Marisol, and Orin Starn. 2007. "Introduction." In *Indigenous Experience Today*, edited by Marisol de la Cadena and Orin Starn, 1–30. Oxford: Berg.

De la Calle, Humberto. 1994. "La Carta del 91: Instrumento contemporáneo." *El Tiempo*, Lecturas Dominicales, November 13.

De León, Sergio. 2007. "Coca-Cola vs. Coca Sek in Colombia." *Washington Post*, May 10.

"De mochila en la Asamblea Constituyente: Rojas y Muelas imponen nueva moda en la política." 1991. *El Tiempo*, February 6.

DeGraff, Michel, ed. 1999. *Language Creation and Language Change: Creolization, Diachrony, and Development*. Cambridge, MA: MIT Press.

———. 2005. "Linguists' Most Dangerous Myth: The Fallacy of Creole Exceptionalism." *Language in Society* 34, no. 4, 533–91.

Del Cairo, Carlos. 2010. "Las encrucijadas del liderazgo político indígena en la Amazonia colombiana." In *Perspectivas Antropológicas sobre la Amazonia Contemporánea,* edited by Margarita Chaves and Carlos del Cairo, 189–212. Bogotá: Instituto Colombiano de Antropología e Historia, Pontíficia Universidad Javeriana.

———. 2012. "Environmentalizing Indigeneity: A Comparative Ethnography on Multiculturalism, Ethnic Hierarchies, and Political Ecology in the Colombian Amazon." PhD diss., University of Arizona.

Deloria, Philip. 1998. *Playing Indian.* New Haven: Yale University Press.

———. 2004. *Indians in Unexpected Places.* Lawrence: University Press of Kansas.

Deloria, Vine. 1969. *Custer Died for Your Sins: An Indian Manifesto.* Norman: University of Oklahoma Press.

Desprès, Leo. 1984. "Ethnicity: What Data and Theory Portend for Plural Societies." In *The Prospects for Plural Societies,* edited by David Maybury-Lewis, 7–29. Washington, DC: American Ethnological Society.

Devereux, George. 1975. "Ethnic Identity: Its Logical Foundations and Its Dysfunctions." In *Ethnic Identity: Cultural Continuities and Change,* edited by George De Vos and Lola Romanucci-Ross, 42–70. Palo Alto: Mayfield.

Dietz, Gunther. 2004. "From *Indigenismo* to *Zapatismo*: The Struggle for a Multi-ethnic Mexican Society." In *The Struggle for Indigenous Rights in Latin America,* edited by Nancy Grey Postero and Leon Zamosc, 32–80. Brighton: Sussex Academic Press.

Douglas, Mary. 1966. *Purity and Danger: An Analysis of Concepts of Pollution and Taboo.* London: Routledge and Kegan Paul.

Dover, Robert V. H., and Joanne Rappaport. 1996. "Introduction." *Journal of Latin American Anthropology* 1, no. 2, 2–17.

Dressler, William W. 2015. "Opinion." *Anthropology News* 56 (May–June), 20.

Dudley, Edward, and Maximillian E. Novak, eds. 1972. *The Wild Man Within: An Image in Western Thought from the Renaissance to Romanticism.* Pittsburgh: University of Pittsburgh Press.

Dudley, Steven. 2005. "Indians Battle Rebels." *Miami Herald,* April 21.

Dugas, John C. 2012. "Paramilitaries and the Economic Origins of Armed Conflict in Colombia." *Latin American Research Review* 47, no. 1, 205–213.

"Editorial: Frente al evangelio y la cultura: ¿Cristianos de verdad o de puro cuento?" 1990. *Selva y Río* 5, 2.

Epps, Patience, and Katherine Bolaños. 2017. "Reconsidering the 'Makú' Language Family of Northwest Amazonia." *International Journal of American Linguistics* 83, no. 3, 467–507.

Epps, Patience, and Kristine Stenzel. 2013. "Introduction." In *Upper Rio Negro: Cultural and Linguistic Interaction in Northwestern Amazonia*, edited by Patience Epps and Kristine Stenzel, 13–50. Rio de Janeiro: Museu Nacional, Museu do Índio–FUNAI.

Erazo, Juliet S. 2013. *Governing Indigenous Territories: Enacting Sovereignty in the Ecuadorian Amazon.* Durham: Duke University Press.

Eriksen, Thomas Hylland. 2010. *Ethnicity and Nationalism: Anthropological Perspectives.* 3rd ed. London: Pluto.

———. 2015. "Opposing the Motion: The Neoliberal Person." In T. H. Eriksen, J. Laidlaw, J. Mair, K. Martin, and S. Venkatesan, "The Concept of Neoliberalism Has Become an Obstacle to the Anthropological Understanding of the Twenty-First Century." *Journal of the Royal Anthropological Institute* 21, no. 4, 911–923.

"'Erradicación' del té de coca perjudica a 2,000 familias del Cauca." 2007. *El Tiempo*, March 12.

Escárcega, Sylvia. 2012. "Authenticating Strategic Essentialisms: The Politics of Indigenousness at the United Nations." In *Indigeneity: Collected Essays*, edited by Guillermo Delgado-P and John Brown Childs, 204–255. Santa Cruz: New Pacific Press.

Escobar, Arturo. 1992. *Encountering Development: The Making and Unmaking of the Third World.* Princeton: Princeton University Press.

———. 2008. *Territories of Difference: Place, Movements, Life*, Redes. Durham: Duke University Press.

Espinel, Adriana. 2005. "Indígenas, en la guerra de las colas." *El Tiempo*, December 11.

Espinosa, Myriam Amparo. 2009. *La civilización montés: La visión india y el trasegar de Manuel Quintín Lame en Colombia.* Bogotá: Ediciones Uniandes.

Fabian, Johannes, 1999. "Remembering the Other: Knowledge and Recognition in the Exploration of Central Africa." *Critical Inquiry* 26, no. 1, 49–69.

———. 1983. *Time and the Other: How Anthropology Makes Its Object.* New York: Columbia University Press.

Farfán-Santos, Elizabeth. 2015. "'Fraudulent' Identities: The Politics of Defining Quilombo Descendants in Brazil." *Journal of Latin American and Caribbean Anthropology* 20, no. 1, 110–132.

Faudree, Paja. 2013. *Singing for the Dead: The Politics of Indigenous Revival in Mexico.* Durham: Duke University Press.

Fernández, Harold. 1990. "Diagnóstico socioeconómico de comunidades indígenas de Amazonia Vaupés: Ríos Cuduyarí, Querarí y Vaupés (bajo)." Unpublished document. Bogotá: Proyecto Gaia.

Field, Les W. 1999. "Complicities and Collaborations: Anthropologists and the 'Unacknowledged Tribes' of California." *Current Anthropology* 40, no. 2, 193–209.

Findji, María Teresa. 1992. "From Resistance to Social Movement: The Indigenous Authorities Movement in Colombia." In *The Making of Social Movements in Latin America: Identity, Strategy, and Democracy*, edited by Arturo Escobar and Sonia F. Álvarez, 112–133. Boulder: Westview Press.

Fleming, Luke. 2016. "Linguistic Exogamy and Language Shift in the Northwest Amazon." *International Journal of the Sociology of Language*, 2016, no. 240, 9–27.

Forbes, Jack D. 2001. "'Indian' and 'Black' as Radically Different Types of Categories." In *The Social Construction of Race and Ethnicity in the United States*, Joan Ferrante and Prince Browne Jr., 164–167. 2nd ed. Upper Saddle River: Pearson/Prentice Hall.

Forero, Juan. 2005. "Colombia War Spills into Indians' Peaceful World." *New York Times*, May 2.

———. 2011. "Colombia to Compensate Victims of Its Long Civil Conflict." *Washington Post*, June 11.

Forte, Maximilian C., ed. 2013. *Who Is an Indian? Race, Place, and the Politics of Indigeneity in the Americas*. Toronto: University of Toronto Press.

Franky, Carlos Eduardo. 2011. "'Acompañarnos contentos con la familia': Unidad, diferencia y conflicto entre los Nükak (Amazonia colombiana)." PhD diss., Wageningen University, The Netherlands.

Franky, Carlos Eduardo, and Dany Mahecha. 2010. "Objetivizar para gobernar: Comunidades indígenas, censos poblacionales, control territorial y políticas públicas en la Amazonia colombiana." In *Ecología política de la Amazonia: Las profusas y difusas redes de la gobernanza*, edited by Germán Palacio Castañeda, 122–144. Bogotá: Instituto Latinoamericano de Servicios Legales Alternativos, Ecofondo, Universidad Nacional de Colombia, Sede Amazonia.

French, Jan Hoffman. 2009. *Legalizing Identities: Becoming Black or Indian in Brazil's Northeast*. Chapel Hill: University of North Carolina Press.

Fried, Morton. 1975. *The Notion of Tribe*. Menlo Park: Cummings.

Friedman, Jonathan. 1992. "The Past in the Future: History and the Politics of Identity." *American Anthropologist* 94, no. 4, 837–859.

———. 1994. *Cultural Identity and Global Process*. Thousand Oaks: Sage.

"Fuete a gobernador indígena." 2000. *El Tiempo*, May 14.

García-Godos, Jemima, and Knut Andreas O. Lid. 2010. "Transitional Justice and Victims' Rights before the End of a Conflict: The Unusual Case of Colombia." *Journal of Latin American Studies* 42, no. 3, 487–516.

Garrett, Paul B. 2004. "Language Contact and Contact Languages." In *A Companion to Linguistic Anthropology*, edited by Alesssandro Duranti, 46–71. Malden: Blackwell.

Gaviria Díaz, Carlos. 2000. "Prólogo." In *La jurisdicción especial indígena*, edited by Esther Sánchez and Isabel Cristina Jaramillo, 15–20. Bogotá: Procuraduría General de la Nación.

Geertz, Clifford. 1973. *The Interpretation of Cultures*. New York: Basic Books.

Geismar, Haidy. 2013. Review of *The Elusive Promise of Indigenous Development: Rights, Culture, Strategy*, by Karen Engle. *American Anthropologist* 115, no. 2, 338–339.

"Gobierno e indígenas no llegaron a acuerdo por productos a base de coca." 2007. *El Tiempo*, March 19.

Godoy, María Ximena. 1988. "Maximiliano Veloz: Un indígena educando a más indígenas." *El Tiempo*, June 3.

Goldman, Irving. 1963. *The Cubeo: Indians of the Northwest Amazon*. Champaign: University of Illinois Press.

———. 1968. *Los Cubeo*. México: Instituto Indigenista Interamericano.

———. 1981. "The New Tribes Mission Among the Cubeo." *Anthropology Resource Center Bulletin* 9, 7–8.

———. 2004. *Cubeo Hehénewa Religious Thought: Metaphysics of a Northwestern Amazonian People*. New York: Columbia University Press.

Gómez-Imbert, Elsa. 1996. "When Animals Become 'Rounded' and 'Feminine': Conceptual Categories and Linguistic Classification in a Multilingual Setting." In *Rethinking Linguistic Relativity*, edited by John J. Gumperz and Stephen C. Levinson, 438–469. Cambridge: Cambridge University Press.

Gómez-Imbert, Elsa, and Stephen Hugh-Jones. 2000. "Introducción al estudio de las lenguas del Piraparaná (Vaupés)." In *Lenguas indígenas de Colombia: Una visión descriptiva*, edited by María Stella González de Pérez and María Luisa Rodríguez de Montes, 321–356. Bogotá: Instituto Caro y Cuervo.

Goodale, Mark. 2007. "Introduction: Locating Rights, Envisioning Law Between the Global and the Local." In *The Practice of Human Rights: Tracking Law Between the Global and the Local*, edited by Mark Goodale and Sally Engle Merry, 1–38. Cambridge: Cambridge University Press.

———. 2009. *Dilemmas of Modernity: Bolivian Encounters with Law and Liberalism*. Stanford: Stanford University Press.

———. 2010. Review of *Rights in Rebellion: Indigenous Struggle and Human Rights in Chiapas*, by Shannon Speed. *American Anthropologist* 112, no. 3, 493.

Gooding-Williams, Robert. 1998. "Race, Multiculturalism and Democracy." *Constellations* 5, 18–41.

Gow, David D. 2008. *Countering Development: Indigenous Modernity and the Moral Imagination*. Durham: Duke University Press.

Gow, David D., and Joanne Rappaport. 2002. "The Indigenous Public Voice: The Multiple Idioms of Modernity in Native Cauca." In *Indigenous Movements, Self-Representation, and the State in Latin America*, edited by Kay B. Warren and Jean E. Jackson, 47–80. Austin: University of Texas Press.

Graham, Laura R. 2002. "How Should an Indian Speak? Amazonian Indians and the Symbolic Politics of Language in the Global Public Sphere." In *Indigenous Movements, Self-Representation, and the State in Latin America*, edited by Kay B. Warren and Jean E. Jackson, 181–228. Austin: University of Texas.

Graham, Laura R., and H. Glenn Penny, eds. 2014. *Performing Indigeneity: Global Histories and Contemporary Experiences.* Lincoln: University of Nebraska Press.

Green, W. John. 2005. "Guerrillas, Soldiers, Paramilitaries, Assassins, Narcos, and Gringos." *Latin American Research Review* 40, no. 2, 137–149.

Greene, Shane. 2007. "Introduction: On Race, Roots/Routes, and Sovereignty in Latin America's Afro-indigenous Multiculturalisms." *Journal of Latin American and Caribbean Anthropology* 12, no. 2, 329–355.

———. 2009. *Customizing Indigeneity: Paths to a Visionary Politics in Peru.* Stanford: Stanford University Press.

Gros, Christian. 1991. *Colombia indígena: Identidad y cambio social.* Bogotá: Fondo Editorial CEREC.

———. 1993. "Derechos indígenas y nueva constitución en Colombia." *Análisis Político*, no. 19 (May–August), 8–24.

———. 1996. "Un ajustement à visage indien." In *La Colombie: À l'aube du troisième millénaire*, edited by Jean-Michel Blanquer and Christian Gros, 249–278. Paris, Éditions L'IHEAL.

———. 2013. "¿Indígenas o campesinos, pueblos de la selva o de la montaña?" *Revista Colombiana de Antropología* 49, no. 1, 45–70.

Grueso, Libia, Carlos Rosero, and Arturo Escobar. 1998. "The Process of Black Community Organizing in the Southern Pacific Coast Region of Colombia." In *Cultures of Politics, Politics of Cultures: Re-visioning Latin American Social Movements*, edited by Sonia E. Alvárez, Evelina Dagnino, and Arturo Escobar, 196–211. Boulder: Westview Press.

Gruner, Sheila. 2017. "Territory, Autonomy, and the Good Life: Afro-Colombian and Indigenous Ethno-territorial Movements in Colombia's Peace Process." *Journal of Latin American and Caribbean Anthropology* 22, no. 1, 174–182.

Gruner, Sheila, Melquiceded Blandón, Jader Gómez, and Charo Mina-Rojas, eds. 2016. *Des/DIBUJANDO EL PAIS/aje: Aportes para la paz con los pueblos afrodescendientes e indígenas. Territorio, autonomía y buen vivir.* Medellín: Ediciones Poder Negro.

Grupo Investigadores Culturales del Vaupés. 1989. "Proyecto propuesto para un centro de investigaciones culturales del Vaupés." Mitú, Vaupés. Unpublished document.

Guevara, Juan. n.d. *Etnodesarrollo y medicina indígena ecológica.* Bogotá: Ministerio de Salud, Servicio Seccional de Salud del Vaupés.

"El güío domesticado" 1989. *Centro Animación Pastoral Indígena* 66, 9.

Gupta, Akhil, and James Ferguson. 1997. "Culture, Power, Place: Ethnography at the End of an Era." In *Culture, Power, Place: Explorations in Critical Anthropology*, edited by Akhil Gupta and James Ferguson, 1–32. Durham: Duke University Press.

Gustafson, Bret, and Nicole Fabricant. 2011. "Introduction: New Cartographies of Knowledge and Struggle." In *Remapping Bolivia: Resources, Territory, and Indigene-*

ity in a Plurinational State, edited by Nicole Fabricant and Bret Gustafson, 1–25. Santa Fe: School for Advanced Research Press.

Guzmán, Ramiro. 1998. "Emberá expulsan a organización indígena." *El Espectador*, March 23.

Hale, Charles. 1997. "Consciousness, Violence, and the Politics of Memory in Guatemala." *Current Anthropology* 38, no. 5, 817–824.

———. 2002. "Does Multiculturalism Menace? Governance, Cultural Rights and the Politics of Identity in Guatemala." *Journal of Latin American Studies* 34, no. 3, 485–524.

———. 2004. "Rethinking Indigenous Politics in the Era of the '*Indio Permitido*.'" *NACLA Report on the Americas* 38, no. 2, 16–21.

———. 2006. *Más que un Indio: Racial Ambivalence and Neoliberal Multiculturalism in Guatemala*. Santa Fe: School of American Research Press.

———. 2011. "Epilogue." In *Remapping Bolivia: Resources, Territory, and Indigeneity in a Plurinational State*, edited by Nicole Fabricant and Bret Gustafson, 195–207. Santa Fe: School for Advanced Research Press.

Hale, Charles R., and Lynn Stephen, eds. 2013. *Otros Saberes: Collaborative Research on Indigenous and Afro-descendant Cultural Politics*. Santa Fe: School for Advanced Research Press.

Hall, Stuart. 1996. "Identity: Who Needs It?" In *Questions of Cultural Identity*, edited by Stuart Hall and Paul du Gay, 1–17. London: Sage.

Handler, Richard. 1988. *Nationalism and the Politics of Culture in Quebec*. Madison: University of Wisconsin Press.

Handler, Richard, and Jocelyn Linnekin. 1984. "Tradition, Genuine or Spurious." *Journal of American Folklore* 97, no. 385, 273–290.

Henríquez, Orlando. 1988. "Barco traza bases para política amazónica." *El Espectador*, April 24.

Hernández, Manuel. 1998. "Laboratorio social." *El Espectador*, September 8.

Hernández Castillo, R. Aída. 2010. "The Emergence of Indigenous Feminism in Latin America." *Signs: Journal of Women in Culture and Society*, 35, no. 3, 539–545.

Hill, Jane. 1991. "In Ñeca Gobierno de Puebla: Mexicano Penetrations of the Mexican State." In *Nation-States and Indians in Latin America*, edited by Greg Urban and Joel Sherzer, 72–94. Austin: University of Texas Press.

Hill, Jonathan. 1996. "Introduction: Ethnogenesis in the Americas, 1492–1992." In *History, Power, and Identity: Ethnogenesis in the Americas, 1492–1992*, edited by Jonathan Hill, 1–19. Iowa City: University of Iowa Press.

Hippert, Christine. 2011. "The Politics and Practices of Constructing Development Identities in Rural Bolivia." *Journal of Latin American and Caribbean Anthropology* 16, no. 1, 90–113.

Hodgson, Dorothy L. 2011. *Being Maasai, Becoming Indigenous: Postcolonial Politics in a Neoliberal World*. Bloomington: Indiana University Press.

Hooker, Juliet. 2005. "Indigenous Inclusion/Black Exclusion: Race, Ethnicity and Multicultural Citizenship in Latin America." *Journal of Latin American Studies* 37, no. 2, 285–310.

Howe, James. 1998. *A People Who Would Not Kneel: Panama, the United States, and the San Blas Kuna.* Washington: Smithsonian Institution Press.

———. 2009. *Chiefs, Scribes & Ethnographers: Kuna Culture from Inside and Out.* Austin: University of Texas Press.

Huarcaya, Sergio Miguel. 2015. "Performativity, Performance, and Indigenous Activism in Ecuador and the Andes." *Comparative Studies in Society and History* 57, no. 3, 806–837.

Hugh-Jones, Christine. 1979. *From the Milk River: Spatial and Temporal Processes in Northwest Amazonia.* Cambridge: Cambridge University Press.

Hugh-Jones, Stephen. 1979. *The Palm and the Pleiades: Initiation and Cosmology in Northwest Amazonia.* Cambridge: Cambridge University Press.

———. 1988. "Lujos de ayer, necesidades de mañana: Comercio y trueque en la Amazonia noroccidental." *Boletín del Museo del Oro*, no. 21, 77–101.

Hunt, Stacey. 2006. "Languages of Stateness: A Study of Space and El Pueblo in the Colombian State." *Latin American Research Review* 41, no. 3, 88–121.

Hymes, Dell. 1968. "Linguistic Problems in Defining the Concept of 'Tribe.'" In *Essays on the Problem of Tribe*, edited by June Helm, 23–48. Seattle: University of Washington Press.

Iglesias, Juliana. 2012. "Coca Nasa e INVIMA, entre la multiculturalidad y la política antidrogas." Unpublished document.

"Indígenas rescatan su alcalde." 2003. *El Tiempo*, April 14.

Instituto Colombiano de Antropología. 1993. "Tutela en territorio de los Nukak." *Boletín Trimestral*, no. 1, 4, 5.

Instituto Colombiano de Bienestar Familiar. 1988. "Atención integral de la familia indígena." Bogotá.

Isaacs, Harold. 1975. *Idols of the Tribe: Group Identity and Political Change.* New York: Harper and Row.

Jackson, Jean E. 1983. *The Fish People: Linguistic Exogamy and Tukanoan Identity in Northwest Amazonia.* Cambridge: Cambridge University Press.

———. 1984. "Traducciones competitivas del evangelio en el Vaupés, Colombia." *América Indígena* 44, no. 1, 49–94.

———. 1989. "Is There a Way to Talk About Making Culture Without Making Enemies?" *Dialectical Anthropology* 14, no. 2, 127–144. Reprinted in Fernando Santos Granero, ed., *Globalización y cambio en la Amazonía indígena*, 439–472. Quito: FLACSO, Biblioteca Abya-Yala, 1996.

———. 1991a. "Being and Becoming an Indian in the Vaupés." In *Nation-States and*

Indian in Latin America, edited by Greg Urban and Joel Sherzer, 131–155. Austin: University of Texas Press.

———. 1991b. "Hostile Encounters Between Nukak and Tukanoans and Changing Ethnic Identity in the Vaupés, Colombia." *Journal of Ethnic Studies* 19, no. 2, 17–39.

———. 1992. "The Meaning and Message of Symbolic Sexual Violence in Tukanoan Ritual." *Anthropological Quarterly* 65, no. 1, 1–18.

———. 1993. "El concepto de 'Nación Indígena': Algunos ejemplos en las Américas." In *La construcción de las Américas* (Memorias del VI Congreso de Antropología en Colombia), edited by Carlos Uribe, 218–242. Bogotá: Universidad de los Andes.

———. 1995a. "Culture, Genuine and Spurious: The Politics of Indianness in the Vaupés, Colombia." *American Ethnologist* 22, no. 1, 3–27.

———. 1995b. "Preserving Indian Culture: Shaman Schools and Ethno-education in the Vaupés, Colombia. *Cultural Anthropology* 10, no. 3, 302–329.

———. 1996a. "Coping with the Dilemmas of Affinity and Female Sexuality: Male Rebirth in the Central Northwest Amazon." In *Denying Biology: Essays on Pseudo-Procreation*, edited by Warren Shapiro and Uli Linke, 89–128. Lanham: University Press of America.

———. 1996b. "Hippocrates in the Bush." *Anthropological Quarterly* 69, no. 3, 120–123.

———. 1999. "The Politics of Ethnographic Practice in the Colombian Vaupés." *Identities: Global Studies in Culture and Power*, 6, no. 2–3, 281–317.

———. 2001. "Treinta años estudiando el Vaupés: Lecciones y reflexiones." In *Imani Mundo: Estudios en la Amazonía Colombiana*, edited by Carlos Franky and Carlos G. Zárate, 373–396. Leticia: Universidad Nacional, Sede Amazonía, and Bogotá: Unibiblos.

———. 2002a. "Caught in the Crossfire: Colombia's Indigenous Peoples During the 1990s." In *The Politics of Ethnicity: Indigenous Peoples in Latin American States*, edited by David Maybury-Lewis, 107–134. Cambridge, MA: Harvard University Press.

———. 2002b. "Contested Discourses of Authority in Colombian National Indigenous Politics: The 1996 Summer Takeovers." In *Indigenous Movements, Self-Representation and the State in Latin America*, edited by Kay B. Warren and Jean E. Jackson, 81–122. Austin, University of Texas Press.

———. 2005. "Colombia's Indigenous Peoples Confront the Armed Conflict." In *Elusive Peace: International, National, and Local Dimensions of Conflict in Colombia*, edited by Cristina Rojas and Judy Meltzer, 185–208. New York: Palgrave Macmillan.

———. 2007. "Rights to Indigenous Culture in Colombia." In *The Practice of Human Rights: Tracking Rights Between the Global and the Local*, edited by Mark Goodale and Sally Merry, 204–241. Cambridge: Cambridge University Press.

———. 2011. "Indigenous Culture-linked Enterprise in Colombia." Paper presented at the American Anthropological Association Annual Meeting, Montreal.

Jackson, Jean E., and María Clemencia Ramírez. 2009. "Traditional, Transnational and Cosmopolitan: The Colombian Yanacona Look to the Past and to the Future." *American Ethnologist* 36, no. 3, 521–544.

Jaramillo, Juan Fernando. 2012. "Colombia's 1991 Constitution: A Rights Revolution." In *New Constitutionalism in Latin America: Promise and Practices*, edited by Detlef Nolte and Almut Schilling-Vacaflor, 313–331. Burlington: Ashgate.

Jarvis, Brooke. 2017. "Who Decides Who Counts as Native American?" *New York Times Magazine*, January 18.

Jimeno, Gladys. 1995. "Programa de apoyo y fortalecimiento étnico de los pueblos indígenas del Colombia 1995–1998." *Anuario Indigenista* 34, 155–182.

Jimeno, Myriam. 1979. "Unificación nacional y educación en territorios nacionales: El caso de Vaupés." *Revista Colombiana de Antropología* 22, 60–84.

———. 1985. "Cauca: Las armas de lo sagrado." In *Estado y minorías étnicas en Colombia*, Myriam Jimeno and Adolfo Triana, 149–212. Bogotá: Ediciones Cuadernos del Jaguar.

———. 1993. "Etnicidad, identidad y pueblos indios en Colombia." In *La construcción de las Américas* (Memorias del VI Congreso de Antropología en Colombia), edited by Carlos Uribe, 243–254. Bogotá: Universidad de los Andes.

———. 1996. "Juan Gregorio Palechor: Tierra, identidad y recreación étnica." *Journal of Latin American Anthropology* 1, no. 2, 46–77.

———. 2014. *Juan Gregorio Palechor: The Story of My Life*. Durham: Duke University Press.

———. 2017. "Emotions and Politics: A Commentary on the Accord to End the Conflict in Colombia." *Journal of Latin American and Caribbean Anthropology* 22, no. 1, 161–163.

Jimeno, Myriam, and Adolfo Triana. 1985. *Estado y minorías étnicas en Colombia.* Bogotá: Ediciones Cuadernos del Jaguar.

"Juicio 'politico' indígena: Jesús Piñacué será juzgado en su comunidad por votar por Serpa." 1998. *El Tiempo*, July 12.

"Una justicia de dolor y leyenda." 1998. *El Tiempo*, July 12.

Kahn, Joel. 1981. "Explaining Ethnicity: A Review Article." *Critique of Anthropology* 16, no. 4, 43–52.

Kaltmeier, Olaf, and Sebastian Thies. 2012. "Specters of Multiculturalism: Conceptualizing the Field of Identity Politics in the Americas." *Latin American and Caribbean Ethnic Studies* 7, no. 2, 223–240.

Kapila, Kriti. 2008. "The Measure of a Tribe: The Cultural Politics of Constitutional Reclassification in North India." *Journal of the Royal Anthropological Institute* 14, no. 1, 117–134.

Keesing, Roger. 1989. "Creating the Past: Custom and Identity in the Contemporary Pacific." *The Contemporary Pacific*, 1, nos. 1&2, 19–42.

Keyes, Charles F. 1976. "Towards a New Formulation of the Concept of Ethnic Group." *Ethnicity* 3, 202–213.

———. 1981. "The Dialectics of Ethnic Change." In *Ethnic Change*, edited by Charles F. Keyes, 4–30. Seattle: University of Washington Press.

Kirk, Robin. 2003. *More Terrible Than Death: Violence, Drugs, and America's War in Colombia.* New York: Public Affairs.

Koch-Grunberg, Theodor. (1906) 2010. "Los Makú." In *Viviendo en el Bosque: Un siglo de investigaciones sobre los Makú del Noroeste Amazónico*, edited by Gabriel Cabrera, 29–55. Medellín: Universidad Nacional de Colombia.

Kolter, Jared. 1998. "Colombian Indians vs. Occidental." Associated Press, May 29.

Kroeber, Alfred, and Clyde Kluckhohn. 1952. *Culture: A Critical Review of Concepts and Definitions. Papers of the Peabody Museum of American Archaeology and Ethnology*, vol. 47.

Kroeber, Theodora. 1961. *Ishi in Two Worlds: A Biography of the Last Wild Indian in North America.* Berkeley: University of California Press.

Kymlicka, Will. 2001. *Politics in the Vernacular: Nationalism, Multiculturalism and Citizenship.* Oxford: Oxford University Press.

Labov, William. 1966. *The Social Stratification of English in New York City.* Washington, DC: Center for Applied Linguistics.

Lame, Manuel Quintín. 1981. *Los pensamientos del indio que se educó dentro de las selvas Colombianas.* Bogotá: Ediciones FUNCOL.

Langdon, E. Jean Matteson. 1992. "Introduction: Shamanism and Anthropology." In *Portals of Power: Shamanism in South America*, edited by E. Jean Matteson Langdon and Gerhard Baer, 1–21. Albuquerque: University of New Mexico Press.

Larson, Brooke. 2014. "Indigeneity Unpacked: Politics, Civil Society, and Social Movements in the Andes." *Latin American Research Review* 49, no. 1, 223–241.

Lasmar, Cristiane, and Cesar Gordon. 2015. "Um antropólogo da civilização amazônica: Entrevista com Stephen Hugh-Jones." *Sociologia & Antropologia*, 5, no. 3, 627–658.

"Indigenous Peoples." 1975. *Latin America* (November 28).

Latorre, Sara. 2013. "The Politics of Identification in a Shrimp Conflict in Ecuador: The Political Subject, 'Pueblos Ancestrales del Ecosistema Manglar' [Ancestral Peoples of the Mangrove Ecosystem]." *Journal of Latin American and Caribbean Anthropology* 18, no. 1, 67–89.

Latorre, Sara, and Katharine N. Farrell. 2014. "The Disruption of Ancestral Peoples in Ecuador's Mangrove Ecosystem: Class and Ethnic Differentiation Within a Changing Political Context." *Latin American and Caribbean Ethnic Studies* 9, no. 3, 293–317.

Laurent, Virginie. 2005. *Comunidades indígenas, espacios políticos y movilización electoral en Colombia, 1990–1998: Motivaciones, campos de acción e impactos.* Bogotá: Institut Français d'Études Andines, Instituto Colombiano de Antropología e Historia.

Lawler, Steph. 2008. *Identity: Sociological Perspectives.* Cambridge: Polity Press.

Lee, Richard. 2006. "Twenty-first Century Indigenism." *Anthropological Theory* 6, no. 4, 455–479.

Leiva, Andrea. 2004. "'Man no sell yuh birthright, man les go fight': Dinámicas de reivindicación y auto-definición del movimiento para la autodeterminación del pueblo Raizal de la Isla de San Andrés (AMEN S.D.), en medio de un escenario 'pluriétnico y multicultural.'" MA thesis, Universidad de los Andes.

León Restrepo, Orlando. 1998. "Para Mitú la guerra era muy lejana." *El Tiempo,* November 8.

Lévi-Strauss, Claude. 1966. *Mythologiques II: Du miel aux cendres.* Paris: Plon.

Li, Tania Murray. 2000. "Articulating Indigenous Identity in Indonesia: Resource Politics and the Tribal Slot." *Comparative Studies in Society and History* 42, no. 1, 149–179.

———. 2001. "Masyarakat Adat: Difference, and the Limits of Recognition in Indonesia's Forest Zone." *Modern Asia* 35, no. 3, 645–676.

———. 2005. "Beyond the State and Failed Schemes." *American Anthropologist* 107, no. 3, 383–394.

Linares, Andrea. 2001. "Proliferación de indígenas." *El Espectador,* March 28.

Lomawaima, K. Tsianina. 1993. *They Called It Prairie Light: The Story of Chilocco Indian School.* Lincoln: University of Nebraska Press.

"Los 82 pueblos indígenas de Colombia: Por la autonomía, la cultura y el territorio." 1996. *Utopías: Presencia Cristiana por la Vida* 4, no. 37, 22–27.

Losonczy, Anne-Marie. 2006. *La trama interétnica: Ritual, sociedad y figuras de intercambio entre los grupos negros y emberá del Chocó.* Bogotá: Instituto Colombiano de Antropología e Historia, Instituto Francés de Estudios Andinos.

Lucero, José Antonio. 2006. "Representing 'Real Indians': The Challenges of Indigenous Authenticity and Strategic Constructivism in Ecuador and Bolivia." *Latin American Research Review* 41, no. 2, 31–56.

Mahecha, Dany, Gabriel Cabrera, and Carlos Eduardo Franky. 1996–1997. "Los Makú del Noroeste Amazónico." *Revista Colombiana de Antropología* 33, 86–132.

Mahecha, Dany, and Carlos Eduardo Franky. 2011. *Los Nükak: El último pueblo de tradición nómada contactado oficialmente en Colombia.* Leticia: Universidad National de Colombia Sede Amazonia, and IWGIA.

———. 2017. "Políticas de la representación y participación entre los Nukak (Amazonia colombiana): Transformaciones y continuidades." In *Política y poder en la Amazonia: Estrategias de los pueblos indígenas en los nuevos escenarios de los países andinos*, edited by François Correa, Philippe Erikson, and Alexandre Surrallés, 162–180. Bogotá: Universidad Nacional de Colombia.

Malkki, Liisa. 1992. "National Geographic: The Rooting of Peoples and the Territorialization of National Identity Among Scholars and Refugees." *Cultural Anthropology* 7, no. 1, 24–44.

Martínez Medina, Santiago. 2009. *Poderes de la mimesis: Identidad y curación en la comunidad indígena Muisca de Bosa.* Bogotá: Universidad de los Andes—Facultad de Ciencias Sociales—Ceso, Departamento de Antropología.

Martínez Novo, Carmen. 2006. *Who Defines Indigenous? Identities, Development, Intellectuals, and the State in Northern Mexico.* New Brunswick: Rutgers University Press.

———. 2009. "Introducción." In *Repensando los movimientos indígenas*, edited by Carmen Martínez Novo, 9–38. Quito: FLACSO and Ministerio de Cultura del Ecuador.

"Más que neutrales, autónomos." 2000. *El Espectador*, December 12.

Maybury-Lewis, David. 2002. *Indigenous Peoples, Ethnic Groups, and the State.* 2nd ed. Boston: Allyn and Bacon.

McCormack, Fiona. 2011. "Levels of Indigeneity: The Maori and Neoliberalism." *Journal of the Royal Anthropological Institute* 17, no. 2, 281–300.

Medicine, Bea, and Liucija Baskauskas, dirs. 1999. *Seeking the Spirit: Plains Indians in Russia.* Watertown: Documentary Educational Resources, Warrior Women, Inc. Video and DVD.

Mehta, Uday. 1999. *Liberalism and Empire: A Study in Nineteenth-Century British Imperial Thought.* Chicago: University of Chicago Press.

Melo García, Yimi. 1997a. "El castigo será en febrero: Los indígenas aplazaron un mes el cumplimiento de la sentencia a implicados en crimen." *El Espectador*, January 11.

———. 1997b. "Es mejor el fuete que una cárcel: Castigo paez no es una tortura, es la forma de asegurar armonía en la comunidad." *El Espectador*, January 12.

———.1997c. "Por tutela se aplazaron los fuetazos en Jambaló." *El Espectador*, January 11.

———. 1997d. "Sí les 'dieron' los fuetazos en Toribío." *El Espectador*, January 13.

———. 1998. "Le cambian fuete por agua a Piñacué." *El Espectador*, July 16.

Mercado, Bibiana. 1993. "'Estamos en el centro de una guerra': Indígenas." *El Tiempo*, November 21.

Merlan, Francesca. 2007. "Indigeneity as Relational Identity: The Construction of Australian Land Rights." In *Indigenous Experience Today*, edited by Marisol de la Cadena and Orin Starn, 125–150. Oxford: Berg.

Merry, Sally Engle. 1997. "Legal Pluralism and Transnational Culture: The *Ka Ho'okolokolonui Kanaka Maoli* Tribunal, Hawai'i." In *Human Rights, Culture and Context*, edited by Richard Ashby Wilson, 28–48. London: Pluto.

———. 1998. "Law, Culture, and Cultural Appropriation." *Yale Journal of Law & the Humanities* 10, no. 2, 575–603.

———. 2001. "Changing Rights, Changing Culture." In *Culture and Rights: Anthropological Perspectives*, edited by Jane K. Cowan, Marie Bénédicte Dembour, and Richard A. Wilson, 31–55. Cambridge: Cambridge University Press.

———. 2006. "Transnational Human Rights and Local Activism: Mapping the Middle." *American Anthropologist* 108, no. 1, 38–51.

Ministerio de Educación Nacional. 1986. "Lineamientos generales de educación indígena." Edición modificada. Bogotá. Unpublished document, 90 pp.

Ministerio de Educación Nacional, Comisión de Asuntos Indígenas del Vaupés. 1987. "Proyecto de Trabajo Interdisciplinario en la Comunidad Indígena de San Miguel (Pirá-Paraná), Comisaría Especial del Vaupés." Bogotá: Ministerio de Educación Nacional.

Ministerio de Gobierno, Departamento Nacional de Planeación. 1984. Dirección General de Integración y Desarrollo de la Comunidad, "Programa nacional de desarrollo de las poblaciones indígenas—PRODEIN." Unpublished document.

———. 1987. "Proyecto de etnoeducación para la Comisaría del Vaupés." Vaupés, Colombia. Unpublished document.

Moerman, Michael. 1965. "Who Are the Lue? Ethnic Identification in a Complex Civilization." *American Anthropologist* 67, no. 5, 1215–1230.

Molano, Alfredo. 1987. *Selva Adentro: Una historia oral de la colonización del Guaviare.* Bogotá: El Áncora Editores.

Mompotes, Andrés. 1997a. "El cepo evita los crímenes en Pitayó." *El Tiempo*, January 10.

———. 1997b. "'Ley blanca no lava las culpas': Paeces insisten en castigar hoy con latigazos a implicados en crimen." *El Tiempo*, January 10.

———. 1998a. "En Paniquitá buscan un fuete: Hoy es el juicio a Jesús Piñacué." *El Tiempo*, July 15.

———. 1998b. "Gota fría para Piñacué: Fué condenado a sumergirse en la laguna Juan Tama." *El Tiempo*, July 16.

Moore, Henrietta L., and Todd Sanders, eds. 2006. *Anthropology in Theory: Issues in Epistemology*. Malden: Blackwell.

Moore, Sally Falk. 1987. "Explaining the Present: Theoretical Dilemmas in Processual Ethnography." *American Ethnologist* 14, no. 4, 727–736.

Moser, Brian, dir. 1975. *War of the Gods*. Granada Television. DVD.

Muyuy, Gabriel. 1992. "Taking Responsibility: Interview with Gabriel Muyuy Jacanamejoy." *Cultural Survival Quarterly* 16, no. 3, 49–52.

Nadasdy, Paul. 2003. *Hunters and Bureaucrats: Power, Knowledge, and Aboriginal-State Relations in the Southwest Yukon.* Vancouver: University of British Columbia Press.

Nagata, Judith. 1974. "What Is a Malay? Situational Selection of Ethnic Identity in a Plural Society." *American Ethnologist* 1, no. 2, 331–344.

Nagel, Joane. 1997. *American Indian Ethnic Renewal: Red Power and the Resurgence of Identity and Culture.* New York: Oxford University Press.

Nash, June. 2001. *Mayan Visions: The Quest for Autonomy in an Age of Globalization.* New York: Routledge.

Native Voices Public Television. 1996. *White Shamans and Plastic Medicine Men.* Written by Terry Macy and Daniel Hart. Montana State University, Bozeman. Documentary video.

Navia, José. 1996. "Protesta sin señales de humo." *El Tiempo*, July 21.

Nelson, Diane. 2001. "Stumped Identities: Body Image, Bodies Politic, and the *Mujer Maya* as Prosthetic." *Cultural Anthropology* 16, no. 3, 314–353.

Ng'weno, Bettina. 2007. "Can Ethnicity Replace Race? Afro-Colombians, Indigeneity and the Colombian Multicultural State." *Journal of Latin American and Caribbean Anthropology* 12, no. 2, 414–440.

Nieto de Samper, Lucy. 2005. "Martín von Hildebrand, un antropólogo dedicado a los derechos de la comunidad indígena." *El Tiempo*, December 7.

Niezen, Ronald. 2003. *The Origins of Indigenism: Human Rights and the Politics of Identity.* Berkeley: University of California Press.

———. 2009. *The Rediscovered Self: Indigenous Identity and Cultural Justice.* Montreal: McGill-Queen's University Press.

"No patentamos genes: U. Javeriana." 1997. *El Tiempo*, October 13.

"Noticias." 1992. *Selva y Río* 14, 15.

"Noticias: El cultivo de la coca." 1991. *Selva y Río*, 9, 16.

"Nuevo amanecer indígena: Desalojada la conferencia Episcopal, cuya mediación fué decisiva." 1996. *El Espectador*, August 10.

Nyamnjoh, Francis. 2007. "'Ever-diminishing Circles': The Paradoxes of Belonging in Botswana." In *Indigenous Experience Today*, edited by Marisol de la Cadena and Orin Starn, 305–332. Oxford: Berg.

O'Brien, Jay, 1986. "Toward Reconstitution of Ethnicity: Capitalist Expansion and Cultural Dynamics in Sudan." *American Anthropologist* 88, no. 4, 898–907.

Occipinti, Laurie. 2003. "Claiming a Place: Land and Identity in Two Communities in Northwestern Argentina." *Journal of Latin American Anthropology* 8, no. 3, 155–174.

"Ojo a los indígenas." 2004. *El Tiempo*, September 15.

Ong, Aihwa. 2006. *Neoliberalism as Exception: Mutations in Citizenship and Sovereignty.* Durham: Duke University Press.

Organización Nacional Indígena de Colombia. 1998. *Memorias: Los pueblos indígenas de Colombia: Un reto hacia el nuevo milenio.* Bogotá: Ministerio de Agricultura, Fondo Capacitar.

———. 2011. *El derecho fundamental a la consulta previa de los pueblos indígenas en Colombia.* Bogotá: Autoridad Nacional de Gobierno Indígena.

Orta, Andrew. 2013. "Forged Communities and Vulgar Citizens: Autonomy and Its *Límites* in Semineoliberal Bolivia." *Journal of Latin American and Caribbean Anthropology* 18, no. 1, 108–133.

Osborne, Ann. 1995. *Las cuatro estaciones: Mitología y estructura social entre los U'wa.* Bogotá: Banco de la República.

Padilla, Guillermo. 1993. "Derecho Mayor indígena y derecho constitucional: Comentarios en torno a su confluencia y conflict." Paper presented at the 13th International Congress of Anthropological and Ethnological Sciences, Mexico City.

———. 1995. "La tutela, la expansión del estado y los pueblos indígenas." *Gaia,* no. 1, 5–8. COAMA, Bogotá.

———. 1996. "La ley y los pueblos indígenas en Colombia." *Journal of Latin American Anthropology* 1, no. 2, 78–97.

"Paeces levantarán 300 veces el látigo." 1997. *El Tiempo,* January 10.

Pardo, Edgar. 1993. "Los descendientes de los Zenúes." In *Encrucijadas de Colombia Amerindia,* edited by François Correa, 225–244. Bogotá: Instituto Colombiano de Antropología, Colcultura.

Paschel, Tianna S. 2010. "The Right to Difference: Explaining Colombia's Shifts from Color Blindness to the Law of Black Communities." *American Journal of Sociology* 116, no. 3, 720–769.

Penny, H. Glenn. 2014. "Not Playing Indian: Surrogate Indigeneity and the German Hobbyist Scene." In *Performing Indigeneity: Global Histories and Contemporary Experiences,* edited by Laura R. Graham and H. Glenn Penny, 169–205. Lincoln: University of Nebraska Press.

Perafán, Carlos César. 1995. *Sistemas jurídicos Paez, Kogi, Wayuu y Tule.* Bogotá: Instituto Colombiano de Antropología.

Pérez, Gustavo. 1971. "Planas: Espejo de la opresión del indígena." *El Tiempo,* February 7.

Perilla, Sonia, 2003. "Una Nukak se 'roba' la pasarela." *El Tiempo,* May 16.

"Piñacué no se posesionará como senador," 1998. *El Tiempo,* July 9.

Pineda, Roberto. 1984. "La reivindicación del indio en el pensamiento social colombiano (1850–1950)." In *Un siglo de investigación social: Antropología en Colombia,* edited by Jaime Arocha and Nina S. de Friedemann, 197–252. Bogotá: ETNO.

———. 1995. "Pueblos indígenas de Colombia: Una aproximación a su historia, economía y sociedad." In *Tierra profanada: Grandes proyectos en territorios indígenas de Colombia.* Bogotá: Disloque Editores.

———. 1997. "La constitución de 1991 y la perspectiva del multiculturalismo en Colombia." *Alteridades* 7, no. 14, 107–129.

Politis, Gustavo G. 1995. *Mundo de los Nukak: Amazonia colombiana.* Bogotá: Fondo de Promoción de la Cultura.

Postero, Nancy. 2006. *Now We Are Citizens: Indigenous Politics in Postmulticultural Bolivia.* Stanford: Stanford University Press.

———. 2013. "Introduction: Negotiating Indigeneity." *Latin American and Caribbean Ethnic Studies* 8, no. 2, 107–121.

Povinelli, Elizabeth A. 2002. *The Cunning of Recognition: Indigenous Alterities and the Making of Australian Multiculturalism.* Durham: Duke University Press.

Pratt, Mary Louise. 2007. "Afterword: Indigeneity Today." In *Indigenous Experience Today*, edited by Marisol de la Cadena and Orin Starn, 397–404. Oxford: Berg.

Programa Colombo/Holandés de Atención Primaria en Salud. 1980. "Informe téchnico y administrativo preparado por la oficina de coordinación general." Bogotá. Unpublished document.

"Protestan por pena de látigo a indígenas: Noventa nativos ocuparon la Basílica Menor de Popayán." 1997. *El Tiempo*, January 9.

Radcliffe, Sarah. 2010. "Re-mapping the Nation: Cartography, Geographical Knowledge and Ecuadorean Multiculturalism." *Journal of Latin American Studies* 42, no. 2, 293–323.

Rahier, Jean Muteba. 2013. "A Self-identified U.S. Black Intellectual-Entrepreneur on Blacks in Latin America." *Journal of Latin American and Caribbean Anthropology* 18, no. 1, 153–156.

Rajagopal, Balakrishnan. 2003. *International Law from Below: Development, Social Movements and Third World Resistance.* Cambridge: Cambridge University Press.

Ramírez, María Clemencia. 2002. "The Politics of Identity and Cultural Difference in the Colombian Amazon: Claiming Indigenous Rights in the Putumayo Region." In *The Politics of Ethnicity: Indigenous peoples in Latin American States*, edited by David Maybury-Lewis, 135–168. Cambridge, MA: David Rockefeller Center for Latin American Studies, Harvard University.

———. 2011. *Between the Guerrillas and the State: The Cocalero Movement, Citizenship, and Identity in the Colombian Amazon.* Durham: Duke University Press.

Ramos, Alcida R. 1994. "The Hyperreal Indian." *Critique of Anthropology* 14, no. 2, 153–171.

———. 1998. *Indigenism: Ethnic Politics in Brazil.* Madison: University of Wisconsin Press.

Rappaport, Joanne. 1990. *The Politics of Memory: Native Historical Interpretation in the Colombian Andes.* Cambridge: Cambridge University Press.

———. 1994. *Cumbe Reborn: An Andean Ethnography of History.* Chicago: University of Chicago Press.

———. 2003. "Innovative Resistance in Cauca." *Cultural Survival Quarterly* 26, no. 4, 39–43.

———. 2005. *Intercultural Utopias: Public Intellectuals, Cultural Experimentation, and Ethnic Pluralism in Colombia.* Durham: Duke University Press.

Rappaport, Joanne, and Robert V. H. Dover. 1996. "The Construction of Difference by Native Legislators: Assessing the Impact of the Colombian Constitution of 1991." *Journal of Latin American Anthropology* 1, no. 2, 22–45.

Rappaport, Joanne, and David D. Gow. 1997. "Cambio dirigido, movimiento indígena y estereotipos del indio: El estado colombiano y la reubicación de los Nasa." In *Antropología en la modernidad: Identidades, etnicidades y movimientos sociales en Colombia,* edited by María Victoria Uribe and Eduardo Restrepo, 361–399. Bogotá: Instituto Colombiano de Antropología.

Rathgeber, Theodor. 2004. "Indigenous Struggles in Colombia: Historical Changes and Perspectives." In *The Struggle for Indigenous Rights in Latin America,* edited by Nancy Grey Postero and Leon Zamosc, 105–130. Brighton: Sussex Academic Press.

Reichel-Dolmatoff, Gerardo. 1967. "A Brief Field Report on Urgent Ethnological Research in the Vaupés Area, Colombia, South America." *Bulletin of the International Committee on Urgent Anthropological and Ethnological Research* 9, 53–62.

———. 1968. *Desana: Simbolismo de los indios Tukano del Vaupés.* Bogotá: Universidad de Los Andes.

Reid, Howard. 1978. "Dreams and Their Interpretation Among the Hupdü Makú Indians of Brazil." *Cambridge Anthropology* 4, no. 3, 2–29.

———. 1979. "Some Aspects of Movement, Growth, and Change Among the Hupdü Makú Indians of Brazil." PhD diss., Cambridge University.

"Renunció ayer el alcalde de Mitú." 1994. *El Tiempo,* September 22.

"Resguardo de avivatos." 2001. *El Tiempo,* December 11.

"Resguardo indígena cierra sus puertas a los violentos." 1999. *El Espectador,* October 14.

Resguardo Yanacona de San Agustín. n.d. *Resguardo Yanacona de San Agustín: Nuestra propia mirada.* Bogotá: Imprenta Patriótica del Instituto Caro y Cuervo.

Restrepo, Eduardo. 1997. "Afrocolombianos, antropología y proyecto de modernidad en Colombia." In *Antropología en la modernidad,* edited by María Victoria Uribe and Eduardo Restrepo, 341–360. Bogotá: Instituto Colombiano de Antropología.

———. 1998. "La construcción de la etnicidad: Comunidades negras en Colombia." In *Modernidad, identidad y desarrollo,* edited by María Lucía Sotomayor, 341–360. Bogotá: Instituto Colombiano de Antropología.

Rivera Cusicanqui, Silvia. (1984) 2003. *Oprimidos pero no vencidos: Luchas del campesinado Aymara y Qhechwa, 1900–1980.* 4th ed. La Paz: Aruwiyiri.

Rojas, Axel. 2011. "Gobernar(se) en nombre de la cultura: Interculturalidad y educación para grupos étnicos en Colombia." *Revista Colombiana de Antropología* 47, no. 2, 173–198.

Rojas, Tulio. 1997. "La traducción de la Constitución de la República de Colombia a lenguas indígenas." In *"Del olvido surgimos para traer nuevas esperanzas": La jurisdicción especial indígena*, Ministerio de Justicia y del Derecho, 229–244. Bogotá: Ministerio de Justicia y del Derecho, Dirección General de Asuntos Indígenas.

Roldán, Roque. 2000. *Indigenous Peoples of Colombia and the Law: A Critical Approach to the Study of Past and Present Situations.* Translated by Efraín Sánchez. Bogotá: Tercer Mundo.

Romero, Mauricio. 2003. *Paramilitares y autodefensas 1982–2003.* Bogotá: Editorial Planeta Colombiana.

Rosen, Lawrence. 1997. "Indigenous Peoples in International Law." *Yale Law Journal* 107, no. 1, 227–259.

Sahlins, Marshall. 1999. "What Is Anthropological Enlightenment? Some Lessons of the Twentieth Century." *Annual Review of Anthropology* 28, i–xxiii.

Said, Edward. 1978. *Orientalism.* Harmondsworth: Penguin.

Salomon, Frank. 1986. *Native Lords of Quito in the Age of the Incas: The Political Economy of North Andean Chiefdoms.* Cambridge: Cambridge University Press.

Sánchez, Enrique, Roque Roldán, and María Fernanda Sánchez. 1993a. *Bases para la conformación de las Entidades Territoriales Indígenas—ETIS.* Bogotá: Departamento Nacional de Planeación.

———. 1993b. *Derechos e identidad: Los pueblos indígenas y negros en la constitución política de Colombia de 1991.* Bogotá: Disloque Editores.

Sánchez, Esther. 2004. *Justicia y pueblos indígenas de Colombia: La tutela como medio para la construcción de entendimiento intercultural.* 2nd ed. Bogotá: Universidad Nacional de Colombia.

———. 2006. *Entre el juez Salomón y el dios Sira: Decisiones interculturales e interés superior del niño.* Doctoral diss., Amsterdam: University of Amsterdam.

———. 2010. *El peritaje antropológico: Justicia en clave cultural.* Bogotá: Deutsche Gesellschaft für Technische Zusammenarbeit.

Sánchez, Luisa Fernanda. 2008. "Trasplantar el árbol de la sabiduría: Malocas, maloqueros urbanos y comunidades de pensamiento en Bogotá." *RITA—Revue Interdisciplinaire de Travaux sur les Amériques* 1, 1–25.

———. 2010. "Paisanos en Bogotá: Identidad étnica y migración indígena amazónica." In *Perspectivas Antropológicas sobre la Amazonia Contemporánea*, edited by Margarita Chaves and Carlos del Cairo, 129–152. Bogotá: Instituto Colombiano de Antropología e Historia, Pontíficia Universidad Javeriana.

Sanjek, Roger. 1983. "On Ethnographic Validity." In *Fieldnotes: The Makings of Anthropology*, edited by Roger Sanjek, 385–418. Ithaca: Cornell University Press.

Santacruz, Jesús. 1985. *Principios fundamentales del Consejo Regional Indígena del Vaupés.* Bogotá: Comisaría Especial del Vaupés.

Santos, Boaventura de Sousa. 2001. "El significado político y jurídico de la jurisdicción indígena." In *El caleidoscopio de las justicias en Colombia*, edited by Boaventura de Sousa Santos and Mauricio García Villegas, vol. 2, 201–216. Bogotá: Siglo de Hombre Editores.

Sawyer, Suzana. 2004. *Crude Chronicles: Indigenous Politics, Multinational Oil, and Neoliberalism in Ecuador*. Durham: Duke University Press.

Schaft, Gretchen E. 2012. Review of *Gender and Culture at the Limit of Rights*, by Dorothy Hodgson. *American Ethnologist* 39, no. 2, 461–462.

Schneiderman, Sara. 2014. "Reframing Ethnicity: Academic Tropes, Recognition Beyond Politics, and Ritualized Action Between Nepal and India." *American Anthropologist* 116, no. 2, 279–295.

Scott, James C. 1990. *Domination and the Arts of Resistance: Hidden Transcripts*. New Haven: Yale University Press.

———, 1998. *Seeing Like a State: How Certain Schemes to Improve the Human Condition Have Failed*. New Haven: Yale University Press.

Segal, Daniel A. 1996. "Resisting Identities: A Found Theme." *Cultural Anthropology* 11, no. 4, 431–434.

Selva y Río. 1992. [Cover.]

Sengupta, Somini. 2016. "Colombian President Cites Forgiveness as Key to Peace Deal with Guerrillas." *New York Times*, September 20.

Sevilla, Manuel, and Elías Sevilla Casas. 2013. *Los Yanaconas y el proyecto posible de "indio urbano."* Cali: Pontífica Universidad Javerana; Popayán: Universidad del Cauca.

Shepard, Glenn. 2017. "A década do contato." In *Povos indígenas no Brasil 2011/2016*, edited by Fany Ricardo and Beto Ricardo, 556–559. São Paulo: Instituto Socioambiental.

Shulist, Sarah. 2018. *Transforming Indigeneity: Urbanization and the Politics of Language Revitalization in the Northwest Amazon of Brazil*. Toronto: Toronto University Press.

Sieder, Rachel. 2002. "Introduction." In *Multiculturalism in Latin America: Indigenous Rights, Diversity and Democracy*, edited by Rachel Sieder, 1–23. New York: Palgrave Macmillan.

"Siempre he obrado de manera limpia." 1998. *El Tiempo*, July 12.

Sierra, María T. 1995. "Articulaciones entre ley y costumbre: Estrategias jurídicas de los Nahuas." In *Pueblos indígenas ante el derecho*, edited by Victoria Chenaut and María T. Sierra, 101–123. Mexico City: Centro de Investigaciones y Estudios Superiores en Antropología Social.

Silverwood-Cope, Peter. 1972. "A Contribution to the Ethnography of the Colombian Makú." PhD diss., Cambridge University.

Simpson, Audra. 2014. *Mohawk Interruptus: Political Life Across the Borders of Settler States*. Durham: Duke University Press.

Smith, Carol. 1996. "Race-Class-Gender Ideology in Guatemala: Modern and Antimodern Forms." In *Women Out of Place: The Gender of Agency and the Race of Nationality*, edited by Brackette Williams, 50–78. New York: Routledge.

Sorensen, Arthur P., Jr. 1967. "Multilingualism in the Northwest Amazon." *American Anthropologist* 69, no. 6, 670–684.

Speed, Shannon. 2006. "At the Crossroads of Human Rights and Anthropology: Toward a Critically Engaged Activist Research." *American Anthropologist* 108, no. 1, 66–76.

———. 2007. "Exercising Rights and Reconfiguring Resistance in the Zapatista Juntas de Buen Gobierno." In *The Practice of Human Rights: Tracking Law Between the Global and the Local*, edited by Mark Goodale and Sally Merry, 163–192. Cambridge: Cambridge University Press.

Speed, Shannon, R. Aída Hernández Castillo, and Lynn M. Stephen, 2006. *Dissident Women: Gender and Cultural Politics in Chiapas*. Austin: University of Texas Press.

Starn, Orin. 2005. *Ishi's Brain: In Search of America's Last "Wild" Indian*. New York: W. W. Norton.

Stavenhagen, Rodolfo. 2002. Indigenous Peoples and the State in Latin America: An Ongoing Debate. In *Multiculturalism in Latin America: Indigenous Rights, Diversity and Democracy*, edited by Rachel Sieder, 24–44. London: Palgrave Macmillan.

———. 2008. "Cultural Rights and Human Rights: A Social Science Perspective." In *Human Rights in the Maya Region: Global Politics, Cultural Contentions, and Moral Engagements*, edited by Pedro Pitarch, Shannon Speed, and Xochitl Leyva Solano, 27–50. Durham: Duke University Press.

Stepan, Nancy Leys. 1991. *"The Hour of Eugenics": Race, Gender, and Nation in Latin America*. Ithaca: Cornell University Press.

Stephen, Lynn, 1997. "Redefined Nationalism in Building a Movement for Indigenous Autonomy in Southern Mexico." *Journal of Latin American Anthropology* 3, no. 1, 72–101.

———. 2002. *Zapata Lives! Histories and Political Culture in Southern Mexico*. Berkeley: University of California Press.

———. 2007. *Transborder Lives: Indigenous Oaxacans in Mexico, California, and Oregon*. Durham: Duke University Press.

Stern, Steve J. 1982. *Peru's Indian Peoples and the Challenge of Spanish Conquest: Huamanga to 1640*. Madison: University of Wisconsin Press.

Stoll, David. 1982. *Fishers of Men or Founders of Empire? The Wycliffe Bible Translators in Latin America*. London: Zed Press; Cambridge, MA: Cultural Survival.

Strong, Pauline, and Barrik Van Winkle. 1996. "'Indian Blood': Reflections on the Reckoning and Refiguring of Native North American Identity." *Cultural Anthropology* 11, no. 4, 547–576.

Sturm, Circe. 2002. *Blood Politics: Race, Culture, and Identity in the Cherokee Nation of Oklahoma*. Berkeley: University of California Press.

Tate, Winifred. 2007. *Counting the Dead: The Culture and Politics of Human Rights Activism in Colombia.* Berkeley: University of California Press.

———. 2015. *Drugs, Thugs, and Diplomats: U.S. Policymaking in Colombia.* Stanford: Stanford University Press.

Taussig, Michael. 1993. *Mimesis and Alterity: A Particular History of the Senses.* New York: Routledge.

"Testimonios: Entrevisa a Lorenzo Muelas." 1991. *Selva y Río,* 7.

"Testimonios: Nuestro Obispo habla en favor de los indígenas ante el presidente de la república." 1991. *Selva y Río,* 9.

Todd, Loreto. 1974. *Pidgins and Creoles.* London: Routledge and Kegan Paul.

Torres, William. 1994. "Nukák: Aspectos etnográficos." *Revista Colombiana de Antropología* 31, 195–236.

"Tregua indígena con 'paras': 60 días para evaluar papel de los indígenas en el conflicto." 1998. *El Espectador,* September 25.

Triana, Adolfo. 1978. "El estatuto indígena o la nueva encomienda Bonapartista." *Controversia* 79, 29–41.

———. 1993. "Los resguardos indígenas del sur del Tolima." In *Encrucijadas de Colombia Amerindia,* edited by François Correa, 99–140. Bogotá: Instituto Colombiano de Antropología, Colcultura.

Trouillot, Michel-Rolph. 1991. "Anthropology and the Savage Slot: The Poetics and Politics of Otherness." In *Recapturing Anthropology: Working in the Present,* edited by Richard G. Fox, 17–44. Santa Fe: School of American Research Press.

Troyan, Brett. 2015. *Cauca's Indigenous Movement in Southwestern Colombia: Land, Violence, and Ethnic Identity.* Lanham: Lexington Books.

Tsing, Anna Lowenhaupt. 2005. *Friction: An Ethnography of Global Connection.* Princeton: Princeton University Press.

———. 2007. "Indigenous Voice." In *Indigenous Experience Today,* edited by Marisol de la Cadena and Orin Starn, 33–67. Oxford: Berg.

Turner, Terence. 1999. "Indigenous and Culturalist Movements in the Contemporary Global Conjuncture." In *Las identidades y las tensiones culturales de la modernidad: Homenaje a la Xeración Nós,* Franciso Fernández del Riego, Marcial Gondar Portasany, Terence Turner, Josep R. Llobera, Isidoro Moreno, and James W. Fernández, 53–71. Santiago de Compostela: Federación de Asociaciones de Antropología del Estado Español.

Ulloa, Astrid. 2005. *The Ecological Native: Indigenous Peoples' Movements and Eco-Governmentality in Colombia.* New York: Routledge.

Valencia, José Luis. 2001. "Indígenas prohibirán paso a actores armados." *El Tiempo,* May 16.

Van Cott, Donna Lee. 1994. "Indigenous Peoples and Democracy: Issues for Policy

Makers." In *Indigenous Peoples and Democracy in Latin America*, edited by Donna Lee Van Cott, 1–28. New York: St. Martin's Press.

———. 2000. *The Friendly Liquidation of the Past: The Politics of Diversity in Latin America*. Pittsburgh: University of Pittsburgh Press.

———. 2005. *From Movements to Parties in Latin America: The Evolution of Ethnic Politics*. Cambridge: Cambridge University Press.

Van Emst, P. (1966) 2010. "Sometimiento voluntario: Los Makú en el Occidente del Amazonas." In *Viviendo en el Bosque: Un siglo de investigaciones sobre los Makú del Noroeste Amazónico*, edited by Gabriel Cabrera, 37–55. Medellín: Universidad Nacional de Colombia.

Varese, Stefano, 1996. "The New Environmentalist Movement of Latin American Indigenous People." In *Valuing Local Knowledge: Indigenous People and Intellectual Property Rights*, edited by Steven B. Brush and Doreen Stabinsky, 122–142. Washington, DC: Island Press.

"El Vaupés: Geografía." 1976. *Unidad Indígena* (November).

Veber, Hanne. 1998. "The Salt of the Montaña: Interpreting Indigenous Activism in the Rain Forest." *Cultural Anthropology* 13, no. 3, 382–413.

Villa, William, and Juan Houghton. 2005. *Violencia política contra los pueblos indígenas en Colombia 1974–2004*. Bogotá: Centro de Cooperación al Indígena CECOIN.

Vincent, Joan. 1971. *African Elite: The Big Men of a Small Town*. New York: Columbia University Press.

———. 1974. "The Structuring of Ethnicity." *Human Organization* 33, no. 4, 375–379.

"La voz del pastor: ¡Bienvenidos al futuro!" 1991. *Selva y Río*, 9, 3.

Wade, Peter. 1993. *Blackness and Race Mixture: The Dynamics of Racial Identity in Colombia*. Baltimore: Johns Hopkins University Press.

———. 1997. *Race and Ethnicity in Latin America*. London: Pluto.

———. 2006. "Etnicidad, multiculturalismo y políticas sociales en Latinoamérica: Poblaciones afrolatinas (e indígenas)." *Tabula Rasa*, no. 4, 59–81.

———. 2009. "Defining Blackness in Colombia." *Journal de la Société des Américanistes* 95, no. 1, 1–15.

———, 2016. "Mestizaje, Multiculturalism, Liberalism, and Violence." *Latin American and Caribbean Ethnic Studies* 11, no. 3, 323–343.

Walley, Christine J. 2004. *Rough Waters: Nature and Development in an East African Marine Park*. Princeton: Princeton University Press.

Warren, Kay. 1998. *Indigenous Movements and Their Critics: Pan-Maya Activism in Guatemala*. Princeton: Princeton University Press.

Westerman, Floyd. 1969. "Here Come the Anthros." *Custer Died for Your Sins*, Track B2. Perception Records, Vinyl, LP, Album.

White, Richard, 1991. *The Middle Ground: Indians, Empires, and Republics in the Great Lakes Region, 1650–1815*. New York: Cambridge University Press.

Whiteley, Peter. 2003. "Do 'Language Rights' Serve Indigenous Interests? Some Hopi and Other Queries." *American Anthropologist* 105, no. 4, 712–722.

Whitten, Norman E., Jr. 1985. *Sicuanga Runa: The Other Side of Development in Amazonian Ecuador.* Urbana: University of Illinois Press.

Williams, Brackette. 1989. "A Class Act: Anthropology and the Race to Nation Across Ethnic Terrain." *Annual Review of Anthropology* 18, 401–444.

Wilson, Richard Ashby. 1997. "Human Rights, Culture and Context: An Introduction." In *Human Rights, Culture and Context: Anthropological Approaches*, edited by Richard Ashby Wilson, 1–27. London: Pluto.

———. 2006. "Afterword to: 'Anthropology and Human Rights in a New Key': The Social Life of Rights." *American Anthropologist* 108, no. 1, 77–83.

Wirpsa, Leslie. 1988. "Un espíritu castigador persigue a los Nukak." *El Espectador*, May 22.

Wirpsa, Leslie, and Hector Mondragón. 1988. "Resettlement of Nukak Indians, Colombia." *Cultural Survival Quarterly*, 12, no. 4, 36–40.

Wirth, Louis. 1961. "The Problem of Minority Groups." In *Theories of Society*, edited by Talcott Parsons, Edward Shils, Kaspar D. Naegele, and Jesse R. Pitts, 309–312. New York: Free Press.

Wolf, Eric. 1982. *Europe and the People Without History.* Berkeley: University of California Press.

———. 1988. "Inventing Society." *American Ethnologist* 15, no. 4, 752–761.

Wolff, Jonas. 2007. "(De-)mobilising the Marginalised: A Comparison of the Argentine *Piqueteros* and Ecuador's Indigenous Movement." *Journal of Latin American Studies* 39, no. 1, 1–30.

Wright, Robin. 1998. *Cosmos, Self, and History in Baniwa Religion: For Those Unborn.* Austin: University of Texas Press.

———. 2013. *Mysteries of the Jaguar Shamans of the Northwest Amazon.* Lincoln: University of Nebraska Press.

Yashar, Deborah J. 1996. "Indigenous Protest and Democracy in Latin America." In *Constructing Democratic Governance: Latin America and the Caribbean in the 1990s—Themes and Issues*, edited by Jorge I. Domínguez and Abraham F. Lowenthal, 87–105. Baltimore: Johns Hopkins University Press.

———. 2005. *Contesting Citizenship in Latin America: The Rise of Indigenous Movements and the Postliberal Challenge.* Cambridge: Cambridge University Press.

Yrigoyen, Raquel. 2002. "Peru: Pluralist Constitution, Monist Judiciary—a Post-reform Assessment." In *Multiculturalism in Latin America: Indigenous Rights, Diversity and Democracy*, edited by Rachel Sieder, 157–183. New York: Palgrave Macmillan.

Yúdice, George. 2003. *The Expediency of Culture: Uses of Culture in the Global Era [Post-contemporary Interventions].* Durham: Duke University Press.

Zambrano, Carlos Vladimir. 1993. "Introducción." In *Hombres de páramo y montaña:*

Los Yanaconas del macizo colombiano, edited by Carlos Vladimir Zambrano, 19–21. Bogotá: Instituto Colombiano de Antropología, Colcultura, PNR.

———. 1994. "El contacto con los Nukak del Guaviare." *Revista Colombiana de Antropología* 31, 177–194.

———. 1995. "Etnicidad y cambio cultural entre los Yanaconas del macizo colombiano." *Revista Colombiana de Antropología* 32, 127–146.

———. 2000. "La inacabada y porfiada construcción del pasado: Política, arqueología y producción de sentido en el macizo colombiano." In *Memorias hegemónicas, memorias disidentes: El pasado como política de la historia*, edited by Cristóbal Gnecco and Marta Zambrano, 195–228. Bogotá: Instituto Colombiano de Antropología e Historia and Popayán: Universidad del Cauca.

Zambrano, Marta. 2014. "Entre el estado y la nación: Ambigüedades de las políticas de comercialización y activación patrimonial de la hoja de coca y sus derivados en Colombia." In *El valor del patrimonio: Mercado, políticas culturales y agenciamientos sociales*, edited by Margarita Chaves, Mauricio Montenegro, and Marta Zambrano, 443–472. Bogotá: Instituto Colombiano de Antropología e Historia.

Zamosc, Leon. 1986. *The Agrarian Question and the Peasant Movement in Colombia: Struggles of the National Peasant Association, 1967–1981*. Cambridge: Cambridge University Press.

Zeiderman, Austin. 2013. "Living Dangerously: Biopolitics and Urban Citizenship in Bogotá, Colombia." *American Ethnologist* 40, no. 1, 71–87.

Zuluaga, Germán. 2009. *La historia del Vaupés desde esta orilla*. Bogotá: Editorial Universidad del Rosario, 41.

Index

Note: Page numbers in italic type indicate illustrations.